Eye, ear… um… Erica, zing! King.

In these troubled times,
let us all band together and intone
a few fortifying gems;
talk them or sing them,
but be sure
to do it aloud

by Carol Fradkin Brown

ODE TO ERICA MYOME
God bless 'em, Erica;
Land, that isle of.
Stand, bee cider,
And guide earth!
Rue the Knight
Wither light
From above.
From the mound, into
The prayer, eat to Theo, shun
White whiff home!
God bless 'em, Erica
Myome, sweet 'ome.

JOSÉ
José, can ewe, see buy?
Thud awn, surly light what
Soap-prowed lea, wee, haled at that
While light-lassed glee mink.
Ooze, broads, tripes and brights,
Tars, threw the peril; us, fie! Tore
The ram—parts we watch—'twere so gal,
Aunt, leased reaming. And the rock—it's
Read; glare the balm's burse, sting in air.
Gay vapor, roof through—then Knight that
Tariff lag was 'til there rose say, does
That? Stars, pang-gilled, ban err—yet
Waive oar—the land-dove, the freehand.
The home of tub. Rave!

OH, BUTTE!
Oh, Butte! If full force space shoes, guys—
For ram. Burr waives; of grey in for purr pull
Mount, tin matches tease, aboveth if rooted plane.
A myrrh reek, ah! A myrrh reek, ah!
Guard sheds his grey son, thee anchor rowen.
Thigh good with broth, ere hood frump's seat
Two shine ink, see?

THE MYCON TREE
Mycon tree! 'Tis of these
Wheat-land, dove-lip,
Burr tea
Of the icing;
Land-dove—the pill
Grimm's pried!
Land, wear
My father's dyed
From ever remount
Inside—
Let free, dumb ring!

Drawing by Wally Neibart

REVIEWERS

Henri Edmonds — Howard University
Evan Ulrey — Harding University
Mary M.B. Hutton — Alabama State University
Eunice W. Moore — Alabama State University
Sennia Mack — Georgia State University
Barbara Blackstone — Slippery Rock
Alice Dyson — University of Florida
James Young — California State-Fullerton
Ralph Hillman — Middle Tennessee State University

VOICE & DICTION
SECOND EDITION

P. JUDSON NEWCOMBE

UNIVERSITY OF SOUTH FLORIDA

CONTEMPORARY PUBLISHING COMPANY
508 ST. MARY'S STREET, RALEIGH, N.C. 27605—(919) 821-4566

Publisher: Charles E. Grantham
Typesetters: Carlisle Graphics
Printer: Edwards Brothers

Illustrations:

Hugh E. Bateman, Ph.D., Robert M. Mason, Ph.D., D.M.D., *Applied Anatomy and Physiology of the Speech and Hearing Mechanism,* copyright   1984, p. 587, Courtesy of Charles C. Thomas, Publisher, Springfield, IL.

David Ross Dickson, Ph.D., Wilma Maue-Dickson, Ph.D., *Anatomical and Physiological Bases of Speech,* copyright 1982, pp. 114, 133. Courtesy of Little, Brown and Company, Boston, MA.

John P. Moncur and Isaac P. Brackett, *Modifying Vocal Behavior,* copyright by John P. Moncur and Isaac P. Brackett. Courtesy of Harper and Row, Publishers, Inc.

C. E. Seashore, *Psychology of Music,* copyright 1983. Courtesy of McGraw-Hill Book Company.

Johannes Sobotta, Frank H. J. Figge, *Atlas of Human Anatomy,* 9th English Edition, copyright 1977, pp. 31, 161, 163, 168, 171. Courtesy of Urban and Schwarzenberg, Baltimore-Munich.

Cartoons:

title page	Wally Neibart-drawing, Carol Fradkin Brown-verse. Courtesy of Esquire Associates, N.Y.
p. 3	Whitney Darrow, Jr., copyright 1966. Courtesy of Simon and Schuster, Inc.
p. 50	Willoughby. Courtesy of *The Rotarian,* Evanston, IL.
p. 80	Copyright by David Pascal. Courtesy of *American Legion Magazine,* Indianapolis, IN.
p. 233	B. Wiseman, Courtesy of The New Yorker Magazine, Inc., 1975.
p. 238	Salo, Courtesy of Curtis Publishing Company.
p. 269	Roy Fox, Courtesy of Curtis Publishing Company.
p. 280	Charles M. Schulz, Courtesy of United Feature Syndicate, Inc., 1970.

ISBN: 0-89892-063-9

Printing 10 9 8 7 6 5 4 3 2 1

PREFACE

When the world was enormous, seldom travelled by most average citizens, and generously populated by uneducated peoples, the need for oral language standards was small. People could be born, live all their lives, and die in a geographical area no larger than today's large towns or small cities. What was good enough for father and mother was good enough for daughter and son! The standards of the family were adequate for a lifetime of talking.

Today, the world has become so small that every valley, mountain peak, and rural plain—every ship at sea, plane in the sky, or orbiting space station—can be contacted with the electronic media. In societies which emphasize freedom of choice, individual initiative, universal public education, and private enterprise, an individual learns that few barriers exist for attaining reasonable goals. The choices we make progressively throughout our lives help or hinder us in our pursuit of these goals.

This textbook addresses this matter of choices. It assumes that the person reading it has no major physiological impairments that will prevent him or her from hearing sounds or producing them accurately. If you have these impairments, the advice of a speech and/or hearing therapist should be sought before, or in addition to, taking this course. This, in itself, becomes a matter of choice since you now know that this textbook and course will not deal with remediation of major impairments.

If you are not aware of your voice and diction errors at the present time, you are not unusual. We become so accustomed to our speaking patterns that we no longer hear ourselves objectively. If you have "picked up" faulty habits from your friends and family, this book, your instructor—and eventually, members of the class will help you to identify some of those problems. Your ears will become better attuned to **specific spoken sounds** (something you probably haven't been aware of since elementary school). Once you can hear distinctions among sounds, you will be able to exercise your right of choice again by deciding whether you want to practice the physical changes needed to modify your current speaking habits.

In addition to working on old habits, you will be learning a new tool: the International Phonetic Alphabet. This will be useful for understanding the sounds being discussed in class since it will give everyone the same symbol system for describing errors and proposed changes. Later on, you may discover this is a handy tool to use as you try to pronounce difficult technical, scientific, or foreign terms, or as you help other persons with their speech patterns.

You will learn the **International Phonetic Alphabet** in progressive steps, as a practical tool, during the first part of the course. You will learn specific sounds, beginning with commonly known symbols. As you use these symbols in oral and written (transcription) exercises, you will gain practical experience in hearing and describing speech sounds that you will hear your classmates use in this course. By the end of this course, you should be able to describe many of the sound substitutions, omissions, and transpositions that you hear outside class. Furthermore, you should be able to describe elements of voice quality, pitch, duration, stress, inflection, volume, fluency, and rate which can change the meanings of words and sentences. These elements, also called paralanguage, often convey as much meaning in your daily conversations as the words you are saying!

This textbook should be looked upon as a supplemental resource to the wisdom, knowledge, interest, and good sense of your course instructor. Exercises will give you clues to ways in which you can practice. However, they can't be considered all-inclusive or definitive in nature. Your instructor will become acquainted with your speaking habits, evidence of your outside practice, and your potential for improving—and then will make suggestions for your **personal improvement.** At that point, this book should become a reference tool for practice sessions—a reminder of some of the ways in which speaking habits may be changed.

In exercising your right of choice, you may decide you need the book only for quick "brush up" exercises in your practice sessions, as you prepare your oral presentations for the class. On the other hand, as a result of your class presentations, you may find you have problems with certain sounds you never recognized before and you will need to return to the chapters dealing with these sounds to spend a considerable amount of time reviewing how to make the correct sounds. Even though the last part of this course emphasizes public presentations, you will be expected to use International Phonetic Alphabet symbols to describe your own speech patterns, as well as the patterns of your classmates throughout this course. Your instructor should be able to use fewer words to describe your problems, once you know how to use this symbol system.

In your lifetime, you probably have become aware of general communication goals, rules, and standards for different situations and populations. These goals and standards develop through common usage—and through written or unwritten expectations, or rules of etiquette. For example, you modify your casual daily oral communication behavior for *certain functions* (saying "Hello" rather than "Hi" when you answer a relative's telephone), *situations* (lowering your volume when you express your condolences to someone who has lost possessions or loved ones), *social classes* (saying "I'm pleased to meet you" with a friendly vocal tone, to newly introduced guests at a formal social gathering) or *professional positions* (quickly reviewing the date and place of a future appointment with a client at the conclusion of a business meeting).

One communication standard you may not have recognized yet is the General American Speech pattern. Some textbooks speak of it as the largest of the three dialects spoken in the United States today. However, General American Speech shouldn't be viewed as a characteristic of only geographical areas in the United States. You will hear it used in many areas of Canada, Bermuda, some of the Caribbean islands, some of the Pacific islands, American overseas schools and military bases, as well as in the United States. It is used in major national *network* radio and television newscasts in the United States and Canada, and on international broadcasts of Voice of America and the U.S. Armed Forces Network.

At first glance, speech improvement looks and sounds deceptively easy. As you learn more about the process of modifying your voice and diction, don't be alarmed or disillusioned if you discover that your personal progress isn't occurring quickly, with little effort on your part. Remember, individual initiative and personal choice are two opportunities that you have right now.

This book encourages you to begin hearing some of the characteristics of General American Speech, and to develop some oral facility for using it easily whenever it may be important to your welfare, success, comfort, and happiness. Your instructor will be the judge of your ability to use General American Speech *in class presentations.* Eventually, **you** must be the judge of whether you will use it in your *daily life.*

I hope your earnest, concerted efforts for improving your voice and diction will reap many rewards, not only in this class, but in your future career. If you make the right choices this year, you may be determining the opportunities that will be available to you next year. Those opportunities, in turn, may limit or extend the choices available to you for attaining the goals you seek to attain throughout the rest of your life.

P. Judson Newcombe
January 1991

TABLE OF CONTENTS

CHAPTER 1

FROM AN ORAL TRADITION TO A LITERATE SOCIETY: AN OVERVIEW

HOW DID WE LEARN TO TALK?

An interesting question which has intrigued scholars of human communication for hundreds of years is "How did human beings learn to talk?" Many interesting theories have been proposed. Among them are the possibilities that humans:

1. Originally communicated on an extra-sensory level and developed their speech from this initial ability to exchange thoughts.

2. Imitated animal sounds (cries, screeches, grunts) or sounds in nature (wind blowing, thunder rolling).

3. Developed speech from working together at difficult tasks which involved rhythmical grunts and gestures which became more and more specific or predictable.

4. First used musical sound combinations or song to express great emotion which gradually evolved into melodic speaking patterns.

5. Received the ability to speak as a gift from their Creator (as several religions teach).

Many primitive human settlements existed in widely separated parts of the ancient world. Probably each depended upon nonverbal communication (gestures, facial expressions, movement, and objects) as well as speech, to convey their messages. We can imagine, for example, that these primitive settlements learned to work together to secure food and water, protect themselves from dangerous animals, and construct shelter for protection from temperature and climate changes. All **communal activities** required a form of communication that could be understood and obeyed by all community participants.

If our ancestors were not born with a fairly sophisticated oral language capacity, they had to develop it through a process of trial and error. Growls, grunts, cries, laughter, sighs, groans and screams which resulted from normal daily activities gradually had to be associated with specific events or feelings. For example, if someone sighed with relief after putting down a heavy burden, and later sighed after a thorn was removed from a foot, the sigh could have communicated a meaning of "relief" to that individual—and to observers of both events. As community members began to understand the similarity of an individual's sounds in two entirely different situations, they would begin to establish a foundation for understanding spoken messages among themselves. That sound now could be imitated by other community members to indicate the same general idea—a feeling of relief. Thus, a common bond would begin to develop through shared sounds and meanings within that community.

The language of one community probably was not similar to languages of distant communities. Each community would have had entirely different experiences, needs, and goals which would have led to the development of their own unique spoken sounds, words, and phrases. Climate, availability of food, water and shelter, congeniality of adult leaders, ability of the population to learn, and threats to life are just a few of the factors that would have influenced the development and refinement of speech in different communities. If, for example, food were always abundant and easy to secure, few terms on ''searching to find food'' would have been necessary. However, if food were difficult to secure, a community's very existence would have been linked with ''searching for food'' terms. Furthermore, words to express procedures for finding, securing, sharing and even preserving food would have been of vital importance to this second community.

DEVELOPMENT OF THE ORAL TRADITION

Whatever the origin of speech, it preceded any form of written communication by thousands of years. This was the period of the ''Oral Tradition'' when law, religion, history, and literature existed **only** in the **spoken word.** Usually, many persons with good memories existed in the same community. They became valuable ''memory banks'' for rulers. Each could be questioned separately about the validity of a statement or the existence of an agreement. When those persons could independently recite **exactly** the same laws, chronology, history, and/or family pedigrees, the rulers knew that truth or fact had been preserved. (This process is similar to our current use of agreement among observers to support empirical research.) Perhaps you can begin to see why, in the ancient world, an individual's spoken word was as good as a written contract today.

Courses in ancient history, history of religion, mythology, and folklore indicate that similar historical events were reported by widely separated civilizations in India, Central America, Africa, Polynesia, and North America. These events include such things as the creation of Earth, creation of human beings, presentation of speech to our earliest ancestors, and destruction of civilization by a great flood. These widely separated civilizations probably did not communicate with one another. Therefore, the similarities among these stories is striking and gives credence to each event's occurrence. Of even greater interest, as you begin to study voice and diction in detail, is the fact that all these stories were transmitted over thousands of years **solely by word of mouth.** Had it not been for this oral tradition, we would not have works such as the Old Testament or the Greek myths today!

Perpetuation of Knowledge through Speech

Today's world depends upon books, computers, microfilm, audio- and videotape for preserving information. You probably have difficulty believing that something as long and complicated as Homer's **Iliad** could have been memorized and passed along through generations of people only through the spoken word.

Before writing developed, all of humankind was dependent upon the memories of a community's elders and scholars. These people knew they had to memorize and recite aloud information exactly as it had been taught to them in order to eliminate the possibility of error in transferring knowledge from generation to generation. Many individuals began to memorize important information and recited it aloud as children, to guarantee that it wouldn't be lost as a result of the untimely death of the community's elders. For example, wherever power was inherited, someone had to be able to recite the blood line of the ruling family. If a name were omitted from the genealogy of a royal family, that individual and his or her offspring wouldn't be considered as heirs in the line of succession.

The Power and Influence of Oral Reciters

Frequently, oral reciters were respected—and were rewarded for their original recitations. They learned that if they purposely complicated rhythm, inflection, and volume changes in their own original stories, they could make their presentations difficult to copy. By doing this, oral reciters preserved their control over their material while guaranteeing themselves continued income and respect! Imitators were easy to identify because they used incorrect words in the wrong order, said words with incorrect inflections, or used an inaccurate metrical pattern.

In some societies, oral reciters could determine their successors. They taught only selected apprentices their techniques for reciting aloud. Often, members of a reciter's family were taught the skills of oral recitation in order to retain a family monopoly on this honored occupation.

In other societies, guilds of reciters arose to perpetuate the telling of certain stories. The Homeridae of ancient Greece, for example, recited the epic tales of Homer. The rhapsodists in ancient Greece, troubadours in France, minnesingers in Germany and minstrels in England all perpetuated the art of oral recitation. They gained reputations as respected, knowledgeable, entertaining story tellers and carriers of recent news. Often, they possessed more knowledge and culture than members of the working class would ever see or hear again in their lifetimes.

Even today, remnants of the oral tradition still exist. Storytellers in some isolated communities can repeat stories exactly as their parents and grandparents repeated them. You might marvel at their memories or even at their ability to hold your attention. However, probably you wouldn't see any continuing need for training other individuals to memorize and recite aloud the same information if you can record or print the information for posterity. Rather than finding these individuals indispensable to modern society, you probably view them as quaint relics of a bygone era.

The Disappearance of Information on Early Civilizations

When civilizations were destroyed by war or natural disasters, their centuries of history, biography, law, literature, and religion disappeared. Only the few preserved, written documents and artifacts of the cultures, or second-hand accounts of the cultures in other languages, remind us of their early existence.

"Can you talk?"

Some of the earliest human bones and artifacts ever discovered have been found in tropical areas of the world. In areas, such as central Africa, written documents could have been made on easily accessible but perishable materials, such as leaves and tree bark. However, these ancient civilizations evidently left no written evidence of their cultures behind. You might assume that these cultures were illiterate and depended entirely upon the oral tradition for perpetuating their cultures. Future discoveries of some forms of preserved writing still may be made. (Remnants of ancient writing from some less tropical areas remain undeciphered today. Keys to their translation remain to be found.) Many early civilizations may have perished because they never "published"— or because they published only on highly perishable materials!

DEVELOPMENT OF WRITTEN LANGUAGE AND LITERACY

Reading and writing (literacy) were not considered essential skills for average citizens to learn during the period of the oral tradition. No great emphasis was placed upon preserving information that was commonly known by most of the citizens.

Writing may have started as simple drawings that were made to illustrate an event, activity, or accomplishment. Ancient drawings and carvings, completed long before any writing was known to have existed, have been found on rocks, cave walls, and pieces of pottery. If you have ever seen primitive petroglyphs (stick-like figures of people and animals), you realize that these early drawings were neither detailed nor anatomically accurate. They communicated basic ideas with a few simple lines. These simple figures communicated general ideas, such as woman, man, child, animal, and could be copied easily by anyone.

Gradually, some of these simple figures began to look more like modern alphabet symbols. They also began to represent specific **sounds** rather than specific objects. With this refinement, "written messages" could deal with more complexity than drawings or pictograms ever allowed. Written number systems for accounting and business purposes also evolved and were combined with alphabets. Practically all of the extant records of early writing have been found on papyrus, clay tablets, skins of animals, tree bark, pieces of wood, or clay pots.

The Power and Influence of Scribes

The oral tradition coexisted with literacy in many civilizations for centuries. Memorization and oral recitation continued to be the primary mode for perpetuating knowledge. Most early written material related to **business** matters but didn't include literature, religion, or laws. The reason was quite simple: cultured people had memorized and could recite these things—or at least had easy access to oral reciters whenever they were needed. Writing was for the practical obligations of keeping track of wealth, fulfilling business transactions, and corresponding with people in distant areas.

As written symbol systems developed, the vocation of scribe also developed. The scribe had to learn a symbol system (alphabet) as well as rules for transcribing certain types of documents. The scribe became especially useful for keeping records and writing letters. Illiteracy was a common, accepted phenomenon. Rulers didn't need to read or write. They could hire a scribe for these tasks, just as a secretary or accountant might be hired today.

Gradually, civilizations became aware of the value of preserving certain information. If merchants and governing leaders believed information should be retained, scribes were called in to copy it, either from existing manuscripts or as oral reciters said the information aloud. (These scribes might be compared with modern court reporters who transcribe oral testimony.) In later years, these scribes gathered together in a common location called a scriptorium, to duplicate important documents.

When transcripts were made of oral recitations, errors could occur if a scribe were inaccurate in spelling, did not hear a spoken message clearly, did not understand the necessity for a poetic or metrical pattern used by the reciter, were inattentive during parts of the recitation, or decided to condense seemingly non-essential components of the oral message. If an illiterate reciter never heard the scribe's written transcription read aloud—or if the scribe were unfamiliar with oral recitation requirements, these errors probably wouldn't be discovered. At that moment in history, the historical prestige of spoken messages was being challenged by the permanency of written messages.

The Permanent Nature of Written Manuscripts

Once information was transformed into writing, it became a permanent, tangible record which did not change (unless it was recopied by someone else at a later time). This aspect of permanency began to be valued highly by many individuals. It also threatened the livelihood of oral reciters because their information could be written and read by any literate person! A later recitation from the written manuscript couldn't be **exactly** accurate (since inflections, rate of speaking, pitch, rhythm, and other oral features were not recorded to specify how the original ideas were expressed.) However, the content of the message usually was close enough to the original meaning to satisfy persons who commissioned transcripts.

Some wealthy individuals began to collect manuscripts and kept them in a special room of their homes. Gradually, rulers also accumulated manuscripts in national or court libraries. They hired scribes to copy important texts, and even encouraged centers of education to develop in conjunction with their personal libraries. Major centers of learning often sprang up near these libraries. They encouraged international scholars to visit the cities where they could study civilization's accumulated knowledge.

Rote memorization and oral recitation continued to be important components of formal education for centuries after the first libraries began. However, as increasing numbers of people learned to read and write, the importance of memorization and oral recitation as the **sole** means for preserving centuries of accumulated information began to diminish. Humankind shifted its trust and allegiance from the spoken word to the printed word—from the oral tradition to the literate tradition.

EDUCATION OF A LITERATE SOCIETY

Mass public education, as we know it today, did not occur in ancient civilizations. Most children were taught to be obedient to their elders and to the state while fulfilling some useful function. Often, this function was learned while the individual was an apprentice to a person with a profession or trade. One did not have to be able to read or write to be a good carpenter, potter, weaver, manual laborer, or farmer. The oral tradition was quite adequate for preparing people to be productive citizens. Higher education usually was limited to children of the ruling class, and later, of successful merchants who could afford this luxury.

The need for *most* citizens to be able to read and write, at least on an elementary level, became evident in modern societies. Children began their early education by copying their parents' oral communication—just as hundreds of previous generations had done under the oral tradition. Then, when they were old enough to learn the alphabet and numbering system, children were taught to use these new tools for simple, functional tasks.

Even though most children didn't develop extensive reading and writing vocabularies, they could follow simple written notices and write simple statements. Furthermore, they learned respect for individuals who surpassed them in ability to read and write. Their limited literacy probably emphasized the value of reading and writing for anyone who wished to change his or her social status in life.

As literacy increased throughout the civilized world, the oral tradition began to wane. A final blow to the primacy of the oral tradition occurred when Gutenberg invented movable type in the mid-1400s, making possible the mass, inexpensive production of manuscripts. For the first time in history, access to humankind's cumulative knowledge could not be limited to selected individuals on the basis of their wealth, family profession, or inherited positions. Any intelligent person who knew how to read could acquire the knowledge and skills preserved in them. The element of personal choice was enhanced significantly at that moment in history.

THE CONTINUING LINK WITH THE ORAL TRADITION

Perhaps you can begin to understand why disagreement arises among theologians and historians about the accuracy and interpretation of ancient holy scriptures and stories that have managed to survive until today. In order to trust the accuracy of these ancient stories, we must place a great amount of faith in the abilities of many generations of oral reciters to tell their stories **exactly** as they had heard them from their ancestors.

Often, this oral tradition "chain" involved translations of stories from one language to another. When the grammatical, poetic and/or syntactic rules of one language were quite different from those of another one, stories were modified to fit the new structural rules. If a language did not have certain vocabulary words, a bilingual scribe (who may not have been as concerned with oral as with written aspects of language) had to use foreign terms, or create or find approximate synonyms in the native language.

Perhaps you can understand the jealousy that must have arisen among illiterate but talented oral reciters and literate scribes, as each group tried to consolidate their positions and future influence in their communities. Ultimately, of course, the oral reciters lost their powerful monopoly on human knowledge. At the same time, scribes were unable to preserve in their manuscripts the exact nuances, emotions, and connotations that the human voice was capable of showing.

As you begin your study of oral components of English, you should remember that most people still learn a significant portion of their knowledge and skills by speaking and listening to other people. You learned most of your earliest information through oral/aural communication. Not until you entered elementary school did you begin to realize the importance of reading and writing to your daily existence. By then, you probably had developed an affinity for oral/aural education. Even now, you may find you can learn easier and faster by listening to someone explain a new approach or idea than by reading about it.

The English language is a relatively young language, when contrasted with some of the ancient languages. It has borrowed words, rules, and traditions from a variety of languages which complicated your task of learning it systematically. You learned the rules for spelling, grammar, and syntax and then incorporated them into your daily life. Once you developed the habits associated with those rules, you probably forgot the rules! As a result, when you are asked for your reason for saying certain things in a certain manner, you may find an explanation impossible.

Unfortunately, the rules for **writing spoken English,** or for **reading written English aloud,** are vague. They don't tell you exactly how things should be said aloud. You must determine your own interpretation of written material. As a result, you may be tempted to read printed material aloud, using rules of written English that are difficult to apply to spoken messages. You also may follow habituated mechanical patterns for reading aloud which you used as a child as you were learning to read, even though those methods destroy the emotional impact and/or meaning of certain ideas.

This course can help you discover some of the elements of the oral tradition that you either never learned as a child—or you learned and then forgot. You will be working on some of the vocal components of language which have been influential in the daily lives of people through thousands of years. As you deal with these components, you will be sharing some of the same concerns for vocal clarity, flexibility, and precision that public speakers and readers throughout history have shared. Furthermore, you should gain a new awareness of the significance of voice and diction in our media-oriented society—and a new respect for accuracy and versatility of vocal messages in all human communication.

CHAPTER 2

ESTABLISHING GOALS AND STANDARDS FOR VOICE AND DICTION

If you have traveled extensively throughout the United States and Canada, you probably are aware of many English dialects spoken by people you met along the way. Some of those dialects were similar to your own but some were quite different. You may have used labels to identify the dialects you were hearing, such as Mountain, New Yorkese, French Canadian, Pennsylvania German, Puerto Rican, Louisiana French or Cajun, Black, Milwaukee German, Deep Southern, Southwest Mexican-American, or Hawaiian Pidgin. These labels served as a frame of reference for you to remember and describe certain features of the dialects, even though the terms were not descriptive in themselves. Actually, these labels probably were generalizations about the oral language patterns of *many* individuals, but were not accurate terms for describing *all* individuals in specific geographic, national or ethnic communities.

WHAT IS A DIALECT?

A dialect generally is considered to be a relatively consistent variation or deviation in speech from the norm or standard of a particular country, region, class, or profession. Probably you associate sound substitutions, omissions, additions, and transpositions most often with dialects. If you hear people saying "bresh" for "brush," "dint" for "didn't," "athaletics" for "athletics," and "calvary" for "cavalry," you may identify these as dialectal changes. However, dialects also can involve changes in vocabulary, speech rhythm, rate, inflections, stress, syntax or structure of sentences, and use of certain idioms.

Because you are of Chinese, German or Italian extraction; or live in Magnolia, Mississippi, Swan River, Canada, or Nanakuli, Hawaii; or are black, white or brown does not mean that you automatically have a dialect that is associated with many of the people with whom you identify or associate. You may have some, but not all of the dialectal characteristics of the group in which you live. Although you have lived your entire life with parents or grandparents who speak little or no English, you may have absolutely no trace of a recognizable accent or dialect. However, you also may be the only member of your family with an identifiable dialect!

How Did Dialects Begin?

In large countries where great expanses of land or natural barriers (such as mountains and deserts) separated early settlers, geographical areas or regions often developed their own unique speech patterns. Since transportation was difficult and expensive, and the oral media of movies, telephones, radio, and television were not available, those early settlers in various regional areas were insulated from other dialects or standards of speech. Educated and uneducated citizens alike used the dialect which had become the standard for their particular region. In the United States, for example, the Eastern American, Southern American, and General American Dialects arose as the three most obvious **regional dialects.** (The Eastern dialect which is most evident in New Hampshire, Maine, and the eastern parts of Connecticut, Vermont, and Massachusetts, sometimes is referred to as the eastern New England Dialect.)

8

Within each of these large regions, however, slight deviations from the regional dialect occurred—again, often as the result of some form of isolation from the general regional population. Metropolitan areas such as New York City and Atlanta and mountainous regions in West Virginia and Tennessee developed their own variations of their regional dialects. These variations became known as **subsidiary dialects.** The subsidiary dialects often were related to national or ethnic origins of one's parents. As long as little communication occurred among various dialectal groups, individuals had no basis for comparing their dialects with anyone else. People could spend their lives in one region and never be aware that they spoke differently from people in other regions.

Becoming Familiar with Our Own Dialects

If you have lived most of your life in relative isolation (regardless of whether the isolation was caused by geographic, social, family, racial, religious, national, ethnic, professional or economic factors) you may be unaware of any dialectal characteristics that you have. You have become so accustomed to your speaking patterns and those of your immediate associates that you probably don't even hear your deviations unless they are pointed out to you by people outside your group. (Often, we have difficulty believing that we say things differently from our friends, associates or our favorite radio and television personalities. Our ears simply aren't attuned to the differences.)

A common experience for voice and diction instructors is to ask a student to repeat certain words exactly as the instructor pronounces them. When a student is corrected on a word's pronunciation and is asked to repeat the word exactly as the instructor says it, the same error is repeated! Not until the student is taught to *hear* differences between the two pronunciations, through listening or ear training exercises, does any change occur.

Therefore, as you begin this course, your instructor will be describing various sounds and deviations from them to familiarize you with General American sound production. Pay close attention to these sounds to be sure you hear them accurately. If you demonstrate you can hear each sound, but you still have difficulty producing certain sounds, your instructor will give you suggestions for changing the location of your tongue, jaw, lips and other articulators. These two steps will be extremely important for eliminating obvious sound deviations from a General American Speech pattern.

WHAT DIALECT IS ACCEPTABLE?

A regular question asked of us is "Who or what determines the acceptability of one dialect over another?" Why shouldn't every English dialect be equally acceptable, as long as individuals can be understood by a majority of their audience? (Individuals who ask this last question often don't realize that speakers seldom are in a position to ask their audiences how many listeners are actually comprehending the total spoken message at any moment.)

Some people associate the interesting nature of various dialects with the old saying, "Variety is the spice of life." They fight concerted attempts to achieve a universal or standard national dialect, saying that such attempts carry a "snob appeal" and try to force everyone into too narrow a mold. (Frequently, one of the fundamental differences between linguists and voice and diction specialists revolves about this issue: should dialects be encouraged/preserved, or modified/eliminated? Linguists study the changes that occur from dialect to dialect or language to language; voice and diction specialists help individuals eliminate obvious deviations from a specific dialect or language.)

Dialects and Non-Native Speakers of English

This interest in dialects is not new, unique to the North American continent, or pertinent only to English. Any language which becomes an international language tends to be pronounced with many variations, particularly by individuals who devote most of their time to reading and writing the language but very little time to speaking it. The fact that non-native speakers "mispronounce" words gives native speakers some cause for believing their language is being "mutilated" by outsiders.

At times, this poor oral facility among non-native speakers of English is fostered by non-native English teachers who have never been required to demonstrate a **high level of oral proficiency.** If the teachers are considered experts in English in their own countries, but regularly misarticulate English words, who will be knowledgeable or bold enough to correct them? (In this respect, they are similar to our own native American elementary teachers who have obvious sound substitutions and omissions. If they teach language arts to children for thirty years, they may perpetuate their own sound deviations in hundreds of individuals. Many of those students never will realize how or where they received their dialects!)

Often, oral language changes among first (and sometimes later) generation Americans are caused by their dependency upon their **native language's sounds and rules** which are used as their only available model for speaking English. An approximation of the correct English sound may seem satisfactory to them. The native language, however, may lack important English sounds or have an entirely different accent and inflection pattern. Non-native English speakers who are incapable of hearing sounds accurately will need to undergo the same period of ear training that native American speakers must experience to modify dialectal patterns.

Dialects and Native Speakers of English

Through the years, English speaking countries have developed national identities which are based, in part, upon their major dialectal patterns. Many independent countries which were once part of the British Empire have maintained English as their primary language for commerce, law, and higher education. Approximately 325,000,000 people speak English as their first language today and at least that number of people use it as their second language. Although only thirteen percent of the world's 4.7 billion people speak English, it continues to function as one of the most important international languages today. Whether one examines popular music, computer technology, international air controller training, fast food franchises, or outer space travel, one runs into English as a universal means of communication.

Among the more populous countries where speakers use English as their mother tongue are: the United States (215,000,000); Great Britain (56,000,000); Canada (17,000,000); Australia (14,000,000); Irish Republic (3,300,000); New Zealand (3,000,000); Jamaica (2,300,000); South Africa (2,000,000); Trinidad and Tobago (1,200,000); Guyana (900,000); Bahamas (250,000); Barbados (250,000); Zimbabwe (200,000); Belize (100,000); St. Vincent (100,000); Antigua-Barbuda (100,000) and Grenada (100,000). Many other populous countries depend upon English for commerce, law, higher education, and/or professional communications including: India, Pakistan, Malaysia, Liberia, Uganda, Tanzania, the Philippines, Ethiopia, Ghana, Hong Kong, Singapore, Malawai, Malta, Namibia, Papua New Guinea, Sierra Leone, Zambia, and Sri Lanka. Although this list is incomplete, it gives you some idea of the number of different English dialects that are possible throughout today's world.

Will citizens from one English speaking country have difficulty understanding people from another one? We are sure you wouldn't believe the variety of dialects used unless you heard them yourself. If typical citizens of Jamaica, India, Australia, Ireland, South Africa, Canada, Singapore, Kenya, Wales, Scotland, Hong Kong, Brooklyn, New York, and Atlanta, Georgia all congregated in the same room to talk together informally, you would have some difficulty in decoding their spoken messages—at least until your ears became attuned to their deviations from your own dialectal pattern.

National Dialects and Employability

In general, the English dialect that is spoken by the greatest number of well educated citizens of a country will tend to be the most influential dialect in that country. It may not be the easiest to learn, most prestigious, or most beautiful dialect. Certainly, it will not be spoken exactly the same way by all the people who possess some facility in its use. However, most of that nation's citizens will hold it in higher esteem than any other nation's English dialect.

Our national dialect, however, does not necessarily limit our employability to positions within our national borders. Rather, the more similarities our dialect has with other English dialects, the more possibilities we have for moving about the English-speaking portions of the world easily without being misunderstood. Because of similarities in the Eastern American and southern British dialects, a Bostonian might be more easily understandable to many British citizens than a person from Chicago with a General American dialect. If, however, the Bostonian also has sound changes which are associated with a particular ethnic group, such as inner city Jews or blacks (subsidiary dialects), British listeners might have difficulty in understanding the person.

On the other hand, a British citizen who is proficient in "Received English" (or BBC English) might be quite acceptable as a news broadcaster with major broadcasting companies in the United States and Canada, whereas an American speaker with an Ozark or mountain dialect might be completely unacceptable. A Sydney, Australia history teacher with no obvious regional dialect might be a better potential representative for a Canadian international business firm than an experienced American radio disk jockey with a definite Texas dialect.

SOME DETERMINANTS OF ACCEPTABLE DIALECTS

With so many English dialects being spoken throughout the world, how do we determine the best, most useful, or most correct dialect to use? The answer must be given in terms of "relativity." The correctness or incorrectness, accuracy or inaccuracy, acceptability or unacceptability of any dialect is determined by the: country in which it is spoken, degree of familiarity existing between a speaker and an audience, formality of a situation in which a message is being given, time of the presentation, general expectations of an audience being addressed, and specific educational, social, professional and economic constraints placed upon the speaker.

Formality of Situations and Familiarity of Audiences

In casual conversations with good friends, we often use disjointed or abbreviated comments, slang expressions, slurred speech, rapid speaking rates and extreme changes in pitch and volume. However, in relatively formal situations with people we have just met (such as job interviews or conferences with professional advisors) we may choose our words carefully, use only moderate pitch and volume changes, speak slowly and distinctly, and strive to speak in complete sentences. Effective oral communicators recognize this ability to adapt to situations as a crucial step for establishing bonds with listeners.

Does this mean that our casual or informal speech is less appropriate than our more formal speech? Not necessarily! Extremely formal, overly precise diction in an informal situation can be as detrimental to a speaker and a social situation as extremely informal or sloppy diction can be in a formal situation. The ability to adapt our dialectal pattern simply indicates we understand when one form is likely to be more effective than the other. (If we are unsure of the degree of formality required in an unknown situation, we usually are safer to begin with a relatively formal or standard dialectal pattern. If the situation becomes less formal and other participants display less concern for accuracy in diction, then we may modify our own speaking patterns.)

If we are aware of our listeners' responses, we try to know when we must modify our speaking patterns in order to be understood easily by them. This becomes particularly important in settings where we do not know our listeners well. If we are not aware of these responses, we probably have people asking us to repeat ourselves—or they may respond to something they thought we said when we actually said something quite different.

11

Choosing Our Own Speaking Pattern

Does this mean that we have an impossible task of determining the dialect that will give us the most benefits throughout our lives? Not at all. We must be willing to take as realistic a look at our futures as possible and determine what our potential jobs and our desired social status will require of us. We also must be able to determine the degree of formality we will be dealing with at any moment in our lives and then develop the facility for adapting to it without undue strain or self-conscious effort.

If we realize we will be competing in our professions with individuals who have excellent speaking skills, we need to determine whether our current level of skills will give us an advantage or place us at a disadvantage. We need to be cautious of deciding that our present oral communication patterns are adequate because no one has ever criticized us for them. (One doesn't make or keep friends easily by criticizing their faults, even, sometimes, when our friends have asked for honest criticism. It's safer to ignore them or pretend that the speech errors we perceive are insignificant.)

Whether we are examining voice quality, degree of loudness, variety of inflections, rate of speaking, clarity of diction, or accuracy of pronunciation, we need to be concerned with their appropriateness to the situation and the audience. Because a loud voice wins your friends' approval in informal storytelling sessions doesn't mean it will win the approval of a potential employer who wants to hire a good public relations representative. You may be able to drop word endings among your friends and family because these people know you well and understand what you intended to say. However, if you do this among strangers, they may conclude you are partially deaf and don't hear ends of words, that you are ignorant of verb tenses or grammatical rules, or that you are just a careless speaker. If you speak with great hesitation, have a slow rate of speaking, or "drawl" words by holding onto certain sounds, you may be perceived by outsiders as having an interesting or "cute" drawl. However, a future national employer may conclude that you can't handle accounts outside the South because you will be perceived as being too slow or too identifiable as a regional rather than a national representative.

This course allows you a chance to modify a particular ethnic, regional, racial, or social identification. It stresses the development of an increased facility in handling a General American Speech pattern in addition to any dialectal pattern you now have. If you have a fairly well developed General American Speech pattern, it encourages you to gain greater vocal variety in using it while modifying any minor deviations you may have now.

WHY ARE WE USING GENERAL AMERICAN SPEECH AS OUR MODEL?

The General American Speech pattern will be used as our class model for several reasons. First, it is the most widely used of all the regional dialects in North America today. Second, it has become the North American dialect that is heard most frequently on national and international radio and television newscasts. Therefore, all American and Canadian citizens (and citizens in other countries who have easy access to North American radio and/or television) should have no difficulty in understanding it.

Furthermore, because General American Speech is heard more than any other North American dialect in motion pictures and television programs distributed throughout the world, it also is understood readily by native English speakers in other countries and speakers of other languages who have learned or are learning English as a second language.

Perhaps you have noticed that no attempt has been made to define either the people who use General American Speech or the characteristics of the dialect. The task of defining the specific population of General American speakers definitively would be impossible. This is due to the ease and frequency with which people change jobs and locations today. Since people carry their dialects with them, you could discover as many speakers of General American Speech in southern California as you would in southern Illinois. In general, the geographical areas with the largest percentage of people using General American Speech are the northcentral portions of the United States and the central portion of Canada.

The chances are excellent that you speak a General American dialect if you were reared in a second or older generation Canadian or American family in one or more of the following locations: Ohio, Michigan, Indiana, Illinois, Wisconsin, Minnesota, Iowa, Kansas, Nebraska, South Dakota, North Dakota, Colorado, Manitoba, Ontario, and Saskatchewan. The chances are very good that you use this dialect if you were reared in one or more of these locations: California, Oregon, Washington, Idaho, Montana, Wyoming, New York, Pennsylvania, Alberta, British Columbia, and Washington, D.C. If you lived your early years in other areas and your later years in one of the areas mentioned above, you also may have developed a very good General American Speech pattern. Also, if the persons who raised you speak a General American dialect, your chances are very good that you also speak the dialect, regardless of where you have lived. (Frequently, we have students who have lived in many areas of the world because their parents were in military service or employed by international firms. Although they have lived little or none of their lives in areas of North America where General American Speech is used, they still have excellent General American Speech patterns because their parents served as their primary models.)

What are the characteristics of General American Speech? Most of the chapters in this book will attempt to define the sounds, describe how they are formed, and give practice words and sentences containing those sounds. If you find you are disagreeing with some of the pronunciations given, you may discover that your dialectal pattern differs from General American Speech for those specific sounds or words.

The degree of proficiency in General American Speech that will be expected of each participant by the end of this course cannot be determined by this book. The final judge of your progress in developing competency in General American Speech will be your instructor. His or her experience, acuity of hearing, and honesty in discussing your major problems will be of major assistance to you as you evaluate your current facility with General American Speech and determine your priorities for improving this facility.

"I must say since we learned to talk, how well you express yourself in a crystalline and often aphoristic manner."

PRACTICE SENTENCES

The following sentences contain sounds that often are changed from one regional dialect to the other in North American English. Read the sentences aloud in class. See if you can hear differences in your fellow students' dialects.

1. I asked for nine and a half dollars' worth of any color of the new house paint to paint our cottage shutters.

2. In June, many of the girls participating in our carnival which commemorated the sun god, could not carry a tune.

3. After passing the farm, we stopped our car and asked a man for directions for finding the old dance hall.

4. The cowboys, who wouldn't admit it, caught five men trespassing on their property late one hot night in July.

5. Often, we would rather go with you to the body shop instead of waiting until noon for Aunt Betty to pick us up.

6. I found the stamp that you said was left outside in the fog for three or four nights, just before you got home.

7. Mike wondered why those examples of primitive life were allowed to be part of your last, leading newspaper story.

8. Now that our department head has met our outstanding worker of the year, she either will find a place for him with our firm, or will encourage him to find a better position elsewhere.

9. They could not hear the loud murmur rising from the crowd standing beside the county highway north of town.

10. Don was very impressed with all of those students and asked them why they hadn't taken a little more time to prepare their biographies for publication.

DIALOGUE FOR ORAL PRACTICE (requires three readers)

Shopper: I'd like to buy my friend a pair of these loafer shoes as a Christmas present, please.

Clerk: What size shoe does s/he wear?

Shopper: Well, let me see . . . I guess I don't really know.

Clerk: That's all right. Do you know what size socks s/he wears?

Shopper: Ummmm, no, I don't know that either.

Clerk: How about her/his coat size? Or do you know what size collar s/he has?

Shopper: Oh, yes! That would be a fifteen. I know because I just bought him/her a shirt.

Clerk: Very good. That means s/he needs a size 8 loafer. If you'll wait, I'll get a pair for you from the storeroom.

Storeroom Worker: That's wonderful! I don't think I've ever seen another clerk who could determine someone's shoe size by simply knowing her/his neck size. How do you figure that?

Clerk: (Quietly) To be perfectly honest, I really can't. However, if the shoes don't fit, s/he will bring them back after Christmas. And I won't be working then!

14

VOCABULARY FOR ORAL PRACTICE

Read the following lists of words as you would say them in daily conversation. Don't pause between syllables or over-articulate sounds, to make the words stilted or pedantic (overly precise).

List A	List B	List C	List D	List E
all	call	tall	hall	fall
welfare	shellfish	Belfast	elfin	selfish
extra	extract	extreme	extraordinary	extremity
blight	trite	fright	night	height
egg	leg	beg	peg	keg
asked	masked	basked	ask	husked
Harry	sherry	Mary	carry	very
murder	girder	herder	further	purser
missed	fished	kissed	hissed	swished
on	operate	option	occupy	Oscar
which	whittle	whistle	whimper	whisper
shout	loud	cowboy	doubts	bounce
mountain	certain	curtain	fountain	hearten
alive	five	dived	chives	hive
thirsty	thirty	thirteen	Thursday	thinker
adore	another	along	around	adopt
out	about	outlook	house	outside
other	mother	another	brother	father
should	would	could	shouldn't	hood
fast	last	cast	mast	past
shouldn't	wouldn't	hadn't	didn't	needn't
spoon	noon	news	knew	tune
much	touch	hutch	such	Dutch
highway	lightweight	byways	plywood	Taipei

15

CHAPTER 3

VOICE PRODUCTION AND MODULATION

BECOMING AWARE OF SOUND AND SENSE

Sound surrounds you from the moment of your birth. Whether it comes from you, from other people, or from nonhuman sources, sound continues to influence you throughout the rest of your life. It may be the pleasant sound of music, the irritating sound of a siren, the soothing sound of a bubbling stream, or the captivating sound of someone telling a story. For the earliest years of your life you give and receive information primarily through the oral/aural (speaking and listening) mode. When you begin to attach meaning to **spoken sound,** you become the most recent link in the oral tradition chain. Thus, spoken sounds become a legacy as old as humankind—a legacy which is preserved or modified by each new generation.

Taking Spoken Sound for Granted

The presence of sound (and the ability to create sound) since birth makes this common element of your life a factor that is easy to "take for granted." Since you learned to speak at a relatively early age, you have forgotten your earliest difficulties in imitating sounds correctly and putting words together in a proper order to create meaningful chains of ideas other people could understand. By the time you reached adulthood, you probably had no difficulty in speaking to friends and associates.

These factors may explain why some adults see little reason for formal courses in speaking. Since they have spoken (and been understood) since childhood, what else needs to be learned about speaking? Many adults view speaking as a mechanical skill that is similar to walking. Both should be capable of being learned in daily experience, rather than in formal courses.

This analogy between the mechanical skills of walking and talking falters if you realize that talking also is based upon continuing, spontaneous intellectual decisions, whereas, in most situations, walking remains an automatic, mechanical activity. Furthermore, few people ever will find that their careers, promotions, friends, salaries, and social influence will relate directly to how they walk. However, careers often are affected by how they talk.

Rediscovering the Importance of Spoken Sound

Thousands of well-educated people seek private or public instruction in voice production and modulation when they are being considered for a position or promotion they want desperately. At this critical moment in their careers, they become aware that competing candidates may have more pleasant vocal quality, more distinct diction, better ability to project their voices in groups, greater inflectional variety, or a less obvious dialect than they have. (In some cases, a supervisor or prospective employer may point out their deficient speech habits.) As a result, they seek a quick solution to well established habits which they never believed would affect their futures.

16

Some people become quite discouraged when they discover they can't break their lifelong speaking habits easily or quickly by themselves. They find that the ability to create meaningful sounds doesn't mean necessarily the ability to speak fluently, accurately, or pleasantly! Neither does it include the ability to assist others with their sound production problems. In fact, many of these adults admit they don't know where or how to begin working on vocal problems. They usually can't hear their own errors. Because they haven't thought about sound formation and modulation since childhood, they can't even describe the process used to create sound.

In this chapter, we will review the process and components of the speech mechanism used to create and manipulate sounds in speaking. We will include some technical terms in parentheses throughout the chapter to assist you in cross referencing terms, in case your instructor uses them in class. (Often, the less technical terms will be adequate for describing how sound is created and used.) Also, we will intermix bracketed sounds and sounds in quotation marks, such as [z] and "uh," to represent **spoken sounds** (not the letter in the alphabet usually associated with the symbol) until we have established a uniform method for describing sounds in a later chapter. By following this procedure, you gradually will begin working with the symbols needed for this course.

THE SOURCE OF POWER FOR SPEAKING

When someone mentions "sources of power," probably you think of sources which generate some form of electricity: movement of **water** for hydroelectric plants, heated **steam** to drive turbines, combustible **fuel** for truck, automobile and airplane engines, **wind** to drive large windmills, and the **sun** to run solar electric cells. All of these **energy sources** provide different forms of energy which can be transformed into action or movement.

The power source for speaking originates in the **air** you breathe. If you have little or no air reserved, you will have difficulty creating and sustaining a loud voice. This same principle is involved with a battery operated radio. If the batteries are weak, you won't be able to sustain a loud volume level. The control you maintain over your air supply will determine your general volume level. This will be important to remember if you find you have a relatively weak voice.

In normal daily activities, breathing (respiration) is a reflex activity. You don't remind yourself to breathe in and breathe out. Instead, the amount of oxygen or carbon dioxide in your blood automatically tells your body when to inhale and exhale, as well as how deeply and how often to breathe. When you speak, however, you learn to control your breathing, including the duration and force of your exhalations.

The **lungs, diaphragm, and chest muscles** are the major parts of the body involved in providing the air or potential source of energy needed for speaking. None of them has as its primary objective the creation or support of voice. In fact, all of the component parts of the speech mechanism actually have other primary functions; their speech function is a secondary (or overlaid) function.

The Diaphragm

The diaphragm is a thin, irregularly shaped, double-domed muscle separating the digestive tract from the lungs. (The spelling of this word gives many people difficulty because of its silent "g.") Only the esophagus, which carries food and water to your stomach, some nerves, and a main artery and vein to and from the lower part of your body, pass through the diaphragm wall. The diaphragm, the principal muscle used for inhalation, accounts for half the air inhaled during quiet breathing. The other half is supplied by muscles in the lower chest area.

The diaphragm's muscular fibers originate from a central tendon just below the heart and radiate out. At its extremities, the diaphragm's fibers are attached to the tip of the breast bone (sternum), lower six ribs on each side of the body, and lumbar section of the spine. This muscle serves as the floor for the chest (thoracic) cavity. If you place your hands on either side of your waist, just below your rib carriage, with your thumbs extended toward the spine and your index fingers extended to the front, you will feel approximately where your diaphragm is located. As you breathe in and out, you should feel your hands move in and out too. If they don't move, you probably are breathing too much from the chest area.

When you **inhale,** the diaphragm contracts (tightens and flattens, pulling downward about half an inch and creating some pressure against the stomach, liver, and intestines). This pressure may

VC vena caval formamen
ES esophageal hiatur
AA abdominal aorta
RC rib cage
S sternum
CT central tendon
→ radiating fibres

Figure 3-1 (A) Photograph of the diaphragm looking up (inferior view) towards the head area, (B) simplified drawing of the diaphragm viewed from the front (anterior) (C) side view (sagittal). Note the muscular connections of the diaphragm to the spine and lower ribs in (C). These connections, along with the one to the breastbone, create a dome-like formation which is obvious when most of the air in the lungs has been expelled. At this point, the diaphragm has a more pronounced dome because the lungs aren't pushing down on it. (From Dickson, Maue-Dickson, Courtesy Little Brown and Company)

force the front portion of the stomach to bulge forward slightly. It also creates additional space allowing the lungs to increase in size in the chest cavity. When you **exhale,** the diaphragm relaxes and resumes its domelike position as the stomach, liver, and intestines push back up toward the lungs. Your chest cage falls slightly and decreases in circumference as the lungs also decrease in size.

The diaphragm is similar to a bellows which takes in and forces out air, depending upon whether it is in an active (contracted) or passive (relaxed) state. It attempts to equalize air pressures inside and outside the lungs. (Remember that any muscle is soft and flabby when it is relaxed. In that state, it is not capable of creating much pressure or force, even though it may take up space. Also, a muscle can expand or contract but it can't push.)

The diaphragm is a striped or voluntary muscle which allows you to maintain conscious or volitional control over its tension. You can determine how quickly and forcefully you will release your exhalations, allowing the diaphragm to attain a relaxed state and bulge upward. The length and strength of your exhalations, determined in part by abdominal muscle contractions, will be two considerations of **breath support** which are extremely important in controlling volume and intensity.

The Lungs

The lungs also are components of the power source for speaking. These non-muscular, cone-shaped, spongy sacs which fill the chest cavity, serve as storage areas for air. At the top of your chest, the lungs are attached to your windpipe (trachea). The bottom of each lung is in contact with your diaphragm's upper surface. Your lungs are *not* capable of inflating and deflating by themselves but respond to muscular and gravity pressures surrounding them. When you inhale, the diaphragm contracts, pulls down and forward and creates a vacuum which causes your lungs to begin filling with air received through the nose or mouth. When you exhale, the diaphragm relaxes and moves upward, allowing the digestive organs to push upward as the decreasing pressure in the lungs equalizes with the outside air.

Your lungs don't have to be filled completely to function efficiently in relaxed activities, including conversations with friends. In fact, many people who have had lung surgery live normal, active lives with only *one* lung. People with breathy voice qualities often are inefficient in their control of air and tend to expel *too much* air as they speak. When you are in a relaxed state, inhaling requires effort and energy but exhaling does not. (Mechanical lungs in hospitals help sick people fill their lungs effortlessly, thereby removing some of the strain that might be placed on their hearts and muscles.)

The lungs are not merely storage areas for air. They also act as filtering mechanisms for purifying your blood, exchanging oxygen from the air during inhalation for carbon dioxide and other harmful gases from your bloodstream during exhalation. The lungs work harder during exercise than during relaxation in order to supply additional oxygen required by the body. Therefore, during animated speaking you will consume extra oxygen which must be replaced by an increased intake of air.

During relaxed or at-rest breathing, the **average time ratio** of inhalation to exhalation is about 1:1. However, during normal speaking this ratio changes to about 1:5. In many speaking situations this ratio can rise as high as 1:15, particularly when little volume or intensity is required.

When you must increase your volume in order to be heard in large groups, or above competing noises, you need to be sure your lungs have an adequate supply of air to create the pressure needed to **produce** sound. By increasing the air supply, you also will provide additional oxygen to muscles that are used to **amplify** sound. (Later in this chapter we will consider how exhaled air flowing through the larynx creates sound.)

19

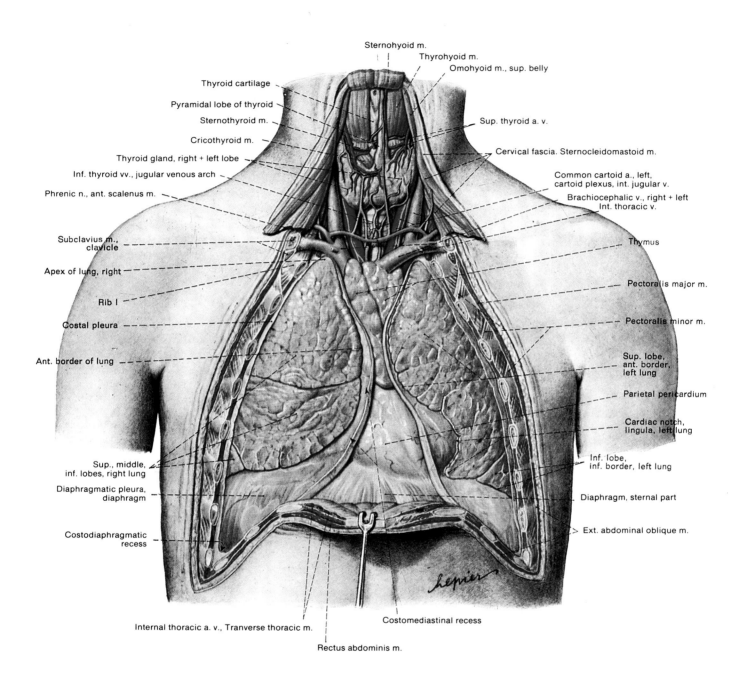

Sternohyoid m.

Thyrohyoid m.

Omohyoid m., sup. belly

Thyroid cartilage

Pyramidal lobe of thyroid

Sternothyroid m.

Sup. thyroid a. v.

Cricothyroid m.

Cervical fascia. Sternocleidomastoid m.

Thyroid gland, right + left lobe

Common cartoid a., left,
cartoid plexus, int. jugular v.

Inf. thyroid vv., jugular venous arch

Brachiocephalic v., right + left
Int. thoracic v.

Phrenic n., ant. scalenus m.

Subclavius m.,
clavicle

Thymus

Apex of lung, right

Pectoralis major m.

Rib I

Costal pleura

Pectoralis minor m.

Ant. border of lung

Sup. lobe,
ant. border,
left lung

Parietal pericardium

Cardiac notch,
lingula, left lung

Sup., middle,
inf. lobes, right lung

Inf. lobe,
inf. border, left lung

Diaphragmatic pleura,
diaphragm

Diaphragm, sternal part

Costodiaphragmatic
recess

Ext. abdominal oblique m.

Costomediastinal recess

Internal thoracic a. v., Tranverse thoracic m.

Rectus abdominis m.

Figure 3-2 Frontal View of the Human Lungs. Notice the size of the lungs in relation to the total chest area. The diaphragm, which separates the thoracic region containing the lungs and heart from the abdominal region, can be clearly seen. Also, at the top, the thyroid cartilage, commonly called the Adam's Apple is shown. This is the front protection for the larynx. (From Sobotta/Figge, Courtesy Urban and Schwarzenberg)

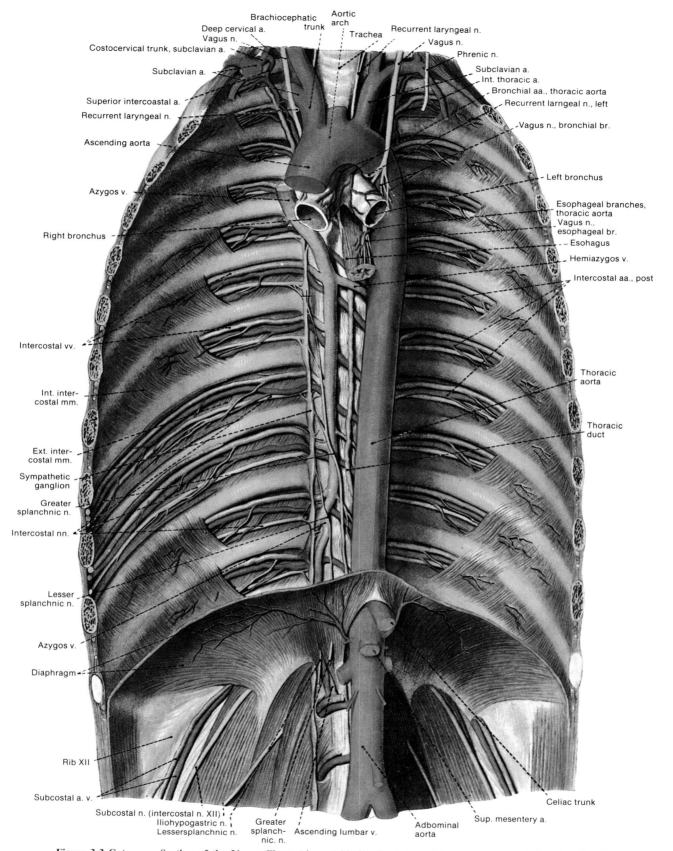

Figure 3-3 Cut-a-way Section of the Upper Chest. (thorax) Notice the intercostal muscles connected to the ribs. When attempting to amplify voice, the diaphragm should be pushed down with the abdominal muscles rather than expanding the short intercostal muscles. Greater force can be created this way. Also, tension of the intercostal muscles will cause constriction in the throat and larynx which may result in a strained vocal quality and increased anxiety during speaking. (From Sobotta/Figge, Courtesy Urban and Schwarzenberg)

21

The Chest (Thoracic) Muscles

The chest muscles are the final components of the source of energy for speaking. Included in this group are the: intercostal muscles between ribs, muscles that connect the breastbone (sternum) to the collarbones (clavicles), and muscles from the spine to the neck. The most efficient method of breathing for relaxed speaking involves using the lower chest muscles, diaphragm, and abdominal muscles. (During inhalation, each curved lower rib swings upward and outward, much like a pail handle as it is lifted away from the pail sides. During exhalation, your chest muscles relax, allowing the ribs to drop forward and downward.)

If you raise your relatively heavy collarbones repeatedly while you speak, you place unnecessary strain on your heart and oxygen supply. Often, people who use upper chest and shoulder (clavicular) breathing when they speak develop tight throats and harsh voices. Their breathing becomes shallow and frequent, sometimes resulting in gasping or "out-of-breath" sounds. Therefore, clavicular breathing is not recommended for speaking. An obvious external indication of clavicular breathing is the amount of shoulder raising that occurs whenever a speaker inhales. This form of breathing can be useful during athletic activities when the lungs must be expanded suddenly to provide a little extra oxygen for a strenuous endeavor.

We have said that **air supplies the power for all human speech.** Remember that air is *not* sound or speech itself, any more than the air in a pipe organ or accordion is the sound that is produced. Air is the necessary "raw ingredient" needed to create sound. This air is captured, stored and controlled by the three components of the power source.

THE SOURCE OF SOUND FOR SPEAKING

When you are sitting in a large audience, you generally are not aware of the breathing of people around you—but it is occurring regularly. When you wake up at night and hear the rustling of leaves or "sighing" of air through tree branches, you know the wind is blowing even though you can't see outside. If you sit in a well-insulated building and look out a window at trees and shrubbery in motion, you conclude that a wind is blowing even if you can't hear the wind. Probably you are not aware of the continuous movement of air that occurs around you unless you can hear it, see effects of its movement, or feel temperature changes from it.

Take a deep breath, round your lips slightly, then exhale through your mouth as quietly as you can. Now take a file card and repeat this process, but move the edge of the card back and forth in front of the escaping air. You can see from this simple activity that quiet air movement can produce sound when it runs into an obstacle. When this occurs, the energy source (moving air) loses part of its movement energy each time it hits a resisting obstacle. This energy changes into sound energy. This same principle is involved in creating sound for human speech. The size, shape, composition, and tension of the obstacle and the speed and regularity of the air movement as it hits the object will determine whether the resulting sound is high or low in pitch, consistent or inconsistent in its strength and pitch, and continuous or intermittent in its duration.

The Larynx

The throat (pharynx) is a common channel for food, water, and air. It divides into the esophagus and the windpipe (trachea) at the "voicebox" (larynx). The windpipe, a semirigid tube consisting of many C-shaped cartilage rings, connects the lungs and throat. The opening of each "C" rests against the esophagus. The two largest C-rings, sitting at the top of the trachea, house the larynx or voice box. When you inhale, air passes through the windpipe to the lungs, regardless of whether you breathe through your nose or mouth. When you exhale, air goes from the lungs back out through the nose and mouth. In both cases, the air passes through the larynx. If you lift your

22

head while looking at a mirror and run a finger down the front of your throat, you will see and feel a slight protrusion, often called the Adam's apple, which shields your larynx. (Actually, this protrusion is the thyroid cartilage, the largest cartilage in the larynx.)

The larynx (which sounds like "lair rinks" rather than "lar nicks") consists of three sets of cartilages (thyroid, cricoid, and arytenoid) which are bound together by ligaments, and muscles. Within the larynx are two narrow folds or flaps of smoothly rounded, mucous-covered muscle tissue called **vocal folds.** Often, they are referred to erroneously as vocal "cords." The vocal folds create an important pressure valve which is used for strenuous tasks such as childbirth, movement of heavy objects, elimination, and tasks requiring the suspension of breathing. They also work in conjunction with the epiglottis to prevent food, water, or other foreign particles from entering the lungs. If you have ever experienced the sensation of choking on food or water, you know the power that can build up behind the vocal folds to expel a foreign object!

During at-rest breathing, the vocal folds are relaxed and drawn apart slightly, leaving a V-shaped opening (glottis) between them, with its vertex pointed to the front of the neck. Air passes easily in and out of the lungs through this opening. The opening narrows for all **voiced sounds** that are spoken aloud. (You can tell which sounds are voiced by placing your index finger on your throat over your larynx and saying "shhh" and "ahhh." The vibration that occurs for "ahhh" but not for "shhh" indicates voicing. This element of voicing will be very important as you study individual sounds.)

The process of creating sound (phonation) is a voluntary or conscious activity. Initial sounds are relatively weak and unpleasant and must be modified further before they can be called meaningful or pleasant sounding "words." You are able to control the elements of quality, intensity, and pitch during this phonation process.

As you exhale, the flow of air through the vocal folds creates vibrations or flutterings that might be compared to sounds created by wind blowing through tree branches. You probably won't make any meaningful sounds in the English language during **inhalation,** with the exception, perhaps, of the startled intake of air you make when you "catch your breath" suddenly.

You may be aware that your normal pitch usually changes when you have a cold. Often, the throat and vocal folds become inflamed and swell, changing their length and thickness enough to change your normal pitch range. Also, when you are under extreme tension, the vocal folds may be so tense that your pitch moves higher than normal. In general, fast vibrations of the vocal folds will create a higher pitch than slower vibrations. (For example, if you sing middle C on the musical scale, your vocal folds will vibrate 256 times or cycles per second. If you move up to high C, your vibrations will double to 512 per second.) The greater the tension in the vocal folds, as air escapes, the higher the pitch will be. However, the length, tension and thickness of vocal folds all can affect their rate of vibration—and therefore, your pitch level.

One word of caution needs to be given here. Often, vocal amplification is handled incorrectly and the vocal folds are strained, particularly at athletic events where shouting and cheering are common. The after-the-game hoarse voice seems to be many students' weekend social status symbol. This hoarseness results from strained, inflamed vocal folds. Continued inflamation can lead to serious vocal difficulties and even permanent damage to the larynx. When you cheer, use your normal pitch range, keep your throat and larynx relaxed, and use your abdomen and diaphragm to increase your volume. Your larynx still is irreplaceable!

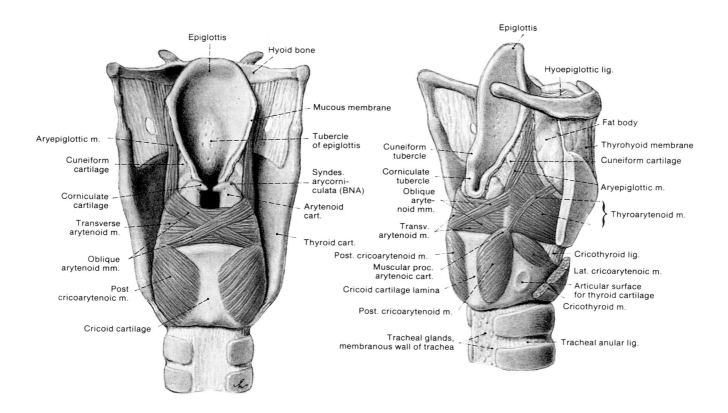

Figure 3-4 Three-dimensional Model of the Human Larynx viewed from the back and from the side. As we swallow, the epiglottis bends down to cover the vocal folds, but during normal breathing, it remains upright. (From Sobotta/Figge, Courtesy Urban and Schwarzenberg)

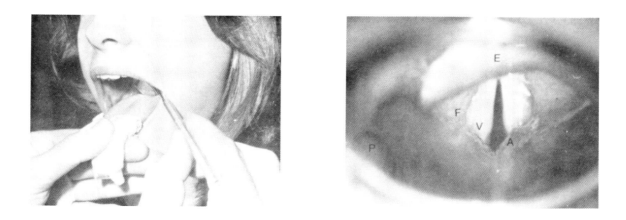

Figure 3-5 Photos Showing a Laryngoscopy. A mirror view of the larynx is shown on the right as a result of using a laryngoscopic technique for examination. Clearly visible are: (**E**) Epiglottis, (**A**) piriform recess, (**P**) ventribular or false folds, and (**V**) vocal folds. The glottis is evident between the folds. (From Bateman/Mason, Courtesy Charles C. Thomas, Publisher)

24

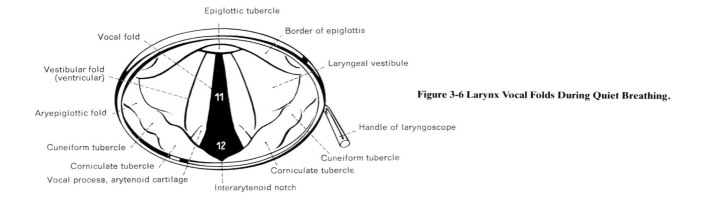

Epiglottic tubercle

Vocal fold

Border of epiglottis

Vestibular fold (ventricular)

Laryngeal vestibule

Aryepiglottic fold

Cuneiform tubercle

Handle of laryngoscope

Corniculate tubercle

Cuneiform tubercle

Vocal process, arytenoid cartilage

Corniculate tubercle

Interarytenoid notch

Figure 3-6 Larynx Vocal Folds During Quiet Breathing.

Figure 3-7 Larynx Vocal Folds for Producing Shrill Tones.

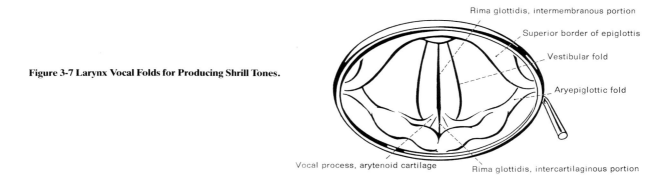

Rima glottidis, intermembranous portion

Superior border of epiglottis

Vestibular fold

Aryepiglottic fold

Vocal process, arytenoid cartilage

Rima glottidis, intercartilaginous portion

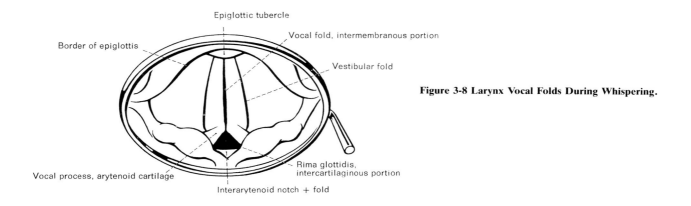

Epiglottic tubercle

Vocal fold, intermembranous portion

Border of epiglottis

Vestibular fold

Figure 3-8 Larynx Vocal Folds During Whispering.

Vocal process, arytenoid cartilage

Rima glottidis, intercartilaginous portion

Interarytenoid notch + fold

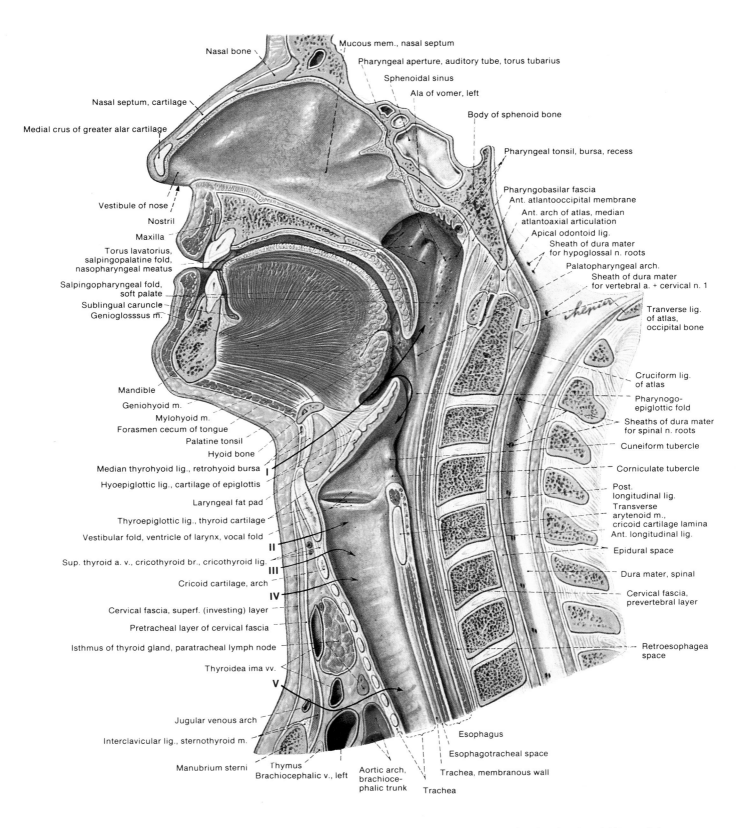

Nasal bone

Mucous mem., nasal septum

Pharyngeal aperture, auditory tube, torus tubarius

Sphenoidal sinus

Ala of vomer, left

Nasal septum, cartilage

Body of sphenoid bone

Medial crus of greater alar cartilage

Pharyngeal tonsil, bursa, recess

Pharyngobasilar fascia
Ant. atlantooccipital membrane

Ant. arch of atlas, median
atlantoaxial articulation

Apical odontoid lig.

Vestibule of nose

Sheath of dura mater
for hypoglossal n. roots

Nostril

Maxilla

Palatopharyngeal arch.

Sheath of dura mater
for vertebral a. + cervical n. 1

Torus lavatorius,
salpingopalatine fold,
nasopharyngeal meatus

Salpingopharyngeal fold,
soft palate

Sublingual caruncle

Genioglosssus m.

Tranverse lig.
of atlas,
occipital bone

Mandible

Cruciform lig.
of atlas

Geniohyoid m.

Pharynogo-
epiglottic fold

Mylohyoid m.

Forasmen cecum of tongue

Sheaths of dura mater
for spinal n. roots

Palatine tonsil

Cuneiform tubercle

Hyoid bone

Corniculate tubercle

Median thyrohyoid lig., retrohyoid bursa

Hyoepiglottic lig., cartilage of epiglottis

Post.
longitudinal lig.

Laryngeal fat pad

Transverse
arytenoid m.,
cricoid cartilage lamina

Thyroepiglottic lig., thyroid cartilage

Ant. longitudinal lig.

Vestibular fold, ventricle of larynx, vocal fold

Epidural space

Sup. thyroid a. v., cricothyroid br., cricothyroid lig.

Cricoid cartilage, arch

Dura mater, spinal

Cervical fascia, superf. (investing) layer

Cervical fascia,
prevertebral layer

Pretracheal layer of cervical fascia

Isthmus of thyroid gland, paratracheal lymph node

Thyroidea ima vv.

Retroesophagea
space

Jugular venous arch

Interclavicular lig., sternothyroid m.

Manubrium sterni

Thymus
Brachiocephalic v., left

Aortic arch,
brachioce-
phalic trunk

Esophagus

Esophagotracheal space

Trachea, membranous wall

Trachea

I

II

III

IV

V

Figure 3-9 Cross Section of the Articulators in Relation to the Larynx. Notice that the soft palate is relaxed (dropped) in a position for producing a nasal sound. The passageway to the lungs (trachea) and the passageway to the stomach (esophagus) separate at the larynx. The mouth is closed and the tongue takes up most of the oral cavity here, as if the individual is producing the (n) sound. (From Sobotta/Figge, Courtesy Urban and Schwarzenberg)

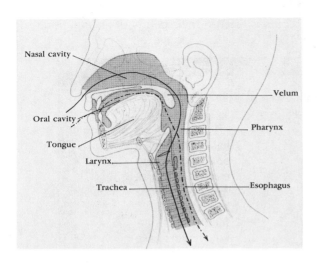

Labeled diagram showing: Nasal cavity, Oral cavity, Tongue, Larynx, Trachea, Velum, Pharynx, Esophagus

ARTICULATION OF SPOKEN SOUNDS

Articulation is the process of bringing movable components of the speech mechanism into greater or less proximity to each other in order to produce, distinguish, or connect different unique sounds. These movements may change the size and/or shape of the vocal tract, bringing greater or less obstruction to the breathstream. Those components, often referred to as **articulators,** include the lips, teeth, tongue, alveolar ridge, hard and soft palate, and lower jaw.

The Lips

The lips are flexible folds of flesh surrounding the opening to the mouth. They are most useful for changing the shape and size of the mouth opening. The terms "labio" and "labial" are used to describe sounds associated with the lips.

Sounds, which have their **place of articulation** (or contact point) at the lips, are classified as lip **(labial)** sounds. They include two sub-categories: two lip **(bilabial)** sounds which are formed by both lips and include the sounds [p], [b], [w], [hw], and [m] and lip/teeth **(labiodental)** sounds which are produced with the lower lip and the upper front teeth and include the sounds [f] and [v]. (Remember, when the term "sounds" is used, we are referring to spoken sounds and not the alphabet letters.)

Some sounds also may be described in terms of physiological changes made by the lips as they produce certain sounds. These may include features such as rounded or unrounded, tense or lax, spread (stretched) or neutral lips. The following chart shows you some of these descriptive possibilities in relation to articulating certain words.

USE OF THE LIPS IN ARTICULATION	
Lip(s) may be:	**In words such as:**
rounded	oh, awed, who, work, rumor
unrounded	ice, loud, name, hat, day
spread/stretched	each, mean, slip, he's
touching (bilabial)	pink, buy, mine, able, kept
in contact with the teeth (labiodental)	five, after, ivory, sleeve

Here is a brief summary chart of the lip sounds in relation to their points of articulation:

SUMMARY OF LIP (LABIAL) SOUNDS

Two Lip	[b]	bake, habit, cab
(bilabial)	[p]	poll, apple, step
	[m]	melt, ample, seem
	[w]	well, away
	[hw]	wheat, awhile
Lip/Teeth	[f]	feel, often, safe
(labiodental)	[v]	void, over, have

The Teeth

Unless you have false teeth, your individual teeth are not movable. Why are they included as movable portions of the speech mechanism? The answer is that the top and bottom teeth can move close together or far apart, in and out of alignment, and the tongue can move in greater or less proximity to them.

The term "dental" is used to refer to sounds whose point of articulation is on or at the teeth. You just saw that lip/teeth (**labiodental**) sounds [f] and [v] involve both the lower lip and teeth. Another class of sounds made between the teeth (**interdental**) is produced with the tongue tip between the upper and lower front teeth, as the upper surface of the tongue tip rests lightly on the biting edge of the upper front teeth. This class of sounds also is called the tongue/teeth (**linguadental**) sounds since both the tongue and teeth are involved in articulation. This class includes the voiced "th" sound in "that" and "feather" and the voiceless "th" sound in "think" and "myth." Soon, you will learn specific symbols for these two different sounds. By placing a finger on your Adam's apple, you can feel the vibrations that occur for the voiced but not the voiceless "th."

SUMMARY OF TEETH (DENTAL) SOUNDS

Lip/Teeth	[f]	few, after, half
(labiodental)	[v]	vain, ivy, leave
Tongue/Teeth	voiceless "th" = [θ]	thimble, wreath
(linguadental)	voiced "th" = [ð]	them, rather,
or (interdental)		bathe

The Tongue

Of all the articulators, the tongue is the most versatile. Although its primary purpose is to taste food and move it about in the mouth, it also is recognized as an essential component in speaking. Throughout history, the tongue has been celebrated, criticized, and studied. For centuries, "tongue" referred to a person's native language and to other languages that he or she

28

spoke. During the period when the oral tradition was at its zenith, references to the tongue would have been very meaningful. Even today, unknown or strange languages are referred to as "tongues."

The terms "lingua" or "lingual" are used frequently to refer to points of articulation involving the tongue. You just learned that "th" sounds are classified as tongue/teeth (**linguadental**) sounds. Other classes of sounds which include the tongue in their point of articulation are the tongue/gum ridge (**lingua-alveolar**) or (**alveolar**) sounds of [t], [d], [l], [n], [s] and [z]; tongue/palate (**lingua-palatal**) sounds of "sh," "zh," "y," [r], and tongue/soft palate or velum (**linguavelar**) or (**velar**) sounds of [k], [g], "ng."

Classifying all sounds that use the tongue in their articulation is impossible. However, the following chart may help you understand *a few* that use different portions of the tongue in their articulation.

USE OF THE TONGUE IN ARTICULATION OF SELECTED SOUNDS

Portion of Tongue Used	To Create These Sounds	Sample Words Containing Sounds
front tip	[t], [d], [n]	test, did, none
blade (behind tip)	[s]. [z]. "sh" = [ʃ] "zh" = [ʒ] "tsh" = [tʃ] "dzh" = [dʒ]	sacks, zoo, ship, leisure check, jail
front	[i], [ɪ], "y" = [j]	siesta, pick, yet
center (mid)	"uh" = [ʌ] "er" = [ɝ]	cut, her
back sides	[u], [ʊ]	suit, put
back	[k], [g], "ng" = [ŋ]	back, gun, sing

Later, you will discover that the tongue plays a crucial role in vowel resonance in three respects.

1. **Tongue tension,** which contracts the tongue's muscle fibers running from side to side, will make the tongue narrower and rounder, thus affecting the passageway's shape where it becomes most narrow. Say the words "keep" and "cup" to feel the difference in tension and rounding.

2. **Tongue height** (toward the hard palate) pushes sound forward, using up part of the oral cavity or creating two cavities that are connected by a narrow passageway. This passageway increases in size as the tongue drops, allowing the front and back chambers gradually to unify and expand. Say these words aloud to feel the gradual dropping of the tongue and a combining of the two chambers: heel, hull, hall.

3. **Location of the tongue's highest point in the mouth** increases or decreases resonance. If the **front** portion of the tongue is elevated close to the front teeth, the forward chamber will have little space for resonance. However, if the **back** portion of the tongue is elevated close to the hard palate, the forward chamber will elongate and allow more resonance. Say these words aloud to

29

feel the tongue position change: he, how—aid, owed.

Because of its great flexibility, your tongue can compensate for changes in size, shape, and composition of other components of the speech mechanism. Even though you may have a shorter tongue, smaller jaws or mouth, fewer teeth, a higher hard palate, or less flexibility in your lower jaw than your parents, siblings, or friends, your tongue can make enough changes in shape and location to allow you to duplicate their sounds.

SUMMARY OF TONGUE (LINGUAL) SOUNDS

Tongue/Teeth (linguadental) or (interdental)	voiceless "th" = [θ] voiced "th" = [ð]	thimble, wreath them, rather, bathe
Tongue/Gum Ridge (lingua-alveolar) or (alveolar)	[t] [d] [l] [n] [s] [z]	tell, attic, pat due, ready, said low, really, all not, and, win see, best, less zip, hazy, craze
Tongue/Palate (linguapalatal)	"sh" = [ʃ] "zh" = [ʒ] "tsh" = [tʃ] "dzh" = [dʒ] "y" = [j] [r]	ship, ashen, cash leisure, beige chide, itches, ditch jam, ledger, edge yes, hoya, yoyo rose, around

The Gum (Alveolar) Ridge

Just behind your upper front teeth is a short extension of the gums which forms the narrow gum **(alveolar)** ridge just before the roof of your mouth slopes upward to your hard palate. Although this articulator doesn't move, your tongue moves to it as another point of articulation for a class of tongue/gum ridge **(lingua-alveolar)** or simply **(alveolar)** sounds. These sounds, mentioned earlier under "The Tongue," include [t], [d], [n], [l], [s], [z]. In the first four sounds, the **tongue tip** makes a firm contact with this ridge; in the last two, the tongue tip is close to, but doesn't touch the ridge (the edges of the tongue make firm contact with inner surfaces of the teeth right up to this ridge.)

30

```
┌─────────────────────────────────────────────────────────────┐
│          SUMMARY OF GUM RIDGE (ALVEOLAR)                      │
│                    SOUNDS                                     │
│                                                               │
│     Tongue/Alveolar       [t]       tell, attic, pat          │
│     (lingua-alveolar)     [d]       die, ready, said          │
│     or (alveolar)         [l]       low, really, all          │
│                           [n]       not, and, win             │
│                           [s]       see, best, less           │
│                           [z]       zip, hazy, craze          │
└─────────────────────────────────────────────────────────────┘
```

The Soft Palate (Velum)

The soft palate or velum is the fleshy extension of the hard palate which terminates in the uvula, the limp protrusion that droops from the middle portion of your soft palate. If you have never been aware of this articulator before, you should look at it in a mirror. Open your mouth wide and breathe in and out slowly, first through the nose only and then through the mouth only. Say ''ahh'' and then ''ng'' and watch the action of the soft palate and uvula.

The soft palate should move up toward the nasal passages for all non-nasal sounds, forcing the air out through the mouth. (If you have a nasal voice, you probably are not elevating the soft palate high enough to shut off the flow of air through the nose for non-nasal sounds, such as the vowel sounds.) However, the soft palate should drop for the three English nasal sounds [n], [m], and ''ng,'' allowing air to escape through the nose rather than through the mouth. The soft palate elevates and drops thousands of times during a normal conversation as speakers constantly intersperse nasal and non-nasal sounds.

The class of sounds associated with the soft palate as its point of articulation is called the tongue/soft palate **(linguavelar)** or simply **(velar)** class of sounds. It includes [k], [g], and ''ng'' mentioned previously under ''The Tongue.''

```
┌─────────────────────────────────────────────────────────────┐
│          SUMMARY OF SOFT PALATE (VELAR) SOUNDS                │
│                                                               │
│     soft palate        [k]          king, asked, lack         │
│     (linguavelar)      [g]          go, again, lag            │
│     or (velar)         ''ng'' = [ŋ] singing, slang            │
└─────────────────────────────────────────────────────────────┘
```

The Hard Palate

The hard palate becomes a point of articulation for the sounds ''sh,'' ''zh,'' ''tsh,'' ''dzh,'' ''y,'' and [r] mentioned previously under ''The Tongue.'' These sounds constitute the class called tongue/palate **(linguapalatal)** or simply **(palatal).** They are formed by the proximity of the upper surface of the tongue to the hard palate.

The hard palate, often referred to as the roof of the mouth, is the bony structure in the upper jaw separating the oral and nasal cavities. Individuals who are born with a cleft palate have an opening directly into the nose from the mouth. This defect makes non-nasal sounds difficult or impossible to say without nasalization since sound that ordinarily bounces against the roof of the mouth now goes up into the nose. If this opening doesn't close, surgical repair is necessary. When the surgery takes place after an individual has learned to talk, that person may need speech therapy to learn to say non-nasal sounds **without** nasalizing them.

SUMMARY OF HARD PALATE (PALATAL) SOUNDS		
hard palate	"sh" = [ʃ]	ship, ashen, cash
(linguapalatal)	"zh" = [ʒ]	leisure, beige
or (palatal)	"tsh" = [tʃ]	chide, itches, ditch
	"dzh" = [dʒ]	jam, ledger, edge
	"y" = [j]	yes, hoya, yoyo
	[r]	rose, around

The Lower Jaw (Mandible)

The lower jaw is included as one of the articulators because of its flexibility in moving up and down, or side to side during sound articulation. Since it doesn't serve as a point of articulation, no one class of sounds is directly related to it. However, the jaw influences all sounds by changing the size of the mouth opening and the oral cavity. Its movement allows the tongue more room in which to move—and allows the teeth to align properly for various sounds.

* * * * * * * * *

The articulators allow you to shape and clarify sounds. When you criticize speakers for poor diction—or comment that you can't understand what speakers are saying—you usually are referring to slovenly, inaccurate use of these components of the speech mechanism. Problems in sound substitution, omission, addition, and transposition all result from improper use of one or more of the articulators.

THE SOURCES OF RESONANCE FOR SPEAKING

The final portion of the speech mechanism concerns the components that affect vocal quality: the resonators. The nose, mouth, and throat (pharynx) cavities are the most important resonators for the human voice. (Often, one cavity will extend, support or complement the resonation occurring in other cavities—particularly when barriers separating the cavities, such as the height of the tongue, are minimal.) Their size, shape, and composition—and the breathing habits of the individual—have a significant influence on vocal resonation, providing each person with his or her unique voice quality.

If you can identify friends and relatives by the "sound of their voices," you probably are basing your judgment on elements of resonance. Often, family members are able to make fairly accurate estimates of other family members' physical and/or mental health states by the timbre, quality, or sound of their voices. Tension, fatigue, alertness and other physical states are suggested by the kind and amount of resonance displayed by a voice.

Resonance is a process that increases and enriches the **intensity** of sound by increasing the **rate** of energy output over a shorter period of time. However, resonators don't add any further

32

energy to the original energy. Resonance further modifies energy (exhaled air from the lungs) which was partially changed into vibrations or sound waves by striking an obstacle (the vocal folds). A well resonated voice becomes louder than it would have been without the resonating facilities—but it also uses up this intensity in a shorter time than without the resonating facilities.

Vocal resonance or quality may be changed with practice. Comedians and impersonators carefully study the vocal quality of people they are mimicking. Often, this quality may be changed simply by tensing or relaxing the muscles controlling the tongue, throat, and/or soft palate. Later in this book the element of vocal quality will be discussed in greater detail. For the moment, you may be interested to know that some of the more commonly used terms for describing vocal resonance are strident, nasal, denasal, breathy, guttural, throaty, hoarse, and resonant.

DISCOVERY EXERCISES

1. Prolong the [s] sound for five seconds, then, without halting the airflow, change to the "sh" sound and hold it for five seconds. Which sound requires: (a) The greatest rounding of the lips? (b) The greatest protrusion of the lower lip? (c) The least dropping of the back sides or edges of the tongue?

2. Hiccups require action by the diaphragm and involve quick, noisy intakes of air. Imitate a hiccup and notice the action of your larynx and abdominal muscles. Now attempt to reverse the hiccup by expelling air and saying "hic!" What happens to your larynx and abdominal muscles during this reversal?

3. Read the following sentences aloud in a conversational manner. What happens at the point of contact of your articulators as you say the underlined portions of the sentences?

a. It took Todd Drew seven nights and eight days to complete his voyage. (tongue-alveolar ridge)

b. Keep Barbara happy by playing some music. (both lips)

c. I've found a cheap, safe van at Steve Foster's Used Cars. (teeth-lip)

4. Say "ahhh" aloud and gradually round (or pucker) your lips as you prolong the sound. What happens to the sound?

5. Prolong a whispered (unvoiced) "th" and gradually move the tip of your tongue behind the upper front teeth, towards your gumridge. How high can you raise your tongue before the "th" becomes totally distorted?

6. Place your hand on your stomach, just below your lower ribs, and forcefully whisper "ha, ha, ha, ha." Do your hand and abdomen move with each repetition? If not, practice until they do. You may need to increase the tension in your abdominal area as your intensity increases. Now say the words quietly but forcefully.

7. Say "ahhhh" aloud while alternately raising and lowering your soft palate. What happens to the sound?

8. Ventriloquists must change certain sounds to ones which are similar, but don't require lip movement. By doing this, they keep their lips in one position and make it appear that their dummies (whose mouths are opening and closing) are speaking. Try to find the best substitutions for the following sounds: [m], [p], [v], [b]. Practice saying words containing these sounds aloud without moving your lips.

DIALOGUE FOR ORAL PRACTICE (requires two readers)

Use slight changes in your normal vocal quality and manner of speaking to suggest the following characters. After the dialogue, tell what you had to do to change your voice.

Angel: You are a bitter person—cold, calculating, and cruel to your neighbor. The Good Lord wants to cure you and has sent me to offer you anything in the world, if you will only let your neighbor have two of them.

Human: Does that mean if I become president of a bank, my neighbor gets to be president of two banks?

Angel: That's correct. That will help you learn the value of sharing your good fortune with others.

Human: If I win a million dollars in the lottery, my neighbor wins two million dollars?

Angel: Exactly! But think of it—you will have a great deal of money, if that's what you ask of me.

Human: Let me get this straight. If I ask for a furnished castle on a mountain, you will give my neighbor two furnished castles?

Angel: That is what I have been ordered to do and I shall give you a fine castle.

Human: O.K., angel, then I'll take a glass eye.

CHAPTER 4

PREPARING MATERIAL FOR ORAL PRESENTATION

If this is the first time you have had a formal course in speaking and listening, you may not be sure of the procedures that will be used to evaluate your oral presentations to your class. You may be unfamiliar with material that can help you demonstrate your oral communication skills—or with ways of locating and preparing that material. The purpose of this chapter is to help you understand the common expectations of oral presentations—and to help you prepare for them.

SOME COMMON ASSUMPTIONS OF SPEECH IMPROVEMENT COURSES

Most speech improvement courses assume that every participant will be present for every class to gain both the knowledge of how to improve speaking and listening skills (cognitive skills), and classroom experiences for actually demonstrating this improvement (behavioral skills). Knowing the substantive content—the facts, practices, and theories about speaking—is only the first step for demonstrating your competence as a speaker and listener. Discovering how these facts, theories and practices are put into practice by your classmates (and yourself) during class presentations is the second step. If you miss presentations by your classmates, you will be shirking your obligations for developing your listening and analytical abilities as an audience member. By following the progress of individuals in your class, you can gain insights into your own progress. Students often can recognize their own errors in other students before they see or hear them in themselves!

A second common assumption is that every participant will have an equal chance for being chosen to speak on the first day of each new oral presentation. A common practice is for the instructor to assign a date on which all class members must be ready to give their presentations. By using a procedure of random selection (such as drawing names at the beginning of the class period—or after each speaker completes his or her oral presentation), your instructor can remain unbiased in determining speaking order. If you are unprepared on the day of your selection, you won't meet the minimal requirements for that particular assignment. (Many instructors require all unprepared students to complete their presentations at the end of graded presentations, but as ungraded experiences. This practice insures that every participant will have the same speaking/listening experiences. Thus, being unprepared for an oral presentation does not eliminate the need to speak!)

A third assumption is that listening will be an important feature of this course. In the early part of the course, you will be developing your ability to hear various sounds in relatively simple listening exercises. You also will be developing your ability to describe those sounds by using a uniform symbol system. As the class progresses, you will demonstrate your ability to hear specific voice and diction changes in classmates as they give practiced and spontaneous oral presentations in class. You can't be selective in determining the speakers you will listen to, as you can when you change channels while watching your television set. (A term commonly used to refer to this type of academic situation is "captive audience," since you are expected to remain in the class and fulfill specific obligations related to each session, regardless of your interest in the speaker or the topic.) Unlike your daily conversations with friends, during which you are listening primarily for information, these oral presentations require you to evaluate each speaker's control of voice and diction as central elements in the communication process.

A fourth assumption is that every student will meet the specific requirements of each different class presentation. In most speech improvement classes, every oral assignment builds upon lessons learned and experiences gained in previous ones. For this reason, you need to be sure you follow the instructor's directions carefully. In the next section of this chapter we will discuss this matter in greater detail.

SOME IMPORTANT INITIAL CRITERIA FOR SELECTING MATERIAL

Before you begin to look for material to present to the class, you should be aware of several factors that will be extremely important throughout this course. First, the material you will read to the class usually will be less than five minutes in length. Therefore, you will be expected to read only a small portion or "cutting" of a selection rather than the entire piece of literature. You will be responsible for making your own cutting. It should be self-contained, or able to stand by itself as a complete, unified episode, without a lengthy explanation by you. In narrative prose or poetry cuttings, the audience should be able to understand what happened to whom and should have a fairly good idea of why it happened. If your selection makes little sense by itself, leaves too many things for your audience to guess, or requires many of your own intervening comments, it probably is a poor cutting and should be bypassed in favor of another selection.

Next, the material you choose should meet the criteria specified by your instructor. Generally, these criteria will involve considerations of:

1. **Time:** You will be assigned a maximum and minimum time limit for giving your oral presentations. This becomes a very important consideration for organizing the course. Your instructor must know how many presentations can be scheduled each session, each week, and throughout the term. When several students exceed the maximum time limit, your instructor must shorten or eliminate important lectures, class discussions, or other assignments. If your assignment specifies a maximum, but no minimum time limit, you should find material that allows you enough time to demonstrate your increasing oral competence, rather than looking for the shortest selection you can find to get through the experience quickly. Always be sure to select material that will allow you to meet the time constraints without having to rush through your presentation. You will be able to judge this, as you practice aloud, by timing yourself with a digital counter, clock, or watch with a sweep second hand. Also, find out if your introductory comments will count as part of your time limit—and if your comments will be evaluated by your instructor as part of your oral proficiency demonstration. When introductory remarks are counted as part of your time limit, or in your oral proficiency evaluation, you should practice your comments as carefully as you do your oral presentation. Since many careers, such as those in broadcasting, involve severe time constraints that must be met to fulfill contract obligations and since many daily speaking experiences must be done quickly and efficiently, you should view the experience of meeting imposed time limits as a practical learning experience.

2. **Literary Genre:** If you are required to find and present material from a specific form or genre of literature (prose, poetry, or drama), you should be sure your selection meets this requirement. If you choose an interesting poem that tells a story but the assignment requires a prose selection, you will not meet the assigned genre category. Often, your instructor will have specific developmental reasons for requiring you to use a certain literary form at a given time.

3. **Discretion and Good Taste:** You are responsible for choosing material that will not offend members of your audience. When material contains excessive, overt vulgarity and profanity, or intentional religious, sexual, ethnic, political, socio-economic, professional, or racial slurs, you need to realize that some members in your "captive audience" may find them offensive. Unless you have time to explain why these elements are important in your selection—or to your oral presentation—you probably would be wiser to select something else. Neither should your oral presentations be viewed as opportunities to proselytize, "witness for," or convert class members to your viewpoint. A good rule-of-thumb to follow in selecting material for this class is to avoid topics that propose or suggest adopting a specific religious, political, sexual, or racial orientation. Also, your material should appeal to the intelligence and maturity level of your audience, rather than to children and young teenagers. You can argue that certain authors write for "anyone who is young at heart," but your audience may find the overly simplistic nature of juvenile literature boring or degrading.

4. **Special Requirements:** Your instructor might ask you to find material that contains specific qualities, approaches, demands, or emphases. For example, if you were asked to find a descriptive prose selection, this assignment would require you to emphasize various sense appeals contained in a short story, novel, essay, or article. On the other hand, if you were required to find a drama selection involving a male and a female speaker, you would need to find a play (drama refers to the genre and not the element of suspense involved) in which your voice would suggest a male and female character talking together. You also might be asked to find a piece of literature that contains numerous words with sounds you are having difficulty saying accurately. Always check your course syllabus and your lecture notes to be sure of any special requirements for each new assignment.

FINDING MATERIAL FOR ORAL PRESENTATIONS

Even though your listeners' primary attention will be focused on your voice and articulation, you must be concerned about their potential interest in your material. If you just transferred to your college, or have taken no recent courses in the Arts and Letters, you may not be aware of resources available to you for finding suitable material that will be interesting to your classmates. You may be wondering where you should begin your search. The purpose of this section is to give you suggestions for finding and adapting suitable materials.

Anthologies

Collections of short stories, poems, essays, speeches, articles, plays and so on, used in other courses can simplify your selection process. General anthologies usually contain works of many different authors; specific anthologies contain either the collected works of one author or literature by different authors on the same theme or during the same era. If you don't like the writing style or subjects of one author, a general anthology allows you to turn immediately to another author's work.

You may discover the literary anthology you are using in an English course contains useful, interesting selections. Since you are analyzing the selections for another course, you should be well acquainted with the meaning and requirements of your selection. Furthermore, by having the book already, you eliminate the necessity for using time to search for a source of literature.

A disadvantage of choosing an anthology used in one of your college courses is that many of your classmates may be taking the same course and may select the same material to read—or may be so familiar with it that they will find your selection uninteresting or boring.

If you like the work of an author in one of your current textbooks, but you want to find a new selection, you may check the author index of your library's card catalog (or computerized catalog) to see if the library has a copy of that author's collected works. If the college has none you also may check under "Literature" and "Anthologies" in the subject index of the catalog to see if the author is included in another available anthology.

Textbooks

Besides literary anthologies, other textbooks may contain pieces of literature that are suitable for your oral presentations. Practice selections, samples of stories, plays, poems or speeches that illustrate particular points being made in a certain class—all may be found in textbooks you are using, or have used, in classes. Some books include selections in an appendix at the end of the books; others, within the chapters; and still others, at the ends of chapters. Again, if you have studied those pieces of literature in other classes, your familiarity with them can eliminate problems in understanding and interpretation that might arise if you were not familiar with a selection.

A disadvantage is the same as for anthologies that are used in other classes: classmates may be so familiar with the literature that they will find the presentation less interesting than a new selection. You will give classmates less basis for comparing your presentation with other ones if you choose something they haven't heard in previous classes.

Novels, Biographies, Histories

Separately published books such as novels, biographies and histories may be excellent sources for prose selections. Novels may be fictional or non-fictional in nature whereas histories and biographies usually are factual—or at least based on fact. Novels and biographies usually combine dialogue, narration, and description, and depending on the cutting that is selected, are suitable for many types of prose presentations. Books permit you to scan several chapters involving the same characters, events, or situations before choosing the best selection to use.

If you never read the books before, a disadvantage of these resources may be their length. Choosing a cutting from the middle of an unfamiliar novel without reading the entire novel may cause you to give an incorrect interpretation to certain events and/or characters. If the instructor or members of the audience have read the novel, they will recognize your error when you read the cutting aloud, even if *you* do not.

Magazines, Journals and Other Periodicals

Periodicals are a readily available source of short stories, poetry, and articles. Popular magazines, trade and professional journals, literary quarterlies, and sometimes newspapers contain a wealth of literature that may be appropriate for your oral presentations. In fact, many famous writers gained their early recognition by publishing their works in contemporary periodicals. Later, the authors published their collected works or anthologies.

One of the advantages of periodical publications is the current appeal the literature will have. Magazine and journal editors want to secure and maintain loyal readers. Therefore, they look for material on topics of current interest. Another advantage is the availability of material. You can pick up a copy of a high quality magazine on any newsstand if you don't already subscribe to one. The most current issues of periodicals in your library will be found, unbound, on the shelves or in the reading racks of your Periodicals Room or Reading Room. Older copies of the same periodicals will be found in bound editions and shelved in their own separate section of the library. (Some periodicals may be on microfiche or microfilm and will be so specified in the card catalog.)

A disadvantage of periodical literature is the uncertain quality of material you will find in some publications. If you have read only a few different magazines and journals, you may not know which ones have acquired consistent reputations among authors and literary critics as ''quality publications'' and which ones are considered ''average'' or ''below average'' publications. Even in some of your average publications you may find a story, article, or poem that has outstanding qualities, so a periodical's reputation isn't always a reliable indicator of the merits of its literature. (Writers frequently determine the quality of a periodical by the amount of money it pays for accepted manuscripts! If you would like to know current rates, ask your reference librarian for a recent annual or index to publishers and publishing rates or look at recent copies of magazines intended for writers.)

SOME WORDS OF CAUTION ABOUT SELECTING MATERIAL

You may be tempted to use readily available material that has unproved literary merit, simply because you have it on hand—or because you wrote it. Our advice is to be cautious. You may be a talented writer and your material—or material written by a friend—may have great potential for interesting your classmates. However, an instructor who has dealt with many, many oral presentations may find the material of questionable value, either as literature, or as a vehicle for demonstrating your growing proficiency in speaking. Students are too emotionally attached to their own or their friends' material to see its limitations. Often, instructors stipulate that all material used for oral presentation must be from national or international published sources.

Generally, you shouldn't select material from your school newspaper—or even from the local newspaper—since newspaper writing style is not the best style for demonstrating your oral capabilities. An instructor may know that an article appeared in a recent edition of the newspaper and may conclude that you either didn't have time to find a better selection, or that you are incapable of evaluating literary merit adequately. Ultimately, the quality of your oral presentation may be determined by the material you select—so choose the best vehicle possible in the time available.

When material relates to your particular areas of interest and expertise, it should be understandable to nonspecialists. An article on the symbiotic relationship of certain algae and fungi in lichens may be fascinating to a botanist, but too technical for other students. Some literary allusions, mathematical equations, foreign language quotations, and technical terms may make your oral presentation partially or totally confusing to many people in your class. One of your goals in selecting any material for oral presentation is to be understood by everyone.

PREPARING YOUR MANUSCRIPT

Your instructor may require a standard format for all manuscripts in order to check them quickly for accuracy, source of origin, required elements, or words and phrases that were not clear during your oral presentation. Your carefully prepared manuscript will serve as evidence that you took time to prepare your material in advance. (Anyone can bring a book or photocopy of a piece of literature to class and "read it off the top of his or her head" with little or no preparation.)

Many speech improvement instructors use the manuscripts either while completing critique forms as they listen to recordings of presentations given in class (to be sure they heard what they thought they heard) or in diagnostic and advisory conferences with individual students following oral presentations. If one of your instructor's special requirements is a correctly prepared manuscript, you should follow his or her specifications exactly. If special instructions are not given, you may find the information in this section helpful for completing useful manuscripts.

Paper Specifications

You probably are aware of the variety of paper that exists today for completing various educational tasks. It may be lined or unlined, white or colored, easy or difficult to erase, loose leaf or bound (either with glue or in spiral notebooks), and in many different sizes. Some paper is intended for rough, quick pencil notes; detailed pen and ink drawings; typewritten copy; computerized printouts; mimeographing; or sketching. If an instructor doesn't give explicit directions on the type of paper you should use for your manuscripts, you may conclude that any paper is adequate if *you* can read from it.

In making this judgment, you may be giving yourself additional burdens when you try to read your material in front of the class. If your notebook paper is small, you may have to flip through numerous sheets of paper. If your paper is highly polished, it may reflect so much overhead light that you will have to hold your pages in just the right position to avoid a glare so you can see your words. If you tear sheets out of spiral ring binders, you may find the ragged edges bind some pages together making the turning of pages difficult at the lectern. If some of your pages are on one type or size paper and the rest are on another, you could have difficulty keeping pages in the right order or in moving smoothly through your manuscript.

If you are in doubt about the paper you should use, you generally will be correct if you choose white 8 ½ × 11 inch typing, computer, or loose leaf notebook paper. You and your instructor can carry, file, and sort these standard sized forms quickly and easily. Yellow or other colored paper usually is used only for rough drafts but not for "finished" papers.

Format of Manuscript

By following the same format in all your manuscripts, you can develop a preparation pattern that will make your work efficient and complete every time. Usually, you should double space typewritten entries or skip every other line for handwritten or printed entries. This system allows your eyes to move easily through your material without getting "lost"—a feature that is particularly helpful if you are experiencing tension in class. Also, your manuscript should indicate the source of your information to allow you to find it again quickly—and to indicate to your instructor that you know how to give credit to the proper source. (Often, a classmate may be so interested in a particular selection that he or she will ask you where you found the material. By having a complete bibliographical citation, you can share your information easily.)

You may find the following format easy to follow.

1. Number all pages except the first one in the upper right corner of each page. The numbers will be easy to see if you place your manuscript in a ring binder.

2. On the first page of your manuscript, place your name, class name, and date in the upper right corner, single-spaced, on three lines.

3. On the first page of your manuscript, place a full bibliographic citation of the source of your selection, single-spaced, in the upper left corner. This citation should follow a format similar to the following:

   a. If a smaller work (poem, article, short story) appears in an anthology, use this format:

      First and Last Name of Author, "Title of Shorter Work," TITLE OF BOOK edited by Name of Editor(s) (Place of Publication: Name of Publisher, Date of Publication), page(s) on which material was found

   b. If a separately published work (novel, play, novella) contains your selection, use this format:

      First and Last Name of Author, TITLE OF BOOK (Place of Publication: Name of Publisher, Date of Publication), page(s) on which material was found

4. Leave at least a one inch margin at the top, sides, and bottom of each sheet. (The information at the top of the **first** sheet does not have to meet this condition.) If your material will be placed in a notebook, you may wish to leave a slightly wider left margin to allow for punched holes.

The following sample of a first page gives you an idea of how your manuscript will look when you follow this format.

Walt Whitman, "I Sit
and Look Out," THE
NORTON ANTHOLOGY OF
AMERICAN LITERATURE,
Vol. I, edited by
Ronald Gottesman, et
al. (New York: W.W.
Norton & Co., 1979),
p. 1941

Mindy Taylor
Speech Improvement I
April 23, 1991

I Sit and Look Out

I sit and look out upon all the sorrows of the world,

   and upon all oppression and shame,

I hear secret convulsive sobs from young men at

   anguish with themselves, remorseful after deeds

   done,

   etc.

You should type or write your manuscript on one side of the page only. This eliminates the potentially confusing possibility of ink or type showing through the copy. It also allows you to develop a consistent pattern of looking at a smaller area (one side of each sheet rather than front and back of each sheet) while reading aloud. Rather than flipping pages as you finish reading them, you can slide the top sheet unobtrusively to one side as you finish reading it while still keeping your visual focus on the same general area of the lectern or your notebook.

Use of a Notebook

Your classroom may contain a permanent lectern for you to stand behind when you give your presentation. It also may contain no lectern at all, or a flimsy reading stand that may or may not be a good place for your manuscript. If you are uncertain whether the lectern will be present during all of your presentations, or if it is too high, too low, or undependable for you, you may decide to hold your manuscript in one or both hands. This decision may involve another consideration regarding your manuscript: whether or not to place it in a notebook or other binder.

A rigid, light weight, ring notebook can be a handy aid for you during oral presentations. It eliminates the need for holding your script with both hands. It can be held with one hand and pages can be turned with the other. It also prevents pages from accidentally slipping out before or during your presentation, assuring you that the pages remain in the order you selected when you closed the rings. Also, the stiff backing of a notebook allows you to control extraneous movement, such as shaking of pages, better than if the script is several sheets of loose leaf paper.

Use of Manuscript Marks as Guides

As your oral presentations develop in complexity, you will be trying to practice several different elements of oral communication simultaneously. You may be trying to remember to voice final [z] sounds, pause at the ends of thought sequences, emphasize key words in each sentence, and use certain inflection patterns you aren't accustomed to using. In addition, you will want your audience to understand the content of your selection and experience the emotional impact of it. These tasks take much practice to control easily in presentations to the class, even in a short selection.

You may wish to use colored pencils or ink to circle, underline, or highlight various parts of your selection. You also may wish to use your own special marks to remind you of needed pauses, thought sequences, points of emphasis, or other features on which you have been working. Your instructor may ask you to underline throughout your manuscript one or two sounds that you have had difficulty with in the past to make you conscious of their recurrence in your oral reading. You also may want to write brief comments or reminders in the margin of your manuscript to help you remember to do certain things when you are practicing. All of these visual guides can assist you in practice sessions and during your actual presentation to the class. Since you are trying to demonstrate your awareness of potential problems and your ability to overcome them in **practiced readings,** you may find some of these reading guides useful, at least until you are confident of your ability to control them spontaneously. If your instructor has no objections, mark your manuscript carefully with as many guides as you find helpful.

PRACTICING WITH THE MANUSCRIPT

The most important thing you can do to prepare for your presentation to the class is to practice it aloud with the same volume and vocal changes you will use in class. Your chances for accomplishing your goals will improve as your practice conditions duplicate the actual classroom situation.

You cannot sit in your room and run through your presentation silently, expecting that this will prepare you for the classroom experience. You must stand up, place your manuscript on a simulated lectern (if one is used in the classroom) or hold it in one hand, and read from it with enough volume to be heard by the group of students who will be seated in your classroom. You must be able to feel the muscles that are working as you maintain a fairly loud volume level. You have to hear your vocal changes enough times so that they will not come as surprises to you while you are speaking to the class. You need to be aware of the sound changes that occur when you intensify your words, change your emphasis, pause for meaning, speed up your rate, and change your vocal quality.

Some students believe they can do an adequate job of practicing if they simply memorize their manuscripts. Your familiarity with your manuscript *can* help make your presentation more interesting to an audience. This familiarity allows you to look at your audience more often and to share information through visual as well as vocal means—a goal everyone in your class should try to attain. However, familiarity with your manuscript will not compensate for a lack of improvement in voice and diction. This improvement will come only as a result of concerted oral practice in a realistic situation.

If you are concerned about disturbing a roommate, members of your family, or other people, find an empty room where you can practice aloud in isolation. Look away from your manuscript at an imaginary audience periodically while you continue to speak, to gain fluency in your delivery and to gain experience in maintaining eye contact with your listeners. Don't be afraid of exaggerating and "playing" with vocal changes and sounds during your practice sessions.

By varying your oral practice techniques, you can discover ways to control and change your habituated patterns. If necessary, prolong or shorten sounds you are having difficulty with; speed up and then slow down your speaking rate significantly; use rising and falling inflection patterns that you don't normally use; give extra stress or emphasis to certain syllables in words; imitate the vocal qualities or characteristics of other people; practice tightening and relaxing your throat and chest muscles while you speak. Try to hear the changes that occur as a result of each of your actions during your practice sessions. These changes may help you hear the areas which you need to improve. They also may give you clues on how you can make these improvements easily and quickly, in your own way.

READINGS FOR ORAL PRACTICE

Read the following selections aloud as if you are telling, not reading the story, to your friends.

1. One bright Spring morning, a lion awoke from a sound sleep, stretched vigorously, then got to his feet. He felt unusually strong and gave a stupendous roar which shook the trees. He held his head high, inhaled the fresh morning air, then sauntered down a dusty trail until he came to a zebra. "Who" he asked, "Is the king of the jungle?" "Oh, sir," said the zebra, "You are the king of the jungle." The lion felt very good. He continued down the trail until he came to a gazelle. The lion threw out his chest and bellowed, "Well, well, Miss Gazelle, and who do you believe is the king of the jungle?" The shy gazelle took two steps backward and replied, "Why, everyone knows you are king of the jungle." The lion felt his heart swelling with pride. He pranced down the dusty trail until he came to an elephant which was enjoying his morning meal under a great shade tree. The lion roared, "Who is the king of the jungle, Mr. Elephant?" The startled elephant turned around, picked up the lion with his trunk, and threw him against a tree. Then he picked up the lion again and threw him against a rock. The lion scrambled to his feet and scurried behind a rock. From there, he shouted, "O.K., O.K., you don't have to get so angry—just because you don't know the answer!"

2. A middle-aged father became concerned that his three young children were becoming couch potatoes because they were spending so much time watching television. He decided it was up to him to encourage their artistic talents. He remembered his own childhood days when he wanted to play the piano, but his parents wouldn't let him because it made too much noise. He decided he would like to hear some piano music in his house. So, one afternoon, before his children returned from elementary school, he had a beautiful walnut console piano delivered to his living room and the television was moved upstairs to the parents' bedroom. All afternoon, he anticipated what he would hear as he walked into his house that evening! It might not be music yet, but someday it would be. When he got home at 5:30 that evening, he listened for the sound of the piano. He heard nothing. He went inside and found his three children standing at the piano, staring at it with great puzzlement. Finally, the father could take the suspense no longer and he said to the oldest, "Well, how do you like it?" The youngsters looked at him, looked at the piano, then looked at him again. After a long pause, the eldest replied, "I guess it's O.K., but how do you plug it in?"

CHAPTER 5

FINDING A UNIFORM WAY TO DESCRIBE SOUNDS

This chapter will remind you of some of the ways in which sounds are classified in the English language. It will help you understand why our non-phonetic language is a difficult one to learn. Also, it will introduce the phonetic system you will be using throughout this course to describe spoken English.

The English language consists of twenty-six written (alphabet) letters but almost fifty different spoken sounds. If each English letter always represented only one unique sound, our language would be considered a phonetic one. You would have only twenty-six sounds to remember since each sound would be represented by a different letter. You would spell and pronounce the same sounds in the same way every time.

INCONSISTENCIES OF ENGLISH

When you're trying to spell an unfamiliar English word you have heard, you can't always "trust your ear" for clues on how to spell the word correctly. Consider the vowel sound in the word "met" for just a moment. The same **sound** appears in all these words "said, heir, friend, leopard, bear, anyone, says." Notice the variety of ways this one sound is spelled in those words!

Since the letter "a" sometimes is pronounced as a long "a" and sometimes as a short one, you must learn specific rules for correct pronunciation of the sound—and then all the exceptions to those rules. The words "phone" and "fact" begin with entirely different **letters,** but the same **sound**. The same sound is produced by doubling the letter "f" in the word "affair."

You can begin to see why you may have difficulty looking for a word in a dictionary if you haven't seen the word in print! The spelling (orthography) of an English word is not a dependable method for determining how it must be pronounced. Neither is its pronunciation a consistent clue for telling you how a word is spelled.

CAN YOU TRUST YOUR DICTIONARY?

Perhaps you depend on a dictionary for determining correct pronunciations of new words you find in your reading. If you have used the same dictionary for several years, you are familiar with its pronunciation key for phonetic sounds of letters (diacritical symbols), usually found at the front of the dictionary, and have little difficulty in determining how a new word should be pronounced. You have learned what all of the symbols mean and can apply them easily and quickly to each new word. Those diacritical symbols generally look like the letters of our alphabet, but have diacritical marks such as lines or points above or through them to indicate sound changes.

For example, if you use **Webster's New World Dictionary,** you find that when the letter "a" appears with "-" above it, the symbol refers to a long "a" sound (as in "late"). However, the same symbol without any mark over it refers to the vowel sound in "patch" and the symbol with two small points or dots above it refers to the vowel sound in "psalm."

If you use different dictionaries for information on word pronunciation, you have discovered a disconcerting fact: **the same diacritical marks are not used by all dictionaries for the same sounds.** For example, in using **The American Heritage, Thorndike-Barnhart, American College, Random House,** and **Webster's New World Dictionaries** to check the pronunciation of the words "truths" and "kitchen," you will discover they don't agree on diacritical marks for the three vowel sounds or the voiced "th" sound.

Your instructor may give you outside readings or dictionary exercises to review the diacritical system if he or she believes it is an important supplementary tool for learning sound production and modulation. However, this book will not use diacritical symbols to describe spoken sounds. They can confuse you if you are trying to learn one consistent system that is readily available to everyone in the class.

THE INTERNATIONAL PHONETIC ALPHABET (IPA)

This book will use a modified form of the International Phonetic Alphabet, an international symbol system for writing or transcribing spoken sounds. Currently, the IPA is used by linguists, foreign language teachers, speech therapists, speech communication teachers, and many other professionals who are concerned with spoken language. You will discover the IPA is a useful tool as you attempt to describe changes in sound that occur in the articulation of your classmates. Before we examine this system further, you might be interested to know how this important tool originated.

Origins of the IPA

In 1886, The Phonetics Teachers' Association began as a result of interests of several language teachers in France who had found phonetic theory and transcription useful in their work. (It voted to adopt its current name, The International Phonetic Association, in 1897.) Its new journal, **Dhi Fonetik Ticer,** published entire articles in tentative phonetic symbols using English as its base language. During 1886, one of the association members, Otto Jespersen, wrote a letter to Paul Passy, editor of that journal, in which he proposed developing a phonetic alphabet which could be applied to all languages. By 1888, the first version of the International Phonetic Alphabet appeared.

Originally, the International Phonetic Alphabet attempted to use a different roman (printed) letter for each distinctive sound. The term "distinctive" refers to any spoken sound change in the same language which changes a word's meaning as, for example, when the single spoken vowel sound in the word "men" changes so that the word becomes "mean," "man," "moan," "moon," "main," or "mine." A nondistinctive sound change could include vocal changes (such as higher or lower pitch, softer or louder volume, faster or slower rate) which would not change the word "men" to another word.

46

The originators of this early version of the IPA, attempted to avoid creating new letters for the IPA. They chose IPA symbols which suggested the sounds they represented (as determined by their frequency of use in other international languages)—and which resembled existing letters whenever possible.

Today, the IPA is a detailed written system which is applicable to all spoken languages. Many of the original IPA letters still are used. However, quite a few of the symbols were changed to remedy some early limitations. A copy of this alphabet may be found in **The Principles of the International Phonetic Association** (1949, 1982), available from the secretary of the International Phonetic Association at University College, Gower Street, London WC1E 6BT, England. This pamphlet also includes samples of phonetic transcriptions of many different languages and dialects.

The association's journal underwent several name changes, finally adopting its current name, **The Journal of the International Phonetic Association**, in 1971. During that same year the association voted to change its official language from French to English. Today, the journal publishes most of its articles in English text, supplemented by many IPA transcriptions.

The IPA Symbol System

The International Phonetic Alphabet uses a different symbol to describe each unique spoken sound (phoneme) or separate family of sounds, regardless of how that sound is **spelled** in a specific language. If the sound [o] were spelled "augh," "agox," "rvyl," and "ookk" consistently in four different exotic languages, their IPA transcription would remain [o]. Let's see how this would work in those four languages. If the [b] and [t] sounds in all four languages were spelled and pronounced exactly as they are in English, here is how the words "oboe," and "boat" would be written in them.

Language # 1	Language # 2	Language # 3	Language # 4		Word
aughbaugh	agoxbagox	rvylbrvyl	ookkbookk	=	oboe
baught	bagoxt	brvylt	bookkt	=	boat

However, the IPA transcriptions would be ['o bo] and [bot] for the words in each language! Doesn't that simplify your task of writing spoken words?

The following chart lists IPA symbols which will be used in this course to describe General American Speech. It doesn't include all the current IPA symbols and it modifies a few symbols to simplify the system you will use in this introductory course. Additional IPA symbols may be introduced periodically throughout this book to serve as a basis for comparing General American Speech to other dialects and/or languages. Those additional symbols are not essential for you to learn in order for you to describe or use General American Speech. Either the sounds don't occur in General American Speech or they are so similar to other sounds that the differences are difficult or impossible for novices to hear. In advanced courses in phonetics, linguistics, or speech science, you would be expected to learn additional symbols in order to do "narrow" or more detailed transcriptions.

INTERNATIONAL PHONETIC ALPHABET (IPA) SYMBOLS
USED FOR GENERAL AMERICAN SPEECH SOUNDS

VOWELS

front	middle	back
[i] east, pizza	[ɝ] ermine, hurry	[u] oops, rule
[ɪ] itch, tin	[ɚ] enter, energy	[ʊ] pull, hook
[e] ache, veil	[ʌ] other, luck	[o] oak, sew
[ɛ] exit, tell	[ə] again, circus	[ɔ] awful, raw
[æ] acid, plaid		[ɑ] odd, knot

CONSONANTS

front		middle		back	
voiceless	voiced	voiceless	voiced	voiceless	voiced
[p] pay	[b] by	[t] take	[d] down	[k] key	[g] go
	[m] mail	[θ] thing	[ð] those	[h] how	
[f] for	[v] voice	[s] so	[z] zone		[j] yet
[hw] when	[w] wait	[ʃ] shell	[ʒ] beige		[ŋ] sing
		[tʃ] check	[dʒ] jam		
			[n] now		
			[l] like		
			[r] rich		

DIPHTHONGS

[ɑɪ] idea, tide	[ɑʊ] out, how	[ɔɪ] oyster, toy

BECOMING FAMILIAR WITH THE IPA

At first glance, you may think that the IPA will require you to learn a totally different symbol system from the English alphabet (orthographic) symbols. However, examine the IPA symbols closely and you will find you already use most of the consonant symbols in your current writing system. Almost sixty-five percent of all spoken English sounds are consonants. You will use sixteen of those twenty-five English alphabet letters as these IPA consonant symbols: [p b t d k g f v s z h l r w m n]. **Each IPA symbol represents a phoneme which is a unique or distinctive speech sound—or sound family.** This leaves only nine new IPA consonant symbols you need to learn. Many of the vowel sounds will be similar to alphabet letters you are accustomed to using too.

Listening to Individual Sounds

Probably your major hurdle in learning the IPA will be to begin thinking in terms of SOUNDS rather than how a word is spelled—or what it means. During the early phases of this course, you may find nonsense transcriptions easier to transcribe into IPA symbols than formal words, simply because you must listen to the way nonsense sound combinations are formed. If you **hear** someone say the meaningless (or nonsense) syllables, "Ik po lat" and you try to write them in IPA symbols, you won't be tempted to figure out what the sounds mean. Instead, you can concentrate on individual sounds and syllables. Your IPA transcription will be:

[ɪk po læt].

By listening for each separate sound and syllable, you can learn to transcribe spoken foreign words and phrases correctly in IPA symbols. For example, you have heard the Spanish and French terms for "yes," although you may not be sure how to spell them. Once you learn that [i] is **always** the IPA symbol for a long "e," you can transcribe the words as follows:

Spanish: "Sí" = IPA [si]   French: "Oui" = IPA [wi]

Once you have transcribed the foreign terms accurately, you also can read your transcriptions aloud repeatedly, using the same pronunciation every time.

Many people even learn to sing or speak short sentences in several foreign languages without ever learning those actual languages, by reading words and phrases written in phonetic script aloud! This can be particularly useful if you expect to travel outside your native country and need to learn a few common phrases such as "Thank you" or "Where is the . . . ?" to use in several different languages. Radio and television broadcasters often find the IPA useful for pronouncing names of foreign people and cities or for quoting brief foreign terms.

Some General Rules for Making IPA Transcriptions

In order to assist your instructor with the task of evaluating your work fairly, you will want to follow several simple rules when you write all your phonetic transcriptions. These rules are.

1. **Always enclose your transcriptions in brackets.** You don't need to place each IPA symbol of a transcribed word or thought unit inside a **separate** pair of brackets (as would occur if you wrote "[h] [i] [ɪ] [z] [n] [u]" for the spoken statement, "He is new."). Brackets indicate the enclosed symbols should be read as IPA transcriptions of spoken sounds and not as spelled words. Your brackets become particularly important in phonetic transcriptions which *appear* to be different words from the ones they actually are. Although you haven't studied the IPA in detail yet, you can see from the following examples that IPA transcriptions and regular words can be confused when brackets are not used.

IPA transcription		Word
[hit]	=	heat
[het]	=	hate
[let]	=	late
[lɛt]	=	let
[sun]	=	soon
[sʌn]	=	sun

2. **Use only lower case (uncapitalized) letters in your transcriptions.** At least two IPA symbols, [ɪ] and [ʊ] *appear* to be like our printed capital "I" and "U" letters but they shouldn't be any taller or larger than [i] or [u]. However, their shapes should be easily discernible for a reader. (Notice that [ɪ] has small top and bottom crossbars but [i] has a small point or dot above it; [ʊ] is shaped like a horseshoe with two crossbars at the top but [u] has a small tail at its right.)

Capital letters won't be used in IPA transcriptions. Therefore, you won't capitalize the first word in a transcribed sentence or a proper noun. For example,

The sentence, "He is new." will not be transcribed as [Hi ɪz nu] but as [hi ɪz nu].

"Rome" will not be transcribed as [Rom] but as [rom].

An instructor is correct to count transcriptions wrong when they contain capital letters.

Willoughby   Courtesy Rotarian

"Is it ◎ before ᗯ, except after 𝍆, or...?"

3. **Use only printed (roman) rather than written (cursive) symbols.** If you are accustomed to putting little loops on the spines of some of your printed letters (especially "p," "b," "d,") or of making no distinction between written and printed letters (especially "l," "k," "h," "n," "e," "u," and "i"), you will need to modify your printing style for IPA symbols.

The IPA can be written in cursive form but this book doesn't deal with the specific cursive symbols. Therefore, all IPA symbols, except [ɛ], which is similar to a small cursive capital "E," should look like printed (roman) symbols. Whenever any doubt arises over whether your transcription contains a written or printed symbol, your instructor will be justified in counting that phoneme wrong.

4. **Leave a space between words in transcriptions of phrases and sentences within one set of brackets.** By keeping all the symbols in each word together (without spaces), you make words in thought sequences easy to see—and to read aloud at a later time. If you transcribed "He is new" as [hiɪznu] rather than [hi ɪz nu], you or someone else could have difficulty reading the transcription aloud immediately. Also, if you are trying to read a transcript of a spoken message you haven't heard before, you would have great difficulty determining where one word begins and another one ends.

5. **Place an accent (stress) mark in front of the syllable it stresses.** In your IPA transcriptions, an accented syllable should be indicated by a short *vertical* line (') slightly above and in front of each stressed syllable. (This is a different procedure from many current dictionaries which place a *slanted* accent mark **after** a stressed syllable.) Your task of reading an IPA transcription aloud quickly becomes a bit easier when an accent mark comes before, rather than after a stressed syllable. The mark prepares you for the stress **before** you actually see the sound(s). When you have plenty of time to analyze a word in a dictionary, you will not find the placement of the accent mark a major consideration.

Determining Syllables in IPA Transcriptions

A syllable is a single vocal impulse or "beat" built around a vowel, diphthong, or syllabic consonant. (Syllabic consonants include [l̩], [m̩], and [n̩] which are capable of standing alone as separate impulses. For example, you can pronounce the words "little," "chasm," and "cousin" correctly without including a vowel sound in the final syllable.) **In most phonetic transcriptions of polysyllabic words, you will be able to determine the number of syllables by counting the number of vowel and diphthong symbols in those words.** One-syllable words and unstressed syllables in polysyllabic words require no accent marks.

A primary accent mark (for the syllable that receives the greatest stress in a polysyllabic word) should be slightly darker or heavier than a secondary accent mark. When a word has two syllables, one of the syllables will be said with a little more pressure or volume and a slightly higher pitch than the other. For example, pronounce the following two syllable words aloud, as if you were saying the words in a conversation. You may hear the stressed syllable more quickly if you use each word in a sentence. Notice where the accent or stress comes in each word.

```
+--------------------------------------------------------------+
|                    TWO SYLLABLE WORDS                        |
|                                                              |
|   First Syllable Stressed        Second Syllable Stressed    |
|                                                              |
|   at/tic, typ/ist, Day/ton,      de/test, im/ply, in/spect,  |
|   rea/son, cap/ture, pack/age    re/ceive, ig/nore, re/sist  |
|                                                              |
+--------------------------------------------------------------+
```

When a word has three or more syllables, the word **can have more** than one stressed syllable. In those cases, the word is described as having one primary stress and one or more secondary stresses, in addition to its unstressed syllables. As a word increases in length, the possibility of having more than one stressed syllable increases. In the following polysyllabic words, you can see how the primary stress or accent shifts. Some of the words also have secondary stresses. Can you find those words?

```
+--------------------------------------------------------------+
|                    POLYSYLLABIC WORDS                        |
|                                                              |
|   The Word Has:        Primary Stress Is On Boldfaced Syllable|
|                                                              |
|   Three Syllables:     des/per/ate          in/spec/tor      |
|                                                              |
|   Four Syllables:      as/pir/a/ted          ap/prox/i/mate  |
|                                                              |
|   Five Syllables:      cap/i/tal/iz/ing      re/cov/er/a/ble |
|                                                              |
|   Six Syllables:       in/ca/pac/i/ta/ted    ar/ti/fi/ci/al/i/ty |
|                                                              |
|   Seven Syllables:     re/pre/sent/a/bil/i/ty                |
|                                                              |
+--------------------------------------------------------------+
```

In the early period of learning to use IPA symbols, your instructor may not require you to break words into syllables or to show stressed and unstressed syllables. However, as you become familiar with the IPA, you should be able to analyze these elements in each word you hear.

OTHER WAYS OF CLASSIFYING ENGLISH SOUNDS

English sounds normally are classified in three groups: consonants, vowels, and diphthongs. Consonants are voiced and voiceless sounds that result from some obstruction of the breath stream; vowels and diphthongs are voiced sounds which are fairly free of obstruction, depending instead on the oral cavity's size and shape for their distinctive resonance. Consonants tend to mark the beginnings and endings of syllables; vowels and diphthongs tend to stand alone as syllables or act as the nucleus around which syllables are built. Consonants usually determine clarity or distinctness of diction; vowels and diphthongs usually determine voice quality, duration of sound, and inflectional variety. A brief review of sound classifications may help you understand their influence on diction.

Consonants

Consonants may be classified in several different ways. The same consonant may fit into several different classes. Although all of these descriptive systems will not be important in an introductory speech improvement course, they are included here in case your instructor refers to them in class lectures and discussions.

Consonants may be classified according to:

1. **Voiced or voiceless (or unvoiced) status.** The larynx must vibrate to create voiced sounds. If no vibration occurs, the sounds are called voiceless sounds. You can use two methods to determine if sounds are voiced: **feeling** the vibration that occurs in your larynx (behind your Adam's apple) with your thumb and index finger, or **hearing** the vibration by placing your hands firmly over both ears as you say sounds. For example, the first sound in these pairs will have no buzzing or vibration but the second sound will: [t] and [d], [s] and [z]. When two sounds are produced in the same way except for the element of voicing, they are called **cognate pairs,** or merely **cognates.**

In English, the voiceless consonants include [p], [t], [k], [f], [s], [h], [ʃ], [tʃ], [θ], and [hw]. All other consonant sounds are voiced (unless they are whispered.)

2. **Primary articulators used for forming.** Chapter 3 enumerated these articulators as the lips (labial), lips and teeth (labiodental), tongue and teeth (linguadental), upper gumridge (alveolar), hard palate (palatal), and soft palate (velar).

3. **Duration.** Consonants which result from a quickly stopped breath stream ([p], [b], [t], [d], [k], and [g]) and are short in duration are called **stops.** Consonants which may be sustained on one breath and are long in duration are called **continuants.**

4. **Manner of production.** Consonants may be sub-divided into these technical categories:

a. **Plosives.** These consonants result from complete stops followed by tiny breath explosions as compressed air is released. (Stops and plosives include the same sounds.) Plosives may be voiced ([b], [d], [g]) or voiceless ([p], [t], [k]).

b. **Fricatives.** These consonants are created by friction as breath is forced through a partially narrowed passage (either in the mouth or larynx). Fricatives may be voiced ([v], [ð], [z], [ʒ]) or voiceless ([hw], [f], [θ], [s], [ʃ], [h]). Fricatives also are continuants.

c. **Affricates.** These consonants have both plosive and fricative qualities. They begin with a plosive position and compression of the breath stream and are exploded through a narrowed opening. The only important General American Speech affricates are the voiced [dʒ] and voiceless [tʃ]. Affricates also are continuants.

d. **Nasals.** These consonants are created as the breath stream flows through the nose, using its chambers for resonance. Only three sounds in General American Speech are nasalized and all are voiced: [m], [n], and [ŋ]. Nasal consonants also are continuants.

e. **Glides.** These consonants glide quickly from an initial sound toward the position of the following vowel. Two General American Speech glides, [w] and [j], are voiced; one, [hw], is unvoiced. Some instructors use the term "semi-vowel" to describe glides because they can be sustained on one breath for a long time and are relatively free-flowing sounds. Glides also are continuants.

f. **Lateral.** This consonant is made as breath escapes over one or both sides of the tongue. Only the voiced [l] is considered to be a lateral consonant in General American Speech. Some instructors include [l] as a glide or semi-vowel also. The [l] also is a continuant.

g. **Retroflex.** This consonant is made with the tongue tip pointing upward and backward. Only the voiced sound [r] is considered to be a retroflex consonant in General American Speech. Some instructors include the [r] sound as a glide or semi-vowel also.

The following chart summarizes the classifications of consonants just described.

CLASSIFICATION OF GENERAL AMERICAN SPEECH CONSONANTS

Point(s) of Articulation	STOPS Plosive	CONTINUANTS Fricative	Affricate	Nasal	Glide	Lateral & Retroflex	GENERAL LOCATION
LIPS	[p] [b]	[hw]		[m]	[w]		**F R O N T**
LIPS/TEETH		[f] [v]					
TONGUE/ TEETH		[θ] [ð]					**M I D D L E**
GUM/RIDGE	[t] [d]	[s] [z]		[n]		[l]	
GUM RIDGE/ PALATE		[ʃ] [ʒ]	[tʃ] [dʒ]			[r]	
PALATE					[j]		
SOFT PALATE	[k] [g]			[ŋ]			**B A C K**
GLOTTIS (LARYNX)		[h]					

Consonant sounds may appear in syllables as single or isolated consonants (as in ep/i/**sod**/ic) or as consonant clusters (as in **stress**/ful or **fra**/**grant**). Consonant clusters may appear in the beginning (initial), middle (medial), or ending (final) position of a word. Since they don't appear in many languages, they can be difficult for international students to learn.

One other quality which affects many consonants is called **aspiration.** An aspirated sound is a voiceless, breathy outflow of sound. Frequently, students have difficulty controlling the amount of air expelled on certain consonants, such as [t] and [p], even though they have no difficulty forming the sounds correctly. Since strong or weak aspiration doesn't change one word to another one, this becomes a *non-distinctive* change. However, excessive hissing or popping of air can be distracting characteristics of consonants. If you have difficulty with strongly aspirated consonant sounds, you may have to practice breath control exercises (such as saying sounds in front of a candle flame or a thin piece of paper to *see* how excessive expulsions of air influence the flickering flame or fluttering paper).

Vowels

Since all vowel sounds are voiced, relatively unrestricted, non-nasal sounds, you can't use the voiced/voiceless, point of articulation (or stoppage), and nasal/non-nasal categories to distinguish one vowel from another. Instead, you will use four other factors to classify vowels. These were discussed briefly in chapter 3.

1. **Degree of lip rounding** used in their formation. Some vowels (such as the long "a" or [e] and long "e" or [i] sounds) require the lips to be spread into a semi-smile. Other vowels (such as the long "o" or [o]) require considerable rounding of the lips.

2. **Amount of muscle tension in the tongue.** A definitive feature of many vowels is the tension of the tongue required to produce them accurately. This tension can be felt by placing your thumb firmly into the fleshy part under your chin and saying the long "e" or [i] and the long "o" or [o]. The amount of tension or laxness for various vowels differs from person to person and vowel to vowel. However, within the same person's articulation habits, this degree can determine whether he or she is saying [i] or [ɪ]; [u] or [ʊ]. Thus, the words "peak" and "pick" or "Luke" and "look" can be created by a slight change in tongue tension.

3. **Height to which the tongue is raised.** Tongue elevation also affects the unique sound that is produced. Usually, vowels are produced with the tongue elevated to high, mid, or low positions in the mouth. In a later chapter, a Diagram of General American Vowel Placement will show these positions in relation to specific vowel sounds.

4. **Place in the mouth where the tongue is raised to its highest point and the specific portion of the tongue that is raised.** Usually the terms "front," "central" or "middle," and "back" will be used to refer to the portion of the tongue which is raised highest in the mouth to form specific vowels. The arch of your tongue can move up and down as well as forward and backward in your mouth. These movements create perceptible changes in vowels. The Diagram of General American Vowel Placement in a later chapter will relate this characteristic to specific vowels.

Duration or length of vowels often becomes a characteristic that affects speaking patterns, although it is not a distinctive feature of vowels. When sounds are clipped or prolonged, you may understand them and the intended message. However, you will recognize the person is not a native of a specific country or region. Vowel length is influenced by factors such as word position, surrounding sounds, appearance in stressed or unstressed syllables, and their tension or laxness. Ultimately, vowel length can affect speaking rhythm.

Two modifications in IPA vowel symbols will be used in this book. First, technically the pure vowels [o] and [e] are different sounds from the diphthongs [oʊ] and [eɪ]. However, the sounds are not distinctive (words containing them will be understood regardless of whether the pure vowel or the diphthong is used in them). You probably won't hear the difference between the sounds in most speakers. Although you use the diphthongs more often than the vowels in your daily speaking, you will find the vowel symbols faster and easier to use in transcriptions. Therefore, only the [o] and [e] symbols will be used throughout this book.

Secondly, the [ɑ] symbol will be used for [a] or [ɒ] since these last two symbols describe more sounds in British, Southern, and Eastern American Dialects than in General American Speech. Although these three sounds are not identical, they are similar enough to allow for this simplification. Your instructor may wish to discuss and/or use these sounds if they are prominent in your class. To carry out this consistency further, [ɑ] rather than [a] will be used for writing both the [ɑɪ] and [ɑʊ] diphthong symbols.

Diphthongs

Diphthongs are voiced, non-nasal combinations of two vowel sounds that are glided together in the same syllable. They tend to be longer in duration than most vowels. Also, they move from one lip and tongue position to a higher one. The three diphthongs which will be used in this book are:

[ɑɪ] in "I" and "type"

[ɑʊ] in "pout" and "how"

[ɔɪ] in "coy" and "loyal"

Since the [j] sound is included under consonant sounds in this text, the [ju] combination (or its allophone or close companion sound [ɪu]) will not be considered a diphthong. Your instructor, however, may prefer to use these as additional diphthongs.

PUTTING THE IPA TO PRACTICAL USE

You are now ready to begin using the IPA to transcribe sounds in a manner that will be understood by everyone in your class. The chapters that follow will give specific details on how different sounds are produced to help you improve your own articulation. They also will give you experience in transcribing what you hear in IPA symbols.

Once you know the IPA symbols fairly well, you will be expected to demonstrate your ability to use these symbols in your class as you listen to fellow classmates give their practiced readings to the class. You should begin to identify their obvious deviations from General American Speech by writing the incorrect and correct IPA symbols as well as the words in which those symbols occur. For example, if someone:

omits the [d] in words, you would write:

omits [d]: didn't, couldn't

substitutes [s] for [z], you would write:

[s − z]: beads, is, words, these

adds [jə] to words, you would write:

adds [jə]: we, they, play, obey

By using this simple method for designating sound changes, you can keep a cumulative critique sheet on each individual in your class. Don't try to write out entire words in IPA symbols during classroom presentations, since this would require you to devote too much of your time and attention to technical details of transcription and too little to identifying different sound changes that occur in relatively brief periods. By using this simple method, you can refer back to your classmates' previous errors each time they speak, to see if they are as numerous or obvious as before. As your listening ability improves, you will begin to hear more sound changes in your classmates—and more variations in those changes. Also, you will develop confidence in your knowledge of the needed IPA symbols—and a faster transcription rate.

At the back of this book are critique sheets which can be used to record errors in diction made during oral presentations in this class. Read the introductory information on using critique sheets at the beginning of the appendix. Beginning with the first IPA symbols at the top left of the sheets, notice where each of the following words would be written to alert a speaker to errors made in class.

	The speaker says:	The speaker intends to say:
Substitutions	miny, iny, tin	many, any, ten
	each, Team	itch, Tim
	A boy, A car	a (uh) boy, a (uh) car
	luke, shoed	look, should
	jist, sitch	just, such
	ma, ah	my, I
	cot, lahn	caught, lawn
	bawdy, naught	body, not
	doin', seein'	doing, seeing
	iss, hass	is, has
	toof or toot	tooth
	wantet	wanted
	jutch	judge
	dat, dem	that, them
	shtrict, exshtra	strict, extra
	laeud, haeuw	loud, how
	sistuh, mothuh	sister, mother
	lock, dock	luck, duck
Omissions	fer, yer	for, your
	shurr, endurr	sure, endure
	lan, dint	land, didn't
	sinificant	significant
	figger, reguhler	figure, regular
	ony	only
	mos, lil	most, little
Additions	athaletics	athletics
	septerate, often	separate, often
	dident, couldent	didn't, couldn't
Transpositions	ax, tacks	ask, task

CHAPTER 6

THE FRONT SOUNDS
[p], [b], [f], [v]

In chapter 3, we learned some of the portions of the anatomy used to articulate sounds. Beginning with this chapter, you will be examining how and where **specific sounds** are produced. Also, you will begin to use the unique IPA symbols representing each phoneme as you identify sounds you are **hearing** rather than letters you are **seeing.** In many cases, the IPA symbols will relate directly to the spellings you are accustomed to seeing. However, periodically you will be learning new symbols. From now on, you should begin to depend upon your ears more than upon your eyes. If you can trust your ears, you will discover that using the IPA is simple and fun. A side benefit will be your increasing ability to write in a code that many of your associates who have not had a course in voice and diction will not be able to understand.

(pay)

Technical Description:	Voiceless, Bilabial Stop Plosive, Cognate of [b]
Physiological Description: **How The Sound Is Made**	Vocal folds not vibrating, both lips used to hold back pressure until a puff of air is released, teeth parted, soft palate raised, aspiration may be quiet or loud, lower jaw drops slightly
Common Spellings:	p in pony, clips, mop, practice pp in clipper, happen, suppose pe in hope, ripe, shape
Periodic Spellings:	gh in hiccough

Technical Description:	Voiced, Bilabial Stop Plosive, Cognate of [p]
Physiological Description: How The Sound Is Made	Vocal folds vibrating, both lips used to hold back pressure until a puff of air is released, teeth parted, velum raised, aspiration may be loud or soft, lower jaw drops slightly
Common Spellings:	b in band, habit, tab, branch bb in cribbage, hobby, Libby be in lobe, gibe, Abe
Periodic Spellings:	pb in cupboard
Note On Spelling:	mb combinations may create a silent "b" as in "bomb" and "plumber" or a pronounced [b] as in "tumble" and "limber"

(boat)

The consonant sounds **[p]** and **[b]** are called plosive sounds. They actually are small explosions occurring as **both lips** (bilabial) hold back the pressure of the breathstream until the sounds are released. Notice that these sounds are produced in exactly the same way with but one exception. The [p] is voiceless and the [b] is voiced. (You can check this by placing a finger on your thyroid cartilage or Adam's apple in your neck and saying [p] and [b] aloud. Be sure you say the **sounds** [p] and [b], not the letter **names** "p" and "b" since the letter names are voiced.) Two sounds which, except for voicing, are produced in the same place and way with the same articulators are COGNATES.

In English, these sounds may be said with very little, or with a considerable amount of escaping air. When you are talking rapidly, or in casual situations, probably you have quiet, unnoticeable explosions. However, when you are talking to large groups without the aid of an amplifying device, or you are making a vigorous oral defense of your position, or you are asserting your command over a group, the explosion of these sounds becomes more forceful. (Recently, a pet trainer indicated that dogs are more likely to obey an owner's commands, such as "stop" and "sit," when final plosive sounds are said with great force.)

COMMON PROBLEMS

If you have been accused of having slurred diction, an angry or "defensive" speech pattern, or too much "spitting" in your speaking, you may be having trouble with your plosive sounds. These are common labels we have heard used by laypersons relative to individuals with faulty [p] and [b] production. Here are a few of the problems you may hear among your classmates as your ears become more accustomed to hearing diction errors:

1. Expelling air with too much force, particularly in the final position of words and in one syllable words such as ship, sweep, slap, sleep, rope, or pronunciation of a silent "b" in words such as lamb, climber, and tomb. In general, voiceless plosives which begin words and are followed by a vowel or diphthong, such as in "poetry" and "power," will have stronger aspiration than in words where the [p] is preceded by another consonant, as in "mapped," and "riptide." Often, little or no breath escapes when these sounds occur at the end of a word before a pause. In normal conversation, when the same plosive ends one word and begins the next word, the sounds are assimilated or combined into one phoneme which seems to have a pause in the middle, as you will hear in the phrases "sip pop," "cab boy," and "ripe pineapple." If you try to pronounce the repeated phonemes, you will sound overly precise or pedantic. This error can be as evident as careless diction.

2. Confusing [p] and [b] (inability to distinguish voicing and unvoicing). When this occurs, the phonetic changes may create changes in meaning (semantic changes) as in the following pairs: paced-based; pat-bat; rapid-rabid; pelt-belt; parking-barking; pull-bull; cap-cab. If your primary oral language is not English, you may tend to confuse these two phonemes regularly if your native language made no distinction between the sounds—or if the spelling rules of your native language were quite different from those of English. As a general rule, non-native speakers of English who are having difficulty with these sounds will need to aspirate or explode [p] more than [b] in the initial position of words— and be sure the larynx vibrates for [b] but not for [p]. If you are a native speaker of English and you are criticized for having blurred or indistinct [p] and [b] sounds, you probably are not bringing the lips together with enough pressure to produce precise sounds.

3. Substituting [f] for [p] and [v] for [b]. This is a fairly common error in individuals who come from bilingual families where parents have never distinguished among these sounds correctly. If your native language is Spanish, you may tend to substitute these sounds most often when they occur in the medial position of words, as in: liberate, lobby, dropping, apples. If you have problems with these substitutions, avoid allowing the upper front teeth to come in contact with the lower lip as you say the sounds.

4. Omitting [p] or [b]. This error occurs frequently in medial and final positions of words. Usually it is an indication of inadequate lip pressure or incomplete lip closure, often called "lazy lips." Say these words but omit the [b]: thimble, rumble, lumber. See why people could be accused of having lazy lips if they omit the sound? When two or more plosives are clustered together, as [spt] in "grasped" and [pt] in "wrapped," one of the plosives may be omitted. Thus, "grasped" may sound like "grassed" and "wrapped" becomes "rat." A common omission occurs when [b] occurs immediately before the suffix "ably" as, for example when "probably" becomes "probly." Since [p] and [b] are **stop** plosives, you must make a **complete** stop in words containing the letters "pf" and "bv" in adjacent positions, as in "cupful" and "obvious" or you will omit the stops.

5. Transposing sounds. This error occurs when two sounds are reversed or exchanged. For example, the word "rasped" becomes "rapsed" when [spt] becomes [pst] and the word "rhapsody" becomes "rhaspody" when [ps] becomes [sp].

A NOTE REGARDING PRACTICE EXERCISES

As we begin the practice exercises for various phonemes, remember that whenever a letter appears in brackets [ ], it will be an IPA symbol and will refer to the SOUND, not the alphabetical letter. If several symbols appear within the same two brackets and are separated by spaces, each sound is to be pronounced separately. Therefore, a transcription of [p p] indicates you are to pronounce [p] twice. Each exercise will begin with practice on sounds in isolation—or by themselves—to be sure you are creating the sound distinctly. If you are certain you have no problems with a specific sound, you will not have to go through all the exercises. Later, if your instructor indicates you should spend time on specific sounds, you should go back to the exercises and **begin** with practice on the isolated sounds before working on words and sentences. Begin your practice sessions slowly, being conscious of what is happening to your lips, teeth, lower jaw, tongue, soft palate, hard palate, alveolar ridge, and larynx. For some sounds, you will find it helpful to check the muscular tension under your chin to see if the sounds are lax or tense.

Practice at a volume level that would be used in daily conversation. Don't whisper or mumble. If you are afraid of bothering other people while you practice, find another place where you can speak aloud. We have found that a major problem of students who are trying to improve their speaking is their tendency to practice their oral exercises in a hushed voice so they won't disturb other people. You must practice in a normal speaking voice to gain the greatest benefit from these exercises.

EXERCISES FOR PRACTICING [p] AND [b]

1. Place a finger on your Adam's apple and say the following. Feel the vibration that occurs for [b] but not for [p].

[p]   [b]   [p p]   [b b b]   [b]   [p p]   [p p b p]   [b p]

2. The following words will give you experience in placing these sounds next to several different sounds.

Initial	Medial	Final
[p] [b]	[p] [b]	[p] [b]
pay/bay	apron/label	ape/babe
pie/buy	wiper/libel	type/vibe
pool/boot	super/tuber	group/lube
pond/bond	optic/hobby	shop/knob
pearl/burn	purple/curbing	slurp/blurb
puff/buff	upon/abound	cup/cub

3. Combinations of plosive sounds in close proximity to each other create a bobbing or rippling effect for listeners. Tongue twisters often use many plosive sounds. Read the following words slowly and feel the motion of the lips. Increase your rate of speaking and see if you can keep the sounds distinct. You will discover that your lips become "tired" after prolonged practice and your sounds may begin to become blurred.

a. dibble, dabble, bobble, bubble, babble, burble, boo

b. poppy, peeper, pepper, purple, puppy, pimple, pope

c. double, pumper, pebble, dumper, popper, pamper, pep

d. blooper, ripple, paper, dribble, rubber, tipple

e. tripper, paper, robber, bopped, popper, bumper, bop

f. upper, hamper, jumper, triple, peppy, ribber, rope

g. baby pony, imperfect bottle stopper, tropic slumber

h. apple pie, sinking bobber, flapping plaster

i. inept but pretty, hamburger platter, deep purple

4. The following sentences contain [p] and [b] in a variety of locations. Say the sentences with the same inflections you would use in daily conversations. Avoid a rhythmical or sing-song approach.

a. Lumber probably will be expensive for paper-making.

b. People picked bell peppers by the bushel.

c. Backpacking brought Pepe popularity at Pepperdine.

d. Practice spying on big, black bears near Bayport.

e. Polly Ripple packed a pistol in her hamper.

f. Probably practice makes habits permanent as well as perfect.

g. Pink paper poppies brightened Bertie's bedroom.

h. Scrupulous paupers tripled their troubles by robbing the Doubloon Hobby Shop.

5. Practice the following selections aloud.

a. Piper Barber's byline in the paper proved that she could whip up popular, believable stories based upon local people. She poked fun at barbers and preachers, trappers and packers, babies and beekeepers. Her superiors never stopped her from poking fun at traditional practices, precious beliefs, or important people. Behind each quip was a passionate hope for less prejudice, more understanding, and open, unhampered, simple humor.

b. Big handpainted signs were posted throughout the preserve to "Protect the Chimps from Poachers." Campers were warned to avoid the scrub land and shrubbery along the east portion of the park. Before daybreak, Paul Bagley had scrubbed the blue dust off his truck, propped open the door of the cage in back of the cab, and was preparing to ignore the posted warnings.

Technical Description:	Voiceless, Labiodental Fricative, Cognate of [v]
Physiological Description: How The Sound Is Made	Vocal folds not vibrating, biting edge of the upper front teeth are touching the upper surface of the lower lip lightly while the airstream pushes through the narrow opening forcefully, creating audible friction, soft palate is raised
Common Spellings:	f in fame, after, deaf, artful ff in muffin, off, coffee, cuff gh in laugh, enough, rough ph in phony, epitaph, euphoric fe in wife, knife, safe, life
Periodic Spelling:	ft in soften lf in half, calf

[f]

(face)

Technical Description:	Voiced, Labiodental Fricative, Cognate of [f]
Physiological Description: How The Sound Is Made	Vocal folds vibrating, and all other information relating to the production of [f] will apply
Common Spellings:	v in vain, heavy, very, avid ve in shave, grieve, groove
Periodic Spelling:	f in of ph in Stephen lve in salve vv in savvy, fivver

[v]

(voice)

The consonant sounds [f] and [v] are called labio- (lip) dental (teeth) fricative (friction) sounds. Since the lower lip is used, they are considered to be frontal sounds, just as [p] and [b] were because they required both lips to be used. They also are cognates of one another since both are produced in the same way with the one exception mentioned before—the element of voicing occurs for one but not the other.

COMMON PROBLEMS

Frequently, we find that students who are unable to distinguish between [f] and [v] in their own speaking either have a hearing loss or come from a foreign background where these sounds don't exist. Both sounds are relatively weak and may be confused with other fricatives found in words that contain "th," "sh," and "ch." (In a later chapter, we will discuss these sounds further.)

Another possible source of problems stems from faulty articulation learned as children and never heard and/or corrected by adults. It is normal for children to "test" approximate sounds before discovering how to duplicate accurately the ones they are hearing. However, in many cases the **approximate** sounds may never be corrected because adults (1) don't hear the differences, (2) find the errors "cute" and never correct them, or (3) think the children will "grow out of" the incorrect sounds. Adult relatives may become so accustomed to hearing incorrectly produced sounds over the years that they won't hear them even after children grow up!

Here are the most common problems related to [f] and [v]:

1. Substituting [f] for [v] or omitting [v] entirely in the word "of." In daily conversation, it's easy to overlook a small word like "of" because it seems relatively unimportant. We say it so rapidly that it often disappears or becomes part of the word that precedes or follows it, as in "kinda" for "kind of," or "someuh" for "some of." In casual or hurried speech, it sounds very much like "uh." Contact must occur between the upper front teeth and the lower lip to create a good [v]. An individual who substitutes [f] for [v] in "of" usually doesn't realize that this is one word in English where "f" is pronounced as [v].

2. Substituting [f] for [v], especially in words ending in "ve," as in "save, believe, leave." Often, this word precedes "to," as in "love to," "have to," and "gave to." Normally, when "ve" occurs in the final position of a word, the vowel immediately before it should be prolonged slightly to give you time to prepare to voice the [v]. If you substitute [f] for [v] in polysyllabic words such as "everyone," you probably do so because of habit, a fast rate of speaking, or inability to hear a difference between them.

3. Substituting other phonemes for [f] and [v]. If your native language is one in which [f] and [v] do not occur, you may be using substitutes which sound similar to you. Filipino citizens may substitute [p] for [f] in certain positions. Speakers of Spanish may interchange [b] and [v] when [v] occurs in the initial position of a word, making "voter" into "boater" and "valid" into "ballad." Persons with a Germanic background often confuse [v] and [w] (because "w" is pronounced as [v] in German) and tend to pronounce the letter "f" as [v] and initial and final [v] as [f]. If your native language is English, but one or both of your parents speak another language as their native language, you may have adopted some of their sound changes without knowing it. Speakers of an American Black Dialect may tend to substitute [b] for [v] in the medial and final position of words such as "river," "leave," and "proverb."

EXERCISES FOR PRACTICING [f] AND [v]

1. Place a finger on your Adam's apple and say the following. Feel the vibration that occurs for [v] but not for [f].

[f]   [f f]   [v v]   [v f v]   [v v f v f]   [f v f v v]

2. Compare the voiced and unvoiced characteristics of [v] and [f] in the following paired sounds as you say them aloud.

Initial	**Medial**	**Final**
[f] [v]	[f] [v]	[f] [v]
fee/V	wafer/waver	a chief/achieve
fan/van	gifts/gives	belief/believe
few/view	leafs/leaves	half/have
fine/vine	Schaefer/shaver	grief/grieve
felt/veldt	shuffle/shovel	shelf/shelve
fain/vein	Joffa/Java	safe/save
first/versed	raffle/ravel	proof/prove

3. Read the following phrases aloud. Be sure your upper front teeth make contact with your lower lip for all [f] and [v] sounds.

a. five voiced frequencies; avid voter fraud failed

b. have a heavy van; if I find affable friends

c. fixed Fred's food first; drove a Ford forward

d. even after five of us; favorite vacations for every

e. raft veered forward forcing Vera forward; top value

f. vacated farms from frosty Vermont; obvious cupful

4. The following sentences contain [f] and [v] in various positions in words. Read them aloud as if you were saying the ideas expressed to friends in a conversation.

a. Several rivals have fought for that viewpoint.

b. Frequent flights of fancy often have been viewed as daydreaming.

c. Be careful as you travel through foggy valleys as evening falls.

d. Deceiving Eva was never a virtue for Floyd.

e. Whenever the chef's food and coffee have given off fragrant vapors, half of our starving team arrives.

65

f. After averting the rough river rapids, Frank travelled for several more afternoons.

g. The volume of advertising in Friday's evening paper gave everyone a negative feeling.

5. Read each of the following phrases aloud, trying to voice the [v] in every "of." Begin slowly, then increase your speed to see if you can continue to maintain the voicing.

a. glass of orange juice; lots of turmoil; round of golf; picture of health; heard of him

b. ahead of us; three of them; field of wheat; garden of flowers; sang of freedom; groups of ghosts

c. land of opportunity; afraid of thunder; herd of elephants; speak of all; roots of weeds

d. claim of those; last of our; test of time; knew of several; height of two; freight of four

6. Read the following selections aloud.

a. Every afternoon when Flora arrived home from school, she found her friendly goldfish waiting for her. Whoever would have thought a fish could rival a dog or a cat for Flora's affections? It never voiced its disapproval if the family forgot to feed it on time. It never infested the living room with fleas. It behaved perfectly when visitors arrived. It was vivacious, colorful, laughable, friendly, and very fond of her favorite music.

b. After Harvey moved away from Hartford, we never heard from him unless he felt lonely. Then our telephone would ring and he would ask to be forgiven for never writing. If he suffered from half the guilty feelings he said he had, he must have felt a vast relief after making his confession to us.

c. Before Blake Fir left Peoria for his first vacation in Happy Valley, Idaho, he invited his office staff to a backyard barbecue at his cabin on the river. His wife, Rebecca, served baked beans, corn on the cob, home-baked bread, freshly picked tomatoes, barbecued ribs, soft drinks, coffee, and strawberries on vanilla ice cream. Everyone felt comfortably full after lunch. The tables were cleared of food. Blake then pulled a big motorized, pontoon raft out of the brush near the river and invited everyone to climb aboard for a ride. Fourteen people carefully left the riverbank and found places to sit on the brightly painted raft. One pull of the rope on the motor, and everyone gave a happy cheer as the vessel moved backwards into the flow of the river. For the rest of the afternoon, the raft cruised peacefully up and down both sides of the pretty blue river.

d. The Balkan Peninsula is found between the Adriatic and Black Seas in southeastern Europe. Yugoslavia, Bulgaria, Greece, Albania, and the European portion of Turkey are parts of that peninsula. After the battles of World War I ended, most of Europe developed ways to live peacefully with neighboring countries. However, the small Balkan nations broke up into mutually antagonistic political entities. As a result, the term "Balkanize" developed as a means of describing small, mutually hostile political units, regardless of where they are located.

e. On a frigid, February evening in Portland, Oregon, a small snail began climbing an Apple tree. Several robins who were resting on the branches above began to laugh at this spectacle. Finally, one of them flew over the snail and said, "Say, my good fellow, don't you know this tree has no apples on it?" The plucky snail continued to crawl slowly up the trunk but managed to say in a puffy little voice, "There will be by the time I get there!"

CHAPTER 7

THE FRONT SOUNDS
[hw], [w], [m]

The final three front consonant sounds, [hw], [w], and [m], all have their points of articulation at the lips. These bilabial sounds also are continuants. The [hw] and [w] sounds are cognates.

Technical Description:	Voiceless, Bilabial Fricative Glide or Semivowel, Cognate of [w]
Physiological Description: **How The Sound Is Made**	Vocal folds not vibrating, both lips rounded and protruded or puckered as sound begins, tip of tongue is behind lower front teeth as back of it arches toward the hard palate, both lips and tongue change to the position that follows [hw], a little more air is expelled for [hw] than for [w]
Common Spellings:	wh in wheat, nowhere

(while)

Technical Description:	Voiced, Bilabial Glide or Semivowel, Cognate of [hw]
Physiological Description: **How The Sound Is Made**	Vocal folds vibrating, both lips rounded and protruded or puckered as sound begins, tip of tongue is behind lower front teeth as back of it arches toward the hard palate, both lips and tongue change to the position that follows [w]
Common Spellings:	w in went, away, inward u in quest, acquire, Maui, guava o in once, anyone
Periodic Spellings:	ju in Juanita

(wait)

The [hw] and [w] sounds are classified as **glides** because the articulators are moving as the sounds are formed. You begin both sounds in practically the same position as the phoneme [u], with your lips rounded and the back of your tongue elevated high toward the palate. Since both sounds always appear immediately before a vowel or diphthong and never in the final position of words, they glide from their initial sound to the following vowel or diphthong sound. Thus, even as you are forming [hw] and [w], your articulators are preparing to glide to the [i] sound in the words "wheat" and "weed."

The [hw] and [w] sounds have become almost indistinguishable during informal speaking in large segments of the North American English speaking population. The less energetic but voiced [w] seems to be replacing [hw] in words such as "when, where, why, what," particularly in casual, rapid conversational situations. As a result, you must listen carefully to determine whether a speaker is saying:

whirred or word; which or witch; whet or wet;

where or wear; while or wile; whey or way;

when or wen; what or watt; whit or wit; why or Y.

Fortunately, one of each of these paired words usually is a different part of speech (or has a different function) and can't be confused easily with the other word. In case you're wondering what these pairs of like-sounding words with different spellings and meanings are called, they are homophones.

Most words which begin with the letters "wh" are pronounced with the [hw] sound. (Many of these words actually were spelled with the "hw" combination of letters in Old English.) A few words, such as "who" and "whole" begin with "wh" which is pronounced as [h].

COMMON PROBLEMS

1. Many people substitute the [w] phoneme for [hw]. If you tense your lips more in a rounded position (as you would to blow out a candle) and force a small puff of air through the lips, you can hear the slight voiceless oral fricative as air escapes through the lips for [hw]. Also, by holding a finger in front of your lips as you say [hw], you should be able to feel its additional air flow (aspiration) through the lips, when contrasted with [w].

2. Some nonnative speakers of English substitute [v] for [w]. This change occurs because the lips are not rounded or puckered and because the upper teeth are allowed to touch the lower lip (changing the point of articulation from bilabial to labiodental). If you have this difficulty, begin your practice with the [u] sound in "cool." Feel the rounded position of the lips for [u] and then glide into the vowel and diphthong sounds as follows: [u]. . .oe (woe); [u]. . .ide (wide); [u]. . .ait (wait).

3. Some nonnative speakers of English add [f] at the beginning of [hw], forming a consonant cluster that doesn't exist in English. Thus, [hwit] (wheat) becomes [fhwit], and [hwɪp] (whip) becomes [fhwɪp]. In some speakers, the [f] is substituted for [hw] entirely, creating [fit] (feet) for [hwit] (wheat), and [fɪp] (fip) for [hwɪp] (whip). If you have either of these problems, don't allow your upper front teeth to touch your lower lip for words which begin with "hw." Be sure your lips are firmly rounded *before* the sound is started.

4. Some people omit the [hw] and [w] sounds when they occur in the medial position of words and word combinations in which one word ends in [m] and the next one begins with [w] or [hw]. This omission is most evident among children and poorly educated adults. These omissions could occur in the words "someone" and "somewhat" and the word combinations "seem why" and "same way." If you have this problem, you probably are not rounding your lips after making bilabial contact for [m]. Instead, you are allowing the lips to relax and spread slightly in a neutral position as your articulators prepare for the next vowel or diphthong sound.

If you have ever heard someone practicing the statements "Which witch is which?" or "We will have weather, whether or not" aloud, you are familiar with the difficulty most people have in distinguishing between the [hw] and [w] sounds. Either they don't hear a difference between these cognate pairs, or they don't use enough escaping air (aspiration) to make the distinction evident. If you have any difficulty in understanding which of two pairs of words containing these cognates is being said, you must depend upon the context of the message for the clues you need.

Using the context or general meaning of surrounding words, choose one of the parenthetical words you believe is correct in each of the following sentences.

1. The (wine/whine) made my head ache!

2. We listen for the (wail/whale) whenever we're at sea.

3. We agreed he needed the (wax/whacks) if he was to succeed.

4. The teacher asked me to spell ("weather/whether") for the class.

5. Annie was the daughter of a (wig/Whig) salesman in the novel we read.

If enough information is supplied in oral messages, you can decode unknown or indistinct words by using the words that surround them (context) to assist you in your decoding endeavors. However, periodically you will hear messages which can be decoded in two or more different ways, as was evident in the five sentences you just read. When this possibility occurs frequently, or at important points in a speech or reading, you will experience one form of listener frustration, referred to frequently as "communication breakdown."

EXERCISES FOR PRACTICING [hw] AND [w]

1. Distinguish between [hw] and [w] by placing a finger in front of your lips to feel the additional flow of air for [hw] as you say the following phonemes in isolation. Remember, [w] is voiced but [hw] is voiceless.

[w]   [w]   [w w]   [hw]   [hw hw hw]   [w]   [hw]   [w]   [hw hw]

2. Read the following paired words aloud. The first word in each pair will contain [w]; the second, [hw].

a. went/when; squeeze/wheeze; wide/why; one/what

b. work/whirl; squeal/wheat; west/when; wilt/whip

c. wine/white; wear/where; wicket/whisk; queen/whee

d. well/whelp; swoop/whoopee; wipe/while; weak/whee

e. wish/which; woke/whoa; wise/why; weight/whey

3. Contrast the [hw], [w], and [v] sounds in the following exercise by reading the horizontal word trios aloud.

	[hw]	[w]	[v]
a.	whine	wine	vine
b.	wheeze	we's	V's
c.	whale	wail	veil
d.	whacks	wax	vaccinate
e.	while	wile	vile
f.	wheel	we'll	veal
g.	when	went	vent
h.	why'd	wide	vied
i.	whys	wise	vies
j.	whet	wet	vet

4. In the following words the [w] and [hw] sounds appear in the medial position. Read the words aloud, being sure your lips move quickly to and from their rounded position. Listen for the longer aspiration for [hw] than for [w].

a. everyone/anywhere; exquisite/horsewhip; inquiry/awhile; tower/meanwhile

b. switching/elsewhere; anyone/awhile; swivel/bobwhite; acquiring/somewhat

c. swimming/somewhere; quit/bullwhipping; acquainted/somewhat; swing/awhirl

d. quiet/bewhiskered; awkward/nowhere; equator/everywhere; squeezing/off-white

5. Practice reading aloud the following words containing [w], [hw], and [v] combinations.

a. whatever words varied; waiting while Vern; verification which went

b. vast woods which; warranted covering awhile; whenever vitamins work

c. questioned why values; whipped virtues wisely; invited whittlers worried

d. Wayne whined vigorously; every which way; wherever voters qualified

e. when Queen Victoria; revealed what would; working whereby voices

6. Read the following sentences aloud, being sure to aspirate your [hw] sounds deliberately until you can hear a distinction between [w] and [hw]. If necessary, place a finger in front of your mouth to feel the greater puff of breath used in articulating [hw].

a. When we were invited to spend awhile with the Howards, we quickly accepted, knowing what fun we would have.

b. Whatever it was that went into Wendy's waffles made everyone whistle with quiet wonder.

c. Walt wanted to go somewhere away from the wheat fields of Saskatchewan—anywhere where he would be warm all winter.

d. While everyone was whispering about the queen's wedding gown, white doves appeared from nowhere.

e. She asked whether or not Wilma and Gwen knew why the quaint wool quilt had been whacked to pieces.

f. The whirring of the wheel made Van's whiskers quiver like seaweed in an undercurrent of rushing water.

7. Practice Paragraphs

a. While riding a western railway, Warren vowed he would stop somewhere in Nevada to write about the whirlwind he had watched near Roswell, New Mexico. The weather had been warm and wonderful just before the wind began whirring huge quantities of white sand out of a field a quarter-mile away. All at once the whisper of the wind turned into a low, steady whine and the whole field seemed to rise halfway into the sky. Then, a high level whistling sound began as a weird funnel of white sand quivered upward and sideways.

b. The cobwebs in her window were welcome sights each morning when she awoke. They would wiggle quietly in the warm breeze while she decided which shoes she would wear or what color would fit her mood. The webs always were her first connection with total reality, somewhat like whispered reminders of her past. Other women would have brushed away the webs quickly before anyone could see them and question what kind of housekeepers they were. Not Vera! Whenever she cleaned her windows, she always watched for telltale wisps of web that warned her to be cautious.

c. "Which one would you like?" he asked, holding up two dwarf, snow-white whelps of the dead mountain lioness. "We will make room somewhere in our wagon, but only for one. They're both males." What a decision to make when one is twelve years old! Which one whined the least? Which one would weather our long highway trip back to Atwater best? Which one was strongest? Which one would I be most proud to show my friends next week? While my father waited and watched, I walked over to the one hanging limply from his right fist and said, "That one. I want to call him 'Buckwheat.' "

Technical Description:	Voiced, Nasal Bilabial or Semivowel Continuant (may be a syllabic consonant in the final position of words such as "prism" and "chasm")
Physiological Description: **How The Sound Is Made**	Vocal folds vibrating as lips are closed, teeth are close together but not touching, soft palate is lowered allowing all air to exit through the nose
Common Spellings:	m in man, women, sham, prism me in homely, handsome mn in columnist, hymn mb in thumbnail, dumb mm in swimmer, stammer
Periodic Spellings:	gm in paradigm, phlegm lm in psalmist, calm

[m]
(meal)

[m̩]
(chasm)

The [m] phoneme is one of the most universal sounds in modern languages. It is easy to say since the tongue remains in a neutral position, the lower jaw doesn't change positions during the sound, the soft palate relaxes and drops, and the lips remain closed. In fact, it is one of the first sounds babies learn to say. When they begin to babble, one of their first meaningful sound combinations is "mama." Few people have any difficulty producing this sound. It is the most common sound used for "humming" musical tunes, a habit you probably associate with physical relaxation and peacefulness.

Perhaps its simplicity of production also has led to its wide use with one or more other consonant sounds to create consonant clusters. The [m] phoneme occurs in nine different consonant clusters in General American Speech.

The syllabic [m̩] is a common occurrence in General American Speech. The IPA symbol contains a small line just below the symbol to indicate that the [m] sound is acting as a separate syllable by itself. Normally, a syllabic sound appears only as the final, unstressed syllable of words.

The words "spasm, protoplasm, chasm, rhythm, cataclysm" and any word ending in the suffix "ism" (such as "socialism" and "egoism") tend to be pronounced with a syllabic sound in General American Speech. Frequently, if words contain a vowel or diphthong immediately before an [m] in a final syllable (as in "column, bottom, Chisholm, atom, and bosom) they also are pronounced with syllabic sounds.

COMMON PROBLEMS

1. The nasality of [m] may be carried over to the vowel or diphthong which comes before or after it. In one-syllable words which begin with [m] and end with a vowel or diphthong, you may hear considerable carry-over of nasality. For example, this could occur in the words "me, may, myrrh, moo, mow, ma, my." In one syllable words which begin with a vowel or diphthong and end with [m], such as "I'm, aim, M, am, ohm, alm," you also could hear this extended nasality on the vowels and diphthongs as the soft palate drops in anticipation of the nasal sound. Nasality isn't a distinctive change, since the change in vocal quality doesn't affect word meaning.

If excessive nasal carry-over is one of your problems, you need to become more conscious of the action of your soft palate as it elevates for vowels and diphthongs and falls for [m]. Also, you may be able to pinch your nostrils closed on non-nasal syllables (syllables which contain no [m], [n], or "ng") to see if you are allowing air to escape through the nose on them. If you are, you will *feel* air trying to escape through the nose.

2. Either [n] or "ng" may be substituted for some [m] sounds. Their nasal characteristics make them similar enough that some people don't make clear distinctions among these three sounds. When syllables or adjacent words contain a medial [m] followed by the "ed" suffix, (such as "clai**m**ed or see**m**ed") or by [t, d, l, n] or "th" (such as "I'**m** done" and "so**m**ething"), an [n] frequently is substituted.

When syllables or adjacent words end in [m] and are followed by a syllable beginning with [k] or [g] (as in "I'**m** king" and "so**m**e give"), the "ng" substitution may occur. This change also occurs less frequently before syllables beginning with [s], [w], [hw], and "sh" (as in "so**m**ewhat" and "a**m** seeing").

3. Nonnative speakers of English often have difficulty with English consonant clusters, if their native language had none. These clusters include: [sm], [md], [mfs], [mp], [mps], [mpst], [mpt], [mz] and [rmθ] as in words such as "**sm**all, see**m**ed, triu**mphs**, whi**m**per, ca**mps**, gli**mps**ed, cra**mp**ed, drea**m**s, and war**mth**." If you have trouble with consonant clusters, practice blending each individual sound in the cluster slowly. Feel the different movements of your articulators for each sound, then gradually increase the speed of these movements until you can blend all the sounds together without hesitation.

4. Some people have a problem with denasalizing the [m] sound. This may sound like a complete omission of [m] in words containing an [m] followed by another consonant (as when "si**m**ple" becomes "sipple" and "pro**m**pt" becomes "propped") or as a substitution of [b] (as when "graha**m**" becomes "grab" and "**m**elt" becomes "belt"). Usually, the soft palate is raised too high, closing the nasal passage and forcing air out through the mouth. However, this also may result from enlarged adenoids which block the nasal passage. If you had your enlarged adenoids removed recently, after years of coping with them, you may still speak with a denasalized vocal quality. You need to make complete lip closure for [m] while lowering your soft palate to force air out through the nose and not the mouth. Practice humming or prolonging [m] while moving your pitch up and down the musical scale. Then add different vowel sounds before and after the prolonged [m].

EXERCISES FOR PRACTICING [m]

1. Practice repeating [m] successively as represented below:

[m m]   [m]   [m m]   [m]   [m m m]   [m m]   [m m]   [m]   [m]

2. Be sure your lips are completely closed so you will produce [m] and not [n] as you **prolong** or hum the following:

    a. Low Pitch: [mmmmmmmmmmmmmm]   [mmmmm] [mmmmmmmmmmm]

    b. Medium Pitch: [mmmmm] [mmmmmmmmmmmmm] [mm] [mmmmmm]

    c. High Pitch: [m] [mmmm] [mmmmmmmmmmmmmmmmmmm] [mmm]

3. Pronounce the following words aloud, prolonging the [m] slightly. Be sure the nasal sound doesn't carry over into the vowels and diphthongs. If necessary, hold your nostrils closed on vowels and diphthongs which occur in the final position and release them for [m].

    a. my, Emma, murmur, Amy, mum, alm, mam

    b. may, I'm, mom, me, Mimi, Mame, memory

    c. mow, Miami, aim, Erma, mama, ohm, mime

    d. moo, Emmy, Maugham, am, mummy, myrrh

4. Pronounce the following words with the syllabic [m̩]. Be sure to close your lips after the consonant which is immediately before the [m̩] to avoid inserting a vowel or diphthong between adjacent consonants.

    a. syllogism, schism, bottom, witticism, chasm

    b. barbarism, spasm, organism, atom, prism

    c. realism, egoism, rhythm, criticism, bosom

    d. fascism, bottom, cataclysm, bedlam, plagiarism

5. Read the following word pairs aloud.

    a. mean/seem; mint/simple; mate/aimed; metal/temple; map/sample; Murphy/Herman; muscle/humming

    b. moving/tombstone; money/humble; mice/time; maw/Maugham; most/showman; modern/ominous

    c. mighty/pieman; musty/lumber; mopping/psalmist; mimic/images; mention/eminent; movies/human

    d. meek/dreamer; moody/groom; meant/emigrate; mobile/Roman; mystical/simplicity; macho/hominy

6. The following words contain consonant clusters involving [m]. Try to read the words smoothly, blending all of the consonants in each cluster together.

a. [sm]: smile, smirk, smelling, small, smooth, smog, smoke, Smith, smudge, smother, smart, smash, smelter, smock, smuggle, smear, smashed, smut, smolder, smattering

b. [md]: calmed, roomed, climbed, presumed, crammed, seemed, beamed, dreamed, drummed, ashamed, schemed, timed, screamed, flamed, hemmed, jammed, maimed, mimed, named, numbed, claimed, primed, rammed, roamed, resumed, wormed

c. [mp]: blimp, clamp, temper, damp, stump, ramp, whimper, dampen, simple, shrimp, cramp, slump, bump, dimple, scamper, ample, limp, champion, sample, Tampa, temple, chomping, lamp, pump, primping, stamp, trample, simper

d. [mps]: stamps, primps, ramps, lamps, blimps, lumps, crimps, vamps, slumps, bumps, limps, stumps, cramps

e. [mpt]: camped, tempted, limped, bumped, cramped, stomped, stamped, dumped, crimped, empty, lumped, clamped, tramped, pumped, chomped, primped, attempt, dreamt, trumped

f. [mz]: primes, dreams, comes, screams, homes, seems, crams, steams, beams, games, foams, reams, streams, jams, chimes, psalms, limes, clams, mimes, poems, trams, rhymes, roams, dreams, stems, germs, gums, palms, times, rams, crimes, fumes, lambs, climbs, creams, teams, sums

7. The following word combinations contain the [m] in initial, medial, and final positions of words. Read them aloud as if they were part of a conversation.

a. main army ham; remember mother's team; some bottom cement; moist foam emission; Rome moves slumber

b. more remarks alarm; lamb empties meal; summer came more; altruism marched amiably; cream makes emphasis

c. murmur hampers blame; chasm ambles mercifully; claim messy emblems; communism matches term; am remitting time

d. trim monk informing; Myrna rambled calm; remaining slim mainly; egoism hampers me; Emma meant prime

8. Practice Sentences

a. Most armies maintain some team spirit by aiming to become homes away from home for men and women who join their membership.

b. Remember that December means much more to many members of our immediate families than any other month.

c. The main terminal for our metro tram system makes our shopping mall seem like a miniature, modern marketplace.

d. Sometimes Michael seems so amused by the remarkable dreams of his mother that he has to muffle his spasms of mirth with his arm.

e. In the dim, moist, morning mists, we dreamed of May when most of us would move to Miami for a warm month of merriment, music, and simply elegant meals.

9. Practice Paragraphs

a. A rambling house in the mountains above Alamosa became their home last summer. From the moment they moved in, Romy was mystified by columns of almond colored steam coming out of the mountain, intermittently, across the valley, and moving gloomily up to its remote peak. Members of the local community told her an Indian myth which maintains the steam is a reminder of a mystical Indian chief who had climbed up the mountain to calm some violent autumn storms that threatened his village. The rising mist is a reminder of the Indian chief with the admirable motives who never came down from that mountain.

b. Amy's most memorable experience was a visit to Memphis, Tennessee in the middle of April. She remembered a magnificent white mansion, partially shaded by a magnolia tree, which her grandmother said she had visited every Monday morning when she was a girl. Many white columns supported upper and lower porches that seemed to encircle the mansion. In the main hallway hung a chandelier with hundreds of crystal prisms which moved merrily about whenever a breeze came through the door. Two rooms in the middle of the house were massive in size. Her grandmother said they were parlors where formal dances, banquets, and musical recitals had been held every month.

c. We combed the Manila markets for an umbrella that would match my mother's favorite aquamarine colored dress. It was to be a simple gift from us, but a colorful reminder, on future rainy mornings in Minneapolis, of her first trip away from Minnesota. Every merchant in the marketplace had umbrellas for sale, but no one had an aquamarine colored one. It seemed our efforts were doomed. Then, a small, old seamstress who spoke excellent English said, "I will make you one if I may have until tomorrow morning to complete it." We were ecstatic! We wanted to tell my mother immediately about our good fortune.

10. Dialogue for Oral Practice (for two readers)

Speaker 1: What do you mean when you say I would save money by using fluorescent bulbs in my apartment? They cost more than this simple 100 watt incandescent bulb, don't they?

Speaker 2: Well, a compact fluorescent bulb will last thirteen times longer than an incandescent one. Why don't you multiply the cost of that bulb by thirteen and compare the result to what this fluorescent bulb costs? Remember, too, that a compact fluorescent bulb burns only about one-fourth the electricity that a regular bulb does.

Speaker 1: Hmmm, I see what you mean! Also, I wouldn't have to make extra trips to the supermarket quite as much to replace burned-out bulbs. That means I'd probably burn less fuel going to the store and I'd put less wear on my car.

Speaker 2: Yes, and I believe you're concerned about energy conservation and environmental pollution, so think of the generating power **saved** over the years. Why, you'd also be eliminating about a half-ton of CO2 from the air over the lifetime of **one** fluorescent bulb.

Speaker 1: Wow! O.K., I'll spend the extra money now to save more money in the future. This compact bulb will be perfect for my blue table lamp. By the way, do you work for this fluorescent bulb manufacturer?

CHAPTER 8

THE FRONT VOWELS
[i], [ɪ], [e], [ɛ], [æ]

If you were asked to name all the English vowels, you probably would say "a, e, i, o, and u—and sometimes y." That would be correct for written English. They are the components of words that connect consonants together to form words. You might be interested to know that in some early written languages the vowels were omitted. The reader was expected to insert the vowels as a manuscript was read. In many cases, written messages don't require vowels in order for the reader to understand them. Look at the following and see if you can figure out the messages.

1. W_ kn_w _ll th_ _nsw_rs.

2. H_ lp! S_nd m_ m_re m_n_y.

3. St_p t_lk_ng _nd st_rt th_nk_ng.

4. Wh_t k_nd _f _ss_gnm_nt _s th_s?

As you can see, the number of written vowels which you may use is limited and this makes your decoding process fairly easy. Also, the context of each sentence helps you to see whether your vowel choices "make sense."

One further consideration which helps you to understand the message is the knowledge that words consist of syllables. Syllables are determined by the number of voiced vowels or diphthongs that occur in a word (a silent "e" at the end of a word wouldn't count) since they serve as the nuclei for syllables. Often, by counting the number of vowels and diphthongs in a word, you can tell how many syllables it has. The word "instigating," for example, has four vowels: "i," "i," "a," and "i." It also has four syllables.

If you were asked to list all of the vowel **sounds** in English, you probably would not find the task quite so simple. You practically need a dictionary to determine how many vowel sounds are used in English because all the written vowels can be pronounced in several different ways. Beginning with this chapter, we will be looking at the various vowel **sounds** and how they are produced. You will begin to discover that our language is not a phonetic language (words are not consistently pronounced the way they are spelled) and this factor creates much difficulty for individuals learning the language for the first time.

VOWEL CHARACTERISTICS AND LOCATIONS

Before we discuss the first groups of vowel sounds, we should review characteristics which all General American vowel sounds have in common.

1. All are **voiced** (except when they are whispered.)

2. The airflow from the lungs is **unrestricted.**

3. The sounds are **not nasalized,** so the velum is raised.

4. Their quality and preciseness are affected by the **size and shape of the resonators.**

It may be helpful if we use a simplified diagram of the location of vowels in the human mouth. Although each person makes sounds according to his or her physiological equipment, we can generalize about locations of sounds to assist you in your studies and practice. If your vowel sounds are too far removed from their correct location, they may not be distinguishable from other vowels. Listeners will perceive them as sound substitutions if they are not familiar with your speaking habits.

DIAGRAM OF GENERAL AMERICAN VOWEL PLACEMENT

	FRONT	MIDDLE/MID	BACK	
	(high)	(high)	(high)	
Lips Spread	[i] eel		pool [u]	Lips Rounded
	[ɪ] ill		pull [ʊ]	
	[e] ale			
	[ɛ] Ella	[ɚ] [ɝ] hurt	pole [o]	
		[ə] [ʌ] hut		
Lips Open			Paul [ɔ]	Lips Unrounded
	[æ] Al		pod [ɑ]	
	FRONT	MIDDLE/MID	BACK	
	(low)	(low)	(low)	

Our diagram of vowel placement assumes that the speaker is facing the left side of the paper and we are able to see a cross section of the mouth's interior. The roof of the mouth (hard palate) is at the top of the diagram and the tongue and lower jaw are at the bottom. The lips are at the front (left) and the throat or pharynx is at the back (right) of the diagram.

THE FRONT VOWELS

Five vowel sounds are created close to the lips or front of the mouth. You will discover that [i], the highest sound, begins with the lower jaw very close to the upper jaw. As the vowels "drop" the lower jaw drops and the upper and lower front teeth separate. You will be able to feel the response of the muscles under your tongue to this drop. Place a thumb firmly in the fleshy portion under your chin and feel how the muscles gradually become more relaxed as the vowel sounds drop. This will be a useful procedure to use with all your vowel sounds as you try to **feel** physiological changes which create sound changes you are hearing. If you fail to tense or relax your tongue muscles for a particular sound, you may get an approximation of the desired sound, but not the exact sound.

As a general rule, you will find that the tip of your tongue is behind your lower front teeth for all your front vowel sounds. The back of your tongue will be arched upward towards the velum or soft palate.

Technical Description:	Tense High Front Vowel
Physiological Description: **How The Sound Is Made**	Vocal folds vibrate, lips are close together and drawn into a slight smile, lower jaw drops slightly, back of tongue draws up close to soft palate and tip is behind lower front teeth while front sides of tongue are in contact with the upper molars, velum is raised closing off nasal passages
Common Spellings:	e in even, scene, be ee in eel, cheese, coffee ea in easy, dream, sea ei in either, leisure ie in relieve, fiend y in Ybor, partying, easy i in Igor, pizza, ski
Periodic Spellings:	ey in monkey, lackey oe in amoebic, supoena ae in Aesop, Caesar eo in people

$$[\overset{\bullet}{\text{i}}]$$

(seed)

We spoke about the International Phonetic Alphabet earlier in this book in relation to its use throughout the world. Many of the symbols selected were representative of how certain sounds were spelled in numerous languages. For this reason, some of the symbols may not seem to apply easily to English. The [i] is one of those symbols and may be confusing at first. If you can remember some words in which the "i" is pronounced as a long "e," (as in piano, antique, and kilo) you will have less difficulty in making future associations with the [i] symbol. If you have had French, Spanish, or Italian, or if your native language is one in which the letter "i" usually is pronounced as [i] (as in the Spanish "adios" and "sí," the French "il" and "oui," or the Italian "appetito" and "musica") you will recognize immediately why this symbol was selected.

COMMON PROBLEMS

Three common problems are associated with producing the [i] sound accurately.

1. It is nasalized when individuals allow the velum or soft palate to fall or "droop." This is a common error in areas of the Southwest and Middle West. It also is a characteristic of many Country/Western singers and entertainers. This error is heard frequently among individuals with cleft palates who learned to speak before surgical repair of their palates. If you have a tendency to nasalize vowel sounds, you will need to become conscious of what your velum feels like when you raise and lower it. You may begin by saying "ah," then, while prolonging the sound, move to the [i] sound without allowing the soft palate to fall. For all nasalized vowels, you should be able to pinch the nostrils shut with your thumb and finger and be able to produce a clear sound. If the nose vibrates and air tries to escape, your velum is not shutting off the nasal passages adequately.

2. The less tense [ɪ] sound, which you will study next, is substituted for [i]. This substitution is common among first generation Americans and foreign students whose native language makes no distinction between these two sounds. Thus, the word "heat" becomes "hit," and "least" becomes "list." The blade (front) of your tongue probably is too relaxed and needs to be elevated slightly higher.

American Legion Magazine

"When I say 'riiiiiich frmmmmmm,' I don't mean 'criiiiii rgmmmmmmm.''

3. A vowel or glide is added immediately after the [i], producing a diphthong-like quality or "drawl." This is a common change in many areas of the South and Southwest. In many individuals the resulting schwa sound of "uh" is added to the end of most [i] sounds. It becomes most obvious in the final position of a word such as "tea" (tea-uh) or before "l" as in "feel" (fee-uhl).

EXERCISES FOR PRACTICING [i]

1. Practice saying the sound aloud in isolation. Remember to repeat the sound each time that a symbol appears within brackets.

[i i]   [i]   [i i i i]   [i i]   [i i i]   [i i]

2. The following list is to test your ability to recognize words transcribed in IPA symbols. Try to determine what each word is.

a. [ti]   f. [fid]
b. [did]   g. [ti vi]
c. [fit]   h. [iv]
d. [it]
e. [tid]

3. Place your thumb firmly under your chin and say the following words. Feel the difference in muscular tension as you say them.

a. please, I, neat, ought, keep, itch, peach, pet

b. grease, old, heat, nest, ski, hut, key, bit

c. meal, mall, preach, inch, queen, said, deed, oh

d. keen, much, tree, pit, we, you, theme, thin

e. knee, knit, reed, red, each, etch, plead, pledge

4. Determine whether the following paired words contain the same or different vowel sounds.

a. thrill/reach
b. tease/left
c. inch/peak
d. trees/these
e. flea/cheese

f. bean/pique
g. gift/least
h. drip/pier
i. field/each
j. team/dealt

5. Read the following groups of words aloud as if you are saying them to a friend in informal conversation.

a. each peach lately; either street deceives

b. safety fleece machine; anemia empty thesis

c. ego needs kilo; donkey perceives easy

d. sweet even Phoenix; people flee dreams

e. Caesar queen lesion; piano seize stream

6. Read the following sentences aloud.

a. We could not conceive of Phoebe being either place.

b. East Street meets Peach Street in Phoenix.

c. "Leave the trees and flee!" screamed the queen.

d. Lately these machines needed greasing daily.

e. We believe relief is easy to dream of.

7. Read the following selections as if you were describing the scene or telling a story. Do not let your volume, rate, or inflections stagnate.

a. We could see the recent excavations made by heavy machinery along the east edge of the stream. She refused to leave until we received assurance that the remaining fields would be left untouched until the local people could be reached by mail or telephone. She knew they were being deceived by promises of flood relief and recreational facilities.

b. At a recent retreat for Eagle Scouts which was held in a renovated cheese factory near Eden Rock, we achieved close harmony. Each of us served briefly as a team leader for some event. Our leisure activities included equal periods of strenuous and easy events. We greeted each meal with anticipation and appreciation. The pleasing menus repeatedly achieved our highest praise. Each evening brought relief from the daily heat and easy, pleasant, and much needed sleep.

Technical Description:	High Front Vowel (less tense than [i])
Physiological Description: How The Sound Is Made	Vocal folds vibrate, lips are drawn into a slight smile but not as broad as [i], lower jaw drops more than for [i], back of tongue is drawn up close to soft palate, tongue tip is behind lower front teeth while front sides of tongue are in contact with upper molars, velum is raised closing off nasal passages, muscles under tongue are less tense and sound is not prolonged as much as for [i]
Common Spellings:	i in itch, ticket, rowing, big e in England, oldest, here u or ui in business, building ea in ear, hear
Periodic Spellings:	y in hymn, bicycle, syntax ie in sieve, friend, pierce o in women ee in sheer ei in forfeiture

[I]

(him)

The [I] sound is a frequently substituted sound for both [i] and [ε]. The vowel diagram shows that it is located between these two sounds. If the tongue muscles are too lax or too tense, you can easily have this error in your daily speaking patterns. Generally, the front of the tongue is slightly lower for [I] than for [i] but it is arched towards the hard palate in both sounds.

COMMON PROBLEMS

1. If you are a non-native speaker of English, or if you were reared in a home by non-native speakers of English, you may have a tendency to substitute [i] for [I] in all positions of words. Thus, someone who is not familiar with your speech patterns may hear you saying, "She had a neat dress and her feet made me jealous" instead of "She had a knit dress and her fit made me jealous." If you have had singing lessons, you may have learned to "raise" your [I] sounds in order to sustain and project them. You may have thought this directive applied to speaking too and changed many or all your [I] sounds to [i]. If you say "wheech" for "which" and "thees" for "this" you are substituting the [i] for [I]. You need to relax the muscles under the tongue and drop the front part of your tongue slightly. Also, if a root word ends in "i" and the suffix "ful" is added to it, the "i" is pronounced [I] and not [i]. As a result, words such as "bountiful," "beautiful," and "merciful" do *not* use [i]. Some words may be pronounced with either [i] or [I]. These include words beginning with a prefix containing "e" (such as "pre," "be," and "de") including "prepare," "between," and "deceive." Words ending in "y" or "ey" such as "money," "happy," and "simply" tend to be produced with an [I] sound in portions of the South and Southwest. However, in General American speech you are more likely to hear [i] in the final position. We prefer [i] rather than [I] since it seems to be easier to understand than [I], particularly when speakers are speaking rapidly before large groups. Probably a sound mid-way between the two is used in casual speech.

2. A vowel or glide (usually sounding like "uh") is added immediately after the [ɪ], producing a diphthong-like quality or "drawl." This change was discussed under [i]. It probably is most obvious when it occurs in the initial and medial position of words. With this habit "him" becomes "hium," and "ill" becomes "iuhl."

3. The sound is nasalized when the velum is allowed to relax or fall. This allows air to escape through the nose while [ɪ] is produced.

4. The [ε] sound which we will be studying later in this chapter is substituted for [ɪ], especially when [ɪ] occurs immediately before an "l" or [l] sound in a word. With this change, the word "fill" becomes "fell" and the word "pick" becomes "peck." In this case, the muscles of the tongue are too lax and must be used to elevate the middle portion of the tongue slightly higher to [ɪ].

EXERCISES FOR PRACTICING [I]

1. Pronounce the following sequences of isolated [ɪ] sounds. Then contrast the sound with [i] in the next series. Feel the change in muscles under the tongue as you move from one vowel to the other. If you can feel no change in tension, you may be making no distinction between them.

a. [ɪ]   [ɪ ɪ ɪ ɪ]   [ɪ ɪ]   [ɪ ɪ ɪ]   [ɪ]   [ɪ ɪ]   [ɪ]

b. [i]   [ɪ ɪ]   [i ɪ ɪ]   [ɪ i ɪ]   [i i]   [ɪ ɪ i ɪ]

2. Determine what the following words are. Read the lists slowly, then repeat the list quickly to see if you can decode the words with equal accuracy.

a	b	c
[ɪf]	[piv]	['pi wi]
[win]	[fɪb]	[wɪmp]
[vi]	['wi pi]	[iv]
[bin]	['ɪf i]	[bif]
[bɪb]	[wiv]	['bi ni]

3. In the spaces provided, transcribe the following words using IPA symbols and brackets.

a. weep _____ , mean _____ , bin _____ , whip _____

b. pimp _____ , beam _____ , beefy _____ , vim _____

c. whip _____ , Fifi _____ , beep _____ , win _____

4. As you read the following words aloud, be aware of the contrasting [i] and [ɪ] sounds in each pair.

a. deep/dip; fill/feel; slip/sleep; eat/it; Tim/team

b. tin/teen; lick/leak; Lynne/lean; deem/dim

c. scene/sin; mitt/meat; each/itch; tick/teak

d. pitch/peach; greet/grit; Kip/keep; leap/lip; green/grin

e. his/he's; greed/grid; kin/keen; feet/fit; feast/fist

5. Practice reading these sentences in which [ɪ] appears frequently.

a. Since that city in Indiana isn't close enough to Cincinnati, we intend to visit one in Michigan instead.

b. If the ink is dry, give him your Indian short story which you intend to submit for publication.

c. Inside his home he was king but at the mill he was indistinguishable from his anonymous co-workers.

d. Cindy lives near the Wilson Shipping Company, just down the hill from our city's busiest intersection.

6. Practice reading these paragraphs aloud.

a. Spring is my time for wishing and planning. I sit on the hill behind my office building during lunch hour and actively scan the crinkly pages of seed catalogs. I imagine my future garden filled with simple, primitive wild flowers; magnificent, crisp vegetables, and luscious fruit. I can see myself in that garden, hidden from public view, enjoying the delights of springtime.

b. If billboards could talk, they would never whisper. In militant voices they would insist on being heard. They would insult, irritate, whittle away at your silly notions on "saving for a rainy day" and insist that your decisions include more frills for your own ecstasy.

c. Linguistics is the science of language. It includes areas such as syntax, morphology, phonology, and semantics. If you decided to major in Linguistics, you might specialize in comparative, historical, descriptive, or geographical sub-divisions of this field. Often, you would be investigating language structure and development, or the relationship of one language or dialect to another. An early term for Linguistics was Philology, which implied a love for learning and literature, especially as it related to determining the authenticity and meaning of written records or literary texts.

d. The mighty Mississippi River begins in northern Minnesota and ends in the Gulf of Mexico. Usually, it flows placidly over 2,348 miles, bisecting the United States as it twists and turns past important cities such as Memphis and New Orleans. Barges filled with coal, grain, machinery and other goods travel its waters regularly. Steamboats filled with people once made continuous trips up and down the river. Now, automobiles and airplanes will make the same trips in a fraction of the time. The river has been immortalized in music as "Old Man River," and in literature, as the background for several of Mark Twain's interesting stories.

[e]

(day)

Technical Description:	Tense, Mid, Front Vowel (or Diphthong [eɪ])
Physiological Description: How The Sound Is Made	Vocal folds vibrate, lips are close together and drawn into a slight smile (not rounded), lower jaw drops more than for [ɪ], back of tongue draws up close to soft palate, tip of tongue is behind or at biting edge of lower front teeth, sides of tongue are firmly against upper molars, front or blade of tongue moves up slightly as sound is prolonged, velum is raised to close off nasal passages
Common Spellings:	a in ache, shaking, today ei in rein, lei ay in player, wayward, Jay ai in aim, prevail, raider eigh in eight, neighbor, sleigh ee in matinee, fiancee, entree e in elite, fiance, risque ea in great, break, steak
Periodic Spellings:	ey in obey uet in bouquet au in gauge ait in parfait, au lait

The [e] sound is listed in the summary above as both a vowel and a diphthong. In English, it tends to be a pure [e] only in unstressed syllables (such as in the words "Daytona," "vacation," and "elite") and at the end of a syllable that is immediately followed by a syllable whose first sound is a stop (such as in the words "atrium," "eighty," or "April.") In most other cases, the sound is a blending of the vowels [e] and [ɪ] in one sound. Unless you are a native speaker of Spanish (in which a fairly pure [e] occurs frequently), you will have difficulty in sustaining [e] without introducing the [ɪ] at the conclusion of the sound. Try it! The front of the tongue moves up slightly as you finish the sound.

In order to simplify future transcriptions in this course, we will *not* use [eɪ]. Only machines and individuals with well trained ears seem to be capable of distinguishing [e] from [eɪ] easily. If you plan to enter speech pathology or linguistics, you may need to make this distinction in the future.

The front of the tongue is slightly lower and, although the muscles under the tongue are more lax for [e] than for [ɪ], they are still quite tense. In some speakers, the tip of the tongue rises slightly, but is still behind the lower front teeth. The lips are unrounded.

COMMON PROBLEMS

The most common problems involving [e] are these.

1. The sound is nasalized when the velum is allowed to relax or droop. This becomes most noticeable when [e] occurs immediately before or after "m," "n," and "ng," as in the words "main," "namely," and "hanger." (See information on correcting nasalized vowel sounds under the [i] sound.)

2. The schwa sound "uh" is added to [e] in syllables ending in "l" or "le." Words such as "tale," "hail," and "jailer" sound like they contain the sound "ay-uh." This is found most often in speakers who were reared in the South. Periodically, one also may hear individuals who add this sound **before** the [e], particularly in one syllable words such as "made," "paid," and "shame," resulting in the sound "uh-ay." These speakers must learn not to drop the middle portion of the tongue when saying [e].

3. The [e] is substituted for [ɛ], the next sound we will be studying, in words such as "head," "extra," "egg," and "said." This is heard frequently among speakers in the South and Southwest and in the Southern Black Dialect. In this error, the muscles of the tongue are not relaxed enough and the tongue pushes too hard towards the hard palate.

4. When [e] appears before a final [l] in words such as "tail, sails, Yale, mail" and "fail," some speakers weaken or slight the sound, making it more like [ɛ]. Thus, they make little distinction between "sell" and "sale."

EXERCISES FOR PRACTICING [e]

1. Say the isolated [e] sound each time it appears in the following sequences.

a. [e]   [e e e]   [e]   [e e e]   [e e]   [e e e e]   [e]

b. [e e]   [e e]   [e]   [e e e e]   [e e e]   [e e e e]

2. Contrast the other vowels studied to date with [e] by saying the following transcriptions aloud.

a. [e]   [ɪ]   [e]   [i]   [ɪ]   [e e]   [ɪ e]   [e i]   [ɪ]

b. [i i]   [ɪ e]   [ɪ]   [i e]   [e e]   [ɪ e]   [ɪ e i]

3. Read the following lists aloud to demonstrate your ability to read IPA transcriptions accurately. Try to read the lists in a regular conversational rate of speaking.

a. [ni], [ep], [pev], [men], [hwɪp]

b. [ɪf], [nem], [wev], [pip], [pen]

c. [min], [wen], [hwɪf], [bin], [fem]

d. [wip], ['mɪn i], ['hwɪn i], [pe], [fi]

4. In the spaces provided, transcribe the following words, using IPA symbols and brackets.

a. waif _____, payee _____, weigh me _____ ____

b. Amy _____, weenie _____, may we? _____ ____

c. if ____, bay ____, knee pain _____ ____

5. Read the following phrases aloud.

a. saving face pay; ate flakes today; Ray delays eight

b. crate display aims; station agent today, Ava's great day

c. April freight play; aiding rate may, chaotic acorn display

6. Read the following sentences aloud.

a. They made their sale a favorite day on the Cape.

b. Able people pay the baker to make their cakes.

c. Mail the neighbors a vacation display from the train station.

d. Whales may stray away to chase their aging, playful partners.

7. Practice reading the following paragraphs aloud.

a. Ada and Dale decided they would wait until May before they announced their engagement. Neighbors waited for them to break the news before they made their way to the city to look at plates, place settings of silver, pillow cases, and other gracious gifts. They scanned the April papers for a portrait of the couple, knowing it would name the long-awaited wedding date.

b. Lately, the days have lengthened, making it possible for us to enjoy our favorite late afternoon pastime—watching the sailing ships racing in the bay—even longer. Their sails billow out gracefully as the breeze plays with them and we wait to see the setting sun bathe the sails in golden splendor. Sometimes our arms ache as we watch the mates raise and lower the sails.

Technical Description:	Mid Front Vowel (less tense than [e])
Physiological Description: **How The Sound Is Made**	Vocal folds vibrate, lips are farther apart and have less muscular tension than for [e] as corners of mouth are not turned up, lower jaw drops considerably more than for [e], tip of tongue is behind lower front teeth while sides of tongue are in contact with upper molars, velum is raised to close off nasal passages, sound is not as prolonged as [e]
Common Spellings:	e in Ed, west, blend, lemon ea in ready, heaven, leather a in anyone, various, warily ai in air, said, again
Periodic Spellings:	ei in heir, heifer, their ie in friendly ae in aesthetic, Aeschylus ay in says u in buried eo in leopard

[ɛ]

(fed)

Of all the front vowel sounds, this sound seems to give native American speakers of English the most difficulty. The [ɛ] sound is not as tense as [i], [ɪ] or [e]. Feel the muscles under your chin as you say each of these sounds and you will discover a noticeable difference in muscle tension.

COMMON PROBLEMS

1. The [ɪ] is substituted for [ɛ] in words such as "guess," "get," "any," "many," "when," and "been." This substitution occurs in all parts of the United States, particularly in rural areas, low socio-economic neighborhoods, and among individuals with little formal education. As a result, to many people, it implies an inadequate education, general carelessness, or impoverished diction due to ignorance and/or environment. Often, laypersons refer to this as "squeezing the vowel sounds" because the mouth is not opened and the lower jaw is not dropped far enough to create a good [ɛ] sound. Ventriloquists learn to produce vowel changes adequately without moving their lips or jaw but the average person does not.

2. As mentioned in the last section, [e] often is substituted for [ɛ] in words such as "egg," "head," and "leg." This is particularly noticeable in the Southern, Eastern, and Black American Dialects. When this substitution occurs, the tongue muscles are too tense and the middle portion of the tongue often is pushing upwards towards the hard palate rather than relaxing and falling towards the lower jaw.

3. The sound is nasalized. This usually occurs just before or immediately after a nasalized sound as in the words "endless," "whenever," and "Bethlehem." However, it also occurs in words such as "let" and "belt" which contain no nasal sounds. As with the nasalization of other vowels, this occurs when the velum is allowed to relax and drop away from the nasal passages, allowing air to escape through the nose. (Remember, all vowels are non-nasal sounds.)

4. The [æ] sound, the next phoneme we will study, is substituted for [ɛ] in words such as "red," "well," and "set." In this error, the lower jaw drops too far and the tongue muscles relax too much. This change occurs frequently among speakers who were reared in New York City and adjacent areas.

5. Non-native speakers of English often have difficulty with the [ɛ] sound because of the inconsistency in spellings that occur for this sound. Depending on the rules of their first language, they may substitute any of the front vowels or the "uh" or schwa sound for [ɛ].

6. The "uh" or schwa sound is added to the [ɛ], creating a diphthong. This change occurs chiefly among speakers who were reared in the South or Southwest and is referred to by laypersons as a drawl. It is most noticeable in one syllable words such as "led," "said," or "when," or before sounds that may be prolonged, such as [l], [m], and [n]. The middle portion of the tongue must not be allowed to drop or relax between the [ɛ] and the final consonant of a syllable if this additional sound is to be eliminated.

To check on your ability to say the [ɛ] sound precisely, read the following sentences aloud and have someone who can't see the script, listen to you. Do they understand what you are saying?

a. Well, we'll willingly will our well to Will.

b. Bill's handmade bells brought cents to the tills and many mints for Bill's best girl, Belle.

c. Since ten cents meant more to Lynn than to Len, we let Len have the tin nickles and Lynn, the ten cents.

d. Many times we send Minny bills which tell how much is left to pay on her bid for the Jenny Lind bed.

EXERCISES FOR PRACTICING [ɛ]

1. The following exercises will give you experience in identifying and using the isolated front vowels studied so far. Read each sequence aloud slowly, then speed up your rate of speaking.

a. [ɛ]   [ɛ ɛ]   [ɛ ɛ ɛ]   [ɛ ɛ]   [ɛ]   [ɛ ɛ ɛ ɛ]

b. [e ɛ ɪ]   [ɛ ɪ]   [ɪ e ɛ]   [ɛ ɪ ɛ ɪ ɛ]   [e ɛ]

2. Read the following sequences aloud.

a. [hwɛn], ['ɛn i], [bɛn], [wɛb], ['mɪn i]

b. ['bɪm ɪn i], ['pɛn i], [ni], ['mɛn i], [pɪn]

c. ['wev i], [eb], [mɛn], ['iv ɪn], [pɛp]

90

3. Write the following words in IPA symbols.

a. hem _____, pea _____, bevy _____, weigh _____

b. if _____, maybe _____, pen _____, whip _____

c. win _____, wen _____, pain _____, beam _____

4. Read the following paired words aloud. Be sure the jaw drops or rises for the second word in each pair. Do not add the "uh" or schwa sound after the vowels in these words.

a. Ben/bin; pit/pet; built/belt; meant/mint

b. bell/bill; ten/tin; picked/pecked; hid/head

c. pig/peg; insist/incest; red/rid; disk/desk

d. Rentz/rinse; Rick/wreck; well/will; till/tell

5. Practice the following sentences aloud at a conversational rate of speaking.

a. Nellie Benson went to Kendall, Indiana to check on metal chicken baskets.

b. Whenever Ted guesses, he gets many items on his examinations incorrect.

c. Denton, Texas had a pet bear with a defective neck which prevented it from turning its head.

d. Our treasure hunt emphasized the ability to get as many mementos of pleasant events as we could find.

e. As we left the Lazy Egg Restaurant, my friend paid the breakfast check by pretending to empty his pockets at the cashier's desk.

6. Read the following paragraphs aloud as if you were telling the ideas to someone in a casual conversation.

a. Their winter wilderness venture led them well beyond the headwaters of Red River to a den of elderly black bears in hibernation. When they recognized the entry to the cave, they felt both terror and elation. Since they had no weapons with them, they could not ignore the treacherous consequences of their next decision. They did not feign contempt for the creatures sleeping inside.

b. Aunt Minnie had many memories of mental games her parents played with her as they went from Benton Harbor, Michigan to Medford, Oregon in the 1920s. She was only seven years old then and her brother, Kenneth, was ten. Whenever they saw a hen in someone's yard, her mother would ask, "What name shall we give this hen that begins with the next letter in the alphabet?" (They kept going through the alphabet, trying not to repeat the same name twice.) Aunt Minnie and Uncle Ken would spend hours in secret deliberation, searching for the next name they would suggest.

Technical Description:	Low, Front Open Vowel
Physiological Description: How The Sound Is Made	Vocal folds vibrate, lower jaw drops considerably from the [ɛ] position and mouth opens wider than for [ɛ], tongue muscles are lax as tongue rests on the floor of the mouth, tongue tip and blade are flattened behind lower front teeth while sides of tongue make contact with upper molars, velum is raised to close off nasal passageways
Common Spellings:	a in ask, pan, thatch, gamble au in aunt, laughter, draught
Periodic Spellings:	al in half, salve ai in plaid

[æ]

(mat)

The [æ] sound often is identified with American English. In fact, some foreign comics use a nasalized version of this sound to imitate the stereotypical American speaker. In the British dialect, this sound usually is softened to [a], a sound mid-way between [æ] and "ah." Your textbook author once had a native French professor who considered this one of the most beautiful sounds in English because it didn't exist in his language! (He also thought the phrase "garbage can" was the most beautiful combination of sounds he had heard in American English.)

COMMON PROBLEMS

1. The [æ] sound can be extremely harsh or tense if the tongue muscles are not relaxed adequately. Constriction of the pharynx and back portion of the tongue can lead to this unpleasant harshness. Frequently, this error is linked with the addition of another vowel to create a diphthong. Some speakers from large cities, such as Chicago, may have this tendency for elevating the [æ] sound by raising the lower jaw and tongue too high. If the fleshy portion under your chin is tense when you say [æ], you need to relax the tongue completely to allow the thumb to push quite far up under the chin.

2. The sound is nasalized. In this case, the velum is allowed to drop away from the nasal passageways and air escapes through the nose. This becomes most evident when the sound is followed by "n," "m," or "ng." (See the information given under the [i] sound regarding nasalized vowel sounds.) If a word such as "at," "plaid," or "sabbath" contains no nasal sound, try pinching the nostrils closed while saying the word to see if you feel any vibration. If you do, you probably are nasalizing the sound.

3. The [ɛ] sound is substituted for [æ]. In this situation, "bag" is pronounced "beg" and "pat" is pronounced "pet." The lower jaw must be dropped even more and the blade or front portion of the tongue should be flattened and relaxed more.

4. The [æ] sound is made into a diphthong by adding a vowel sound immediately after this phoneme, especially in the medial position of one syllable words such as "hand," "aunt," and "man." If your words sound like "ha-yund," "a-yunt," and "ma-yun," you probably are accused of having a Southern drawl. This habit is most noticeable among speakers of the Southern and Southern Black Dialects. However, it also is associated with some "mountain dialects" which laypersons frequently call "hillbilly dialect." The tongue must not be allowed to drop or relax between the [æ] sound and the following consonant sound if this habit is to be changed.

5. Non-native speakers of English may tend to substitute the [a] sound (which is similar to our "ah" sound) for [æ] because the [æ] doesn't exist in their languages. Frequently, foreign students who received their English language training from British teachers are easily identified because they don't say [æ]. If you intend to improve your General American Speech pattern, you must work on the [æ] sound since it is an important characteristic of it. If you plan to return to your home where a British dialect is spoken (or if you will spend the rest of your life in New York or New England) this may not be a crucial phoneme to change since it tends to be heard often in those areas. Americans who substitute [a] for [æ] tend to be perceived by citizens outside New England and New York as somewhat artificial, overly dramatic, or even snobbish. This may be because stereotypes of "overly cultured" or artistic characters in stage and television productions often are portrayed as using a dialect which emphasizes the softer [a] for [æ].

EXERCISES FOR PRACTICING [æ]

1. Practice the following isolated phonemes aloud.

a. [æ] 　　[æ æ æ] 　　[æ æ] 　　[æ] 　　[æ æ] 　　[æ æ]

b. [e] 　[æ] 　[ɪ] 　[æ] 　[ɛ] 　[e æ] 　[i e æ] 　[ɛ]

2. Pronounce the following words aloud, slowly at first and then with conversational speed.

a. [hæv], [næb], ['pæp i], [fæn], ['vɪ vi ɪn]

b. [væmp], ['iv ɪn], ['mæp mæn], [næp], ['feb i ɪn]

3. Transcribe the following into IPA symbols.

a. Pam _____, baby fee _____ _____, pan fan _____ _____

b. maybe _____, happy _____, If we nap ___ ___ _____

4. Read the following pairs of words aloud, being sure the vowel sounds are distinctly different.

a. mass/mess; met/mat; head/had; shall/shell; ten/tan

b. dead/dad; bland/blend; blessed/blast; sat/set

c. man/men; leg/lag; add/Ed; gnat/net; Ken/can

d. bed/bad; hams/hems; said/sad; mesh/mash; pack/peck

e. Beth/bath; sacks/sex; cat/kit; led/lad; past/pest

5. Read the following phrases aloud.

a. bad red snake; last friend's aim; hate mental jams

b. glass head came; shake less mats; heed Jane's plan

c. tackle metal tables; save temper stacks; he met at

d. glance back and; carrot and apples; chap planned it

6. Practice reading the following sentences aloud. Start slowly, being sure each vowel is produced distinctly, then increase your rate of reading.

a. Had the facts been accurate, Dan would have packed and left the camp.

b. The hand that grabbed the can of apples was not the hand of Alice.

c. The trash truck slammed on its brakes, banged into the Mass Transit Office, and smashed into a hat shop.

d. The tramp wrapped his ham shank in a piece of wax paper, packed it in a ragged cloth bag, and glanced up the railroad track.

e. Mrs. Lashley said a gallon of molasses was ample pay for the fancy satin sham she had made.

7. Read the following paragraphs aloud.

a. On Saturday afternoon we always had ham sandwiches and fresh radishes when Aunt Madge came for a visit. We wrapped the ham in freshly baked bread, chattering all the while about our ample harvest of vegetables from our garden patch in back of the house. She would laugh quietly behind her cup of black coffee, encouraging us to ramble on about our annual accomplishments.

b. Catching fish was not a matter of chance for half the population of Cash County. Rather, it became a consuming pastime for most of the men and an ample number of women. They called themselves "anglers," because they always were looking for a new angle to catch the most fish. Tanks of newly hatched minnows stood in back yards. Fifty gallon drums of hand-sorted night crawlers were everywhere. Dozens of yards had handpainted signs announcing new fish traps and lures for sale.

c. In mid-January, when Eve left for Miami, we went to the train station to bid her farewell. She sat with us on the platform until the very last minute, laughing at the tales being told about her past travel ventures. She seemed giddy, happy, and excited. When the conductor made a final announcement that the train was about to depart, she kissed all of us quickly, gathered her carry-on luggage in both hands, and swept them onto the train steps in one magnificent leap. Then, turning quickly for one last glance at us, she shouted, "Watch the mail for my cards. You'll each get at least one—maybe even two, if I get bored—in the next two weeks. The rest of the time, I'll be relaxing on the warm sands of the beach—and I hope I won't be alone! If you don't hear from me, you'll know I'm having a spectacular time." Then she slipped into the car. We stood in the growing gloom of a New Jersey January morning, envious of our friend and wishing we could share her experiences.

CHAPTER 9

THE MIDDLE SOUNDS
[θ], [ð], [t], [d]

Our discussion of **middle** consonant sounds begins with sounds which use the upper front teeth as their point of articulation. These middle consonant sounds gradually will move in their points of articulation from the front teeth to the gum (alveolar) ridge, and then back to the hard palate. You can use this arbitrary "middle" classification to visualize approximately where certain sounds should be located or "placed" in relation to the front consonant sounds which originated at the lips. Also, this classification may help you discover you are using the same **general** area of the mouth where some sounds **should** be formed, to create substitutions for those sounds.

You will find the IPA symbols for the voiced and voiceless "th" sounds are quite different from any modern English alphabet letters. (Remember, the International Phonetic Alphabet uses more than English alphabet symbols for sounds.) Therefore, they can be confusing as you begin your listening and transcription exercises. The symbol for the voiceless "th" is the Greek **Theta** [θ] symbol (which actually stands for the spirant or fricative "th" in the modern Greek alphabet). You may have seen this symbol in scientific and mathematical discussions or in organizational names written in Greek symbols.

If you are a native speaker of English, you probably acquired your [θ] and [ð] sounds near the end of your language acquisition period. Unless you could see a speaker, you may have thought persons were saying [f], [t], or [s] for [θ] and [v], [d], or [z] for [ð]. These sounds do resemble one another. You had to learn that the upper front portion of the tongue had to be placed lightly on the biting edge of the upper front teeth to form these sounds correctly. You still may have difficulty hearing which of these sounds is being said by some speakers. In these cases, you will depend upon contextual clues to tell you what the person probably is saying.

If you are a nonnative speaker of English, you probably find the voiced and voiceless "th" sounds particularly difficult to hear and pronounce, simply because they may not occur in your native language. You may substitute [d] and [t] for voiced and voiceless "th" sounds because you had these sounds in your language. If you learned your spoken English from nonnative speakers of English, your chances for substituting other sounds for "th" increase.

Substitutions of [d] and [t] for "th" sounds also occur frequently among first generation North Americans, and periodically among second and third generation North Americans, if they hear the sound substitutions regularly at home and in their neighborhoods. In Hawaiian Pidgin English, a dialect spoken in casual or informal settings by many well educated people in the islands, the substitutions occur regularly among third and fourth generation Americans. The substitution also occurs often in black American dialects and in numerous ethnic dialects in large metropolitan areas. American movies and television shows still portray the stereotypical first generation American down-and-out boxer as someone who pronounces most of his "th" sounds as [d] or [t] (as in "dose guys," "dey tole me," and "gimme dem tings."

[θ]
(theme)

Technical Description:	Voiceless Linguadental (or Interdental) Fricative Continuant, Cognate of [ð]
Physiological Description: How The Sound is Made	Vocal folds not vibrating, tongue tip lightly on biting edge of upper front teeth (incisors), soft palate raised as breath passes between tongue tip and upper front teeth with some friction. (Some people produce the sound accurately with the tongue tip behind the upper front teeth but many people substitute another sound when they say the phoneme in this manner. For this reason, we don't recommend this procedure for people who have any difficulty with the sound.) The sides of the tongue are pressed against the inside surfaces of the upper teeth. The tongue is farther forward for both "th" sounds than for any other English sound.
Common Spellings:	th in thin, nothing, mouth
Periodic Spellings:	tth in Matthew

[ð]
(those)

Technical Description:	Voiced, Linguadental (or Interdental) Fricative Continuant, Cognate of [θ]
Physiological Description: How the Sound is Made	Vocal folds vibrating, tongue tip lightly on the biting edge of upper front teeth (incisors), soft palate raised as breath passes between the tongue tip and upper front teeth with some friction. (Some people produce the sound accurately with the tongue tip behind the upper front teeth but many people substitute another sound when they say the phoneme in this manner. For this reason, we don't recommend this procedure for people who have any difficulty with the sound.) The sides of the tongue are pressed against the inside surfaces of the upper teeth. The tongue is farther forward for both "th" sounds than for any other English sound.
Common Spellings:	th in those, either, with the in bathe, breathe

You will hear quite a few nonnative speakers of English substituting [z] for [ð] and [s] for [θ]. Actors and actresses who must speak English with a French or Spanish accent for a particular part they are playing, and comedians who tell ethnic stories, learn to incorporate these substitutions in their dialects.

Try this simple exercise. See if you can determine how to substitute sounds for "th" and then listen to the results. Purposely substitute the *first* sound in each of the following brackets for the voiced and voiceless "th" sounds in the words provided:

1. [d-ð] in: breathe, bathe, their, they, lathe

2. [t-θ] in: both, path, thrust, thin, math, wrath

3. [z-ð] in: breathe, lathe, these, then, with

4. [s-θ] in: think, bath, math, thing, thin, thank

5. [v-ð] in: leather, clothing, brother, smoother

6. [f-θ] in: throws, threads, north, mouth, path

Can you begin to see why consistent changes in one or two sounds can become extremely confusing to listeners who don't make the same substitutions? If context clues in face-to-face communication situations are inadequate, or if an individual's general diction is difficult to understand, you will face numerous semantic (word meaning) decisions each time a person speaks.

The Ben Roth Agency

"That tape-recorder you thold me yethterday lithps."

The significance of "th" sounds in English becomes even more evident when you examine how often you use them in daily speaking. The following list may help you see this.

THE IMPORTANCE OF "TH" IN ENGLISH SPEECH

Several of the frequently used words in oral English contain voiced "th" sounds: the, that, they, this, with, and there.

Family references such as "father, mother, brother, grandfather, grandmother, and brother-in-law" all contain the voiced "th" sound.

Quite a few pronoun references depend upon "th" sounds. They include: them, they, their, theirs, these, those, this.

Many of the most frequently used English consonant clusters contain the voiceless "th" sound. Look at the consonant clusters in the words: **thr**ead, wa**rmth,** hundre**dth,** hundre**dths,** de**pth,** de**pths,** le**ngth,** le**ngths,** mo**nth,** mo**nths,** di**phth**ong.

The "th" sound appears repeatedly in ordinal numbers (which show the order of a number in a series, such as "third, fourth" and so on) between:

"third" and "twentieth"

"twenty-third and fortieth"

"forty-third and fiftieth"

"fifty-third and sixtieth"

and so on.

Any sentences incorporating such useful words as "birth" or "death," "breath" or "breathe," "Thursday," "thank you" or "Thanksgiving," "earth," "either" or "neither," "thirst," "month," "warmth," "youth," "thick" or "thin," "clothing," "truth," "think" and "thoughts," "theory," and "north" and "south," will use the sounds. Even many common references to the human body, such as "throat," "teeth," "mouth," "thorax," "thigh," and "thyroid" use the "th."

You can begin to see how important [θ] and [ð] are in the English language. Avoiding words with these sounds in them because you don't pronounce them clearly or accurately would be only slightly easier than avoiding getting wet while walking in the rain with a leaky umbrella. Practically every time you see the spelling "th" or "the" (except for words such as Thailand, Thompson, and Thames) you will produce the voiced [ð] or the voiceless [θ].

COMMON PROBLEMS:

1. One of the voiced sounds [d], [z], or [v] is substituted for the voiced [ð], as in the words "their, either," and "writhe." In all of these, the point of articulation changes as tongue and teeth (linguadental) sounds become gum ridge (alveolar) or lip and teeth (labiodental) sounds. The tongue is at fault in the first two sounds because it hides behind (rather than resting lightly on) the biting edge of the upper front teeth. In the [v-ð] substitution, the upper teeth touch the lower lip rather than the tongue tip. To change this substitution, take a good breath and say a vowel sound. Gradually lift a small portion of the upper surface of the tongue tip to the biting edges of the upper front teeth while sustaining the voicing. The vowel sound will change automatically to the voiced "th" sound.

2. One of the voiceless sounds [t], [s], or [f] is substituted for the voiceless [θ], as in "thirty, birthday," and "fourth." Except for the element of voicing, these substitutions duplicate the problem discussed in item number 1 above. In all of these, the point of articulation changes as tongue and teeth (linguadental) sounds become gum ridge (alveolar) or lip and teeth (labiodental) sounds. The point of articulation must be changed back to the upper surface of the tongue tip and the biting edges of the upper front teeth. Once the tongue is resting on the teeth, air may be forced gently or blown between the tongue and teeth to create the voiceless fricative sound.

3. Some people are unsure whether "th" sounds in words should be pronounced as voiced or voiceless sounds. They may substitute one for the other. This may not be as much a problem of forming the correct sound as it is of knowing the rules for producing a voiced or voiceless sound. These generalizations may be useful as you try to be correct in your use of [θ] and [ð]. When "th" occurs in the:

a. **Initial** position of NOUNS, VERBS, and ADJECTIVES, it usually is voiceless, as in "thimble, thinks, thin."

b. **Initial** position of PRONOUNS, CONJUNCTIONS, and ADVERBS, it usually is voiced, as in "they, than, then."

c. **Final** position of words and is followed by "e," it usually is voiced, as in "lathe" and "bathe."

d. **Final** position of words and follows a voiced consonant sound, it is voiceless, as in "length, width, month."

e. **Medial** position of words, as in "worthless, worthy, without, anything, mythical," no consistent rule can be followed. Ordinarily, if a medial "th" is followed by "er," as in "brother, bother, another, gather, rather, mother," it will be voiced.

4. The voiceless "th" sound in consonant clusters often is omitted when an adjacent consonant sound is produced at the gum ridge, teeth, or lips, and the word ends in [s]. For example, the word "depths" would become [dɛps], "fifths" would become [fɪfs], and "months" would become [mons]. This omission also may occur when the voiceless "th" is the final consonant sound before an [s] in a plural word, as in "deaths" and "births." Special care must be given to forming the voiceless "th" before the tongue tip glides to the gum ridge for [s].

5. Some people add a very short "uh" or schwa sound after some voiced [ð] or voiceless [θ] sounds. At times, this sounds like another syllable is added to words. Often, this occurs immediately after the "th" in consonant clusters, as in "three, thread, thrill, threaten," and at the ends of words such as "writhe, breathe, loathe" when they end in "the." Thus, "thrill" sounds like "thuhrill" and "breathe" sounds like "breatheuh."

6. Children frequently thrust their tongues too far beyond their upper front teeth when they are learning to make their "th" sounds. As a result, they protrude their tongues excessively for both [θ] and [ð]. This habit doesn't change the sound, but it does become distracting to people who are watching them. When they are unaware of their habit, they need to be told by parents and teachers to place only the tip and not the upper middle surface of the tongue on the biting surface of the upper front teeth. Occasionally, adults will still have this distracting habit.

7. The voiced and voiceless "th" sounds are substituted for [z] and [s] when individuals have a frontal lisp. Actually, this is a problem that concerns the formation of [z] and [s], but it should be mentioned here too. The point of articulation needs to be changed from the tongue and teeth (labiodental) to the gum (alveolar) ridge. This is a common substitution among children who are acquiring language skills. Parents think it is a "cute" habit when children are small. Unfortunately, some parents become so accustomed to the lisp that they don't hear it after awhile. Some adults retain their childhood lisps, either because, as they were growing up, no one recognized their errors or no one dared to mention them. A frontal lisp is no longer "cute" in adult speakers. College students with obvious lisps should consult a speech therapist.

EXERCISES FOR PRACTICING [θ] AND [ð]

1. Say the following sounds aloud. Pronounce each symbol enclosed in brackets as many times as the symbol appears.

   a. Voiceless "th": [θ] [θθθ] [θ] [θθθθθ] [θθθ]

   b. Voiced "th": [ðð] [ð] [ðð] [ð] [ððð]

   c. Voiced and Voiceless "th": [θ] [ð] [θðθ] [θ] [ððθð] [ð] [θ] [θ] [θððθ] [θθð] [θ]

2. The following words contain IPA symbols you have studied. Determine what each of these words is without looking back at symbols studied previously. Then, when you have finished all the words, check your work with the chart of IPA symbols.

   a. [pæθ] _____   b. [wɪð] _____   c. [mɪθ] _____

   d. [θim] _____   e. [dɛθ] _____   f. [θɪn] _____

   g. [ði] _____   h. [bæθ] _____   i. [ðɛm] _____

100

Now transcribe these words into IPA symbols:

j. tame _____   k. maid _____   l. math _____

m. teeth _____   n. weed _____   o. deemed _____

3. Contrast the voiced and voiceless "th" sounds with the [d] and [t] sounds by using each of them with the following vowel sounds. Many of the results will form nonsense syllables, so don't worry about "making sense."

VOWEL		[d]	[ð]	[t]	[θ]
a. [i]	in:	['idi]	['iði]	['iti]	['iθi]
b. [e]	in:	[de]	[ðe]	[te]	[θe]
c. [æ]	in:	[æd]	[æð]	[æt]	[æθ]
d. [o]	in:	['dodo]	['ðoðo]	['toto]	['θoθo]
e. [ɪ]	in:	[ɪd]	[ɪð]	[ɪt]	[ɪθ]

4. Read the following pairs of words aloud. Be sure your point of articulation changes to distinguish "th" from its paired sound.

a. thought/fought, boat/both, van/than, though/dough

b. sued/soothed, cloves/clothes, offer/author, myths/mitts

c. fin/thin, debt/death, they/day, loathes/loaves

d. dare/there, clothe/clove, thanks/tanks, frill/thrill

e. thread/Fred, doze/those, thinker/tinker, vat/that

f. fodder/father, wreath/reef, vie/thigh, throws/froze

5. Contrast the following voiced and voiceless "th" sounds as they occur in the words given.

Voiced [ð]	Voiceless [θ]	Voiced [ð]	Voiceless [θ]
a. either	ether	lathe	lath
b. this'll	thistle	bathe	bath
c. soothe	soothsayer	then	thin
d. thy	thigh	teethe	teeth

101

6. The following lists are arranged according to the position of the "th" sound in each word. Read each list aloud to be sure you can control the sound in each position.

	Initial	**Medial**	**Final**
Voiced	then	father	scathe
[ð]	this	leather	breathe
	them	breathing	clothe
	that	loathing	tithe
	the	withered	soothe
	though	clothing	with
	than	although	smooth
	those	southern	scythe
	they	feathered	seethe
	there	heathen	wreathe

	Initial	**Medial**	**Final**
Voiceless	thief	filthy	path
[θ]	through	mythical	month
	third	pathway	sleuth
	thousand	healthy	north
	Thursday	bathrobe	myth
	think	arithmetic	wealth
	theater	wealthy	worth
	thoughtful	ethical	south
	thumb	birthday	ninth
	theories	cathedral	length

7. Read the following word combinations as if they appeared side by side in a normal conversation. Be aware of changes in inflections so you won't read the words in a monotone.

a. the tithe weathered; either those breathe; bathing them with; thus either scythe

b. thereafter smooth breathing; other than soothe; writhe northern though; they gather unclothe

102

c. anything north thought; both thank faithful; atheist think growth; thin truthful sleuth

d. thumbtack everything length; athlete thinks health; thrifty myth author; bath thermostat forthcoming

8. Read the following word combinations aloud. Notice that in each sequence, the point of articulation changes in the words but the vowels and diphthongs remain the same.

a. thumb, some, dumb; though, so, doe, foe, toe; day, they, say; sink, think, zinc; face, faith, fade, fate, phase; truce, truth, trues, truths

b. their, dare, tear; thigh, dye, tie, sigh, thy, vie; thimble, cymbal; threw, zoo, sue, due, too; sick, thick, tick, Dick

c. see, three, D, tea; boat, both, bode; sued, sooth, sues, soothe; wreathe, read, wreath, Reece; zing, sing, thing, ding; letter, lesser, leather

d. load, lows, loathe, loath; either, Easter, eater, ether; thence, dense, tense, sense; a thorn, adorn, a torn; fills, filled, filth

e. lays, lace, laid, lathe, late; looser, Luther, looter, loser, lewder; Ruth, rude, root, ruse; those, toes, doze, sews; ladder, lather, latter

9. Consonant clusters are relatively difficult to say unless you are accustomed to them. The following words contain two or more consonants in clusters. Read the words aloud, being sure to pronounce the "th" sounds, rather than a [t] sound. Read them slowly first, then read them faster a second time. Feel the changes that occur in your articulators as you say these clusters.

a. bir**ths**, brea**dth**, wrea**thes**, six**th**, seven**teenth**, forty-**fifth**

b. le**ngths**, wi**dths**, wri**thes**, anes**th**esia, eleve**nth**, dea**ths**

c. stre**ngth**, wrea**ths**, aes**th**etic, de**pths**, fi**fths**, wri**thed**

d. **th**roughout, ba**thes**, mo**nths**, sca**thed**, ni**nth**, di**ph**theria

e. hundre**dths**, smoo**thed**, **thr**eaten, anes**th**etist, pros**th**etics, clo**thes**

10. **Practice Sentences**

a. My grandfather thinks anything that is worthwhile is a threat to apathy.

b. Our forefathers sailed from Plymouth with absolute faith that their strength would help them withstand their journey.

c. Martha thought that her brother and another anthropologist were gathering worthless information on teeth.

d. On Thursday, three southern authors met in our theater to tell us their theories about doing thorough research for lengthy manuscripts.

e. Neither this authorization nor that other written threat will make me believe those wealthy brothers have either a legal or an ethical right to this property.

f. Although they thought he would rather be an athlete than an ornithologist or mathematician, they weren't sympathetic with his goal.

g. The first three Anglo-Saxon sovereigns of England were Egbert, father of Ethelwulf, and grandfather of Ethelbald.

11. Practice Paragraphs

a. The three Mather children, Kathy, Matthew, and Anthony, met their grandmother at Smith's Clothing Store near the Catholic church on Thursday afternoon. It was the fourth year she had gathered her grandchildren together to buy them new clothes to wear to school when the new term began. She was always sympathetic to their wishes, knowing that they would have to wear the clothes throughout the year. Whether they preferred athletic shoes; smooth, synthetic fabrics; three piece suits, unorthodox colors, or some other current fad in clothing, Grandma Mather always agreed. "That's the way to learn the value of clothing," she would say to their mother. "If they get bored with it, they have themselves to blame."

b. They sailed southward over a smooth sea towards the thriving village of Southport. Although the village had little wealth, it seemed to thrive on the sun's gentle warmth, the thick, rich soil, and a splendid beach that ran the length of the village. Some tourists enthusiastically called it the "Athens of North America." Businessmen found its charms therapeutic, whether they arrived in a thunderstorm or on a cloudless day. The rhythm of Southport was rather slow. Everything from youthful athletic games to middle-aged mirth seemed to adapt to this leisurely rhythm.

c. My father and mother told about their early childhood in tiny Ethelbert, Manitoba, northeast of Baldy Mountain. My mother's grandfather lived farther north in Duck Bay, just three steps from a huge lake. My father's grandparents lived in Cowan, which also was north of Ethelbert. During their youth, neither my mother nor my father ever ventured south of Ethelbert and never north of Duck Bay and Cowan. Throughout the winters, the thermometer hovered near zero for months. Their faithful radio was considered something of a luxury at that time. It served as a mouthpiece to the world, teaching them the mysteries of math, the mastery of myths, and the magic of imagination. Neither of them thought they would ever see a house with an inside bathroom and a real bathtub, although they had seen one in a magazine once!

d. Finally, just for fun, see if you can say this classical tongue twister containing many "th" sounds:

Theopholus Thistle the successful thistle sifter

In sifting a sieveful of unsifted thistles

Thrust three thousand thistles

Through the thick of his thumb.

Technical Description:	Voiceless Alveolar (or Lingua Alveolar) Stop Plosive, Cognate of [d]
Physiological Description: How the Sound Is Made	Vocal folds not vibrating, soft palate raised, upper surface of tongue tip pressed firmly against upper gum ridge as sides press firmly against upper teeth, capturing and holding the breath stream under pressure until its abrupt release with slightly more aspiration than for [d]
Common Spellings:	t in type, rating, sat tt in attic, mattress, tattle th in Thomas, Thames, Thailand te in bite, kites, appetite ed in shipped, snapped, packed ght in light, frighten, caught
Periodic Spellings:	pt in Ptolemy, receipt tw in two bt in debtor, debt cht in yacht ct in indict

[t]
(try)

Technical Description:	Voiced Alveolar (or Lingua Alveolar) Stop Plosive, Cognate of [t]
Physiological Description: How the Sound Is Made	Vocal folds vibrating, soft palate raised, upper surface of tongue tip pressed firmly against upper gum ridge as sides press firmly against upper teeth, capturing and holding the breath stream under pressure until its abrupt release
Common Spellings:	d in dome, alderman, nod dd in added, faddist, Judd ed in paired, stirred de in lemonade, suede, Swede
Periodic Spellings:	ld in should, wouldn't ddh in Buddha

[d]
(dollar)

Only two English stop plosives are formed on the gum (alveolar) ridge: [t] and [d]. The sounds are created when the flow of air out of the mouth is blocked by the upper surface of the tongue tip at the gum ridge, and then released suddenly. Usually, final [t] and [d] sounds in words are exploded when they are followed in the same phrase by a word which begins with a vowel or diphthong, as in "she could if" or "if Pat asked us." Some [t] and [d] sounds are released quietly. Most people don't explode final [t] or [d] sounds when they complete a sentence such as "You asked him to say what?"

These sounds are among our most widely used consonant sounds. You may have noticed that these two sounds may be spelled at least seventeen different ways in English. They also occur in numerous common consonant clusters. The [t] and [d] are not as far forward as the "th" sounds. They will be classified as middle sounds.

COMMON PROBLEMS

1. Many students have difficulty determining whether the past tense of verbs requires [t] or [d] in their transcriptions. A generalization may be useful for regularly conjugated verbs. If the past tense or past participle is formed by adding the suffix "d" or "ed" to the root verb, listen to the SOUND just before the suffix. If it is voiced, as in "stabbed" or "starved," the suffix also will be a voiced [d]. If it is voiceless, as in "stopped" or "laughed," the suffix will be a voiceless [t]. This rule won't apply to verb roots ending in [t] or [d] since these will require an additional vowel sound plus [d], as in "rented" and "traded."

2. The [t] sound is omitted frequently in words. When it occurs in the medial position after another consonant or in a consonant cluster (either in or between syllables, or in connecting words within a phrase), the [t] often is omitted completely. The following words and phrases provide a sample of consonant clusters containing [t]. Read them aloud, first without the [t] and then with it to hear and feel what happens when it is omitted. In those clusters ending in [fts], [kts], [pts], or [sts], pronounce the final [ts] as the same blend which occurs in "it's." Rather than trying to attach the [t] to the preceding consonant, practice until you can say [ts] as a blend by itself. Then attach this blend to the preceding consonant.

omission of [t] in   [ft]:   tuft, graft, drift, craft, left, drafting, rafter, cleft

         in   [kt]:   act, defect, tract, picked, dejected, rejecting, inactive

         in   [nt]:   planter, bantam, phantom, granted, twenty, interfere, planting

         in   [pt]:   crypt, rapt, slept, ripped, dropped, crept, shipped

         in   [st]:   mystery, custard, eastern, faster, must, last, fast, first, waste

         in   [ftl]:   swiftly, softly, laughed Lee, draft less, shift late

         in   [fts]:   shifts, grafts, crafts, gifts, left simple, drift slowly

         in   [ktl]:   directly, matter-of-factly, react less, cracked like

         in   [kts]:   infects, facts, rejects, expects, affect some, tracked several

         in   [ptl]:   abruptly, aptly, interrupt laws, intercept level, accept Leslie

         in   [pts]:   interrupts, disrupts, kept some, helped so, dropped such

         in   [stl]:   lastly, justly, mostly, test looks, taste like, chest lay

         in   [sts]:   crests, persists, trusts, mists, last snowfall, best song

3. The [d] also is omitted frequently in consonant clusters. This omission occurs most frequently in the clusters [dʒd] as in "bridged" and "hedged," [ld] as in "called" and "sold," [ldz] as in "molds" and "welds," [md] as in "slammed" and "seemed," [nd] as in "extend" and "send," and [ndz] as in "wounds" and "brands."

4. The [d] often is substituted for [t] in the medial position of words. This may be an actual substitution, or simply a weak or light formation of the [d]. In some words, such as "city, party, pretty, partner," this may not be very confusing since similar words wouldn't be constructed with this substitution. However, in many words, especially words with a double "t" in the medial position, a distinction must be made to avoid confusing them with similar sounding words. For example, here are some easily confused words:

matter/madder; Patty/paddy; catty/caddy;
written/ridden; betting/bedding; wetting/wedding;
putting/pudding; patting/padding; rotting/rodding;
butting/budding; fattest/faddist; otter/odder;
whiter/wider; metal/meddle; petal/peddle;
waiting/wading; biting/biding; debtor/deader;
rating/raiding; citing/siding

5. Some people explode or aspirate their [d] and [t] sounds too forcefully. Although aspiration doesn't create a distinctive change, its continual popping and hissing can be distracting. If you have extra-plosive sounds, you probably place too much force behind your tongue's contact and release against the gum ridge. Imagine you are whispering these sounds to someone and are trying to create very little pressure against the gum ridge as you say them. Be sure the tongue tip is on the gum ridge and not against the upper front teeth.

When two "t" or "d" letters occur in words such as "matter" and "ladder," or next to each other in a phrase such as "right turn" and "said dumbly," only one [t] or [d] should be exploded. You may view this in one of two ways. Either you are producing an unexploded (soft) first [t] or [d] as your tongue tip lingers on the gum ridge, and a second one when you release the tongue, or you are assimilating the second letter because your meaning is clearly understood without it.

"Shod, I thought you said shot."

6. Many people substitute a glottal stop for [t] or [d] whenever a syllabic consonant follows it. (The syllabic [m] was discussed in Chapter 7.) A glottal stop is a plosive sound produced at the vocal folds as pressure builds up behind them and then is released explosively. (The sound resembles a hiccough, except the flow of air is reversed outwardly.) It is a substandard sound in all American dialects. Usually, when this error occurs, the tongue tip either makes no gum ridge contact for [t] or [d], or substitutes a [t] for a [d], or voicing is eliminated creating a [t] for a [d]. The glottal stop sometimes sounds like a quietly aspirated [t] sound. When the [t] actually is substituted for [d], it tends to occur in contractions such as "couldn't, wouldn't, shouldn't, didn't, hadn't."

To form a correct contracted sound, keep the tongue tip on the gum ridge after forming either [d] or [t] and glide into the syllabic sound that follows it. For example, in "didn't" the tongue tip remains on the gum ridge for [d] while air is forced out through the nose to create the syllabic [n̩]; in "little," the tongue remains on the gum ridge for [t] while air flows over the sides of the tongue to produce the syllabic [l̩] sound. If the tongue moves even momentarily away from the gum ridge, either another [d] or [t] or an additional vowel sound will be created. Syllabic sounds are **important** characteristics in General American Speech.

7. Some medial [t] and [d] sounds are silent in General American Speech. A few native and many nonnative speakers pronounce the letters. No universal rule for determining silent sounds is available. However, this information may help you.

a. Words containing "stle" (gristle, mistletoe, hustle) or "stl" (hustling, rustling) often have a silent "t."

b. Verbs containing "sten" in a medial or final position (christen, fastening, listen) often have a silent "t."

c. Some commonly used words such as "often, soften, Christmas, grandparent, grandson, grandfather, grandmother, Wednesday, handsome" contain silent medial [t] or [d] sounds.

EXERCISES FOR PRACTICING [t] AND [d]

1. Practice reading the following isolated sounds aloud to become familiar with both the IPA symbols you have studied so far, and with their sounds.

a. [t]	[d]	[p]	[t]	[i]	[θ]	[w]	[hw]	[d]	[e]	[m]	[t]
b. [m]	[æ]	[b]	[t]	[ɪ]	[f]	[d]	[ð]	[hw]	[ɛ]	[d]	[v]
c. [p]	[i]	[v]	[hw]	[ɪ]	[m]	[v]	[e]	[p]	[θ]	[w]	[t]
d. [d]	[i]	[p]	[v]	[e]	[t]	[ð]	[ɛ]	[w]	[ɪ]	[m]	[b]

2. Write the following words in IPA symbols. Be sure to include brackets around your transcriptions.

a. Thee _____   Maybe _____   Fame _____

b. Baited _____   Dimwit _____   Them _____

c. That _____   Dame _____   Beet _____

d. Path _____   Timid _____   Whip _____

e. Baby _____   Patted _____   Whim _____

3. Translate the following transcriptions.

a. [ðe] _____   b. [mit] _____   c. [wet] _____

d. [dɪpt] _____   e. [pev] _____   f. [hwæm] _____

g. [dæbd] _____   h. [pit] _____   i. [dɛf] _____

4. Read the following paired words aloud, being sure to voice the [d] sounds wherever they occur.

a. want/wand; built/build; fond/font; pant/panned; canned/can't; to/due; Adam/atom; written/ridden

b. meant/mend; felled/felt; bent/bend; bold/bolt; send/sent; hat/had; dual/tool; Etna/Edna

c. belled/belt; guilt/guild; pined/pint; lent/lend; hauled/halt; not/nod; lewd/loot; madder/matter

d. need/neat; lit/lid; lied/light; gnawed/nought; node/note; laid/late; loud/lout; batman/badman

e. Dade/date; metal/medal; eaten/Eden; and/ant; suit/sued; bed/bet; awed/ought; town/down

5. The following word combinations contain [t] and [d] sounds in all positions of words. Read the combinations aloud.

a. Ted doesn't predict; debts reduced kind; take into account; fat totally decided; mists tried late

b. little time left; Dora hadn't heard; tattled without deciding; murdered Duane's favorite; I'd do Eddie's

c. idiots hide definite; delay didn't prod; timely item not; producer heard during; situation takes part

d. left tiny items; dumped hundreds beside; most teams attribute; decided riding made; today Betty thought

e. raid drew bidders; turkey hadn't details; predictable maid delays; isn't too pretty; dyed dark sided

6. Read the following sentences aloud with as much fluency and careful articulation as you can manage at a conversational rate of speed.

a. Yesterday Tim and Dorothy fished for trout in Lake Tyler while their parents started a fire on shore to fry the trout.

b. They went downtown to try to find the Austrian pastry shop Aunt Dolly had told them about on Tuesday night.

c. The haughty tiger sat on top of a metal box and waited to be coaxed to step into the ring with its master trainer.

d. The Texas twins, Dottie and Marty Thompson, traded their saddles for paddles when they took up canoeing at Camp Tate.

e. We couldn't decide whether the riddle about cotton was written by Doug Atkins or Toby Dawkins, but we liked it.

f. When she said ''led us,'' Tom thought she said ''let us,'' and Estelle thought she said ''lettuce.''

7. Here is another classical tongue twister for you to try. Begin slowly, and then see if you can increase your speed without destroying the [t] sound.

Betty Botta bought some butter

''But,'' said she, ''This butter's bitter.

If I put it in my batter

It will make my batter bitter

But a bit o' better butter

Will make my batter better.''

So she bought a bit o' butter

Better than the bitter butter,

Made her bitter batter better.

So 'twas better Betty Botta

Bought a bit o' better butter.

8. Practice Paragraphs

a. We heard the truck when it crashed through the bolted door of a deserted building, hit a light pole, knocked over a metal shed, and came to an abrupt halt at the top of an incline. From our second floor window, even though it was quite dark outside, we could see its headlights looking crosseyed down the incline towards our city dump. The light pole had exploded into fragments

110

of cement and had scattered about in the impact. Later, as the truck driver sat in our dining room, waiting for a telephone call from Detroit, he told us of his sadness. This was his first accident in thirty years of driving.

b. In the first act of the play, Todd enters the room, tastes the punch on the table, mutters some comment under his breath, clenches his fists, and asks softly, "Who made this ghastly drink?" Then he moves swiftly downstage, turns abruptly to the two dark masks above the fireplace, and says in a ghostly voice, "This is exactly what I was told would happen on the fifth day of August—and you are to blame!" Just then, the butler enters upstage as the grandfather clock stops striking the hour. It is eight o'clock.

c. She caressed the ancient gold and topaz locket her grandmother had just given to her for Christmas. Its design was intricately wondrous. She noticed a faint inscription on the inside front cover. She read it aloud. "To My Friend of Fifty Years. DLT. 1893." Her grandmother reached for her hand, patted it gently, smiled, and said in a hushed voice, "It was your great-grandmother's locket. She wanted her first great-granddaughter to have it when she reached her twentieth birthday. That was just how old she was when she received it from *her* grandmother. Those initials 'DLT' remained a secret until we discovered some old letters in the attic from DLT. They were written by the Royal Prince who eventually became King of his country. Would you like to guess which country he governed?"

9. Dialogues for Oral Practice (for two readers)

Newsperson: With all the building that has been going on in this community in recent months, has your pawnshop done much business?

Trader: Oh, business has been great! Three days ago I bought a used television set for $63. I traded it for thirteen new thermos jugs, then swapped those jugs for a month's supply of health food. This morning I sold all that health food to two different people. They both paid me $32.

Newsperson: Then you've **only** made a profit of a dollar in three days?

Trader: That's true . . . but look at the business I've done! That's worth something.

* * * * *

Oldtimer: Back in the thirties, when I was your age, I had three cousins who lived way out in the country. Each morning they walked to school and every night, they walked home, along a dirt path, through rain or cold weather, sometimes without warm clothing.

Youngster: **Every** day? That was a long walk back then, wasn't it?

Oldtimer: Yes, it was. Thelma was only a month past her fifth birthday, Arthur was in his eighth year, and Martha was just ten. Think of it! They all grew up and became responsible, successful, worthwhile citizens. Isn't that something?

Youngster: All **three** became successful? That IS something. That must have made their parents very happy—especially since they missed the schoolbus all those years when they were in school!

CHAPTER 10

THE MIDDLE SOUNDS
[s] [z] [ʃ] [ʒ] [tʃ] [dʒ]

In this chapter you will learn about the production of sounds which give practically everyone some difficulty at one time or another in their lives. They are difficult for children to distinguish, difficult for children or adults who have lost their front teeth to say correctly, and difficult for broadcasters and other speakers using microphones to say without excessive hissing or sibilance. In tense situations people often produce high frequency variants of these sounds, simply because their tongues are so tense. Nonnative speakers of English have difficulty in hearing and saying some or all of these sounds in the early stages of learning English.

[S]

(see)

Technical Description:	Voiceless, Alveolar (or Lingua-Alveolar) Sibilant, Fricative Continuant, Cognate of [z]
Physiological Description: How the Sound is Made	Vocal folds not vibrating, lips open and spread, front teeth are slightly parted (not clenched), soft palate raised, tongue tip near lower front teeth as the upper surface (blade) immediately behind it touches upper gum (alveolar) ridge on both sides leaving a front opening, tongue's sides are in continuous contact with inside surfaces of upper back teeth while air escapes down its midline, hitting the front teeth with friction
Common Spellings:	s in say, best, packs c in cedar, decimal, decipher sc in scene, descent, Pisces ss in glassy, pass, loss se in loosely, case, debase ce in graceful, place, Luce st in moisten, hasten, whistle
Periodic Spellings:	x (as in [ks]) in axis, taxi, fix ps in psychic, psalm, psycho z in waltzing, quartz, blitz sse in impasse, noblesse sch in schism sw in answering

Technical Description:	Voiced, Alveolar (or Lingua-Alveolar) Sibilant, Fricative Continuant, Cognate of [s]
Physiological Description: How the Sound is Made	Vocal folds vibrating, lips open and spread, front teeth are slightly parted (not clenched), soft palate raised, tongue tip near lower front teeth as the upper surface (blade) immediately behind it touches upper gum (alveolar) ridge on both sides leaving a front opening, tongue's sides are in continuous contact with inside surfaces of upper back teeth while air escapes down its midline, hitting the front teeth with friction
Common Spellings:	z in zebra, crazy, hazard, Oz zz in blizzard, buzzard, fuzz ze in brazen, freeze, breeze s in feasible, has, is, fleas se in used, choose, tease x in xylophone, xanthin, Xerox
Periodic Spellings:	cz in czar, czarina ss in scissors

[z]
(zone)

In any voice and articulation class, an instructor finds [s] and [z] among the most frequently misproduced sounds, even among speakers who use a good General American Speech pattern. Although speakers may say the sounds without **distinctive** changes, they may say them in a manner that is distracting to listeners. Excessive high frequency hissing from a compressor or air hose wouldn't be tolerated very long because of its distracting qualities. Excessive hissing of [s], [ʃ] or [tʃ] can be just as distracting.

In the last chapter you discovered the many spellings for [d] and [t] sounds required you to make numerous decisions about pronouncing words. The same may be said about [s] and [z]. When you see a new word, you must decide whether the letters create a voiced [z] or a voiceless [s] sound. This can be confusing to natives and frustrating to nonnative speakers of English because we have no simple, consistent rules to follow.

COMMON PROBLEMS

1. The substitution of [s] for [z] or [z] for [s] is a persistent problem for native and nonnative speakers of English. Actually, this involves one simple decision: whether or not to use voicing for letters. Generally, you will have no difficulty with initial [s] and [z] letters in words since they remain fairly consistent (except for a few words beginning with "su" which are pronounced as "sh" as in "sugar" and "sure.") Probably the most noticeable changes occur in verbs, plural nouns, and possessive nouns.

The following chart tries to simplify several important decisions you have to make in relation to using [s] or [z] sounds in the final position of words. Read the words in this chart aloud, giving particular attention to voicing final [z] sounds. If you will sustain the voiced sound which precedes the [z] while blending the two sounds together, you may have less difficulty hearing the buzzing sound which is characteristic of [z].

GENERALIZATIONS FOR PRONOUNCING FINAL [s] AND [z] SOUNDS

WHEN A WORD ENDS IN THE LETTERS "s," "es," " 's," OR "s'," LOOK AT THE **SOUND** IMMEDIATELY BEFORE THIS ENDING.

For Plural Nouns And Pronouns	For Possessive Nouns and Pronouns	For Verbs

If it is:

a. A **voiced** sound (other than [z], [dʒ], or [ʒ]), the ending usually will be pronounced as a voiced [z] as in:

bird + "s" = [z]	her + "s" = [z]	stab + "s" = [z]
tree + "s" = [z]	party + " 's" = [z]	trade + "s" = [z]
hobo + "es" = [z]	shed + " 's" = [z]	leave + "s" = [z]
their + "s" = [z]	Miami + " 's" = [z]	play + "s" = [z]

b. A **voiceless** sound (other than [s], [ʃ], or [tʃ]), the ending usually will be pronounced as a voiceless [s] as in:

plot + "s" = [s]	Bert + " 's" = [s]	jump + "s" = [s]
ship + "s" = [s]	chief + " 's" = [s]	kick + "s" = [s]
broth + "s" = [s]	Perth + " 's" = [s]	roof + "s" = [s]

c. [s], [z], or [tʃ], [dʒ], or [ʃ], [ʒ], usually another vowel sound such as [ɪ] or the schwa "uh" sound will be said immediately before a final [z] as in:

brush + "es" = [ɪz]	Tess + " 's" = [ɪz]	miss + "es" = [ɪz]
grass + "es" = [ɪz]	lunch + " 's" = [ɪz]	hitch + "es" = [ɪz]
bridge + "s" = [ɪz]	Liz + " 's" = [ɪz]	nudge + "s" = [ɪz]
cruise + "s" = [ɪz]	nurse + " 's" = [ɪz]	use + "s" = [ɪz]

NOTE: Several widely used words always end in [z] including: is, was, has, because, as, ways, always, says

2. Excessive sibilance, hissing, or whistling are nondistinctive changes which occur frequently when [s] is produced. In the typical speaker, no mouth or teeth abnormalities usually are present. Instead, the individual presses the blade and/or tip of the tongue too hard against the gum ridge, creating too small an opening for air to escape through. If an individual also substitutes [s] for [z] (unvoices [z]) consistently, this increased sibilance becomes even more obvious, since the number of [s] sounds almost doubles.

114

By relaxing and flattening the blade and tip of the tongue while holding onto [s], you should be able to hear a change in the sound of expelled air. Try it! Force the blade of the tongue firmly against the gum ridge and begin an [s] sound, then gradually relax and flatten the front of the tongue. Many people can whistle in this manner, raising and lowering the pitch and intensity by tensing and relaxing the tongue at the gum ridge! The whistle is very similar to the sound made when one whistles with rounded lips and the tongue tip positioned near the lower front teeth.

Excessive sibilance may be compounded if the flow of air on [s] is prolonged. Since much unvoicing of [z] occurs at the **ends** of words, this air flow may be shortened by either closing the lips quicker at word ends or by stopping the outward flow of breath from the lungs quicker.

Anyone who will be working with telephones, public address systems, or microphones for long periods of time should beware of excessive sibilance in their speech patterns. When sibilance is amplified, it becomes extremely distracting and difficult to listen to for long periods of time. Unless you have an expert in the control room who can compensate for this problem, you could lose some of your most enchanted listeners.

3. Many speakers have what could be called a frontal blockage to the air flow for [s] and [z] sounds. Some persons describe this as a lisp. In reality, it is a deflection of the breath coming down the midline groove of the tongue. In some speakers, the result is similar to the sound that would result if they tried to make [s] or [z] with the tip of the tongue turned up and curled backwards in a retroflex position. Their breath hits the slightly raised tongue tip, flows upward and hits the gum ridge, then exits through the parted teeth. Frequently, speakers sound like they have something (such as peanut butter or candy) on the front portion of their tongues as they are speaking. "Fuzzy" or blurred [s] and [z] sounds result.

Some people have learned to make good [s] and [z] sounds with the tongue tip raised towards the gum ridge. Speakers who use this method and have no difficulty with either sound, shouldn't change their speaking habits. However, this book doesn't recommend elevating the tongue tip toward the gum ridge to anyone having problems with either [s] or [z]. Instead, we recommend that the tongue tip remain behind the lower front teeth while the upper surface of the tongue (blade) rises to the gum ridge. Our students have eliminated both excessive sibilance and fuzzy [s] and [z] sounds by making this simple change.

4. Consonant clusters containing [s] and [z] are particularly difficult for people who have no other obvious diction problems. Some people omit portions of the clusters because they don't seem to be very noticeable. Since script writers aren't always alert to the difficulties caused by consonant clusters, they may include strings of clusters in adjacent words that make the reader's job particularly distressing. (When you begin looking for material to read aloud, you should be aware of these potential problems.)

All of the difficulties encountered in consonant clusters can't be discussed here. Your instructor will be able to assist you with your own unique problems. However, a quick discussion of one typical consonant cluster problem may be helpful to you as you begin listening for the accurate pronunciation of [s] and [z] in these clusters. Often, people have difficulty saying the [str] cluster. Instead of saying [s], whose point of articulation is at the gum ridge, they substitute [ʃ], whose point of articulation is at the hard palate. This change occurs in single words (as in "**str**eam" [ʃtrim], "e**x**treme" [ɛkʃ 'trim], "Ca**str**o" ['kæʃ tro]), or in adjacent words (as in "thi**s tr**ee" [ðɪʃ tri], "it'**s tr**im" [ɪtʃ trɪm], or "mo**st wr**aps" [moʃt ræps]).

The following chart will familiarize you with some of the common consonant clusters that can include [s] and [z].

COMMON ENGLISH CONSONANT CLUSTERS CONTAINING [s] OR [z]

Initial Position:

[sk]: ski	[skr]: screen	[skw]: squeeze
[sl]: slow	[sm]: small	[sn]: snap
[sp]: spy	[spl]: splice	[spr]: spread
[st]: story	[str]: strange	[sw]: switch

Medial Position:

[kspl]: explicate	[kspr]: express	[kstr]: extract

Final Position:

[bz]: grabs	[dθs]: breadths	[fs]: thiefs
[fθs]: fifths	[gz]: begs	[ks]: fix
[kst]: waxed	[ksθs]: sixths	[kts]: inspects
[lfθs]: twelfths	[lz]: bells	[mbl̩z]: crumbles
[mfs]: triumphs	[mpl̩z]: dimples	[mps]: cramps
[mpst]: glimpsed	[mz]: themes	[ndl̩z]: handles
[ndz]: friends	[nst]: danced	[nts]: mints
[nθs]: months	[nz]: canes	[nzd]: bronzed
[nglz]: shingles	[ŋks]: thanks	[ŋθs]: lengths
[ŋz]: things	[ps]: ships	[pst]: collapsed
[pts]: disrupts	[pθs]: depths	[ɝgz]: morgues
[rst]: forced	[ɝz]: bars	[sks]: desks
[sps]: clasps	[st]: first	[stl̩]: justly
[sts]: fists	[ts]: bits	[tst]: blitzed
[tθs]: eighths	[vz]: sleeves	[znt]: isn't

Speakers also may make voiced [ʒ] substitutions in adjacent words containing [z] and [tr] (as in "his **tr**aits" [hɪʒ trets], and "fees **tr**eat" [fiʒ trit]). In both of these changes, the front (blade) of the tongue is allowed to drop too far and pull back away from the gum ridge in preparation for the [tr] sounds. By forming a clear [s] or [z] sound and prolonging it while slowly lifting the tongue tip to the gum ridge for [t], one may practice gliding gradually into this consonant cluster. Persistent practice should bring positive results.

5. Lisping is a problem which involves incorrect production of [s] and [z]. If your instructor is not a trained speech therapist, he or she may wish to refer students with obvious lisps to one. Individual conferences will be more beneficial than classroom exercises for changing lisps. If you *are* receiving help from a speech therapist, then the

116

classroom exercises in this course will provide additional public practice for you. Your instructor will be able to give you some indication of your progress toward eliminating the lisp.

You will hear two types of lisps. Our discussion of them will be an oversimplification in order to help you understand what is occurring. The **frontal lisp** occurs when the tongue tip either touches the upper front teeth (dental lisp) or protrudes between the upper and lower front teeth (protrusion lisp) for [s] and/or [z]. The frontal lisp sounds similar (or even identical) to voiced and voiceless "th" sounds. By keeping the tongue tip behind the lower front teeth for [s] and [z] and using the tongue blade to create the friction point on the gum ridge, a speaker can change this habit with careful, spaced practice.

The **lateral lisp** is the second type of lisp. It occurs when the tongue tip touches the upper gum ridge while one or both sides of the tongue drop for [s] and/or [z]. Air passes over the side(s) of the tongue, rather than down the middle. The resulting sound is somewhat slushy and has characteristics of a voiced or voiceless [l]. By keeping the tongue tip behind the lower front teeth for [s] and [z], and keeping the sides of the tongue pressed against the upper molars, air will be forced down the middle groove of the tongue. Again, careful, spaced practice will help eliminate lisps.

As with all sounds that are being modified, both [s] and [z] should be practiced in isolation until they can be produced correctly. Then they should be placed before, after, and between various other sounds (usually beginning with vowels and diphthongs) to link them with adjacent sounds, as happens in daily speech. Next, they should be placed in practice words (in initial, medial, and final positions), sentences, and paragraphs. Finally, they should be practiced in spontaneous conversational and public presentation situations.

EXERCISES FOR PRACTICING [s] AND [z]

1. Contrast the isolated cognate sounds of [s] and [z] in the following transcriptions by reading them aloud. If you have trouble distinguishing between the two, prolong the sounds while reading slowly.

a. [s]   [s]   [z]   [s]   [s s]   [z]   [z s z]   [s s z]   [s z z s]

b. [z z]   [s]   [z s]   [z z z]   [s s]   [z z s s]   [s s z]   [z]

2. Translate the following IPA transcriptions and write the words in the spaces provided.

a. ['tizɪz] _____   [pes] _____   [best] _____

b. [wedz] _____   [pɪts] _____   ['tæsɪt] _____

c. ['fɪzi] _____   [stez] _____   ['pæsɪz] _____

d. [dɪpt] _____   ['fezɪz] _____   [spid] _____

e. [tæbz] _____   [hwɪpt] _____   [twid] _____

117

3. Transcribe the following words into IPA symbols. Be sure to include stress or accent marks when they are needed. Place your transcriptions inside brackets.

a. Bathe _____   Tasty _____   Pete's _____

b. Teams _____   Seeped _____   Thieves _____

c. Dates _____   Whipped _____   Maybe _____

d. Spaced _____   Tempted _____   Pets _____

e. Stamped _____   Webs _____   T.V. _____

4. Read the following word combinations aloud to contrast the voiced and voiceless sounds of [s] and [z].

a. sip/zip, face/phase, dose/doze, bus/buzz, dice/dyes, muscle/muzzle

b. boost/boozed, muscle/muzzle, seal/zeal, hiss/his, zip/sip, racer/razor

c. sue/zoo, advice/advise, zing/sing, braise/brace, price/prize, loose/Lew's

d. vice/vies, fuss/fuzz, fist/fizzed, fleece/fleas, niece/knees, maze/mace

e. once/one's, plays/place, laws/loss, pace/pays, peace/peas, lazy/lacey

f. raced/razed, cops/cobs, hers/hearse, lies/lice, zone/sown, sane/Zane

g. cease/seize, codes/coats, saws/sauce, zinc/sink, rise/rice, Jews/juice

5. The following word combinations include consonant clusters which make them difficult to say easily. Practice them aloud, starting slowly and gradually increasing your speed of reading.

a. explain misquoted expressions; display elapsed strength; discriminate extra thrusts; discredit backstrokes mostly; coughed so loud; best speech given; bathes them once

b. hasn't danced discreetly; commenced explosive contacts; reached drenched desks; taxed misprinted jingles; list some states; left such gifts; first spotted them

c. strengths disqualified friends; grounds mixed unquestioning; ghostly masks bounced; hands wedged discs; missed Spanish plays; wreathes they made; laughed so hard

d. wasn't condensed discreetly; strengthened expressions crisply; extravagance extends mixed; beasts hatched acts; casts such glances; praises those two

e. against fixed bursts; spread waxed lengths; squirrel splattered pastry; contacts glanced angles; blessed certain boys; lost special pets; fist so hard

118

6. Read the following words and word combinations aloud. Keep a clear [s] or [z] sound in the [str] and [ztr] consonant clusters within and between words.

a. these traps; extra; administration; least wrong; x-ray; fast roll; least rhyme; stroke

b. best try; chemistry; stretching; history; is trying; astride; next right; has tried

c. instructor; stringing; most wretched; constructive; was tripping; passed ranches; strong; astronaut

d. cost rolled; stressful; cashed right; administrator; taste rich; strapped; past Ryan; waste rough

e. first rate; pressed right; extraordinary; pastry; expressway; nice try; kissed Trudy; pleased trying

7. The following words are arranged according to the adjacent positions of front vowels and [s] and [z] in words. Say the words clearly, taking time to allow for voicing and tongue changes when they are required.

	Initial	**Medial**	**Final**
[i]	seat/zeal	eastern/easiest	beasts/teases
[ɪ]	silver/zipped	diseased/busiest	this/his
[e]	satan/zany	basic/hazing	ace/stays
[ɛ]	settle/zeppelin	festive/hesitant	confess/says
[æ]	saddle/Zack	Astor/hasn't	pass/has
[i]	seem/zebra	decent/eastern	geese/please
[ɪ]	sick/zig	distant/dizzy	hiss/whiz
[e]	save/Zane	wasteful/gazing	base/Jay's
[ɛ]	said/Zed	Hester/president	guess/fez
[æ]	sash/Zantha	rascal/dazzle	mass/jazz

8. Practice reading the following sentences aloud.

a. He's teasing Esther when he says he loves her mystic smile more than his car's smooth finish.

b. This is a strange but feasible story about South Pacific zombies, isn't it?

119

c. Sue cares for her horses by serving them steaming buckets of oats whenever ice forms on her glass windows.

d. Cincinnati is not the same since the snow storm swept through the central part of our business district in December.

e. Remember the days when some of us wore gloves to school to disguise the walnut stains on our hands?

f. Whenever she finds that wolves have started to sniff at her smokehouse near the woods, she loads her shotguns and waits for their return.

g. Describe the noisy Portuguese music you heard in Brazil last Tuesday while taking the bus to the train station.

9. Practice Paragraphs

a. A strong south breeze was streaming through the windows of our Alaska summer home. The strong scent of wild flowers was in this afternoon's breeze. Sunshine wrapped its arms about our cottage, insisting it was staying awhile. The bees sang tunes of curious delight as they searched for drops of nectar in our one lonesome rosebush. In the distance, we still could see snow on the glaciers in the mountains. Soon we would start our backpacking scramble towards Circle Springs to spend several days in isolated splendor beside the Yukon River.

b. She was certain the rooster had passed her school door several times, although it had displayed no curiosity about the noise inside. He was so red, the sun seemed to have tossed its tarnished rays away—and he had soaked them up. He strutted, silently, but splendidly, and gracefully! Some of the second grade students noticed him just as the recess bell sounded. They stood beside her, struck by the splash of color he displayed against the dark green grass— speechless. Slowly, he stretched his rusty neck, assuming a pose of frozen elegance. Then, seeing he was being observed by the insiders, he crowed so loud that he startled the children—and scampered off into the woods.

c. Our Thespian Society's annual scavenger sale was the most eagerly awaited surprise event in Scottsdale. Ever since a prize dress from the movie "Lost Horizons" had made its unannounced appearance there in 1976, townspeople speculated about the next sale. We assembled goods for each spring sale for months. Brass pots, used boots, cider barrels, dried gourds, new gloves, bottles of herbs, ancient books, knives, beads, and even a shiny statue of Zeus—all were placed on display in our storeroom. Boxes of things were stacked to the ceilings until the Saturday before the sale. Then the members gathered together to sort, catalog, price, and display the items. We called it Circus Saturday.

d. Albert Einstein's early research assisted in the development of the atomic bomb during World War II. Later, when friends asked Einstein what new weapons might be used if we had World War III, he shook his head slowly, several times and meditated several minutes. Finally, he said, "I don't know what weapons might be used in World War III, but there isn't any doubt what weapons will be used in World War IV." Someone asked, "And what will those be?" Einstein responded soberly, "Stone spears."

Technical Description:	Voiceless, Linguapalatal Fricative Continuant, Cognate of [ʒ]
Physiological Description: How the Sound is Made	Vocal folds not vibrating, tongue drawn back farther than for [s] creating a flatter, broader surface without a midline groove down which the air flows, passing through a wide but narrow passage between tongue and front part of hard palate, tongue blade lightly touches hard palate just behind gum ridge, tongue tip may be down by lower front teeth or up near upper gum ridge, sides of tongue are against inside surfaces of upper back teeth (as far forward as premolars), soft palate raised, lips may protrude slightly and may be almost oval (not round) in shape
Common Spellings:	sh in show, fashion, banish si in expansion, tension ss in pressure, issue s in sure, sugar ci in socialize, specialty ti in lotion, motion, ration ch in champagne, machine
Periodic Spellings:	sch in schnauzer, Schmidt sc in conscientious c in oceanography ssi in missionary

$$[ʃ]$$

(shade)

Technical Description:	Voiced, Linguapalatal Fricative Continuant, Cognate of [ʃ]
Physiological Description: How the Sound is Made	Vocal folds vibrating, tongue drawn back farther than for [z] creating a flatter, broader surface without a midline groove down which the air flows, passing through a wide but narrow passage between tongue and front part of hard palate, tongue blade lightly touches hard palate just behind gum ridge, tongue tip may be down by lower front teeth or up near upper gum ridge, sides of tongue are against inside surfaces of upper back teeth (as far forward as premolars), soft palate raised, lips may protrude slightly and may be almost oval (not round) in shape
Common Spellings:	ge in massage, rouge, beige s in pleasure, invasion, casual z in seizure, azure, glazier
Periodic Spellings:	j in Jacques

$$[ʒ]$$

(measure)

121

The cognates [ʃ] and [ʒ] are quite similar to [s] and [z] in their physiological characteristics. They introduce two new IPA symbols which need to be learned. The voiceless [ʃ] looks like an elongated, narrow "s" which must be made carefully so it won't resemble a capital "s" in your transcriptions. The voiced [ʒ] resembles a written or script "z" and must be distinctly different from the [z]. These four sounds are all fricatives with the point of friction changing slightly from the tongue blade and gum ridge for [s] and [z] to the tongue blade and the area just **behind** the gum ridge (postalveolar or prepalatal) for [ʃ] and [ʒ]. Probably one of the first sounds, besides humming, that babies learn from their mothers is the voiceless "shhhhh." Its cognate [ʒ] is not used as frequently in English as it is in French. Many English words containing this sound have their origins in French. Neither of these sounds gives speakers great difficulty.

COMMON PROBLEMS

1. A few native and nonnative speakers of English substitute [ʃ] for [s] and [ʒ] for [z]. Usually, this is a result of not hearing a difference between the sounds. (This substitution often sounds like the lateral lisp mentioned above, in which air was allowed to flow over the sides of the tongue, rather than down the midline indentation.) The voiced and voiceless sounds should be contrasted in isolation and then in various positions of words until they can be heard and said correctly.

2. Some people substitute the voiceless [ʃ] for the voiced [ʒ], particularly at the ends of words. This actually occurs because an individual eliminates the element of voicing too quickly. This elimination of voicing may be encouraged by a drop in volume and/or fast speaking rate.

3. Periodically, people substitute the voiceless [ʃ] for [ʒ] or for [tʃ] or [dʒ] (which will be described in the final section of this chapter). This is a fairly common occurrence among native speakers of Spanish who learn English as a second language. Thus, "chicken" is pronounced incorrectly as "shicken" and "mirage" is pronounced "miratsch." This error usually is due to an inability to hear a difference among these sounds and to an attempt to correlate English spelling and pronunciation with their native language's pronunciation rules.

4. A nondistinctive change occurs when individuals use too much pressure to press the tongue blade upwards towards the gum ridge. This creates a higher frequency sound (or pitch) than is needed for the voiceless [ʃ]. By relaxing the front portion of the tongue and avoiding drawing the corners of the mouth up slightly, much of this tense friction will be eliminated.

EXERCISES FOR PRACTICING [ʃ] AND [ʒ]

1. Contrast the isolated voiced and unvoiced cognates below.

a. [ʃ]   [ʒ]   [ʒʃ]   [ʃ]   [ʃ]   [ʒʃ]   [ʒ]   [ʃ]   [ʃ]   [ʃʒʃ]

b. [s]   [ʃ]   [z]   [ʒ]   [z z]   [s s]   [ʒ]   [ʃ]   [zʃ]

122

2. Determine which of the sounds is contained in each of the following words and place an X in the appropriate column.

	[s]	[z]	[ʃ]	[ʒ]		[s]	[z]	[ʃ]	[ʒ]
a. Business					f. Asiatic				
b. Erosion					g. Mission				
c. Missile					h. Pleasant				
d. Passion					i. Vision				
e. Using					j. Reason				

3. The following words contain the voiceless [ʃ] in various positions of words. Practice saying these words aloud.

Initial	Medial	Final
a. shallow/shoulder	dashes/insurance	flash/mustache
b. shouted/shrinking	precious/flashlight	punish/Irish
c. sugar/shocking	national/crochet	relish/burnish
d. shrewd/shield	pushing/commercial	vanquish/marsh
e. shrimp/shower	passion/brushed	foolish/English

4. The following words contain the voiced [ʒ] in various positions of words. Practice saying these aloud, giving special attention to adequate vibration to create voicing.

Medial	Final
a. derision/Asia/pledging	corsage/menage/garage
b. treasures/regime/delusion	mirage/entourage/rouge
c. precision/leisure/casual	camouflage/massage/beige
d. explosion/measures/vision	persiflage/prestige/collage
e. pleasure/evasion/cohesion	sabotage/barrage/cortege

5. Practice reading the following sentences aloud.

a. Charlotte's casual facial expressions were a camouflage for her drastic social decisions.

b. All his leisure activities vanished when his conscience unleashed a stream of guilt.

c. In her dreams she had visions of unblemished Persian melons, shining in a profusion of sunlight next to her shop.

d. Persuasion was less than an illusion when reason supported his unblemished version of how the action had occurred.

e. We gathered a corsage of flowers along the azure-colored Danish marshes to bring pleasure to our mother.

6. Practice Paragraphs

a. During the regime of the first Czar of Russia, Ivan Vasalitch made a decision to sell his business, secretly invest in Swiss securities, take a leisurely summer vacation in Switzerland, and there, to shed his Russian citizenship. His vision was to fashion a life for himself in a society which valued freedom of conscience as well as personal industriousness. Patiently, he planned the mission which would take several months to complete. A fictitious uncle in Lucerne suddenly needed his financial assistance to set up an international business which would furnish Russia with much-needed finished cloth. Ivan sold his house, sent the proceeds to Switzerland, and rented a simply furnished room. His business colleagues understood it was a temporary situation until the new business would bring him and the community great rewards.

b. The seamstress shouted harshly at the shaggy British sea captain who was standing on his deck. He had just showered sticky soot from his rusty steamship all over her freshly painted oceanfront cottage. As usual, he was too far away to hear her loud, passionate cries, but she knew he could see her as she brandished her tarnished copper frying pan over her head. He merely shrugged his shoulders, lit his pipe, and turned to face a friendlier ocean. Blowing the stacks was a necessary operation, so his conscience was clear of any wrongdoing.

c. At the sound of the doorbell, Shannon blushed slightly and raised her patient, green eyes expectantly from the azure colored shawl she was knitting. She had just come to the conclusion that Jacques would not be visiting her this evening. Her seven-year-old son, fatherless for the past three years, raced to the door and flung it open. "Mama," he squealed, "It's Jacques!" Even before the front door closed, she could smell his spicy after-shave lotion. Now Shannon's cheeks looked like dusty rose rouge had just been applied to them. She anticipated his usual appearance in the living room door, squeezing Shawn close to his cleanly shaven face, and smiling confidently.

d. Sara Frazier sat on her front porch, swinging leisurely in her old fashioned porch swing, enjoying the fresh fall air. She smiled with pleasure at the vision of her small daughter tugging tenaciously at a beige colored cornstalk in the garden beside their garage. After several ferocious tugs, the cornstalk came out of the ground and the little girl raced to the house to show her mother the treasure she had acquired all by herself. Mrs. Frazier chortled, "Well, well, aren't you a strong girl!" The little girl shouted, "Yes, and just think—the whole world was holding onto the other end!"

124

Technical Description:	Voiceless, Linguapalatal Affricate Continuant, Cognate of [dʒ]
Physiological Description: How the Sound is Made	Vocal folds not vibrating, tongue tip touches gum (alveolar) ridge to hold back the flow of air until it is released without an obvious explosion, sending air down a flattened tongue blade (which glides quickly to a position required for the voiceless [ʃ]) and out through the parted front teeth as lower jaw drops, soft palate raised, lips may be slightly protruded and in an oval (not round) shape
Common Spellings:	ch in cheese, peaches, each tch in catches, wretched, itch
Periodic Spellings:	ti in questionable te in righteous tu in nature

[tʃ]
(chip)

Technical Description:	Voiced, Linguapalatal Affricate Continuant, Cognate of [tʃ]
Physiological Description: How the Sound is Made	Vocal folds vibrating, tongue tip touches gum (alveolar) ridge to hold back the flow of air until it is released down a flattened tongue blade (which glides quickly to a position required for the voiced [ʒ]) and out through the parted front teeth as lower jaw drops, soft palate is raised, lips may be slightly protruded and in an oval (not round) shape
Common Spellings:	j in jelly, judge, rejoinder g in genius, ginger, magic ge in pigeon, urge, orange dg in pledging, wedging dge in badges, hedge, fudge dj in adjacent, adjective
Periodic Spellings:	di in soldier d in graduate de in grandeur gg in exaggerate

(jolly)

125

The cognate sound [tʃ] and [dʒ] are classified as **affricates** rather than fricatives. Affricates actually begin as the plosive sounds [t] and [d] but change quickly into the fricative sounds [ʃ] and [ʒ]. In fact, even before air is released for the fricative sounds, the lips and tongue are preparing for the terminal portions of these sounds. In saying these sounds, you hardly pronounce the plosive sounds (or simply produce them as "soft" or quietly exploded sounds.) The IPA symbols for these sounds combine the plosive and fricative symbols into two new symbols. Therefore, in counting numbers of phonemes in words, the [tʃ] and [dʒ] combinations are each considered one sound—not two.

COMMON PROBLEMS

1. Since the voiced [dʒ] doesn't appear in many foreign languages, including French, Spanish, and German, it may be difficult for nonnative speakers of English to hear or say easily. Fortunately, it usually is represented by spellings containing the letters "j," "g," or "dge" whereas, the voiceless [tʃ] usually is represented by the letters "ch" or "tch." The tongue tip *must* be placed on the gum ridge in order to produce these sounds. Otherwise, the resulting sounds will be either [s] and [z], [ʃ] and [ʒ], or the initial sound in the word "you."

2. Probably the only major problem encountered by native English speakers with these two sounds is the elimination of voicing for [dʒ], especially at the ends of words. Frequently, this is because the speakers are unsure of how combinations of letters should be pronounced. If you look at the number of different spellings available for these two sounds, you can begin to understand the reason for this confusion. Try to remember the spelling combinations given in item number 1 above, if you have difficulty knowing which sound to produce.

3. An occasional nondistinctive error is evident when some people prolong either or both of these sounds. Generally, when this error occurs the individuals also are prolonging [s] and/or [z]. This prolongation may be compounded if the tongue blade is pushed with excessive pressure towards the gum ridge, creating a higher pitched fricative sound than is heard normally. The tension in the tongue must be relaxed slightly by dropping the blade back and down away from the gum ridge. The excessive flow of air may be eliminated by learning the same breath control discussed for excessively sibilant [s] sounds.

EXERCISES FOR PRACTICING [tʃ] AND [dʒ]

1. Practice the following sounds in isolation, contrasting the voiced and voiceless qualities of each.

a. [tʃ]   [dʒ]   [tʃ tʃ dʒ]   [tʃ]   [dʒ dʒ tʃ]   [tʃ]   [tʃ dʒ dʒ tʃ]

b. [s]   [t]   [ʃ]   [ʒ]   [tʃ]   [dʒ]   [ʒ]   [tʃ dʒ]   [s tʃ]   [dʒ ʒ]   [ʃ]

126

2. Translate the following IPA transcriptions.

a. [dʒɪp] _____   [mætʃ] _____   [fɪʃ] _____

b. [tʃit] _____   [titʃ] _____   [pætʃ] _____

c. [tʃɛst] _____   [dʒɪm] _____   [wɪtʃ] _____

d. [hwɪtʃ] _____   ['mɪdʒɪt] _____   [tʃes] _____

e. ['ɪmɪdʒ] _____   [bitʃ] _____   [wɛdʒ] _____

3. Transcribe the following words into IPA symbols.

a. Thatch _____   Shamed _____   Pages _____

b. Weeds _____   Jimmy _____   Batches _____

c. These _____   Gem _____   Cheese _____

4. Read the following words aloud. Contrast their fricative and affricate sounds in relation to the front vowel sounds in each word.

	[s]	[ʃ]	[tʃ]	[z]	[ʒ]	[dʒ]
a.	see	she	cheese	Z's	adhesion	genes
b.	sip	ship	chip	zip	visionary	gyp
c.	sane	Shane	chain	Zane	occasion	Jane
d.	said	shed	cheddar	Zed	pleasure	Jed
e.	mass	mash	match	as	azure	Madge
f.	decent	species	preach	sprees	lesion	legion
g.	misty	dishes	ditches	dizzy	collision	pigeon
h.	faced	facial	H's	A's	deja vu	waged
i.	professor	fresher	wretched	says	treasure	wedged
j.	Cass	cash	catch	hasn't	casual	agile

5. Read the following word combinations aloud as if they were part of a phrase in a conversational dialogue.

a. bachelor chose March; short prestige explosion; children catch merchants; camouflaged negligee shop

b. each grandchild chased; Persian rouge showed; reached cheese merchants; measured Sherry's corsage

c. jolly witch joined; managed fudge judging; chilled teacher's lunch; orange ginger hedge

d. major general change; richest church checked; jack matches pitchers; carriage chain reaches

e. chocolate chip merchant; speech registered joy; image matched jests; agent's language much

6. Practice reading the following sentences aloud, using the same inflections you would use if you were saying these things to someone—rather than reading them out of the book.

a. Jonah's entourage of tourists was besieged by jovial street urchins who gesticulated wildly.

b. When we teach English in China on an exchange program, we will search for a larger jade brooch.

c. The jogger adjusted his patched cap, moistened his parched lips with orange juice, and joined his group.

d. Chester searched for matches to light the strange, giant candles in the shop windows.

e. Every January, the jeweled bridge served as a graceful arch over the raging stream.

7. Practice Paragraphs

a. A carriage shop stood at the edge of a sponge dock near the ocean. Legions of soldiers marched past it every week on their way from their ships up to the ridge where the battle would be waged. Charles, the jovial giant who managed the shop, shouted encouragement to the soldiers as they passed, urging them to honor their country with their courage. Barges of equipment arrived daily, discharged their goods, and disappeared. Soon, the warehouses bulged with enough supplies to feed and clothe the village for several years. Charles watched for the ship that would bring the generals. That would be the signal for him to jump into his sailboat and join his family on an offshore island.

b. Geraldine reached for either the wrench or hatchet she knew was on the top shelf in her kitchen cabinet. In spite of the darkness, she felt self-assured. Her fingers searched carefully as she tried not to make any noise. There was the sound again—like someone was just outside her kitchen door, trying to wedge a screwdriver between the frame and door. Geraldine's rage grew. She wasn't just an average housewife, fearing for her life. She was a judo expert and an amateur weight lifter. She enjoyed challenges—even when they surprised her out of a sound sleep.

c. During their leisure hours, the Cortez family enjoyed telling jokes while they shelled popcorn to store for the winter. Their joviality often culminated in crescendos of laughter that streamed through their apple orchards and echoed throughout their valley. Just as their chortling began to wane, someone else would launch into a new, far-fetched tale, finely interspersed with descriptive adjectives and exaggerated facial expressions. Smiles of anticipation turned into grins of appreciation, and finally, wild guffaws and uninhibited gales of laughter, until tears streamed down the faces of everyone present. It was sweet revenge to watch a sister or brother, doubled up with laughter, unable to shell another kernel of corn!

128

CHAPTER 11

THE MIDDLE VOWELS
[ʌ] [ə] [ɝ] [ɚ]

Two middle vowel sounds occur in General American Speech: the schwa and schwa-r. However, four IPA symbols will be used to transcribe these sounds in order to show whether they are used in stressed or unstressed syllables. These symbols are unlike any of our English letters unless you are willing to think of them as reversed or upsidedown English letters. The two sounds are extremely important in relatively fast, connected or assimilated, speech for maintaining smooth (fluent) and connected (assimilated) rather than choppy and overly precise (pedantic) diction.

The first two symbols [ʌ] and [ə] represent the weak "uh" or schwa sound pronounced either "schwa" or "schva," (a Hebrew word originally used to describe an obscure written Hebrew vowel ":") which is the chameleon of vowel sounds. It represents so many different spellings and can involve so many vowels that a complete cataloging of its spelling combinations will be impossible. Your ears must tell you of its presence in conversational speech, since spelling rules won't be of much help. As your ears become attuned to sound production in words, you will be amazed how often you use the schwa sound.

Technical Description:	Stressed Middle (or Central) Vowel
Physiological Description: How the Sound is Made	Vocal folds vibrating, lower jaw drops, lips and tongue muscles are lax, central part of tongue is lifted slightly towards hard palate while tip is flattened and resting behind lower front teeth, soft palate is raised; sound usually is briefer than most vowels and appears only in stressed syllables of words in the initial and medial (never final) position
Common Spellings:	u in us, upright, shut, puppy o in other, brother, love, won ou in double, couple, enough oo in blood, flooded
Periodic Spellings:	oe in does

(fun)

Technical Description:	Unstressed Middle (or Central) Vowel
Physiological Description: How the Sound is Made	Vocal folds vibrating, lower jaw drops, lips and tongue muscles are lax, central part of tongue is lifted slightly towards hard palate while tip is flattened and resting behind lower front teeth, soft palate is raised; sound usually is briefer than other vowels and is only in unstressed syllables (including unstressed one-syllable words in phrases and clauses, such as ''of,'' ''from,'' ''was,'' and ''the'')

[ə]

(adore)

Common Spellings:	any vowel in an unstressed position has the capability of being said as a schwa, as in:

a: aloud, telepathy, China
e: listen, society, system
i: ability, citizen, similar
ia: Portia, parliament, militia
io: action, section, religion
iou: precious, spacious
o: official, prison, anodize
ou: grievous, famous, porous
u: upon, circus

Periodic Spellings:	

ah: rajah, Dinah
au: Chautauqua
ea: Jeanette
eo: surgeon, righteous
he: behemoth
ie: mischievous, deficient
oi: porpoise

Whether it is in a stressed or unstressed syllable, the schwa sound, is a relatively neutral sound. It is the same sound you hear: (1) In vocalized pauses of speaking North Americans who want to let listeners know they haven't finished speaking yet, even though they are pausing; (2) American Indian chiefs use in their grunt ''ugh''; (3) In both syllables of the colloquial expressions ''uh'huh,'' [ə'hʌ] (affirmative or ''yes'' response) or '' 'huh uh,'' ['hʌə] (negative or ''no'' response) to questions.

The schwa sound is a relaxed, relatively effortless sound. You should be able to feel the muscles under the tongue relax completely when you say the sound. This is fortunate, since it probably is the most commonly used vowel sound in English. It also is the lower of the two medial vowel sounds in relation to the hard palate.

Many students wonder why two different IPA symbols are used to represent the schwa sound. You will discover they help to make stressed syllables clearer, especially if you are not using primary and secondary stress marks in your transcriptions. In words such as ''rumpus,'' ''onion,'' and ''ultra'' which contain both stressed and unstressed schwa sounds, your transcriptions make immediate sense. This becomes particularly important in longer polysyllabic words you are trying to read aloud without the assistance of accent marks. For example, the word ''unaccommodating'' has three schwa sounds which occur on the vowel letters ''u,'' ''a,'' and ''o.'' When the word is written [ˌʌnə'kɑməˌdetɪŋ], you know *precisely* where the stresses go.

130

COMMON PROBLEMS

1. The first problem involves using the correct IPA symbols rather than saying the schwa sound. The stressed schwa looks like an upsidedown "v" and the unstressed schwa looks like an upsidedown "e." If you have a scrap of paper, print the letter "e" on the paper and then turn it upsidedown to see what happens. Beginning students frequently turn the upsidedown "e" around to face the wrong direction, creating an incorrect IPA symbol which your instructor should mark wrong on transcriptions.

To use the correct IPA schwa symbol, you must know where primary and secondary stresses occur in polysyllabic words. Remember, if a syllable is stressed, regardless of whether the stress is primary or secondary, the stressed schwa symbol [ʌ] must be used. All stressed syllables will be slightly longer, louder, and perhaps higher in pitch than unstressed syllables will be. The following chart may help you remember which schwa symbol to use in your transcriptions.

USING STRESSED [ʌ] AND UNSTRESSED [ə] SYMBOLS

One Syllable Words:	Examples
1. In all one syllable words, the stressed schwa will be used unless the words are considered relatively unimportant, in the context of a phrase or clause. One syllable nouns, pronouns, verbs, adjectives and adverbs normally will be considered important context words.	luck, trust, spud, cuts, rough, fuss, clutch, hug, tough, cuff, suds, bust, much, such
2. One syllable conjunctions, prepositions, and helping or auxiliary verbs usually are considered relatively unimportant function words and would require the unstressed schwa	the, from, of, was, up

Polysyllabic Words:	
In words of two or more syllables, at least one syllable will be stressed or accented. If a schwa sound appears in the accented syllable, use a stressed schwa [ʌ] symbol.	'cupboard, re'but, in'duct, 'suddenly
If a schwa sound appears in an unaccented syllable, use an unstressed schwa [ə] symbol.	a'lone, 'famous, Ma'nila
Many polysyllabic words will have both stressed and unstressed schwas.	re'luctant, an'nul, in'dustrious

As you become aware of sounds in words, you will discover that certain prefixes such, as "a" (above, alone, about, around, astride, across) and "un" (unnoticed, unwanted, unduly, unseen, unscathed) and certain suffixes, such as "ous," "eous" and "ious" (porous, righteous, previous, virtuous, spacious) usually contain the unstressed schwa sound. When you discover these generalizations, you will be able to apply them automatically to most of your transcriptions.

2. When untrained speakers appear on radio or television to read their own ads for their products or businesses, they often display their lack of training by using two obvious pedantic pronunciations. They are the interminable pronunciations of "the" as [ði] and "a" as [e]. (You may react to these speakers exactly as you reacted to unprepared readers

131

in elementary school who tried to "fake" their preparedness. You wanted to correct them for their repeated mistakes, but knew it wouldn't be polite to do so in public. Their disfluency was agonizing, and the mistakes were so obvious that everyone recognized them. However, if the teacher didn't correct the errors, no one else would. It always was a relief for them to finish their selections so a competent or practiced reader could read.)

Many speakers and oral readers use the overly precise (pedantic) pronunciations [e] and [ði] for the words "a" and "the." Often, people become habituated to saying these articles in a pedantic manner because they don't understand very simple rules for pronouncing articles. In most cases unstressed schwas will be used. The rules are given below.

RULES FOR PRONOUNCING THE ARTICLES "THE" AND "A"

	examples
When the article "the" appears before a word:	
1. Beginning with a consonant **sound**, it will be pronounced [ðə].	boy, house, rain, woods
2. Beginning with a vowel or diphthong **sound**, it will be pronounced [ði].	author, act, east, hours, orchid
When the article "a" appears before a word:	coat, word, mink, step
Beginning with a consonant **sound,** it will be pronounced [ə].	
(When a word begins with [j], the initial sound in "yet," or [ju] as in "useful," this pronunciation also will be used.)	yearning, usual, yell
When a word begins with a vowel or diphthong sound:	old, ice, easy, other
It will be introduced by "an."	
The pronunciations [ði] and [e] are used to **underscore** this one word or to speak about the letter A in the alphabet	not **the** boy, Check **A,** not B

3. Nonnative and a few native speakers of English often substitute another vowel sound for the schwa sound. (Some languages, including Spanish and Italian, don't have this central vowel.) The most common substitution is "ah" or [ɑ] for stressed and unstressed schwa sounds. Thus, "what" becomes [hwɑt], "of" becomes [ɑv], and "from" becomes [frɑm]. In many words, this simple phonetic shift creates semantic problems. Here are a few examples:

Intended Message	**Message Actually Sent**
a. Store the **nuts** in the shed.	Store the **knots** in the shed.
b. Where is the **cut**?	Where is the **cot**?
c. Where did you get **stuck**?	Where did you get **stock**?
d. I hit a **duck** with a stone.	I hit a **dock** with a stone.
e. He took his **luck** with him.	He took his **lock** with him.

To correct this error, speakers must shorten the duration of the vowel sound and be sure the central portion of the tongue moves up slightly towards the hard palate. Since some speakers don't hear the difference between the two sounds, they should listen while someone reads lists of words containing both "ah" and "uh" sounds until they can identify correctly which sound occurs in the words. After this period of ear training, they need to produce the sound in isolation, contrasting it with the "ah" sound they *can* produce.

EXERCISES FOR PRACTICING [ʌ] [ə]

1. Since the stressed and unstressed schwa sounds are the same sound, it is impossible to contrast their sounds in isolation. The symbol for "ah" hasn't been studied yet so it won't be used here. Contrast the sounds as follows:

a. [ʌ]   [ə ə]   [ʌ]   [ə]   [ʌ]   [ʌ ə ʌ]   [ə]   [ʌ]   [ə ə ʌ]

b. [ɪ]   [ʌ]   [e]   [ʌ]   [i]   [ə]   [æ]   [ə]   [ɪ e ʌ]   [æʌ]

2. Read the following lists of words aloud. Be sure to drop your lower jaw for stressed and unstressed schwa sounds.

Initial	Medial	Final
a. about/us/avoid	thus/puppy/stubborn	Malta/sofa/delta
b. achieve/utter/along	nothing/ambition/cut	Emma/Cuba/henna
c. Athena/ajar/onion	truck/movable/dusty	hyena/the/Linda
d. usher/upper/above	shut/telepathy/but	data/China/Rita
e. ugly/against/ultra	funny/persevere/cup	vita/Mecca/sofa
f. apply/announce/up	youngest/dump/levity	sierra/Eva/Silva

3. Transcribe the following words into IPA symbols. Include accent marks to help you determine whether a stressed or unstressed schwa symbol will be used.

a. Amazed _____   Sheba _____   Hushed _____

b. Fuzzy _____   Does _____   Achieve _____

c. Ablaze _____   Above _____   Zeta _____

d. Hump _____   Dubbed _____   Ahead _____

e. Ashamed _____   Stumped _____   Touch _____

4. Translate the following into words.

a. [ʃʌt] _____   ['tʃʌbi] _____   [mʌts] _____

b. [pʌmp] _____   ['stʌbi] _____   [tʃʌmp] _____

c. [sʌtʃ] _____   [səb'mɪt] _____   ['bɪzməθ] _____

5. Read the following word combinations aloud.

a. ushering nothing ugly; avoid Cuban petunias; such astounding affairs; arriving Baltimore Orioles

b. stigma touched others; ancient zealous deacons; patrol around Luntstown; someone reluctant suspended

c. reluctantly acquired study; undaunted cherubs hunted; era lengthening occurred; doubled Malta's royal

d. Alabama wondered about; Iowa's circus allowed; supposed lava against; banana's addition again

e. Emma awaited much; subtle attention abounded; militia afforded another; balloons' appearance against

6. Practice reading the following sentences aloud. Try to retain fluency in reading without overstressing the schwa sounds.

a. Bertha didn't announce a decision until the end of the last business meeting.

b. His suggestion was to allow other hunters to have the run of the more rugged country above us.

c. Edna mumbled under her breath that the punishment was unjust for all the trouble her uncle had caused.

d. Gus couldn't afford to suspend the club's action until other members arrived.

e. Our cousin in Ulster announced the annulment of his mother's marriage to Buddy Hubbard.

f. The rugged rubber baby buggy bumpers ushered in another era.

g. The monkey got in trouble when he stuck one thumb into the honey, assuming it was water.

7. Practice Paragraphs

a. Wanda visited the circus for the first time. Under the tent the place was ablaze with lights. What wonderful aromas scented the air: chocolate, vanilla, and cinnamon! Multi-colored balloons were everywhere. The drama began to unfold as the orchestra played a polka. Wanda watched the chubby tuba player as he vigorously puffed away at his instrument. Then the entry parade began. Elephants, acrobats, lions, horses, trapeze artists, a gorilla, and even a zebra passed in front of her. She was close enough to touch some of the animals. Just before the acts began, her mother bought her a can of diet soda and a carton of pop corn.

b. Breakfast was a necessary evil for Elsa before she left for the university. Other students seemed to love their omelets, cereal, toast and juice. Not Elsa! She was always too tired or in too much of a hurry to eat much of anything. A cup of Sanka and either a banana or a bran muffin was about all she wanted. She always thought breakfast was dull—an utter bore—but she knew she needed something to keep her stomach from gurgling during her Russian history class just before lunch. Lunch was a different matter. She adored lunch!

134

c. The ultimate action of the umpire was to dust off the home plate with a subdued green handkerchief and shout, ''Play ball!'' Suddenly, the stands were alive with thousands of tongues shouting the names of teams and players. The pitcher looked around the bases, struck his glove against his hip, touched his cap, and nodded to the catcher. The first batter stepped up to the plate. He was not very tall but he stood so straight that he aroused everyone's curiosity immediately. ''Who is he?'' Dudley asked of his half-asleep brother. His brother grunted, shrugged his shoulders, and slumped back in his seat.

d. As a youngster in Sacramento, Tina learned to love the cinema. She was allowed to go once in a great while, but always with a relative. Her father continued to remind her to leave the drama at the theatre and not to annoy him with tales of what she experienced there. The element of suspense would grow daily as she anticipated the long-awaited experience. She was extra cautious to complete her chores at home so she would be allowed one Sunday afternoon at the cinema. Just about the time she was to leave, her older brother gave her a big hug, slipped a dull, folded dollar bill into her hands, and whispered, ''Tell me all about it when you come home.''

Technical Description:	Stressed Middle (or Central) r-Colored Vowel
Physiological Description: How the Sound is Made	Vocal folds vibrating, teeth slightly apart and lips unrounded but slightly tense, front of tongue raised slightly (some people curl it backwards slightly in a retroflex position) while middle and back portions rise towards hard palate, back sides of tongue firmly touch inside portions of back molars, soft palate is raised; appears only in stressed syllables of words and most contextually important one syllable words
Common Spellings:	er in erg, hers, berth, defer ur in urgent, curse, incur, fur ir in Irwin, first, stir, fir ear in earth, heard, yearn or in word, worst, working our in tournament, journey urr in hurried, burr, purr re in are, care, more
Periodic Spellings:	orr in worry yrr in myrrh olo in colonel

[3ʋ]

(early)

The second middle vowel sound is variously described as the schwa-r, the r-colored vowel, and the hooked reversed epsilon. The first two terms relate to the classification of the sound as a vowel with some characteristics of the consonant letter ''r.'' The third term relates to the IPA symbol which is used to identify the stressed sound. It is made like the fifth letter and second vowel in the Greek alphabet called epsilon, only the symbol is turned upsidedown (reversed) and a small hook or tail is placed at the top. This hook or tail indicates the r-coloring—and resembles a tiny uncapitalized script ''r.''

$$[\,\mathrm{\partial\!\iota}\,]$$

(over)

Technical Description:	Unstressed Middle (or Central) r-Colored Vowel
Physiological Description: How the Sound is Made	Vocal folds vibrating, teeth slightly apart and lips unrounded but slightly tense, front of tongue raised slightly (some people curl it backwards slightly in a retroflex position) while middle and back portions rise towards hard palate, back sides of tongue firmly touch inside portions of back molars, soft palate is raised; appears only in unstressed syllables of words and contextually unimportant one syllable words.
Common Spellings:	ar in nuclear, dollar, pillar er in shivering, silver, mister or in favorable, author, actor ur in usurpation, murmur, augur ure in measure, leisure, pressure
Periodic Spellings:	yr in satyr, zephyr ir in fakir, tapir re in theatre, euchre oar in starboard, cupboard

Just as the schwa sound has two symbols to represent stressed and unstressed sounds, so does this sound. The stressed [ɝ] appears only in accented syllables; the unstressed [ɚ] appears only in unaccented syllables; the unstressed [ɚ] looks like an unstressed schwa with the addition of a hook or tail to show the r-coloring. Again, you will need to be careful that you don't face the schwa and its hook in the wrong direction as this would be an incorrect IPA symbol which your instructor would count incorrect in transcriptions.

This sound probably is one of the most important ones for distinguishing General American Speech from other regional and subsidiary dialects in North America. It certainly is an important factor in distinguishing General American Speech from most British dialects. Whenever the spellings "er, ir, or, ur, our, ear," and "yr" appear in one syllable, they are produced as either the stressed [ɝ] or the unstressed [ɚ] in General American Speech. They are never "dropped."

In General American Speech, the [ɝ] and [ɚ] sounds also are preferred over the [r] sound in words when they occur between vowels in medial positions and after a vowel in the final position. (You will study the [r] sound in the next chapter.) In words such as "ear," "bearing," and "boring," the [ɚ] sound usually is glided with the preceding vowel, creating a glide which is similar to a diphthong. A clear retroflex [r], in which the tongue tip turns up towards the hard palate, usually doesn't occur. This is quite different from Eastern and Southern dialects where the [r] sound seems to be preferred in many words. Thus, the word "peering" would be pronounced ['pɪɝɪŋ] in General American Speech but ['pɪɝrɪŋ] in the Southern dialect.

136

When "er, ir, or, ur, our, ear," and "yr" are spoken by people with Southern, Eastern, and British dialects, these combinations of letters may be pronounced as a schwa, a retroflex [r], a silent letter, a "one tap trilled r," or a reversed epsilon [ɜ] sound. The reversed epsilon looks like the reversed hooked epsilon **without** its hook or tail—or like a small number 3. Since the sound doesn't occur in General American Speech, the [ɜ] won't be discussed in detail in this book. It is, however, a legitimate IPA symbol your instructor may wish to use in discussing [ɝ] and [ɚ], particularly if many students in your class use it in their daily speaking. (General American speakers often describe the substitution of [ɜ] for [ɝ] as a dropping of the "r" sounds.)

COMMON PROBLEMS

In dealing with common problems for creating [ɝ] and [ɚ], we are examining the sound from a General American Speech perspective. Many speakers of regional or subsidiary dialects of English are trying to modify their dialects within this class for some personal, social, professional, or academic purpose. The "problems" of producing this sound to gain a better General American Speech pattern may not be considered problems within another regional or national dialect where the schwa and/or reversed epsilon sounds are standard replacements for these sounds.

1. The sounds [ɜ], [ʌ] or [ə] are substituted for [ɝ] and/or [ɚ]. This becomes particularly obvious at ends of words such as "mother, sister, other, brother, father, and teacher." (Comedians frequently use this substitution to tell dialectal jokes involving their relatives including their "fadduh" and "brudduh.") In some dialects, this substitution can be confusing to outsiders who don't understand its application. If the changes are applied consistently, the confusion is less than if they are applied only in certain locations or to certain types of words. This consistency must apply to single sounds as well as glided or diphthongized sounds. For example, consistently substitute [ɜ] or [ʌ] for [ɝ], and [ə] for [ɚ] in the underlined sounds below and notice the results:

over/ova	bore/boa	knower/Noah
pastor/pasta	farther/father	Carmen/common
barber/baabaa	larder/lotta	tardy/toddy
part/pot	bird/bud	word/would/wood

The middle portion of the tongue is allowed to relax and fall away from the hard palate too far as the tongue tip drops behind the lower front teeth rather than rising slightly (or even curling up in retroflex) towards the gum ridge. Often, the back sides of the tongue fall down and away from the back molars rather than maintaining firm contact with their inside surfaces. Also, the lips may be relaxing too much, rather than rounding slightly.

2. A nondistinctive change in these sounds occurs when individuals curl up the tongue tip too far and/or pull the tongue back and up towards the hard palate with too much pressure. This habit produces tense, harsh metallic [ɝ] or [ɚ] sounds which sound forced and are unpleasant to hear. One popular British comedian is unsuccessful in his attempts to characterize American speech because he is unaccustomed to producing these sounds and has to strain to create approximations of [ɝ] and [ɚ] sounds. His struggle to attain even these gross exaggerations is humorous to Americans. Less tension should occur in the front of the tongue than near the back when forming these sounds correctly.

3. In some sections of the United States, people tend to add either the schwa or [r] sound after these sounds. This happens most often in the final position of words. Thus,

137

the word "sir" would sound either like [sɜ˞r] or [sɜ˞ʌ]. Either the tongue and jaw are allowed to drop after [ɜ˞] is said, or the tip of the tongue pulls up and retracts slightly after [ɜ˞] is produced. This added tongue and jaw movement creates a brief additional sound.

4. Another nondistinctive change occurs when these sounds are nasalized. Although the sounds have r-coloring, they are considered vowel sounds. Since all vowel sounds in English are not nasalized, these sounds both should be produced with a raised soft palate. If the velum drops, air will escape through the nose rather than (or in addition to) the mouth. If you have this problem, use the list of words below which contains schwa-r sounds but no nasal sounds. Hold your nostrils shut and say the words aloud until you can say them without hearing or feeling nasal emissions.

purse, heard, fear, four, either, cure, core, better, burst, third, curl, adore, bother, setter, flutter, search, perked, works, spirit, earth, turkey, were

5. When some students transcribe words containing a vowel or diphthong which is followed immediately by a schwa-r, they omit the sound before the schwa-r. Often, this is because they don't stop to analyze the quick glide which occurs before that sound and the schwa-r. Technically, a new diphthong (or triphthong) is being formed. However, since this book uses only three diphthongs in order to simplify your learning of the IPA, you may count these as two separate sounds in your transcription exercises. Look at the following groups of words. Can you find the glides which occur in each group? a. are, sharp, card; b. air, share, error; c. ear, fears, theory; d. ire, buyer, admire; e. bluer, newer, detour; f. ower, lower, blower; g. our, tower, coward; h. lawyer, Sawyer, foyer; i. player, sprayer, mayor; j. fewer, cure, reviewer; k. eerie, cheery

EXERCISES FOR PRACTICING [ɜ˞] AND [ɚ]

1. Since no distinction other than stress will be made for the [ɜ˞] and [ɚ] sounds, it is impossible to contrast them in isolation. Read the following sounds aloud.

a. [ɚ]   [ə]   [ɜ˞ ʌ]   [ə ɜ˞]   [ʌ]   [ɜ˞əʌ]   [əɚ]   [ɜ˞]   [ɚ]   [ə ɚ]

b. [iɚ]   [ɜ˞]   [eɚ]   [ɜ˞]   [ɚɚ]   [ɪɜ˞]   [ɚ]   [æɜ˞]   [ɚ]   [ɜ˞ɚ]

2. Translate the following into words. Write the words in the spaces provided.

a. [hɜ˞d] _____   [stɜ˞d] _____   [wɜ˞dz] _____

b. [ʃɜ˞t] _____   [wɜ˞st] _____   [stɪɚ] _____

c. [tɜ˞m] _____   [ə'fɜ˞m] _____   ['mɜ˞si] _____

d. ['sɜ˞vɪs] _____   ['iðɚ] _____   ['pɪtʃɚ] _____

e. ['mɛʒɚ] _____   [ɜ˞θ] _____   ['mɜ˞mɚ] _____

3. Transcribe the following words into IPA symbols. Include primary and secondary stress marks in your transcriptions.

a. better _____   murder _____   germs _____

b. urged _____   thirty _____   worried _____

c. avert _____   wither _____   cellars _____

d. Bert _____   whisper _____   church _____

e. birch _____   sisters _____   slithers _____

4. The following lists of words include the sounds you have been studying in the initial, medial, and final positions.

Initial	**Medial**	**Final**
a. earl/Ernest/urbanity	person/spurn/curve	inter/myrrh/spur
b. urn/Irma/Erkstine	curtain/skirt/word	defer/blur/sir
c. irk/urbane/Ursla	worry/searched/turn	her/inter/purr
d. urchin/Ernest/irked	Myrtle/third/Saturn	occur/aver/fur
e. erstwhile/earn/early	eagerly/concern/Kirk	were/recur/stir

5. Read the following groups of words aloud.

a. Birmingham earned her; Herbert urged Burr; Earlham's first sailor; eastern tar urns

b. American hamburgers irk; urchins' personalities blur; modern erg measure; heard nurse aver

c. early broker purr; Ernest tenderly urge; ergosterol churned inner; earthen repercussions occur

d. measure ermine information; reserve later urgent; greater furniture earnings; squander Erv's faster

e. assure Erpingham's opportunities; turn Earl's picture; prefer earthen circumference; intermix other herbal

6. Read these sentences aloud with the same inflections and fluency you would find in casual conversation. If you have difficulty with [ɜ] and [ɚ], read the sentences slowly at first. Then speed up your rate as you practice.

a. Erwin persuaded the burglar to enter the chamber under the church where they could confer further.

b. My brother is taller and better looking than Robert's brother and he never hurries his searches for words.

c. Early every morning the birds gather near the garbage cans to search their feathers and argue about the weather.

d. We squandered an afternoon to hear a worthless lecture on the repercussions of nuclear war.

e. She swerved on the curve when the surface of the road was slicker than liquor.

7. Practice Paragraphs

a. Jennifer Bannister had just turned four years old. She was perched on her grandmother's front porch railing, watching the perspiring painter next door. He had sandpapered the exterior surface of the house for hours before she learned what he was doing. At first, she wondered if he was brushing it to make its boards look better. When she heard her grandmother say he was a painter, she imagined he would paint pictures all over the house. Her major concern was that he paint at least one picture of a horse. She admired horses more than any other animal.

b. Sooner or later his mother would discover his bedroom door ajar and would hurry downstairs to search for him. She learned to slumber a little later in the summer, knowing he would survive a later breakfast. He took his paper and pencils out under the trees. There, he worked on his poetry while the birds chirped in the branches overhead. His teacher had persuaded him to keep a journal over the summer and to write poetry every day. Neither the warm weather nor the pressure of his farm chores interfered with these daily writing exercises.

c. Irma yearned to have an ermine coat to wear to her thirtieth high school reunion. Yes, it might be a bit overdone. But then, she had earned a reputation as the class clown during her junior and senior years in school. She had deferred her purchase purposely. If her husband, Birch, would bestir himself from his current, worthless pastime of searching for earthworms in their backyard—he could take her. In that case, her present wardrobe would be satisfactory and she would delay her purchase until the summer sales began. However, if he insisted on searching for worms, she would go to her reunion alone—but in good company, in a full length ermine coat. Birch could worry about paying for it while he was digging his worms.

140

CHAPTER 12

THE MIDDLE SOUNDS
[r] [l] [n]

In this chapter you will learn about the three remaining sounds which are produced in the middle portion of the mouth: [r], [l], and [n]. They are extremely versatile sounds as you will see shortly. All of these sounds are consonants and continuants.

Technical Description:	Voiced Palatal (or Linguapalatal) Semivowel Consonant Continuant (or Glide) and Fricative
Physiological Description: How the Sound is Made	Vocal folds vibrating, lips slightly rounded, soft palate is raised, sides of tongue pressed against inside upper back teeth while central portion is raised towards hard palate, and blade and tip either are raised up near (but not touching) the upper gum ridge or are pulled back from lower front teeth, tongue is in motion
Common Spellings:	r in row, reach, bread, crime rr in arrange, barrage, arrive rh in rheumatic, rhyme, rhythm wr in wrong, wrestle, awry

[r]
(rust)

The [r] sound is another mercurial sound in English. Depending on its location in words, and the dialect of the person saying the words, the sound can change considerably. These changes are not due to recent dialectal differences, however, since [r] has been a fluctuating sound for hundreds of years in English.

If you still spoke the type of English used in Chaucer's time (1340–1400), you would be trilling your "r" sounds in all positions of words! This would require you to be able to flutter your tongue tip on or behind the upper gum ridge (or to flutter the uvula) while voicing the [r] phoneme. Since the trilled "r" no longer exists in our dialect, most Americans have some difficulty saying one. However, this sound is common in other languages. If you expect to speak a language such as Spanish or Russian correctly, you probably will learn to trill the "r" in certain words. Many British speakers still use the "one tap trill" in a word such as "very." In this case, the tongue tip taps the gum ridge once, creating a sound which many Americans think sounds like [d] rather than [r].

141

As the spoken language evolved in England, the trilled "r" began to disappear. One hundred years after Chaucer, vowels had shifted and lengthened, often dominating adjacent [r] sounds and reducing them to [ɜ] and [ə] vowel sounds. You will recall that the [ɜ] sound was called a reversed epsilon in the previous chapter. The sound still may be heard as a substitution for [r] in Southern and Eastern dialects in the United States. In southern England, including London, this r-coloring was disappearing in medial and final positions of most words containing the letter "r." In fact, if you read English poetry composed during the early 1600s, you will be amazed to discover that words such as "thirst" and "lust" often rhymed!

When the early English colonists arrived in North America in the 1600s, they brought some of the changing pronunciations with them. However, these widely separated settlements were not all heavily influenced by continued changes in British speech. Some people in the southern and eastern sections of the United States followed the London and southern England custom of "dropping" the "r" but many early colonists followed the northern England custom of pronouncing the [r]. From these early beginnings developed our own current dialects.

Since this book uses the General American Speech pattern for its model, little more attention will be given to the various types of [r] sounds which occur in other national, regional or subsidiary dialects. If your instructor believes they are important for you to learn, he or she will teach you the IPA symbols for the sounds, as well as the general rules that are followed to produce them.

Some phonetics texts classify various types of [r] in relation to their location in words or proximity to other vowels and consonants. An understanding of the technical complexities relating to "after vowel" (postvocalic) and "between vowel" (intervocalic) [r] sounds is not essential in a beginning speech improvement text. In General American Speech, these sounds have less [r] quality and more [ɝ] or [ɚ] quality. Therefore, for the purposes of transcribing phonemes in this book, words such as "merry," "barbaric," "chair," and "tearful" and phrases such as "are Ed's," and "for us" won't be transcribed as containing an [r] **sound**. (The symbol [r] will be used only when the letter "r" begins a word or syllable.) Instead, these words would be transcribed with either [ɝ] or [ɚ]. Since this is a change from some current phonetics books, your instructor may wish to elaborate upon or modify this attempt to simplify your in-class transcription practices.

You will be relieved to learn that a fairly consistent pattern is followed in pronouncing [r] in General American Speech. The [r] always is pronounced. At first, you may find the letter "r" confusing when it appears as a middle or final letter in a word. In Chapter 11, we indicated this book will use the [ɝ] or [ɚ] symbols to refer to *all* spellings which result in the "er" sound, regardless of their location in a word. If you can hear the difference between the letter "r" in "**run**" and "earn," you will be well on your way to keeping these symbols clearly delineated.

To assist you in your future transcriptions, look at the following chart. It will help you understand when [r] and [ɝ] or [ɚ] should be used in your transcriptions. Ultimately, you will find your ears must be able to distinguish which sound is being said by a speaker.

You may begin to see from this chart that, although both sounds involve the letter "r," the IPA symbol [r] generally will function as a consonant in General American Speech; [ɝ] or [ɚ] will function as a vowel.

Use the IPA Symbol [r] in Transcriptions:

1. For **all words beginning** with the **letters** "r," "wr," "rh," as in "romantically wrong rhetoric."

2. For **all words beginning** with a **consonant cluster** containing the **letter** "r." When this same consonant cluster **begins** a syllable in a **medial** position of a word, it also will contain the [r] sound, as in:

[br] brood, abroad	[dr] drapery, adrift
[fr] frank, afraid	[gr] grape, aground
[kr] crisp, decrease	[pr] print, apprehend
[skr] script, ascribe	[spr] spring, respray
[str] stretch, destroy	[ʃr] shred, enshrine
[tr] true, retread	[θr] thread, enthrall

3. In **all medial syllables beginning** with the **letters** "r," "wr," and "rh" as in the words "de/rive, a/wry, un/rhythmical." (The words, "gal/ler/y, der/i/va/tion, ex/hort/ing" would contain [ɝ] or [ɚ] since the letter "r" either **ends** or is in the **middle** of a syllable.) The [r] sound won't appear as the final phoneme in a word.

4. In words containing a **doubled** "r" where the pronounced "r" begins a new syllable, such as in the words "arrange, arrive, barrage" and "correct." (Only one [r] is pronounced in words with adjacent "r" letters.)

Use the IPA Symbols [ɝ] or [ɚ] in Transcriptions:

1. In **all words ending** with a **consonant cluster** containing the **letter** "r." When this same cluster **ends** a middle syllable of a word, it also will contain the [ɝ] or [ɚ] sound, as in:

[ɝd] spurred, herding	[ɝgz] ergs, icebergs
[ɝm] worm, determine	[ɝst] worst, thirsty
[ɝθt] berthed, unearthed	[ɝz] burrs, hers
[ɝʒ] Persian, diversion	[ɝtʃ] church, birch
[ɝdʒ] surge, merging	[ɝtʃt] perched, searched
[ɝdʒd] urged, submerged	

2. In **all syllables** beginning with the **letters** "ur," "ir," "ear," or "er," as in "urging, irked, earnest, err."

3. In **syllables ending** in the **letters** "r" or "re." The vowel or diphthong **blends** with "r" or "re" and affects the [ɝ] quality slightly creating either two (diphthong) or three (triphthong) blended vowel sounds in one syllable. Common spellings of [ɝ] include:

"air": fair, pair	"ar": tar, disbar	"are": care, blare
"ear": ear, endear	"eer": deer, steer	"eir": their, heir
"er": her, infer	"ere": were, there	"ir": fir, astir
"ire": hire, fire	"oar": oar, boar	"oor": poor, door
"or": or, decor	"our": four, tour	"re": care, store
"ur": fur, blur	"ure": pure, endure	"urr": burr, purr

4. In words containing **doubled** "r" where the pronounced "r" ends a syllable, such as in the words "carrot, error, marriage, irrigate, terrible, worry, merry, Harry" and "scurry."

COMMON PROBLEMS

1. A common problem involves the transcription of the letter "r" into IPA symbols. Many students are uncertain of when to use [r] and when to use [ɜ˞] or [ɚ]. You must listen to the way a word is pronounced and stressed in order to make this determination accurately. If classmates speak a definite regional or subsidiary dialect, you may hear changes from the general rules given in the chart above. Medial sounds probably will give you the most difficulty. In words such as "hero" and "perish" you could hear speakers attach the letter "r" to either the first or the second syllable. Speakers of General American Speech usually **end** the **first** syllable with it, creating [ɜ˞]. However, speakers of an Eastern or Southern American dialect may **begin** the **second** syllable with it, using [r] instead. Be sure you listen to and transcribe the sounds the way each speaker says them. Avoid the temptation to transcribe them the way *you* say them.

2. The substitution of [w] for [r] is fairly common among children who are still developing their linguistic competencies. They may say "Woby saw a wed wobin" for "Roby saw a red robin." This [w-r] substitution occurs periodically among some native adult speakers and often in nonnative speakers of English. This change usually is caused by a dependence upon the lips rather than the tongue for forming the [r] sound. Both sounds require some lip rounding, but the [w] sound requires a more tense lip rounding than [r]. The [w] sound doesn't involve much tongue action but the [r] sound does. If you have this problem, relax the lips slightly and move the tip of the tongue up close to (but not touching) the upper gum ridge as [r] is said. Nonnative speakers often have some success if they curl the tongue tip up and backwards slightly in what is called a retroflex position.

In words containing [wɜ˞] in the first syllable, such as "worm, worry, worse," some speakers often encounter a reversal of the problem mentioned above, substituting [r-w]. They attempt to form either [r] or [ɜ˞] **before** they have formed the [w] in anticipation of the [ɜ˞] sound which is difficult for them to say. As a result, the tip of the tongue is "bunched" tensely near the upper front of the mouth while the lips pull into a tense rounding which results in a combination of [rɜ˞], the sound which occurs in the initial position of the word "rural." This lip and tongue tension for [r] must be released in order for a good [w] sound to be produced.

3. Another common substitution which occurs frequently among children who are learning to speak, and among nonnative speakers of English, is [l] for [r]. Later in this chapter, the [l] sound will be described and discussed. The [l-r] substitution occurs when the tip of the tongue touches the upper gum ridge, and air flows over its sides rather than down the middle of the tongue. As a result, a person may have some interesting semantic problems. For example, if the substitution were consistent throughout a speaker's vocabulary, here would be a few of the word changes that would occur:

lib/rib; lay/ray; led/red; light/right; loot/root; laughed/raft; law/raw; lobbed/robbed; loosed/roost; limb/rim; lamb/ram; lot/rot; lice/rice; lust/rust; lye/rye; lift/rift; lied/ride; laced/raced; low/row; plays/prays; flies/fries; glue/grew; clue/crew

Perhaps you can understand why an individual with this sound substitution would confuse listeners by saying the statement, "We watched the red light grow as the crews changed."

4. In previous chapters you learned that consonant clusters are difficult for people to say. Many English consonant clusters contain the letter "r." Some of the most frequent ones were indicated in the chart on "Determining the Use of [r] or [ɜ˞] in General American Speech." In all consonant clusters, the first sound must be formed completely before gliding into adjacent sounds, even though the articulators are anticipating the following sounds. For example, in [tr] the tongue tip must touch the gum ridge for [t] while the lips begin to round for [r]. As soon as air is released for [t] the tongue tip pulls down quickly, voicing begins, and the lips purse or round slightly. This sequence of actions is very rapid. If speakers are unaccustomed to making one sound in a consonant cluster, they may tend to anticipate it in advance and prepare for it instead of the sounds that precede or follow it.

When a consonant cluster begins with sounds formed near the back of the throat, such as the [k] in "crime" and [g] in "green" (which will be studied in the next chapter), the tongue pulls back quite far in preparation for these sounds. The sounds should be released quickly to eliminate excessive back-of-the-throat friction before [r] is produced. (Some nonnative speakers who have learned to trill the uvula, the small fleshy flap that hangs from the soft palate in the back of the oral cavity, must be especially careful to make a quick release or a uvular trilled "r" may result.)

5. If the [r] sound doesn't occur in a language, the sound will be difficult for speakers of that language to produce. Nonnative speakers of English may have more success in beginning with [ɝ] than with [r]. By prolonging [ɝ] for a word that begins with the letter "r" while concentrating on elevating the central part of the tongue and keeping it fairly tense, they will be able to feel the approximate location of a good [r] sound. The back sides of the tongue should be in contact with the inside surfaces of the back teeth and the back of the tongue should pull up towards the soft palate while the sound is prolonged. When the prolonged sound has a distinct r-coloring; it should be blended quickly with the vowel that follows it.

The next step is to eliminate, gradually, the prolonged [ɝ] and extend the time given to the vowel that follows. The following words contain the various English vowels and diphthongs and may be helpful for you if you need to practice initial [r] sounds. Begin by sustaining [ɝ] and then glide into the remaining portion of each of these words:

ream, read; rim, rid; Ray, race; rest, rent; ram, rant; rub, rough; rude, room; roof, rook; wrote, roast; wrong, raw; rob, rocks; round, rowdy; right, rice; Roy, royal; rural

6. One final difficulty involving the letter "r" is titled an **intrusive "r."** Some speakers, particularly from New York and New England, add [ɝ] or [r] to vowels at ends of words, or to words ending in vowels which are followed immediately by another word beginning with a vowel. This habit seems most evident in words ending in the unstressed schwa sound. You may have heard this in words such as: polka, Atlanta, naptha, area, Canada, pizza, Sylvia, Cuba, Vienna, Hawaii, Florida, saw, banana, Africa, Santa, vanilla, Alabama, Maria, tapa, drama, sofa, idea, plaza, law, Havana, jaw, Alaska, Anna, potato. It also would be obvious in combined words such as "manil**a e**nvelope," "obi**e is**," "s**aw it**," and "dat**a on**."

EXERCISES FOR PRACTICING [r]

1. Contrast the [r] and [ɝ] sounds by reading the following symbols aloud. Be careful not to prolong the [r] sound too long.

a. [r]   [ɝ]   [r ɝ r]   [r r]   [ɝ ɝ]   [ɝ ɝ r]   [r ɝ]   [r]   [ɝ]

b. [r]   [ri]   [ɝ]   [ɪɝ]   [r]   [re]   [ɝ]   [eɝ]   [r]   [ɝ]   [ræɝ]

2. Transcribe the following words into IPA symbols. Include primary and secondary stress marks. Use General American Speech as your model.

a. their _____   propose _____   dreamer _____

b. rusty _____   other _____   wretch _____

c. brother _____   crafts _____   promote _____

d. tramped _____   hurries _____   bearded _____

e. warm _____   eraser _____   braided _____

3. Translate the following IPA transcriptions into words and write them on the lines provided.

a. [brevd] _____   ['ræpɪd] _____   [sə'prim] _____

b. ['trɛʒɚ] _____   ['ɪɚətet] _____   [rɪtʃ] _____

c. ['brevɚ] _____   ['istwɚd] _____   ['rædɪʃ] _____

d. [prez] _____   ['tʃitɚ] _____   [fremz] _____

e. [træpt] _____   [ri'mɛmbɚ] _____   ['bɝmə] _____

4. Determine the number of syllables and phonemes in each of the following words. Transcribe the word and circle the correct numbers.

Word	Transcription		Syllables	Phonemes
a. barrier	[	]	1 2 3 4 5	1 2 3 4 5 6 7
b. redeemed	[	]	1 2 3 4 5	1 2 3 4 5 6 7
c. murderer	[	]	1 2 3 4 5	1 2 3 4 5 6 7
d. traced	[	]	1 2 3 4 5	1 2 3 4 5 6 7
e. wretched	[	]	1 2 3 4 5	1 2 3 4 5 6 7

5. The following words contain consonant clusters with the letter "r" in them. Determine whether the General American pronunciation should be [r] or [ɝ]/[ɚ] by saying the words aloud. If you have difficulty, look back at the comparison chart in this chapter for these two sounds.

a. **fr**eight [ ],   de**pr**ive [ ],   sea**rch** [ ],   a**rr**ow [ ]

b. ap**pr**ise [ ],   **wr**ought [ ],   end**ur**ance [ ],   **pr**actice [ ]

c. **br**ight [ ],   **str**etched [ ],   co**rps** [ ],   [wa**rt**] [ ]

d. de**scr**ibe [ ],   **shr**edded [ ],   wo**rds** [ ],   ent**r**usted [ ]

e. a**str**ide [ ],   **tr**icky [ ],   ab**r**upt [ ],   **pr**aised [ ]

6. Read the following combinations of words aloud. Avoid prolonging the [r] sounds.

a. probably reason arose; rhubarb arrived presently; arranging regular breakfasts; struggled around risks

b. arrange river crossings; decreased routine arrests; Roy's products deregulated; biracial representatives pressed

c. create responsible decrees; pressed roughly across; products reached degrees; critical roads enraged

d. stretching aroused rheumatic; wrecked arrangements expressly; pried engraved wrenches; Rob's tragic arraignment

e. rescued from arrears; retried rockets derived; already strengthened wrists; enraptured Spring rotated

7. Contrast the [w] and [r] sounds in the following word pairs by reading the words aloud and being conscious of the lip and tongue movement required for each sound.

a. weep/reap; red/wed; reading/weeding; west/rest; Wong/wrong

b. we're/rear; rude/wooed; ways/raise; rose/woes; wise/rise

c. rouse/wows; wipe/ripe; rooster/Worcester; row/woe; rang/Wang

d. rots/watts; run/won; weed/read; wing/ring; rate/wait

e. Wayne/rain; womb/room; rare/wear; raced/waste; wage/rage

8. Practice reading the following sentences aloud.

a. A straight road ran past the Arapaho reservation.

b. He grinned as he rode all the way around the race track.

c. Rusty wrote his Arabian friend about enrolling in a trade school.

d. Miss Muffet rose rather rapidly when she was frightened by a resting arachnid.

e. We tried to enroll in the enriched arithmetic class, but the roster was full.

9. Practice Paragraphs

a. Ross Trumbull sounded great when he played the trumpet in Aruba. He drew quite a strange crowd to the arena last Friday evening. We tried to get reserved tickets from the hotel three times and finally succeeded. We arrived by taxi right at eight o'clock and found a group of rowdy people at the front entrance. They had almost wrecked the front ticket office trying to get in without reservations. One distraught woman was shrieking that someone had grabbed three tickets and was running through the crowd into the arena. The police caught the crafty robber and dragged him away just as we approached the entrance with some reluctance.

b. Tracey stressed again that the trail would seem to be almost straight down from the canyon rim. The donkey ride might be slightly threatening, but if we remained seated and watched the brush along the trail, we wouldn't be frightened. I glanced at Randy Brill, who usually was making wisecracks or poking fun at everyone. His legs wrapped tightly around his donkey's mid-section. His face was red and his eyes focused on the brush. "I'll race you to the bottom," I mumbled.

c. Aunt Rita's raspberry rolls always smelled heavenly when we arrived home from school on Fridays. They would be fresh out of the oven, resting on the cooling rack, and ready to be tasted by three hungry children. Aunt Rita had trained us to race upstairs quietly, deposit books and tablets in the bedrooms, wash grimy hands and faces, then present three scrubbed, expectant faces around the dining room table. We completed the routine rapidly, always trying to pretend that we had no idea she had just made red raspberry rolls.

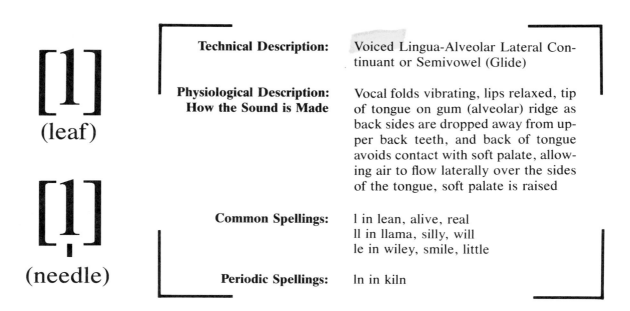

	Technical Description:	Voiced Lingua-Alveolar Lateral Continuant or Semivowel (Glide)
[l] (leaf)	**Physiological Description: How the Sound is Made**	Vocal folds vibrating, lips relaxed, tip of tongue on gum (alveolar) ridge as back sides are dropped away from upper back teeth, and back of tongue avoids contact with soft palate, allowing air to flow laterally over the sides of the tongue, soft palate is raised
[l̩] (needle)	Common Spellings:	l in lean, alive, real ll in llama, silly, will le in wiley, smile, little
	Periodic Spellings:	ln in kiln

The [l] sound is the only English sound that is emitted over the sides of the tongue (laterally). It is produced with the tongue tip in the same location on the gum ridge as [t], [d], and [n]. Two types of [l] can be produced: one with the back of the tongue held low (called a light or clear [l]) and the other, with the back of the tongue raised to the approximate position for producing [o] (called a dark [l]). The clear [l] usually appears at the beginning of a word, just before a vowel; the dark [l] appears in medial and final positions of words. Like [m] and [n], this sound may appear by itself as a separate syllable and is then referred to as a syllabic [l̩]. To distinguish a syllabic [l̩], a small dot or slash is placed below the symbol.

COMMON PROBLEMS

1. The substitution of [o] for [l], particularly in the final position of words, is a fairly common error. This occurs when an individual either doesn't hear the difference between [l] and [o], or allows the tongue tip to drop away from the gum ridge before the [l] is formed. You may hear this in words such as "tell, will, shall, still, little, battle, middle."

148

2. In the discussion of [r], we mentioned one error that is fairly common among nonnative speakers of English: the substitution of [l] for [r]. This is particularly evident among international students from the Far East. In Japanese, the [ɝ] and [ɚ] sounds don't exist and the closest Japanese equivalent sound for our English [r] is somewhere between [l] and [r]. As a result, Japanese speakers of English have great difficulty hearing any difference between "glue" and "grew" or "lice" and "rice."

If you have difficulty with these two sounds, you should be aware of these features:

PHYSIOLOGICAL CHANGES INVOLVED IN SAYING [l] AND [r]

To Say [l] Correctly:	To Say [r] Correctly:
1. The tongue tip must touch the upper gum ridge or front teeth.	1. The tongue tip must NOT touch the upper gum ridge or front teeth.
2. The flow of breath should be over the sides of the tongue.	2. The flow of breath should be down the middle of the tongue.
3. The sound will be formed near the front of the mouth.	3. The sound will be formed behind the area where [l] is formed—not as far forward.
4. The sound usually is sustained longer than [r].	4. The sound usually isn't prolonged as much as [l].
5. The lips should be lax and unrounded.	5. The lips should be slightly tense and rounded.
6. The back sides of the tongue shouldn't touch the back teeth.	6. The back sides of the tongue should press firmly against the back teeth.

3. Some people nasalize the [l] sound when they allow the soft palate to drop while [l] is being vocalized, or to remain down after a nasal sound is followed by a vowel and [l] in words such as in "meal, nail, mail." By pinching the nostrils shut while saying words which contain the [l] sound but no nasalized sounds, you may hear and feel some vibration in the nose if you are making this error. The soft palate must be raised in a manner similar to a yawn and held in that position while saying aloud words such as:

early, Lester, leaves, elevate, little, loaded, less, liberty, really, cattle, telepathy, bridle, Australia

4. Another fairly common problem is the omission of [l] in the medial position of words, such as "only, old, always, cold, already, told" or between adjacent words, the first of which ends in [l] and the second of which begins with [r], [w], or [j] (which is the initial sound in the word "yet"). The phrases "call right," "all weighed," "stool you" would be examples of phrases in which these substitutions could occur. Usually, this problem is caused when the tongue tip doesn't touch the gum ridge long enough to allow air to flow over the sides of the tongue for the [l] sound. For example, if the error occurs in the word "only," the tongue tip touches the gum ridge for [n] but the sides of the tongue remain against the upper back teeth, resulting in the production of ['oni].

5. Many people avoid making syllabic [l] sounds. Instead, they either add a vowel sound immediately before the sound, or they substitute a glottal catch (created by stopping the flow of air quickly at the opening or glottis of the larynx—much like a reversed hiccough) for it. Syllabic [l], [m], and [n] sounds are important characteristics of General American Speech. They either are separate sounds which stand alone as syllables, creating [l] in the words "little, battle, metal" or form vowel-less consonant clusters which create separate syllables such as [dl] in "needle, bundle" or [tl] in turtle."

To form the syllabic [l] correctly, keep the tongue tip on the gum ridge after forming the sound which precedes it (usually [d], [t], [n], [s], [z]) and allow the **sides** of the tongue to drop for the release of air. Final [d] and [t] sounds aren't exploded. If the tip drops even slightly, you probably will say a vowel sound before the [l], thus destroying the syllabic sound. If you substitute a glottal catch, you probably are producing the same stop which occurs between syllables in the idiomatic expression "'huh uh" which we use to replace "no" in casual conversation. If you have problems making the syllabic [l], practice saying these words slowly.

beetle, beagle, regal, needle, little, fiddle, riddle, middle, whittle, ladle, kettle, metal, nettle, petal, peddle, settle, battle, cattle, paddle, rattle, saddle, tattle, tangle, chattel, straddle, strangle, bundle, huddle, jungle, muddle, puddle, subtle, trundle, shuttle, girdle, hurtle, hurdle, curdle, Myrtle, turtle, doodle, noodle, poodle, strudel, total, yodel, modal, nautical, bottle, coddle, model, toddle, waddle

6. A child frequently has difficulty with [l] during early language development and tends to substitute [w-l] in the initial and medial positions of words. Thus, a sentence such as "I saw a little lamb lying down fast asleep" becomes "I saw a wittle wamb wying down fast asweep." (Frequently, a child also substitutes [o-l] in the final position of words. Since both [w] and [o] require considerable lip rounding, the changes appear to be fairly consistent with the [w-l] substitution from a physiological viewpoint.) A period of ear training is necessary to familiarize the individual with differences in [l] and [w] sounds. The child also must be taught to unround the lips and to hold the tongue tip against the upper gum ridge in order to allow air to flow over the sides.

7. A minor problem that is heard periodically is the pronunciation of silent "l" letters in words. This usually is due to our inconsistent rules for spelling, rather than an individual's pronunciation difficulties. In words such as "chalk, talk, half, palm, would, could, salve, salmon" the letter "l" shouldn't be pronounced.

8. Nonnative speakers of English have some difficulty with consonant clusters containing the [l] sound. They can't blend two consonants together easily. Often, consonant clusters don't occur in their native languages. When the cluster appears in the initial position of a word, the [l] always follows the consonant. When it is in the medial or final position of the word, the [l] precedes the consonant. In all clusters, the tongue tip must touch the upper gum ridge to avoid substituting [w] or [r]. If you have difficulty handling consonant clusters, the following list may be helpful in your practice sessions.

150

Common Clusters Appearing in the Initial Position of Words:

[bl]: bleed, blister, blaze, blessed, blast, blush, blurt, blue, bloat, block, blight, blouse
[fl]: flea, flip, flake, fleck, flash, fluff, flirt, flu, flush, flow, flaw, flop, fly, flower, Floyd
[gl]: glee, glib, glade, glen, gland, glove, glue, globe, glory, glottis, glide, glower
[kl]: clean, clip, claim, Clem, clam, club, clergy, clue, close, claw, clock, climb, cloud, cloister
[pl]: please, plain, plenty, plastic, plus, pleurisy, plume, plosive, plot, ply, plough, ploy
[sl]: sleep, slip, slay, sled, slant, sludge, slurr, sloop, slope, slaw, slop, slight, slouch
[spl]: spleen, split, splash, splurge, sploosh, splotch, spline

Common Clusters Appearing in the Final Position of Words:

[ld]: healed, filled, sailed, shelled, dulled, curled, cooled, pulled, rolled, hauled, dolled, dialed, howled, boiled
[lfθ]: twelfth
[lθ]: filth, health, wealth, stealth
[lʃ]: Welsh, Walsh
[lʃt]: filched, welched, squelched, mulched
[lt]: built, belt, shalt, difficult, bolt, halt, salt, vault, Walt
[lz]: eels, hills, pails, bells, pals, dulls, girls, duels, bulls, coals, hauls, isles, owls, oils

EXERCISES FOR PRACTICING [l]

1. Contrast the following sounds by saying them aloud.

a. [l]   [r]   [l]   [ɝ]   [l r l]   [ɝ l ɝ]   [l l l]   [r l r]

b. [il]   [ril]   [ɝl]   [lɝ]   [ɪl]   [le]   [li]   ['eli]   ['ili]

2. Translate the following IPA transcriptions into words and write them in the spaces provided.

a. [lidz] _____   ['ʌltɪmət] _____   ['strædl̩] _____

b. ['pristli] _____   [dɪs'tɪld] _____   ['θɪsl̩] _____

c. [ri 'lɪvd] _____   [lif] _____   ['lɛtɚ] _____

d. ['lɪtɚdʒi] _____   ['dɪmpl̩] _____   [lætʃ] _____

151

3. Write the following words in IPA symbols. Include primary and secondary accent marks. Use General American Speech as your model.

a. slithers _____   telltale _____   table _____

b. battles _____   material _____   pleasure _____

c. little _____   delayed _____   shall _____

d. elderly _____   revealed _____   missile _____

e. wrestle _____   prevail _____   listless _____

4. Read the following word pairs to contrast the [w], [r], [ɝ], [o], and [l] sounds.

a. Lido/little; wed/red; leave/weave; rear/real; we'll/we're; hold/hoed; late/rate

b. severer/several; owed/old; rotation/location; peel/peer

c. code/cold; meadow/metal; berry/belly; wheel/real; surrender/slender; Rhine/line; wrestle/Lester

d. lime/rhyme; Toto/total; fear/few; loom/room; we/Lee; relented/rerented; ear/eel

e. lip/rip; praying/playing; load/rode; tire/tile; island/Ireland; cold/code; believed/bereaved

5. Determine the number of syllables and phonemes in each of the following words. Write the transcription of each word before you make these determinations. Circle the appropriate numbers.

Word	Transcription	Syllables	Phonemes
a. Placid	[ ]	1 2 3 4 5	1 2 3 4 5 6 7 8 9
b. Embellish	[ ]	1 2 3 4 5	1 2 3 4 5 6 7 8 9
c. Abbreviates	[ ]	1 2 3 4 5	1 2 3 4 5 6 7 8 9
d. Trills	[ ]	1 2 3 4 5	1 2 3 4 5 6 7 8 9
e. Rebottled	[ ]	1 2 3 4 5	1 2 3 4 5 6 7 8 9

6. Read the following word combinations aloud as if they were part of a sentence, with normal conversational inflection patterns.

a. last allowed Carl; little lone bulldog; already left Merle; labelled all loose; held all losers

b. drill lost almost; lamps aligned while; pelted loose mail; pull less startled; silver looked all

c. official lies allowed; islands looked neutral; gentle healing let; wall built largely; general looked almost

d. riddle leaned heavily; liberty resulted while; animal lacked elaborate; ill sleep alone; Eldon tell Lefty

e. beautiful railroad labored; Lucy wouldn't smile; less alert patrol; pole applied along; vital industrial hall

7. Practice reading the following sentences aloud.

a. The Pilgrim colony kept its children busy learning their numbers and letters in a tiny school built by the laborers.

b. Next to the wall was a table covered with a neutral colored cloth and a little glass bowl that was filled with holly.

c. Our family's oil field stands all alone on land between two hills, just outside the city limits of Dallas.

d. Unless the lawyer calls to explain what she is doing, we'll consider making our wills ourselves.

e. We had a wild pool party at Leslie's colonial mansion while her relatives from Labelle, Canada looked for work.

8. Practice Paragraphs

a. When I was eleven, I learned to bowl. Soon, bowling was the love of my life. Almost daily, I would haul out my bowling bowl, cotton towel, and bowling shoes, holler to my mother that I would be back by twelve o'clock, and leave for the bowling alley that was several blocks away. I always had the feeling I could lick anyone my size at bowling—even the town bully, who looked like he had two left feet when he got on the alley. He didn't belong in my league, but he was usually loafing about the place whenever I was there. I think he was looking for a chance to put glue in the finger holes of my bowling ball!

b. Larry couldn't believe he was really leaving for Milwaukee. All year, he had planned for this day when he would hear the train whistle blow a long blast, signaling the start of his journey. Although it would take less than twelve hours, he would have to ride all night long. He was willing to sleep a little while, but he wanted to see the lights along the way too. Last year when he rode the rails to Laramie, he had learned how to live on a train. This year he had brought a large, fluffy pillow, several comic books, and a lunchbox that was filled with little surprises his stepmother had made.

c. She longed to be alone on an island, all by herself, lying in the sun and watching beautiful, fluffly clouds drifting by. Instead, she looked out of her Long Island apartment at endless yellow walls only eleven feet away from her living room window. The pleasant blue flowered wallpaper and frilly lace curtains in her living room relieved some of the dullness—but not enough. She felt shackled to the city and she yearned to wriggle out of those shackles. There was always noise (whistles, squeals of tires, sirens, yelling children)—always smells—always the wall clock reminding her to get up, leave for work, or go to sleep. Life was dull—unendingly boring.

[n] (name)	**Technical Description:**	Voiced Nasal Alveolar (or Lingua-Alveolar) Continuant or Semivowel
	Physiological Description: How the Sound is Made	Vocal folds vibrating, soft palate lowered, tongue tip firmly touches the upper gum (alveolar) ridge while sides touch the inside surfaces of the upper back teeth forcing the breath through the nose, the lips are slightly open and lax
[n̩] (button)	**Common Spellings:**	n in nose, any, tan, didn't nn in running, funny, tunnel kn in knot, knife, unknown ne in ninety, finely, dine gn in gnome, feign, campaign en in suddenly, rotten, wooden on in button, mutton, cotton pn in pneumatic, pneumonia
	Periodic Spellings:	nd in handsome gne in champagne yne in Wayne, Haynes, Payne mne in mnemonic dne in Wednesday mp in comptroller

The sounds of [n] and [m] are very similar to the ears. At times, if you're unsure which sound a speaker is saying, you may watch that person's lips to see if they are closed for the [m] sound, or opened for the [n] sound. Ventriloquists, who must always speak with the lips slightly open and not moving, learn to substitute [n] for [m] sounds in all positions of words. Our ears play tricks on us if the ventriloquists are experts.

The [n] sound is the second of three nasal sounds to be discussed in this book. It is capable of standing alone as a syllable, particularly at the ends of words such as "sudden, reason, season, button, kitten." Therefore, a syllabic [n̩] will contain a small dot below the symbol but the non-syllabic [n] will have no dot below the symbol. The syllabic sound will appear only in unstressed syllables and may appear in the middles of words such as "suddenly" and "heavenly." As mentioned in the discussion of [l], syllabic sounds are important characteristics of General American Speech.

COMMON PROBLEMS

1. Rather than producing a syllabic [n̩], many speakers of other English dialects (including "pidgin English") and nonnative speakers of English add a short vowel such as [ɪ], [ɛ], or [ə] before a final [n]. This occurs even in contracted words such as "couldn't, wouldn't, didn't, wasn't, hadn't, shouldn't, isn't" where the vowels should be omitted in the spellings as well as in the pronunciations. Thus, contracted sounds are said **incorrectly** as "couldint, wouldint, didint" and so on. The vowel sound results when the tongue is allowed to move briefly away from the gum ridge immediately before the [n] is said. No matter how brief this movement is, it will result in an additional vowel being inserted before [n].

154

If you have difficulty with syllabic sounds, imagine that a bit of glue on the end of the tongue prevents the tongue from moving away from the contact made just before the [n] is nasalized. If the sound is [t] or [d], this contact will feel exactly like a final unexploded [t] or [d] in the last word of a sentence. If it is a [z], the tongue will remain on the gum ridge for [z] and the lowered tip will be raised to make a complete blockage for the following [n], as in "isn't" and "wasn't." Practice the following words to see if you can keep your tongue from making this extra movement.

    a. shouldn't, mitten, cotton, written, lesson, button

    b. fission, sudden, wooden, hadn't, bitten, wouldn't

    c. couldn't, curtain, sadden, certain, flatten, isn't

    d. laden, maiden, didn't, pigeon, moisten, suddenly

    e. fasten, personality, wasn't, rotten, hasten, mutton

    f. redden, needn't, hasn't, certainly, Sutton, chosen

    g. batten, deaden, widen, wouldn't, leaden, mountain

2. The substitution of [m-n] may occur in words which have a prefix ending in the letter "n" if the adjacent sound's point of articulation is the lips. Thus, the lip sounds [p], [b], [f], [v] and [m] could influence the [n] in such prefixes as "un," "in," and "con." In this error, the tongue tip doesn't touch the gum ridge. Instead, the lips close, producing [m]. Pronounce the following words aloud to see if you make this change.

    a. unprepared, investment, unbowed, confined, inbred

    b. invisible, converge, inmost, unbothered, enmeshed

    c. confront, conviction, unproductive, conflagration, unmannered

    d. influential, unfettered, inviolate, convinced, infant

3. The substitution of "ng" for [n] occurs frequently when [n] is followed by either [k] or [g]. These are sounds we haven't yet discussed, since they are back-of-the-mouth sounds. The back of the tongue is allowed to touch the soft palate while [n] is being said, changing the point of articulation from the gum ridge to the soft palate. Read the following words aloud to see if you make this substitution.

a. inculcate, uncooked, inquiry, unconfirmed, ingrate

b. ingredient, ingrained, uncrushed, unqualified, unkempt

c. uncrossed, uncoated, unquotable, unkind, ingroup

d. incapacitated, incapsulate, uncomputed, unkept, ungraded

    4. Some people omit [n] from words or between words when it is followed by [m] as in "environment" and "can mobilize."

5. Individuals who have nasal congestion or adenoid problems may denasalize [n], forming a sound that is very similar to [d]. Since both sounds have their point of articulation on the gum ridge, the error is a lack of adequate nasalization rather than a change in location of articulation. People who have had their adenoids removed may continue to form the sound as they did when they couldn't use their nasal cavities. They must learn to relax the soft palate, allowing it to drop far enough to allow air to escape through the nose.

EXERCISES FOR PRACTICING [n]/[n̩]

1. Contrast [n] with the following sounds.

a. [n]   [m]   [n]   [l]   [n]   [d]   [n n]   [m m]   [n l m]   [n r n]

b. [in]   [ni]   [im]   [mi]   [nem]   [men]   [len]   [nel]   [æn]

2. Translate the following transcriptions and write the correct words on the lines provided.

a. ['nidl̩] _____   [ni] _____   ['ɛni] _____

b. [θɪn] _____   [tɛnst] _____   ['mɪdl̩] _____

c. [ɪn'stɪl] _____   ['lemən] _____   ['mɛntl̩] _____

d. [ɪn'tɛnsɪv] _____   ['sɪmbl̩] _____   [lenz] _____

3. Transcribe the following words into IPA symbols, using General American Speech as your model. Include primary and secondary stress marks.

a. lender _____   annul _____   lesson _____

b. nettles _____   Nellie _____   another _____

c. synthesis _____   nestles _____   lands _____

d. lurch _____   needy _____   inch _____

e. any _____   didn't _____   winds _____

4. Determine the number of phonemes and syllables in each of the following words after transcribing them in the spaces provided.

Word	Transcription	Syllables	Phonemes
a. tentative	[ ]	1 2 3 4 5	1 2 3 4 5 6 7 8
b. necessary	[ ]	1 2 3 4 5	1 2 3 4 5 6 7 8
c. unneeded	[ ]	1 2 3 4 5	1 2 3 4 5 6 7 8
d. tension	[ ]	1 2 3 4 5	1 2 3 4 5 6 7 8
e. managed	[ ]	1 2 3 4 5	1 2 3 4 5 6 7 8

5. Read the following word combinations aloud.

a. when nimble cannibals; nervous respondent began; brown nasty candy; naughty Dean defended; began nasal connections

b. mean new defenses; ten natural sponges; telephoned again knowing; fine narrow spinet; nine spoons standing

c. bonfire turned nippy; sinner nailed down; noose again fainted; kindly near heaven; nose began finer

d. noise hinted sudden; niece's fenced kitten; nice bean thinner; stone gnashed when; open bound noose

e. seven dandy gnomes; can't screen nasal; necessary fan burning; responses taken nightly; pneumonia meant open

6. Read the following sentences aloud, as if you were telling the ideas to someone in a daily conversation.

a. Benton ended his new relationship with Nelda when he knew he wouldn't be invited to the dance.

b. Anyone who knows another language, in addition to their native language, can act as an interpreter.

c. Tension mounted as the inquisitor gained renewed vigor at the annual banquet.

d. Ann turned again to her friend, Myrna, and inquired about the name of the founder.

e. During the open discussion, Nancy and Andy hinted they would not consider an amendment if it involved more money.

7. Practice Paragraphs

a. A dozen brown chickens fanned about the yard, looking for anything edible they could find. Inside the barn, Dan had started the morning chores by sorting lemons into neat piles of ten each, making sure no bruised or rotten ones were included. Southern California was well known for its fine lemons, thanks to the knowledge and skill of men and women like Dan and his wife. He knew their unsprayed, natural lemons always won praises in any national citrus competition and he was proud of their accomplishments. Only the sun and the chickens outside knew how early Dan began his inspections of lemons every market morning.

b. Whenever she listened to her nutrition professor's lectures, her mind would try to do mental gymnastics. Nothing meant much. He never helped her make associations with her own life—her own meals. Instead, the vitamins went into one category; the minerals, into another; the amino-acids, in another, and so on, and so on. She couldn't remember if niacin was related to zinc or to pantothenic acid. She knew the names of various dietary elements but she didn't know their relationships to one another. She kept telling herself that she *wasn't* dumb. However, on tests, the questions never made sense—and neither did her answers.

c. We longed for the grandeur of trees when we went to the university in Arizona. Instead, we had the elegance of palm fronds and straight tree trunks. When we went walking on the campus, nothing shielded our eyes from the burning sun and only the skinny shadows of cactus and palm trees even suggested genuine shade. We couldn't believe at least one gnarled tree trunk or one magnificent, sprawling limb wouldn't be found at the corner of some building. A token tree had been planted next to the student lounge, but it looked anemic compared to the walnut tree back home. It never had many leaves on it—and it never was undeniably green.

8. Dialogue for Oral Practice (requires two readers)

Youth: I remember reading about you in the local newspaper. You're the oldest living resident in Valley County, right?

Old Timer: That's right. Last February, I celebrated my ninety-first year in Valley County—right here in this old rocking chair that belonged to my Uncle Bart.

Youth: That must be a new record! In ninety-one years, you must have seen many changes around here.

Old Timer: I sure have—and can honestly say I've been against almost every one of them.

Youth: I only arrived here a little over a month ago, so I think I'm one of the newest residents of Valley County. I've got a lot to learn! You know, this place is really much drier than where I used to live. I'm wondering if we'll ever get a real rainstorm. You can tell me, does it rain at all here?

Old Timer: My young friend, there are frogs in this county, over eleven years old, that still haven't learned to swim yet!

Youth: I must remember to tell my friends that. They warned me it would be dry here, but I didn't believe them. Now I do! You know a lot about this place and its people. Do you have any advice for someone like me who is just starting a business?

Old Timer: Hmmm, well, I've always been cautious about giving any advice to strangers. I'll tell you what my older brother told me when I started my own business many years ago. He said, "If at first you don't succeed, you're running about average."

CHAPTER 13

THE BACK SOUNDS
[j] [k] [g] [ŋ] [h]

In this chapter you will learn about our final consonant sounds. They all are produced near or at the back of the throat. All of them require an elevated soft palate and most of them also require the back of the tongue to be raised quite high.

A new symbol will be introduced for the "ng" sound which will be [ŋ]. The IPA symbol [j] represents a sound which usually isn't spelled with the letter "j" in English. We use the letter "y" as in the word "yes" more often to produce the sound [j]. These will be the only IPA symbols that may be slightly confusing. The [k], [g], and [h] sounds will follow our basic English spellings.

Technical Description:	Voiced Palatal Semivowel Glide or Continuant
Physiological Description: How the Sound is Made	Vocal folds vibrating, front part of tongue lifted high towards hard palate in almost the same place as for [i] and is moving continuously to form the vowel sound following it, tip of tongue may be behind lower front teeth, edges of tongue are on inside surfaces of upper back molars, lips are parted, forming a slight smile, soft palate is raised
Common Spellings:	y in yes, yearn, lawyer i in opinion, familiar, million e in Europe, Eurasian
Periodic Spellings:	j in hallelujah, Johansson, Jung g in monsignor
Combined Sound With [u]:	u in usual, evacuate, reunite ue in imbue, cues, hue ie in view, preview eu in Eugene, euchre, eunuch ew in few, pew, mew

[j]
(you)

Students often are surprised to discover the IPA symbol [j] represents a sound that usually is written with either the letter "y" or "u" in English. They often transcribe the sound as [y] in beginning transcriptions because they still are thinking in terms of spelling. If you were from Germany, Switzerland, or a Scandinavian country, the [j] would seem quite natural to you. If you think of Johann Sebastian Bach, Carl Jung, or the term "ja" which is equal to our "yes," you will begin to see that the [j] sound often is spelled as "j" in other languages.

The [j] sound is an extremely flexible sound and doesn't belong in only the front, middle, or back categories of sounds. Because of its continuous movement, it is similar to the diphthongs which will be studied in the next chapter. Although it has open, vowel-like qualities, it is classified here as a consonant—even when it blends with a sound such as [u] in the word "few." Some books view [j] as a vowel and classify [ju] as a diphthong.

This sound begins in a position used for [i] and immediately begins gliding to the position of the sound which follows it. It won't appear as the final sound in English words and will always be followed by a vowel or diphthong.

COMMON PROBLEMS

1. We have mentioned the initial confusion of the letter "y" for the IPA symbol [j] by American students. For the purposes of this class, no [y] will be used. Thus, you can remember any transcription will be wrong if it contains a "y."

2. Some students are unsure whether they should pronounce a [j] in medial positions of all words with spellings such as "ue, eu, ew, uc, eau, u." Some broadcasting majors, for example, wonder if they should pronounce "Tuesday" and "news" with a [j]. A general rule (which has many exceptions) states that [j] will be used after the consonant sounds [k, g, b, p, f, v, h, m] in conjunction with the above spellings. In General American Speech, when a choice may be made between either [u] or [ju], the [j] is NOT used. Using this general pronunciation rule, the following words would be pronounced:

Without a [j]:	•	**With a [j]:**
dues, drew, do, duel, duped	•	beauty, bugle, rebuke, abuse
jewel, Jew, June, juice, jute	•	few, refuel, fumigate, future
loose, gloom, luminous, loop	•	cute, cumulative, coupon, cue
new, nude, nuclear, news, noon	•	huge, human, hue, Hugh, humid
rude, roof, rouge, root, rules	•	amused, music, mucous, mute
sue, suit, soon, soup, sewer	•	impugn, puberty, pure, pews
tune, tooth, two, tomb, tour	•	view, reviewer, preview
wooed, wound, womb	•	regulate, legume, regular
zoo, zoom, Zeus		
choose, chew		
shoe, sure, shoot, assured		
who, whom, whose, hoosier		

3. Nonnative students who are unaccustomed to using the letter "y" for the [j] sound make just the opposite error in **pronunciation**. They pronounce every word or syllable beginning with "j" as [j], following the pronunciation rules of their native languages. Actors and actresses who must portray a Scandinavian person speaking English will try to incorporate this change as an important characteristic of their stage dialects. Thus, "Jingle Bells" becomes "Yingle Bells." You might compare this with the common [dʒ-j] substitution made by Spanish speaking students in words such as "yesterday, Yule, yeast" and their reverse substitution of [j-dʒ] in words such as "judge, juice, German."

EXERCISES FOR PRACTICING [j]

1. Contrast the [j] sound with the following sounds by reading these transcriptions aloud.

a. [j]   [dʒ]   [j]   [ɪ]   [j ɪ ɪ j]   [dʒ ɪ j dʒ]   [j]   [dʒ]

b. [ji]   [je]   [jæ]   [jɪ]   [eji]   [ijɪ]   [jɪpt]   [jild]

2. Translate the following IPA symbols into words and write them on the spaces provided.

a. [jɛt] _____   ['mejɚ] _____   [jild] _____

b. ['dʒiniəs] _____   [jɛld] _____   ['spænjl̩] _____

c. [jæm] _____   ['bɪljən] _____   ['jʌkə] _____

d. ['jʌngɚ] _____   ['dænjl̩] _____   ['dʒiniəl] _____

e. ['ʌnjən] _____   [jɛn] _____   [jɛs] _____

3. Transcribe the following words into IPA symbols, using General American Speech as your model for their pronunciation. Write your answers on the blanks provided.

a. yearning _____   companion _____   senior _____

b. vineyard _____   yearly _____   million _____

c. younger _____   pavilion _____   Yale _____

d. brilliant _____   Spaniard _____   bunion _____

e. valiant _____   civilian _____   yea _____

4. Read the following combinations of words aloud.

a. Tuesday's yacht interview; beyond new views; familiar retinue uniform; student opinion review

b. unique onion stew; yesterday's noon news; using valiant crews; useless yarn residue

161

c. few yellow onions; yearly duty utilized; useful vineyard companions; your yapping spaniel

d. genius yelled unity; few curfews yield; youthful unicorn yanked; units you interviewed

e. beautiful centrifuge used; huge senior medallion; future yucca volume; units induced arguments

5. Practice reading the following sentences aloud, using a conversational mode of delivery.

a. Daniel, who was born in York, England, uses a leather lanyard as a yoke on his mules.

b. Europe expressed its gratitude in a eulogy to millions of military personnel, including Yankee soldiers, who endured the D-Day invasions.

c. A genial duke tried to usurp the power of a popular, young companion of your granddaughter.

d. The yak was reviewed by a Humane Society public opinion poll and was found to be useful, humorous, and genial.

e. "As usual, my mother is playing cupid," he yelled to the yeoman on his yacht, "and I'm not amused by her newest inducements."

6. Practice Paragraphs

a. Whenever Hugh completed a unit of work on his computer, he paused to do some yoga exercises. He refused to yield to the temptation to do just a few more pages in order to increase his daily computing volume. He knew he could reduce his future fatigue by instituting this practice. His employer had her own opinion about the usefulness of yoga, saying she thought he might be abusing his responsibilities. Hugh didn't yield to her futile criticisms. "I refuse to become a puny computer genius who never moves from his station," he said. "Stiff necks are not amusing, tired eyes are confusing, and I have no yearning to be reduced to a robot."

b. Yolanda Ying's early youth in a commune on the Yangtze River had made her realize how important farming was to society. Her parents moved to Yugoslavia to begin a grape vineyard when she was ten. Suddenly, her view of the world matured. She was confused because no one spoke the Chinese language. The Yings used their puny life savings to buy their future farm in a rocky canyon near Split. They used some land to grow green onions which they traded with neighbors for yellow squash, cherries, grains and other useful items. In two years, their vineyard yielded enough fruit to remove them from the destitute category. Then Yolanda began to enjoy her Yugoslavian home and companions.

c. Yesterday, Lillian, my genial Yiddish-speaking neighbor became so anxious for her mail to arrive that she yelled to her young son, "Sit by the box already. Watch the mailman until he comes." Since neither she nor her younger sister in Brooklyn had telephones, they used the daily mail to carry on a running feud. The feud was about whether they should use an old billiard hall, which they had inherited jointly from an uncle, as rental property for an amusement arcade or a union hall. I had become familiar with all of Lillian's arguments supporting its use as a union hall and found them quite amusing.

162

Technical Description:	Voiceless Velar (or Linguavelar) Stop Plosive, Cognate of [g]
Physiological Description: How the Sound is Made	Vocal folds not vibrating, upper back portion of tongue presses against soft palate (velum) and holds back air while building up pressure for its release with noticeable aspiration, soft palate is raised, lower jaw drops slightly and lips are lax, tongue tip behind lower front teeth and sides are touching inside surfaces of upper back teeth
Common Spellings:	k in kept, akin, rank c in cane, because, disc ck in tacking, clock, black cc in accuse, hiccough, occur ke in cake, flake, awoke que in oblique, plaque, opaque qu in quiet, quick, liquid x in boxwood, foxes, ox, hoax lk in chalked, talking, walk ch in charisma, chelate, echo
Periodic Spellings:	kh in Khartoum, khan, khaki che in ache cque in lacquered, Tocqueville q in Qantas, Qatar cch in saccharide, saccharin

[k]
(kick)

Technical Description:	Voiced Velar (or Linguavelar) Stop Plosive, Cognate of [k]
Physiological Description: How the Sound is Made	Vocal folds vibrating, upper back portion of tongue presses against soft palate (velum) and holds back air while building up pressure for its release with less aspiration than for (k), soft palate is raised, lower jaw drops slightly and lips are lax, tongue tip behind lower front teeth and sides are touching inside surfaces of upper back teeth
Common Spellings:	g in guess, again, tag gg in mugging, sagging, egg gh in ghastly, ghetto, aghast gu in guess, guide, guard x in exam, exist, exhaust gue in brogue, prologue, vague

[g]
(gum)

You can see, from the many spellings of these cognates that [k] and [g] aren't easily identifiable in words by consistent rules of spelling. The letter "x" is a challenge in transcriptions, since it may represent either of these sounds.

Both [k] and [g] are stops rather than fricatives. Often, careless speakers treat them as fricatives by not allowing the back of the tongue to make firm contact with the soft palate. This becomes particularly evident when the sound is in the medial position of words such as "raking" or "dragging." Remember, stop plosives require a complete stoppage of the breath. Fricatives, on the other hand, creative friction as air slides through a small opening without complete closure or stoppage.

COMMON PROBLEMS:

1. Some speakers make little or no distinction between [k] and [g]. They may substitute [k-g] or [g-k]. Nonnative students often confuse these sounds. Many of these people eliminate the voicing for [g] in the final position of words. When [g] appears at the end of a word, a solid (but not always exploded) contact must be made between the tongue and soft palate. Some people substitute [g-k], usually in the medial position of words. In practice sessions, try to sustain vowels when they occur before the [g] in medial or final positions of words. You may be able to feel and hear the difference between the voiced [g] and unvoiced [k] sounds better by doing this. If you have problems substituting [g-k] or [k-g], contrast these sounds as you read the following words aloud:

a. **INITIAL**: Cal/gal; cool/ghoul; cord/gourd; code/goad; cod/god; curd/gird

b. **MEDIAL**: shacks/shags; wicks/wigs; Chuck's/chugs; tacking/tagging; tocks/togs; tricker/trigger; fox/fogs

c. **FINAL**: knack/nag; sack/sag; black/Blagg; crack/crag; tuck/tug; leak/league

2. Consonant clusters containing [k] and [g] give some speakers problems, particularly when the adjacent sound is produced near the front of the mouth. For example, some common consonant clusters are: [gl] in "gland, glide"; [kl] in "close, class"; [gr] in "great, green"; and [sk] in "scratch, scream."

CONSONANT CLUSTERS INVOLVING [k] AND [g]

A. ax/axed/axes; act/acted/acts; ask/asked/asks; pact/packs; pack/packed/packs; sex/sect/sexes/sects

B. track/tracked/tracks; truck/trucked/trucks; trick/tricked/tricks; duck/ducked/ducks; duct/ducted/ducts

C. risk/risked/risks; kick/kicked/kicks; desk/desks; mask/masked/masks; bask/basks/basked; fix/fixed; Fisk/Fisks;

D. task/tasks, tax/taxed; flex/flexed; risk/risks; disk/disks; neck/necks/next; tusk/tusks; Borg/Borgs

E. six/sixth/sixtieth/sixteenth; desk/desks; frisk/frisks/frisked; mix/mixed; flick/flicked/flicks

F. plan/bland/bran; glad/gland/grand; green/glean; clean/claim; grin/grown; clear/Greer; Clyde/glide

G. close/grows/glows/crows; scare/score/skirt/square; grace/grass/group/grope; skate/school/skill/scald

---

164

In the final position are: [sk] in "task, desk"; [skt] in "husked, frisked"; [sks] in "masks, whisks"; [kts] in "pacts, sects"; and [ɚgz] in "icebergs," and [ɝgz] in "ergs." Probably the most frequently mispronounced clusters appear in the final positions of words. If you have difficulty with consonant clusters, practice the words aloud in the chart on "Consonant Clusters Involving [k] and [g]" slowly until you can hear and feel all of the sounds being produced.

3. Some speakers develop an exaggerated or pedantic pronunciation when they try to explode every plosive sound with equal force. Frequently, two plosives will occur side by side, either in a word or in adjacent words in a phrase. When this happens, the usual rule is to hold on to the first plosive while gliding into the second one, and then explode the second plosive in a normal manner. Thus, whenever [p], [b], [t], [d], [k], or [g] appear adjacent to one another, you will have only one sound explosion—not two. Here are some words and phrases for you to practice if you have this problem. Read them slowly at first, then speed up your rate of speaking.

WORDS AND PHRASES CONTAINING TWO ADJACENT STOPS/PLOSIVES

A. sagged, rigged, dragged; rocked, packed, licked; pricked, flicked, knocked; tagged, flagged, pegged

B. subgum, acting, octave, chalkboard, octopus, brickbat, backboard, legbend, back-breaking, bagboy

C. cup came, rug cost, lid crossed, hug too, sick girl, that kind, pick both, cab could, flag cost

D. take care, dig twice, picked by, slapped Corry, taxed Brenda, built gas, duck built; stick to

E. stick tight, big glass, taste good, missed carrying, kick grew, packed groceries, Herb growled

---

4. Because of their formation against the soft palate, very close to the nasal passages, some people nasalize [k] and [g]. Usually, they don't raise the backs of their tongues high enough. Instead, they relax or drop their soft palates away from a complete closure of the nasal passages to make the tongue and soft palate contact. This habit allows air to escape through the nose while [k] and [g] are said. If you have this difficulty, practice yawning and at the end of the yawn raise the back of the tongue firmly to the soft palate while it is still elevated. As you do so, form either the [k] or [g] and then say a vowel immediately after the sound. When you can feel solid contact being made, hold your nostrils shut and practice saying non-nasal words aloud. You should feel no vibration in the nose and no air should escape through the nose. The following words may be used for this practice.

WORDS WHICH CONTAIN [k] AND [g] BUT NO NASAL SOUNDS

[k] [g] in initial positon:
    A. key/geese; kick/giddy; cake/gate; kept/guess
    B. capped/gap; cup/guppy; curds/girdle; cool/goulash
    C. cook/good; code/ghost; cost/gauze; coddle/got
    D. kite/guide; cow/gouge; coy/Goyer

[k] [g] in medial position:
    A. beaker/beguile; biscuit/biggest; takes/plagues
    B. Becker/begger; stacked/baggage; lucky/luggage
    C. lurked/burger; spooky/cougar; cookie/sugar
    D. poked/ogre; talked/logger; rocked/jogger; hiked/tiger

[k] [g] in final position:
    A. seek/league; sick/kick; take/vague; check/leg
    B. tack/tag; duck/Doug; irk/erg; Luke; look; luck
    C. oak/vogue; hawk/dog; clock/hog; Ike

---

5. Since the letter "x" is sometimes pronounced as [ks] and sometimes as [gz], it becomes confusing for some speakers to pronounce correctly. A generalization exists for pronouncing "x" correctly. It is shown below in chart form.

DETERMINING THE PRONUNCIATION OF THE LETTER "X"

In most words containing the letter "x," it will be pronounced as:

[ks] when it is
    A. In the final position as in: hex, fix, tax, sex, Tex, fox, vex, lax, box, wax, flux, tux, ox, ax, fix, lox, six
    B. Followed by a consonant sound as in: expect, except, expand, extend, exclude, extern, extra, expense, expose, extract, expound, extrinsic, extravagant, axle, axman
    C. In a word in which the accent or stress is placed on a vowel **other** than the one immediately **following** the "x" as in: exit, execute, exedra, exhibition, exercise, exodus, exorcism, luxury, anxious, axiom, taxidermy, taxi, oxalate, oxygen

[gz] when it is
    In a word in which the primary stress is placed on the vowel following the "x" as in: examination, exert, exacting, exhaust, exempt, example, anxiety, exonerate, executive, exhibited, exasperation, exhume, exorbitant, exotic, existence, luxurious

    (exceptions: taxation, taxonomy, oxalic)

EXERCISES FOR PRACTICING [k] AND [g]

1. Contrast the two sounds by reading the following aloud:

a. [k]   [g]   [k k]   [g]   [k g g]   [k g k g k]   [g g k k]

b. [ik]   [ki]   [ek]   [ke]   [æg]   [gæg]   ['ikæg]   ['kæki]

2. Translate the following IPA transcriptions into words and write them in the spaces provided.

a. [kæpt] _____   [tik] _____   ['lıkwıd] _____

b. [steks] _____   [lækt] _____   [kid] _____

c. [spiks] _____   [dıgz] _____   [gred] _____

d. [klinz] _____   ['dikæl] _____   ['græsız] _____

e. [skwild] _____   [wılz] _____   [lægd] _____

3. Transcribe the following words into IPA symbols, using General American Speech as your model. Include accent marks.

a. thrill _____   Welch _____   chicken _____

b. kneels _____   endless _____   castle _____

c. indelible _____   liquor _____   kelp _____

d. sickness _____   pleasure _____   really _____

e. metal _____   clear _____   eligible _____

4. Read the following word combinations aloud as if they were part of a regular conversation.

a. keep looking back; sick chorus because; snug goose began; morgue got engulfed; clown took blocked

b. comic required clues; wicked captain like; dug good engravings; gauze disguised rig; mistook cracked kit

c. regulate goiter plague; Hague tiger growled; Turk caught looking; attacking cosmic characters; boxed sick cod

d. Klondike booked across; take blackened calf; quack inquired quietly; regulated ghost fatigue; lug single grain

e. misguided gull's egg; iceberg ground again; call boxed cork; stork wrecked courtly; forget goat tangled

5. Read the following sentences aloud. Be sure to distinguish [k] from [g] sounds.

a. Our guide took a shortcut through quite a haggard-looking section of the ghetto.

b. A copper bucket filled with gold glowed on the carefully lacquered dugout deck next to the canoe.

c. Kurt liked Connie's gauze-like gown because it glided lazily across the carpet.

d. Our clean dog dragged a dark green bag filled with garbage back to our cottage.

e. When we got closer to the group, we could see it was struggling with a water-soaked, checkered cloth.

6. Practice Paragraphs

a. Our custom cake-maker talked about resigning six weeks before he left. We were lucky because he could have cancelled his contract any time after his sixtieth birthday. We had grown accustomed to his quiet, kindly manners. He worked constantly on new techniques for baking cakes, coloring frostings, and making exotic designs. He could make the best dark German chocolate cake this country has ever known, and his broiled coconut caramel frosting was an exquisite finishing touch. When he left, he took his baker's cap to keep as a constant reminder of twenty-six years of continuous quality baking at the Monarch Bakery.

b. From her gate she looked out on a picturesque landscape of green grass, gigantic trees, and a magnificent flower garden with acres of multi-colored blossoms. She was grateful that her country neighbors were connoisseurs of color as they grew their gladiolas to sell at the market. She never had to cultivate the ground, brave the grasshoppers, or gather the blossoms—but she felt like she was queen of the country when those flowers began to blossom. The golds, pinks, crimsons, purples and yellows could lift her spirit higher than a kite and keep it there for weeks.

c. "Back in Gunnison, Colorado," he would crow to his new group of friends, "We knew what cold water was! The water came right out of the mountains, down Taylor River. My friends from Crested Butte never could take warm water—or even cool water to swim in. They got accustomed to swimming while chunks of ice still were coming down from the dam. We would climb up on a rock, back up a couple of paces, run and jump into the water. Each time we came up for air, we could feel the color coming back into our necks and faces—and we felt good again. If we didn't tingle, we figured we weren't exercising."

d. Several of Great Britain's literary figures gathered together for an evening of vigorous conversation and general discussion. Someone asked the question, "If you were stranded on a desert island, what one book would you choose to have?" One writer chose the complete works of Shakespeare and another, the Bible. When it came G.K. Chesterton's time to respond, the portly author quipped, "I would choose *Thomas's Guide to Practical Shipbuilding*."

168

Technical Description:	Voiced Velar (or Linguavelar) Nasal Continuant or Semivowel
Physiological Description: How the Sound is Made	Vocal folds vibrating, lips open, upper back surface of tongue firmly pressed against soft palate (velum) while sides are against the inside surfaces of the back molars, soft palate is relaxed or lowered allowing all air to escape through the nasal passages, tongue tip is behind lower front teeth
Common Spellings:	ng in wing, spring, dealing n in bank, think, sphinx, anchor
Periodic Spellings:	nd in handkerchief ngue in meringue, tongue

(ring)

The IPA symbol [ŋ] might be compared, figuratively, to a mermaid. It has the head and torso of the [n] phoneme but the tail of the [g] phoneme. Indeed, the tail even looks a little like a fishhook! The [ŋ] sound appears only in the medial and final positions of English words. The sound isn't pronounced "ing" since that pronunciation contains the vowel sound [ɪ]. It is the same sound you can create by humming with your lips **open**, while the **back** of your tongue touches the soft palate and the front of your tongue remains near the lower front teeth. In transcribing "sing" you would add an [ɪ] before [ŋ] to create the ending sound and in transcribing "rang" you would add an [æ].

In some languages, including several of the Far Eastern languages, [ŋ] can appear in the initial position of words. In fact, "Ng" is a surname in parts of the Orient. We would pronounce this name "ing." In Vietnamese, this sound is found frequently in place names.

The [ŋ] sound is a new sound—not simply a combination of [n] and [g]. Say these two sounds in close succession and you will discover the tip of the tongue goes to the upper gum ridge for [n] and drops for [g]. However, for the [ŋ] sound, the tongue tip **doesn't** touch the gum ridge. Instead, the point of articulation is the **back** of your tongue and the soft palate. Furthermore, [ŋ] doesn't contain the explosion or stop that you hear for [g]. As a continuant, it can be prolonged indefinitely. A word such as "singing" is pronounced as ['sɪŋɪŋ] and not ['sɪŋgɪŋg].

COMMON PROBLEMS

1. One of the most common articulation errors made in all areas of North America is the substitution of [n-ŋ] in the final position of words ending in "ing." In practically all cases, this habit isn't caused by one's inability to hear the difference between the two sounds. Neither is it due to a physiological abnormality. To put it bluntly, it is caused by tongue laziness which becomes so well habituated that the speakers don't realize their speech is sloppy or inaccurate—or don't care. The same people who criticize or belittle other dialects, foreign or domestic, assume they speak "good English" even as they substitute [n-ŋ].

Actually, a fairly practical reason exists for this [n-ŋ] substitution. Speakers take the path of least resistance in producing a phoneme that resembles [ŋ], is easier to say, and generally is understood by listeners. Since most of our consonant sounds are produced in the middle or front of the mouth where [n] is formed, rather than in the back where [ŋ] is formed, the [n] sound is easier to say quickly. The tongue usually is in position for the front [n] sound and many people simply don't use the extra effort needed to raise the back of the tongue for [ŋ]. If a "lazy tongue" is an appropriate reference in diction, this would be one time we could use that reference.

Actors and actresses who play stereotyped roles of "hillbillys," "southern white trash," or "lazy hayseeds" often use the [n-ŋ] substitution to attain their dialects. Many people seem to associate this substitution with casual or informal speaking and perceive the placement of [ŋ] at the ends of words as a formal form of speaking. In reality, they have become accustomed to their own manner of speaking and feel uncomfortable when they must form the sound correctly.

Most users of this substandard substitution are convinced that they can switch to the "proper" way of saying the sound in formal conversations when they *have* to speak correctly. It has been our experience that most of them cannot. Unless your class is very unusual, you will hear this substitution in several of your classmates—even during practiced readings. If you suspect you may make this substitution, practice reading lists of words ending in "ing." Hold onto the final sound in each word until you are sure your tongue and soft palate closure is firm. As you become accustomed to using some of the muscles you haven't used enough, you will be able to say the sound quickly, at the right time, thus, eliminating the excessive, artificial prolongation of the sound. The following words may be useful in your practice.

WORDS CONTAINING THE SUFFIX "ING" OR [ɪŋ]

With Front Vowels:

a. seeing, seating, being, keeping, weeding, peaking
b. ticking, fixing, kicking, ripping, whipping, winning
c. baking, faking, making, breaking, skating, raining
d. decking, getting, checking, lending, tenting, wedding
e. packing, stacking, banning, tanning, mashing, cashing

With Medial Vowels:

a. ducking, dusting, cussing, plucking, rusting, cunning
b. working, flirting, occuring, burning, nursing, purring

With Back Vowels:

a. cooling, chewing, doing, stewing, losing, choosing
b. looking, bushing, pushing, booking, pudding, hooking
c. rowing, knowing, flowing, growing, showing, snowing
d. crawling, thawing, drawing, sawing, falling, calling

With Diphthongs:

a. typing, biting, finding, lying, mining, siding
b. bowing, vowing, doubting, mounting, counting, crowding
c. boiling, annoying, destroying, joining, pointing, oiling

170

Another [n-ŋ] substitution occurs most often in the final consonant cluster [ŋkθ] of the words "strength," and "length." Since this cluster requires three distinct tongue movements, most people find it easier to work on linking sounds in progression, rather than trying to say them all at one time. Begin by connecting the vowel [ɛ] with [ŋ]. Next, blend these two sounds with [k] as in the word "Schenk." When you can do this easily, move the tongue tip quickly to the front teeth to blend the next sound, the voiceless [θ], *without* exploding the [k]. Be sure, however, that the back of your tongue presses long enough against the soft palate to form the soft [k].

2. Some people add [g] after [ŋ] in the medial and final portions of words and between words when [ŋ] is followed by a vowel or diphthong, as in "hanging," "singer," and "Long Island." Often, this habit is learned from parents, grandparents, or close neighborhood friends who speak another language where the [g] usually follows [ŋ]. The sound frequently is associated with ethnic neighborhoods in New York City and other large Eastern United States cities.

However, some of the problem is due to the unpredictable influence of English spelling on pronunciation. For example, look at the root words below and determine why one group requires the addition of [g] and the other doesn't.

WORDS NOT REQUIRING [g]			WORDS REQUIRING [g]		
Root Word	Add "ing" to Root	Add "er" to Root	Root Word	Add "ing" to Root	Add "er" to Root
sing	singing	singer	strong		stronger
bring	bringing	bringer	young		younger
spring	springing	springer	linger	lingering	lingerer
fling	flinging	flinger	finger	fingering	fingerer
sting	stinging	stinger	angle	angling	angler
hang	hanging	hanger	hunger	hungering	hungerer
clang	clanging	clanger	long	(longing)	longer

Do you see any rational reason for this change? First, the words **not** requiring [g] all are one-syllable root **verbs** which end in [ŋ]. When a suffix (including "s" or "ed") is added to them, they keep their original [ŋ] sound. One-syllable **adjectives**, on the other hand, contain [ŋ] in the root word but add a [g] sound when most suffixes (including "est") are added. (Did you notice that "long" can be a verb or an adjective? When "er" is added, it appears to defy the generalization. However, if you look closely, you'll find the word "longer" as a verb isn't common. If it were, we would probably follow the rule of keeping [ŋ] without the [g]. This would complicate pronunciations by giving us two different pronunciations!) The verbs, on the other hand, are **two** syllable words in which [ŋ] appears in the **middle** of the words—not at the end.

Can we simplify the procedure for determining when [g] is added? These general rules may help:

a. When a word or root ends in "ng," "ngue," "nk," or "nc": USE [ŋ] or [ŋk], as in "thing, tongue, wink, lung, rung, zinc, think, sink, sing, wring, hang."

b. When a suffix (such as "er," "ing," "ly," "ish") is added to a word or root ending in "ng," in **most** cases: USE [ŋ], as in "spring" or "king." (Exceptions will involve comparative and superlative degrees of some adjectives, such as "long" and "young.")

c. When "ng" appears at the end of a stressed syllable in a polysyllabic word or root, in **most** cases: USE [ŋg], as in "jungle, mango, tangle, anger, finger, tango, ingot, single."

If you consistently add [g] to [ŋ] practice the following words and phrases to be sure you can blend from [ŋ] to the following vowel without raising the back of the tongue to make a **second** contact with the soft palate for [g]. None of the following require an added [g].

a. singing, ganging, bringing, clanging, hanging, ringing, stringing, banging, flinging, thronging, wringing, stinging, longing, belonging, springing, haranguing

b. wringer, swinger, singer, hanger, slinger, stinger

c. bring us, hang out, string up, sing after, ring around, fling at, wing out, sting each, strong around, young of, evening off, swing about, ring evenly, among all

3. Speakers who had their adenoids recently removed, or now have nasal obstructions, may substitute a sound that resembles [g] for [ŋ]. It is the same sound most people make when they have colds and extreme nasal congestion. The breath is forced out of the mouth rather than through the nose. The result becomes an attempted non-nasal [ŋ]. The soft palate must be dropped enough to allow air to escape through the nasal passages. If you have this problem, contrast the sounds in word pairs such as: fog/Fong, rig/ring, juggle/jungle, sprig/spring, jiggle/jingle, hug/hung, tag/tang, log/long.

EXERCISES FOR PRACTICING [ŋ]

1. Contrast [n] and [ŋ] in the following transcriptions by reading them aloud.

a. [n] [ŋ] [n ŋ n] [ŋ ŋ] [n ŋ ŋ n] [ŋ] [n] [ŋ]

b. [iŋ] [ni] ['eŋi] [æŋ] [ɪŋ] [ɪŋ] [næ] [niŋ] [nɪŋ]

2. Translate the following IPA transcriptions into words and write them in the spaces provided.

a. [slæŋ] _____ [θɪŋk] _____ ['tekɪŋ] _____

b. [drɪŋks] _____ [spræŋ] _____ ['itɪŋ] _____

c. ['kætʃɪŋ] _____   ['sprɪŋkl̩] _____   [rʌŋ] _____

d. ['ɪŋglənd] _____   [lɪŋkt] _____   ['tɪtʃɪŋ] _____

e. ['blæŋkɪt] _____   ['dʒæŋgl̩] _____   ['tizɪŋ] _____

3. Using General American Speech as your model, transcribe the following words into IPA symbols. Include accent marks.

a. Fleming _____   canker _____   learning _____

b. hangar _____   bringing _____   having _____

c. ranks _____   gaining _____   strength _____

d. linger _____   lengthen _____   banged _____

e. hungry _____   entering _____   weighing _____

4. Determine the number of syllables and phonemes in each of the following words. Transcribe the words and circle the correct numbers.

Word	Transcription	Syllables	Phonemes
a. entering	[ ]	1 2 3 4 5	1 2 3 4 5 6 7 8 +
b. crinkles	[ ]	1 2 3 4 5	1 2 3 4 5 6 7 8 +
c. angle	[ ]	1 2 3 4 5	1 2 3 4 5 6 7 8 +
d. malingers	[ ]	1 2 3 4 5	1 2 3 4 5 6 7 8 +
e. swinging	[ ]	1 2 3 4 5	1 2 3 4 5 6 7 8 +

5. Read the following combinations of words aloud.

a. sing/single/singer/singing/sink; rang/wrangle/rank/wrangler/ranking/range/ranging; hang/hanger/hanging

b. young/younger/youngest; strong/stronger/strongest/strongly; long/longer/longest/longing

c. gunslinger/gunslinging; slink/slinkier/slinkiest/slinker; ring/ringer/ringing/rang/rung

d. Congo/monkey; penguin/flunking; uncle/mingled; Bangor/conquer; language/sinking; drink/dangled

e. frank/anger; larynx/lingered; function/bankrupt; triangle/twinkled; banker/bungled; conquer/Rangoon

6. Read the following sentences aloud, being sure to use a conversational inflection as you do so. Try to maintain a smooth, fluent pace.

a. An English youngster in dungarees was asking the banker about buying his drawings.

b. She belonged to a strong congressional committee which was handling inquiries of anguished, retired mining personnel.

c. Ingrid was laughing at the mockingbird which was singing mangled songs all evening.

d. Throngs of single women, chanting "Drinking brings us grief," were picketing the wrong building.

e. Uncle Gordon plunked a shining nickle on the table, winked at me, and drank his steaming coffee.

7. Practice Paragraphs

a. Georgia was willing to play ping pong if I would go swimming with her afterwards. Harriet was watching us from the porch swing as we began, but found the game boring. She began singing a song—something about a skunk and a monkey getting into an argument. She paused to drink her lemonade and then began again, "The monkey banged his pudding cup against the trunk where the skunk lived. 'You are jiggling my ceiling,' said the skunk. 'If you think I am a mink, then you'd better think again or I'll give you something quaint to clear your mind.' " Georgia started giggling while swinging at the ping pong ball—and missed.

b. As a youngster, I admired the strength of Lincoln. He represented Yankee understanding and everlasting patience which I longed to have. I visualized him as an undistinguished looking man with gangling arms and legs, but with eyes that hungered for something more than what he already knew. When he failed, he was willing to try again. I was trying to learn, somewhat grudgingly, that single, simple lesson: how to return to tasks after failing them. Nothing made me work harder during my youth than thinking about those strong, lingering eyes of Abraham Lincoln.

c. The old monk stopped to drink from the clear, refreshing spring which was gushing out of the mountain. He was walking again, after months of illness, and nothing escaped his twinkling eyes. A hummingbird seemed anchored on motionless wings as it stuck its beak and tiny tongue into a single, crimsom blossom hanging over the spring. The monk lifted a finger toward the bird and said, "Don't let me interrupt you from your feeding, little one. I'm stopping for a moment. Evening is coming so I must be moving on. My strength is gaining and you have helped renew my faith."

d. On his long trip back to Washington from Shanghai, China, Frank spent one day in Bangkok, Thailand. That evening, just as the sun sank behind the palm trees, he was riding in a water taxi past throngs of people shopping in outdoor markets and spotted a long piece of yellow, crinkled silk hanging from a banyan tree. It was partially hidden among cotton blankets, silk shirts, and strings of tinkling bronze bells. He asked his driver to stop under a mango tree. He scrambled up the embankment where a young, smiling, languid looking girl was sitting. She asked him in fairly good English if she could help him. He pointed to the silk, saying, "I'm thinking about buying that piece of silk." Obligingly, she scrambled up the tree, gently lifted the golden fabric from the banyan tree limb, and brought it back for Frank's closer inspection.

174

Technical Description:	Voiceless Glottal Fricative Continuant
Physiological Description: **How the Sound is Made**	Vocal folds not vibrating, air flows through the glottis of the larynx creating friction without creating fold vibration or voicing, soft palate is raised forcing the stream of air out through the mouth, the lips and tongue are relaxed in a neutral position
Common Spellings:	h in hold, behave, Ohio j in Jose, jojoba, Navajo wh in whom, whole, whose

(home)

The last consonant sound of [h] is another mercurial sound, since it has no distinctive tongue or lip pattern. Like the [j] sound studied at the beginning of this chapter, [h] moves quickly into the vowel sound which follows it. It doesn't occur in the final position in English. This sound gives few people any difficulty, since it resembles the sound of anything that is whispered. The vocal folds are held fairly close together and air passes through them, creating friction without voicing.

If you whisper the vowel sounds [e] [i] [o] [ɪ] [æ] and then [h], you will discover the fricative quality remains the same. However, the lips and tongue change positions from [h] for each of the whispered vowels. Even though you are whispering, your vocal folds are working. This is one reason why a doctor tells patients not to talk or **whisper** when they have laryngitis. Inflamed vocal folds have no rest when you whisper.

COMMON PROBLEMS:

1. Some speakers who come from families which speak a language such as Spanish, Japanese or Hebrew at home, or nonnative speakers of English may confuse the [h] sound with another sound we won't be studying in this class (whose IPA symbol looks like an ''x''). That sound requires the back of the tongue to be held close to the soft palate or hard palate where its point of articulation creates a sound that resembles the clearing of one's throat. If you have this problem, you will need to drop the back of the tongue to avoid this added point of friction. The [h] sound is a relatively unobstructed sound.

2. Many speakers omit the [h] sound from most words containing the sound [ju] as in ''human, huge, humid.'' They also may omit the sound when it begins a syllable after a vowel or a continuant as in the words ''ahead, unheard, preheat, behold.'' Again, the fact that we have changes in pronunciation rules, depending upon where a word originated, creates confusion among some speakers. For example, words beginning with the letter ''h'' which came from French often contain a silent or unspoken ''h'' as in the words ''honorable, hour, heiress.'' When the letter ''h'' begins an **unstressed** medial or final syllable, as in ''vehicles,'' or ''shepherds,'' the ''h'' is silent. Otherwise, it usually is pronounced as [h].

3. A nondistinctive change occurs when some people aspirate their [h] with too much force. Often, speakers who are accused of having breathy voices expel too much breath for this sound. If you have this problem, you need to limit the flow of air, particularly at the beginnings of words, for [h] sounds. Since most of the words will begin with either ''h'' or ''wh,'' this sound should be easy to perceive in advance.

EXERCISES FOR PRACTICING [h]

1. Contrast the following sounds as they are transcribed.

a. [h]   [h h]   [hw]   [h]   [hw h hw]   [h]   [w]   [h]   [hw]   [w h]

b. [he]   [hi]   [hæ]   [h]   [hwe]   [he]   [we]   [hi]   [wi]   [hwi]

2. Translate the following transcriptions into words and write them on the lines provided.

a. ['hidɪd] _____   [ə'hɛd] _____   ['helɪŋ] _____

b. [ɪn'held] _____   [bi'hev] _____   [ri'hɛdʒ] _____

c. [ri'hɝsl] _____   [ɪn'hæbɪt] _____   [pri'hit] _____

d. [hætʃ] _____   [hʌl] _____   [bi'hɛld] _____

e. [hɪmz] _____   [ri'hæʃ] _____   [hid] _____

3. Transcribe the following words into IPA symbols, using General American Speech as your model for pronunciation.

a. he's _____   heathen _____   mayhem _____

b. perhaps _____   ahead _____   hinted _____

c. hens _____   happiest _____   half _____

d. heady _____   hellish _____   handy _____

e. heater _____   humming _____   hatcheck _____

4. Read the following word combinations aloud. Avoid reading them in a monopitch and be sure to emphasize the stressed syllables as you would in normal conversation.

a. her mahogany home; he helped overhaul; who behaved heroically; had overheard Hannah; perhaps he unhooked

b. had half mohair; horse rehearsing behind; grasshopper held behind; overhauled Helen's hair; whole lighthouse heard

c. anyhow Harold hid; adulthood hurried ahead; Heidi inhaled whole; hadn't prohibited horses; hated Hoagy's house

d. healing inhabitants' hearts; upheld hillside homes; hastily beheaded him; somehow hauled ahead; Hal's hat helped

e. heeded Ohio humor; healthy hunger somehow; exhaling humid heat; harmful cowhide hasn't; hazardous adhesive had

176

5. Read the following sentences aloud. Control the amount of aspiration on [h] to be sure it isn't excessive.

a. Henry Humphries was humiliated by his horrible name and had it changed to Hartley Humphrey.

b. Instead of exhaling, she held her breath for a whole minute until the hospital had disappeared from view.

c. Even if he was an unholy heretic, Horatio shouldn't have been hurt.

d. How humid does Houston become in June when the heat hovers in the high nineties?

e. He held out a huge hand to her in her moment of happy, unhurried glory.

6. Practice Paragraphs

a. We had rented a hot room in a horrible, rundown hotel just outside Havana. Behind it stood a huge mango tree, whose fruit was ripening fast. At night, we heard it dropping with heavy thuds on the hotel roof outside our window. We had never eaten mangoes before until the yardman handed us several the next morning, insisting we must try them. With good humor, we took them. We wondered if they might be hazardous to our health. After washing and peeling one, we tasted it cautiously. "Hmmm, not bad," Hilda said. "I haven't any idea what it resembles. Peaches? Apricots? Pineapples? I'll have another piece." In half an hour we both agreed they tasted heavenly. After two weeks and a whole tree to ourselves, we hadn't changed our minds.

b. The helicopter hovered over two horizontal human figures on the housetop. A rescue team rehearsed a hand-over-hand slide down the rope. Two other figures huddled at the edge of the roof, behaving as if they were hoping to be helped. The rescue team members had to holler to be heard, but they behaved as if this were a routine job rather than a potentially heroic act. When they had helped the horizontal figures, they put them in a sling, and their cohorts in the chopper hauled them up. Everyone was happy when the sling hung empty outside the hovering craft.

c. Her husband called her "Hildegard from Idaho" every time she wore her hiking hat. She had never visited Idaho, but somehow she associated it with Lake Tahoe which she had visited. Maybe it was just because they rhymed. At any rate, she liked her hat, even if it did have holes in it. It made her feel happy, uninhibited, lighthearted, and healthy. Her husband called it "prehistoric and dehydrated," but she said it was moderately handsome and very human. "It upholds the tradition of healthy living in a hardy family," she said. "I hope it holds together until I stop hiking."

d. Hilo, Hawaii, located half-way up a mountainside, has an expansive view of the Pacific Ocean. Homes, stores, hotels, and apartment buildings, cling to the side of the lava hillside and have equally beautiful views of the ever-changing sea. First-time visitors chat happily while they hike up the hillsides. Tradewinds gently moderate the high humidity and bring waves of fragrant aromas from neighborhood trees, vines and bushes. Among the most fragrant blossoms are the jasmine or pikaki, white ginger, and the Tahitian plumeria, whose pungent aromas hang heavily in the evening air, especially after light rain showers.

CHAPTER 14

THE BACK VOWELS
[u] [ʊ] [o] [ɔ] [ɑ]

The back vowels are produced near the back of the throat. All are related to the height of the back of your tongue in relation to the roof of your mouth. The jaw drops progressively from the highest back vowel [u] to the lowest back vowel [ɑ]. You also will discover that the shape of your lips and the tension of muscles under the tongue will give you clues to the production of each sound.

[u]

(sue)

Technical Description:	Tense, High, Back Vowel
Physiological Description: How the Sound is Made	Vocal folds vibrating, soft palate elevated forcing the breath out through the mouth, back of tongue is elevated high towards palate, tip of tongue remains near lower front teeth as its sides press lightly against upper back teeth, tongue muscles are tense, lips are firmly rounded
Common Spellings:	u in ukulele, umlaut, Ruth, Chu oo in ooze, oolong, stoop, too ou in ouzel, soup, you, cougar ew in hewing, ewe, knew, stew ue in clues, blue, due, Tuesday o in movies, doing, into, who
Periodic Spellings:	ui in juice, fruit, cruise oe in canoe, shoe eu in maneuver, rheumatic wo in two ous in rendezvous ough in through ioux in Sioux ieu in lieu

The [u] sound involves the tightest lip rounding of any of our vowel sounds. When making the IPA symbol for this sound, you must include a small tail on the right (much as you would print a small case letter "u") so it won't be confused with the next phoneme we will study. Usually, you will protrude the lips considerably to make the [u] sound. Most people also raise their tongues higher in the mouth when making [u] than for any other English vowel. If you place a thumb in the fleshy portion under your chin as you say this sound, you will discover that [u] is quite a

178

Technical Description:	Lax, High, Back Vowel
Physiological Description: How the Sound is Made	Vocal folds vibrating, soft palate elevated forcing the breath out through the mouth, back of tongue is elevated high towards palate, tip of tongue remains near lower front teeth but sides of tongue have little or no contact with upper back teeth, tongue muscles are lax, lips are less rounded than for [u], the jaw drops slightly from the [u] sound
Common Spellings:	oo in woolen, good, looking u in bullish, bushel, push ou in wouldn't, could, should
Periodic Spellings:	o in bosom, wolf, woman or in worsted orce in Worcestershire

[ʊ]

(full)

tense sound. Since this sound often is confused with [ʊ], the next sound, we will describe it before discussing the problems involved in producing either of these sounds.

The [ʊ] sound requires the back of the tongue to drop slightly from its position for [u] as the muscles under the tongue relax. This sound is not held quite as long as [u] in most words and the lips are not quite as tensely rounded or protruded for [ʊ] as for [u]. The IPA symbol for this sound resembles a small horseshoe or a short capitalized letter "U." However, in transcriptions it shouldn't be taller than [u] or it will appear to be a capitalized IPA symbol (which you already know isn't acceptable in IPA transcriptions). In some ways, these two sounds are similar to the front vowel sounds [i] and [ɪ]. Both pairs of sounds involve IPA symbols which appear to be capitalized and small case letters of the same letter, and both involve a slight relaxing and dropping of the tongue and lower jaw.

COMMON PROBLEMS:

1. Many speakers who come from bilingual families where a romance language is spoken at home and many nonnative students confuse [u] and [ʊ] in their diction. This may be due to an inability to hear the difference between the two sounds, since [ʊ] may not exist in the other language. Often, it results from maintaining too much tension in the tongue while attempting to produce a good [ʊ] sound. If you substitute [u-ʊ], place a thumb in the fleshy portion under your chin and practice paired words containing [u] and [ʊ]. The thumb should be pushed down by the muscles under the tongue for [u], but not for [ʊ]. Also, shorten the length of the [ʊ] sound and relax the rounding and puckering of the lips more than for [u]. Practice reading the following list of words aloud. Listen for the changes in sounds which occur for [u] and [ʊ].

2. Some people nasalize both vowel sounds. Since these sounds are produced close to the soft palate, some speakers allow the soft palate to drop or relax rather than to rise to block off the nasal passages. Some air escapes through the nose rather than totally through the mouth. If you have this problem, practice reading words aloud that contain

```
            WORDS CONTAINING [u] AND [ʊ]


Words Containing [u]                    Words Containing [ʊ]

pool, pooled, pooling, pooler    •    pull, pulled, pulling, puller
fool, fooled, fooling, fooler    •    full,                  fuller
Luke                             •    look, looked, looking, looker
coo, cooed, cooing, cooer        •        could
stew, stewed, stewing, stewer    •        stood
shoe, shooed, shoeing, shoer     •        should
woo, wooed, wooing, wooer        •        would
suit, suited, suiting, suiter    •    soot, sooted, sooting, sooter
      gooed                      •        good
```

the [u] and [ʊ] sounds but no nasalized sounds. Yawn before each group of words to be sure you can feel the soft palate rising. If necessary, hold the nostrils closed as you say the words to be sure no air escapes. The following words may be helpful as you practice eliminating nasalized sounds.

```
    NON-NASAL WORDS CONTAINING THE [u] AND [ʊ] SOUNDS


        Words Containing [u]              Words Containing [ʊ]

A.   rude/shoe/hoop/do/flew/cue         could/wolf/bull/cook/shook
B.   too/Sue/boots/rulers/stewed        cookies/book/put/wood/hoof
C.   fruits/truth/food/tool/you         bush/stood/brook/pull/hood
D.   suited/dues/cruel/sued/use         push/book/should/took/good
```

3. Occasionally, speakers relax their tongues too much and drop the middle and back portions too low for either (or both) [u] or [ʊ]. The resulting vowel is similar to a schwa sound. To avoid this error, the back of the tongue must be raised slightly higher and the lips must be rounded. If you have this problem, practice reading the following words aloud. Feel the change in tongue tension that is required as you move from the first words containing the schwa sound to the following words containing [u] and [ʊ].

　　a. bud/booed/bush; suds/soothed/shook; love/lose/look

　　b. bum/boom/bull; sun/soon/sugar; cud/cooed/could

　　c. campus/pools/push; tuck/tool/took; cuss/coos/cushion

4. A characteristic of some American dialects is the addition of the schwa sound to many vowels. The [u] sound is one in which this occurs frequently, particularly in the medial position of words. A word such as "fool" sounds like "foouhl," making the word sound like it has either a diphthong in the center of the word or two syllables rather than one. Frequently, this characteristic, which is common among speakers of the Southern American dialect, is called a "drawl" by laypersons who don't understand what is happening. To add the schwa sound, you must drop your tongue position from a high back [u] to a mid-high middle schwa sound, and from a tense to a lax sound. If you tend to add the stressed and/or unstressed schwa sounds to vowel sounds, you may need to

180

evaluate the movement of your lower jaw and tongue for the [u], and to a lesser degree, the [ʊ] sound. Say the following words to see if you tend to drop your jaw for [u], thus creating a drawl: you'll, school, pool, cool, duel, tool, fuel, cruel, jewel, mule, stool, rule, spool, yule.

EXERCISES FOR PRACTICING [u] AND [ʊ]

1. Compare the [u] and [ʊ] sounds by reading the following aloud.

a. [u]   [u]   [ʊ]   [u]   [ʊ ʊ]   [u u]   [u ʊ]   [u]   [ʊ ʊ u]   [ʊ]

b. [tu]   [ut]   [tʊ]   [ʊt]   [up]   [pu]   [ʊp]   [pʊ]   [tut]

2. Translate the following IPA transcriptions into words and write them on the lines provided.

a. ['dui] _____   ['wʊdn̩] _____   ['krʊkɪd] _____

b. [stʊd] _____   [sup] _____   [mɪs'tʊk] _____

c. ['rʊki] _____   [ful] _____   ['bʊkes] _____

d. ['fʊtstul] _____   [tuts] _____   ['bʊlɪtɪn] _____

e. [ɪm'pruv] _____   [bæm'bu] _____   [plæ'tun] _____

3. Transcribe the following words into IPA symbols, using General American Speech as your model for pronunciation. Include primary and secondary stress marks.

a. resume _____   sugar _____   choose _____

b. soothing _____   booth _____   should _____

c. pudding _____   newscast _____   looking _____

d. understood _____   enthusiasm _____   doomed _____

e. overlook_____   tattoo _____   truthful _____

4. Determine the number of syllables and phonemes in each of the following words. Write the transcription of each word before you make these determinations. Circle the appropriate numbers. Use General American Speech as your model for pronunciation of these words.

Word	Transcription	Syllables	Phonemes
a. bushel	[ ]	1 2 3 4 5	1 2 3 4 5 6 7 8 9 +
b. improvement	[ ]	1 2 3 4 5	1 2 3 4 5 6 7 8 9 +
c. neighborhood	[ ]	1 2 3 4 5	1 2 3 4 5 6 7 8 9 +
d. toothbrush	[ ]	1 2 3 4 5	1 2 3 4 5 6 7 8 9 +
e. waterproofed	[ ]	1 2 3 4 5	1 2 3 4 5 6 7 8 9 +

181

5. Read the following combinations of words aloud. Contrast the [u] and [ʊ] sounds in the words by sustaining the [u] sounds longer than the [ʊ] sounds. Also, be sure you are not adding the schwa sound to either of these sounds.

a. book boosted good; fools overlook truth; snooping Butch looks; cashew pudding cools; sooty tools grew; spool used to

b. Ruth pulled caribou; full blue cushion; who'll rule you; Kalamazoo could boost; good shoe would; youth drew crooked

c. push cool wool; crew shook pulley; foot glued fully; crook grew sullen; tooth looked wooden; whose smooth pool

d. bullet blew bamboo; cushions drew good; who could wound; clues mistook recruiting; rude bully pushed; nut rolls could

e. cook's soup stood; school glue shook; Luke pulled bushy; true rook looked; boots mistook roosters; whole school used

6. Practice reading the following sentences aloud, using the same inflections and fluency you would use in daily conversation. Do not try to exaggerate the [u] or [ʊ] sounds.

a. Lucille took sugar cookies to school to share with her drama department costume crew.

b. Using a bushel of cucumbers, Susan brewed a kettle of stew that couldn't be used until it was cool.

c. Whoever stole her coupons for oolong tea got fooled because they should have been used by last Tuesday.

d. Lewis and Drew took a wooden canoe ride during our noon visit to the zoo.

e. The unlucky sailor's newly issued shoes grew too tight whenever she played the tuba on the muddy river banks.

7. Practice Paragraphs

a. Matthew moved to Kalamazoo, Michigan from Eugene, Oregon in June, just after turning twenty-two. His amused friends couldn't believe the rumor he was moving soon. "Whoever heard of a place called Kalamazoo, except in a song?" they chortled. "Isn't it a little like Oz? Do they have a wizard there too?" Matthew nodded his head and smiled. He knew it was useless to show the group of hooting friends the university bulletin he had received. He stood among them, put his hands on two of their shoulders, and replied, "I know of two! Both are full of knowledge. They are computer wizards."

b. Her smooth brown skin was beautiful in the morning moonlight. The papoose on her back was sound asleep. She moved through the bushes with firm, soothing strides, giving her companions approving nods as they stooped to pick the mushrooms that had sprung up overnight. The cool morning dew seemed to soften and cushion their footfalls. They must not overlook even one pale mushroom if they were to have food enough this day. One woman paused to push her papoose higher on her shoulders. Off in the distance, a rooster crowed two times and each woman stood upright. They knew that daylight soon would rule the earth again and they would have to leave the foothills for their Sioux village.

182

c. The bulldozer crew was working to remove the top soil in order to begin footings for the Truesdale Community Stadium. Drivers took great care to push the soil to one side where the rookies would remove the rocks. The crew's output had improved every afternoon for the past two weeks. They had learned to maneuver machinery in small areas. They utilized space as if it were invaluable and executed turns uniformly. Then, blue trucks scooted in between the bulldozers, after each turn, and raced to the other side of the field. The football field should be ready on time unless something uneventful happened.

8. Dialogue for Oral Practice (for two readers)

Tracey: I've been gathering unusual information to include in my next two journalism papers.

Marty: Could you use some help? I took good notes when Lou and I gathered quiz questions for the annual Junior Quiz Bowl in June.

Tracey: Do you have anything like this: Many newsmen believe W.C. Fields said, "Anybody who hates children and dogs can't be all bad." However, Leo Rosten, who was introducing Mr. Fields at a dinner, actually said, "Any man who hates dogs and babies can't be all bad."

Marty: Would this be useful: Chop suey is not a traditional food from China. Chinese immigrants created it in California for Americans.

Tracey: That's good! Speaking of California, I have a friend in San Diego who claims one of its streets, Haveteur Way, was named by a tract developer who loved puns. He actually meant "have it your way." To add insult to injury, he made sure it intersected with Unida Place.

Marty: You're kidding! You need a place, huh? That's as good as the rumor about how the Yucatan area got its name in 1517. Francisco Fernandez de Cordoba asked the native Mayans what the region was where he had landed and they replied, "Yucatan," which meant, "I don't understand you."

Tracey: Do you know where the original London Bridge is?

Marty: In London?

Tracey: Wrong. It was sold to McCulloch Corporation for about two and a half million dollars in 1968 and was shipped in 10,000 granite blocks to Lake Havasu City, Arizona where it was reconstructed to span one of Lake Havasu's channels.

Marty: Really? Here's one for you. The words yo-yo, linoleum, cube steak, and dry ice have something in common! Originally, they all were used as new trade or brand names!

Tracey: Well, do you know what Mark Twain, Ulysses S. Grant, Mickey Rooney, and Walt Disney had in common? They all were bankrupt at one time in their lives.

Marty: O.K., give me a clue. How are you going to use so many unique pieces of information in your paper?

Tracey: Who knows? I'm still looking for a way to be inspired.

[o]
(oat)

Technical Description:	Tense, Mid-High, Back Vowel (or Diphthong [ou])
Physiological Description: How the Sound is Made	Vocal folds vibrating, back of tongue drops lower than for [u], tongue muscles are tense as back edges touch the cutting edges of the lower teeth and tongue tip remains close to the floor of the mouth, soft palate is raised, lips are rounded, the jaw drops slightly from the [u] sound
Common Spellings:	o in obey, total, fiasco, go oa in oat, boast, float oe in hoeing, woe, foe ow in Owen, snowing, pillow ou in boulder, shoulder, mould
Periodic Spellings:	ough in though, dough, thorough au in au gratin, chauffeur eau in tableau, beau oh in oh, Noh, Shiloh owe in owed, owe eo in yeoman oo in brooch

As the back of your tongue moves down from the palate to form back vowel sounds, its mid-high location becomes the place where [o] is formed. If an imaginary line were drawn through the middle portion of the mouth from front to back, the vowel sounds [e], [ʌ], and [o] would be produced in this section. Generally, people produce the pure [o] sound only in unstressed syllables as in the words "obedient, ovation, oregano" and when it occurs before voiceless consonants as in "total, topaz, hope." In final positions of words, stressed syllables, and before voiced sounds, the tongue moves upwards from [o] and the lips close and relax slightly to the [u] position creating the diphthong [ou]. Most people have great difficulty distinguishing between [o] and [ou]. To simplify the transcription process, this book will not use the diphthong symbol, but will transcribe all sounds as [o].

COMMON PROBLEMS:

1. Many people add the [ɛ] sound before [o] sounds, creating a diphthongized glide which results in [ɛo]. They begin their voicing by elevating the front portion of the tongue close to the lips for [ɛ] and continuing the voicing as the tongue drops until the back of the tongue reaches its mid-high position for [o]. To avoid this addition at the beginning of [o] speakers must keep the front of the tongue down quite low while raising the back of the tongue. Words containing [o] in the initial and final positions probably will be easiest to work on first. If you have this difficulty, practice reading the words in the exercise section, keeping the front of the tongue flat and relaxed, and the lips rounded.

2. A second problem involves the addition of the schwa sound between [o] and voiced consonants, particularly [l], [m] and [n]. This addition creates a diphthong and has the effect of adding another syllable to words. This addition is heard frequently among speakers of the Southern American dialect and is often a characteristic of the "southern drawl." If you have this difficulty, try to avoid dropping the lower jaw and tongue quickly after [o] sounds. Practice the following words by prolonging the [o] sound and then quickly adding the consonant which follows it.

    a. roll, zone, shown, whole, known, home, phone

    b. troll, known, dome, scroll, lone, bowl, comb

    c. control, unknown, bemoan, regrown, intone, ozone

3. Rather than merely adding the schwa, some people substitute it for [o], particularly in unstressed syllables. This becomes particularly obvious at the ends of words such as "billow, meadow, oratorio, borrow." However, it also occurs in beginning and medial positions as in "Olivia, opaque, convocation." It is interesting that when [o] occurs in an unstressed syllable, the unstressed schwa often is an acceptable substitute for [o] in words such as "opinion, original, convolute, disobey." As a result of current usage, it would appear that only in the *final position* of words has the schwa not become a legitimate substitution at *some* time. If you have this tendency to substitute the schwa for [o], you should examine your lip rounding, tongue tension, and tighter jaws which must be present for [o] but not for the schwa.

4. As mentioned in the discussion of [u] and [ʊ], the nasalized back vowel is fairly common in some parts of North America. This occurs when the soft palate relaxes and drops, allowing air to escape through the nose rather than through the mouth. If you nasalize your [o] sounds, refer back to the "Problems" section of [u] and [ʊ] for information on modifying this habit.

EXERCISES FOR PRACTICING [o]

1. Contrast the following sounds by reading the IPA transcriptions aloud.

a. [o]   [e]   [o]   [æ]   [o o]   [i o]   [o e]   [i o]   [o]   [o o]

b. [ol]   [om]   [mo]   [lo]   [ol o]   [ro]   [ot]   [to]   [to to]

2. Translate the following IPA symbols into words. Pronounce the words aloud as you are doing so.

    a. [o'bed] _____   [bost] _____   ['totl̩] _____

    b. [o'lɪmpɪk] _____   [fi'æsko] _____   [noz] _____

    c. [ri'mot] _____   ['robot] _____   ['mostli] _____

    d. [goz] _____   ['potn̩t] _____   [di'notɪd] _____

    e. ['kozi] _____   [on] _____   [soks] _____

3. Transcribe the following words into IPA symbols, using General American Speech as your model. Include primary and secondary stress marks if they are needed.

a. showboat _____   fellow _____   soda _____

b. cooperate _____   erosion _____   ocean _____

c. soaking _____   total _____   hotel _____

d. potential _____   holiness _____   doped _____

e. snowbird _____   growth _____   colder _____

4. Determine the number of syllables and phonemes in each of the following words. Transcribe each word and circle the correct numbers.

Word	Transcription	Syllables	Phonemes
a. location	[ ]	1 2 3 4 5	1 2 3 4 5 6 7 8 9
b. shoulder	[ ]	1 2 3 4 5	1 2 3 4 5 6 7 8 9
c. mobility	[ ]	1 2 3 4 5	1 2 3 4 5 6 7 8 9
d. posting	[ ]	1 2 3 4 5	1 2 3 4 5 6 7 8 9
e. ghosts	[ ]	1 2 3 4 5	1 2 3 4 5 6 7 8 9

5. Practice reading the following sentences aloud. Try to maintain fluency without prolonging the [o] sounds. Use a conversational inflection pattern in your reading.

a. Joe and Toby spent their whole vacation in Cleo Springs, Oklahoma, very close to the Cimarron River.

b. Only the broker knows who wrote the note that was tied to a stone and thrown through the hotel window.

c. Ohio froze under seven feet of snow which choked the roads and even closed the weather bureau.

d. Olaf lived in Anoka, Minnesota over sixty years in his own stone home overlooking the road to Minneapolis.

e. The ivory keys on her open piano had grown yellow over the years, but her music was still mellow.

6. Practice Paragraphs

a. Joan's associates had phoned to say their radio program appearance had been cancelled. Nobody had told them until moments before they were scheduled to go to the studio. As she stood alone for a quiet moment in front of her window, she wondered if the station's program

186

director, owner, or the local political boss had made this decision. She tried to control her emotions. There would be no way of knowing the answer until her associates arrived. She had hoped a new era of cooperation had opened in her city after they spoke with the mayor. Now they might have to expose him for his failure to cooperate.

b. A menu and notice was posted outside the hotel dining room. It would open at five o'clock. As they looked at the menu, they spoke in hushed voices. "Smoked ocean trout, fresh cold salad, baked potato, and whole wheat muffins—that sounds good to me," she said. He peered over her shoulder. "Oh, and for dessert—colonial apple pie a la mode!" She lifted her head and touched her nose against his chin. "Since nobody else is here, maybe we can get that table by the window that looks out on the rose garden. Who knows, maybe the yellow roses are in bloom—just like last year!"

c. The motorcoach approached the castle by a narrow side road, avoiding the lines of slowly moving automobiles on the main street. The tour guide chose this route because it also followed the river. The tourists always enjoyed watching the unhurried cargo boats, small coastal vessels, and ocean barges through their windows. No one every complained about the slow progress they were making. The guide spoke to them about the city's program to protect both the commerce potential and the environment along the waterfront, even though the property had been sold recently. "The old buildings will be torn down to make room for new condominiums," she said. "Now we all can own part of our riverfront."

7. Dialogue for Oral Practice (requires two readers)

Anchorperson 1: Little hope remains for locating the sailboat, Lucy C. or its four crew members, which disappeared three days ago off the coast of Nova Scotia. Rain, cold weather, and high seas prevented the local air-sea rescue team from conducting a thorough search of the coastline. The Lucy C. had no radio on board and contained provisions for only 24 hours at sea. The skipper of the Lucy C. was 22-year old Joe Tully, son of Boston hotel magnate, Hobart Tully, III.

Anchorperson 2: In a vote of 4 to 3, the local school board decided at last night's board meeting to renovate Oak Grove Junior High School. Oak Grove is the oldest school building now being used in the district. You may recall the board voted, at its November meeting, to close Oak Grove unless taxes were increased at Tuesday's general elections. A two percent tax increase was accepted by voters. Bids for the renovation will be accepted by the school board through March.

Anchorperson 1: Who stole the bowl of donuts from Maude Cole's kitchen? That's the sole question facing local police chief, Bigelow Jones, tonight. Mrs. Cole had made three dozen sourdough donuts for her church's bazaar. She left them on the counter to cool near an open window while she swept her front porch. When she returned to cover the donuts, they were gone! So was the bowl. Chief Jones has his detectives looking—and probably smelling—for the stolen goods.

Anchorperson 2: No one knows yet when Coastal Hospital will lower its longterm care rates. Hospital administrator Clayton Mobley told the Oceanic Rotary Club members today that he is awaiting the opening of the newly endowed wing before making a public announcement of rate changes. However, he assured members that newly admitted patients will receive retroactive refunds, once the rates are set. The endowed wing for longterm care was made possible through a bequest of 22 million dollars by the late Josie Roma of Old Town.

Anchorperson 1: And who will be going to Toronto for the Great Hockey Playoffs? We'll tell you when we come back. Stay tuned!

[ɔ]

(caught)

Technical Description:	Lax, Middle, Back Vowel
Physiological Description: How the Sound is Made	Vocal folds vibrating, soft palate elevated forcing the breath out through the mouth, back of tongue raised slightly towards palate as tongue tip remains near lower front teeth and sides touch inside surfaces of lower back teeth, lips are slightly rounded but not protruded as for [o], the jaw drops slightly from the [o] sound
Common Spellings:	o in office, cloth, ignore au in author, jaundice, Wausau aw in awkward, fawn, Paw Paw augh in naughty, taught, slaughter ough in thought, fought, bought a in warden, wart, warble
Periodic Spellings:	oo in floor, door ou in pour, your

The IPA symbol [ɔ] resembles a backwards letter "c." It is a sound that confuses many students, both in transcriptions and in pronunciation. Frequently, they fail to associate the sound "aw" with the symbol and in the rush of transcribing a word, will use either [o] or the lowest back vowel, [ɑ], which will be discussed next.

To make matters even more confusing, many words have at least two pronunciations which are heard frequently—and which seem to be interchangeable, even in the same word within the same speaker's vocabulary. In other words, the person may use one vowel sound in a word in one sentence and then change to another vowel in that same word in another sentence. For example, here are a few words on which no general agreement exists for a preferred pronunciation in General American Speech:

sorrow, tomorrow, borrow, sorry, horrify, horrible,

Forrest, forest, Forester, foreign, Florida

office, officer, offer, offering, awful, waffle, coffee

orange, on, upon, onto; frog, hog; doll, moral

washing, wash, Washington, washer, wanton, want, wanted

COMMON PROBLEMS

1. In its low middle back position, this sound often is confused with the back vowel sounds that are immediately above and below it: [o] and [ɑ]. It is difficult to talk in generalities about the correct formation of this sound because of interchanges of sounds, some of which were described above, which have become acceptable. Speakers of the Eastern and Southern American dialects probably prefer [ɑ] over [ɔ] when choices are available for words such as "coffee" and "orange." Speakers of the General American dialect prefer [ɔ] over [ɑ].

188

The words in the practice section will give you some guidance in determining words which contain the [ɔ] sound. If you substitute either [o] or [ɑ] for this sound, you must be alert to words which already exist and which could be misunderstood on a semantic as well as a phonemic basis by listeners who are not familiar with your dialect. For example, the chart below attempts to show some of the words which will result in cross-substitutions of sounds.

WORDS WHICH RESULT FROM INTERCHANGING [o] [ɔ] [ɑ]

[ɔ]	[ɑ]	[o]	[ɔ]	[ɑ]	[o]
awe	ah	oh	jaw		Joe
awed	odd	ode	law		low
awning		owning	nought	not	note
ball/bawl		bowl	ought		oat
bought	Bott	boat	pall/Paul		pole
call		coal	pause/paws	pa's	pose
called		cold	raw	rah	row
caught	cot	coat	Saul		soul
claws/clause		close	saw		sew/so
cawed	cod	code	sawed	sod	sewed
cost		coast	Shaw/pshaw	shah	show
craw		crow	shawl		shoal
dawn	Don		slaw		slow
fall		foal	sought	sot	
fawn		phone	stall		stole
flaw		flow	talk	tock	
gnawed	nod	node	taught	tot	tote
hall/haul		hole/whole	wrought	rot	wrote/rote
hawed	hod	hoed			
hawk	hock				

2. Some speakers, particularly in the southern regions of the United States, add the schwa sound to [ɔ]. This probably is most noticeable in the final position of words. Thus, "awe" becomes ['ɔə]. As mentioned in previous sections of this chapter, the addition of the schwa to vowels creates a diphthongized vowel or, in many cases, an additional syllable. To eliminate this addition, you must prevent the tongue and jaw from moving downward or relaxing even slightly, once a good [ɔ] sound has been produced. Also, the lips must continue to be rounded slightly throughout the sound. If the lips become too lax, your chances of producing a schwa sound increase.

3. Some speakers, particularly from cities in New York and the Middle Atlantic states, begin the [ɔ] sound almost as an [o] and then glide into [ɔ]. In some speakers, this creates diphthongized vowels, and often an additional syllable. Thus, "call" becomes ['koɔl] and "song" becomes ['soɔn]. Usually, the individual is pulling back or retracting the tongue, which creates an unpleasant back-of-the-throat sound. To begin the sound correctly the back of the tongue must be dropped slightly, and relaxed rather than being pulled back tensely. Tension in the lips must be relaxed, although some lip rounding still should be present.

189

4. Another sound addition that is heard more often in the Eastern portion of the United States than in most other regions of North America is the addition of [ɚ] or [ɝ] to the [ɔ] sound, especially at the ends of words. Thus, no distinction is made between "saw" and "soar" or "raw" and "roar." The front of the tongue moves up and forward slightly after forming [ɔ] and the lips quickly relax their rounding when creating this addition. To eliminate the addition, the lips must maintain their slightly rounded position and the front of the tongue should not be allowed to move towards the hard palate. The tip of the tongue should be close to the lower front teeth and the muscles under the tongue should be fairly lax. Also, when [ɔ] appears in the final position, no movement in the lower jaw should occur after [ɔ] has been voiced. This sound addition is very similar to the addition of the schwa sound to [ɔ].

5. A nondistinctive change results from nasalization of the [ɔ] sound in some speakers when they allow the soft palate to drop as the sound is produced. If you have this problem, see the information given previously for [u] and [ʊ] regarding nasalized vowels.

EXERCISES FOR PRACTICING [ɔ]

1. Contrast the following sounds by reading the IPA transcriptions aloud.

a. [ɔ]   [ʌ]   [ɔ]   [o ɔ]   [ɔ ʌ]   [e]   [o]   [ɔ]   [ʌ ɔ]   [ɔ]

b. [tɔ]   [ɔt]   [kɔ]   [ɔk]   ['ɔki]   ['ɔsi]   [ɔf]   [fɔs]

2. Translate the following IPA transcriptions into words and write them on the blanks provided.

a. ['kɔstli] _____   [ə'kɔstɪd] _____   ['frɔstɪŋ] _____

b. [skwɔʃ] _____   ['nɔti] _____   [flɔst] _____

c. [bɔt] _____   ['tɔkətɪv] _____   ['ɔfn̩] _____

d. ['krɔsɪz] _____   ['wɔkɪŋ] _____   ['tɔfi] _____

e. [mɔd] _____   [wɪθ'drɔɪŋ] _____   [gɔz] _____

3. Write the following words in IPA symbols, using General American Speech as your model for the way the words should be pronounced. Include primary and secondary stress marks.

a. authors _____   yawning _____   auburn _____

b. autumn _____   causing _____   squaw _____

c. tossed _____   slaughter _____   hawk _____

d. thoughtful _____   seesaw _____   chalk _____

e. cause _____   drawing _____   distraught _____

190

4. Determine the number of syllables and phonemes in each of the following words. Transcribe each word and circle the correct numbers.

Word	Transcription	Syllables	Phonemes
a. caution	[ ]	1 2 3 4 5	1 2 3 4 5 6 7 8 9
b. formula	[ ]	1 2 3 4 5	1 2 3 4 5 6 7 8 9
c. majority	[ ]	1 2 3 4 5	1 2 3 4 5 6 7 8 9
d. exhausted	[ ]	1 2 3 4 5	1 2 3 4 5 6 7 8 9
e. chords	[ ]	1 2 3 4 5	1 2 3 4 5 6 7 8 9

5. Read the following groups of words aloud.

a. saw tall awnings; straw auction stalled; August lawns draw; wrong jaw also; hawks saw all

b. often thought law; audio broadcast thaw; Norman Shaw audited; Australia taught paw; McGaw coughed awfully

c. orchids brought awed; ignore Auburn's law; raw authority called; Shah augmented Raleigh's; Paul saw autos

d. tawny oars gnaw; withdraw north's autumn; claw always caused; squaw also walked; author's flaw fought

e. withdraw almost caustic; awkward Choctaw wall; awed guffaw caught; already pawed straw; wrong draw ought

6. Practice Paragraphs

a. George and Audrey were talking at their office picnic in Shawnee State Park while enjoying hot dogs, coffee and chocolate malted milk cake. They thought it was the wrong time to discuss business—so they talked about the softball game they had watched that morning. They spoke in laudatory terms about their boss, who had fought their coworkers to a six to six draw in the last inning. They had expected to chalk up an easy victory over the "authorities." "If Austin hadn't dawdled at first base in the fourth inning, we would have won," Audrey said with a naughty toss of her head. "Who would have thought the boss would hurl that horrible last pitch and get a called strike on Laughton? If Laughton hadn't been so tall, the ball would have been way outside. Or is it inside? I always get the two mixed up."

b. Normally, they would have walked along the beach. However, when a storm looked like it was coming in off the ocean, Doris and Laura decided to take a shortcut back to town through a forest. They had to walk cautiously to avoid thorn bushes and when an awesome rain squall began, they quickly sought shelter under a huge, faltering, old oak tree. The tree was covered with soft, green moss. When the wind stopped blowing, the rain stopped. Off in the distance, they heard frogs croaking. After about forty minutes, they came out of the forest. At first, they thought they were lost. A field of tall grass still dripped water from its recent washing. Then, almost half a mile ahead, they caught a glimpse of the flag on top of their resort. They rushed forward eagerly.

c. Each fall, in spite of his careful organization, Lorenzo fought the urge to walk back into his house and delay the onslaught of another tour. However, in the bright early morning sunshine, a transformation occured regularly. All his worries seemed to dissolve as the asphalt unrolled ahead of his automobile. For a quarter century, Lorenzo Moore had played pipe organs for a large manufacturing corporation. He travelled across the country at least four times during an ordinary year, giving absorbing demonstrations of the versatility of his organization's products. He wasn't expected to sell or moralize—only to inform and transform. He always was cautious to play many songs his audience already knew. However, his formula for success also included a few absorbing pieces that were foreign to his listeners because they taught them to enjoy new experiences.

The IPA symbol for the "ah" sound is [ɑ]. This resembles a small script or written letter "a." If you were trying to do narrow (extremely precise) transcriptions of sounds, you would need to learn other symbols that are close to, but variations of, this sound. In the Southern and Eastern American Dialects and in several British dialects, these other sounds appear frequently. However, in this beginning class, unless your instructor decides to teach you those symbols, you won't be required to use them in transcriptions. General American Speech tends to use [ɑ] in most positions, rather than these other sounds.

[ɑ]
(art)

Technical Description:	Lax, Low, Back Vowel
Physiological Description: How the Sound is Made	Vocal folds vibrating, soft palate elevated forcing the breath out through the mouth, tongue is totally relaxed except for a small portion of the back, tip of tongue is near lower front teeth and sides rest against the lower back teeth, lips are unrounded and lower jaw drops considerably
Common Spellings:	o in opera, stop, Oshkosh a in are, father, wants
Periodic Spellings:	ea in hearth, heart ow in knowledge ho in honest, honor al in almond, palm, alms, calm eois in bourgeois as in faux pas ah in ah, hah, shah e in sergeant

The [ɑ] sound is the lowest back vowel sound in the English language. As a result, the tongue and lower jaw are very relaxed and drop to their lowest positions. This may explain why doctors ask you to open your mouth and say "ah" when you have an oral or throat examination. They can see farther back and down in your throat for this sound than for any other one. It also may explain why this sound is preferred for vocal music warm-up exercises. By relaxing the muscles, less strain is placed on the neck, throat, and larynx as pitch rises and falls, and as volume increases and decreases.

192

COMMON PROBLEMS:

1. Many people substitute [ɔ] for the back vowel [ɑ]. If you make this substitution, the back of your tongue and lower jaw are not dropping far enough and your lips are rounded slightly. The lips should have absolutely no rounding, just as the front vowel sound [æ] had no rounding.

Some people don't open their lips wide enough to create a clear [ɑ]. Frequently we find that they keep their jaws too close together, almost in a clenched position, rather than dropping the lower jaw easily. Because of their long-practiced habit, they feel they are dropping their jaws excessively when they try to practice this sound with looser jaws.

If you are criticized for blurred or tight [ɑ] sounds, look in a mirror and watch how far you must drop your jaw to create a full, clear [ɑ]. Learn to feel the difference between your old physiological pattern and this new position. When working on distinguishing between [ɔ] and [ɑ], you may wish to refer back to the chart which compared these sounds in the last section of this chapter.

2. Some speakers, including many nonnative students, have difficulty distinguishing this sound from the schwa sound. As a result, they often confuse the two in pronouncing words. A period of ear training becomes crucial for clarifying these sounds. If you have this difficulty, contrast word pairs containing both sounds by listening to someone else read the pairs aloud as you attempt to determine which sound is being said. Then practice saying the words aloud yourself. The word may be paired as follows:

    a. rot/rut; luck/lock; balm/bum; not/nut; snob/snub

    b. cut/cot; dock/duck; sub/sob; come/calm; poppy/puppy

    c. rob/rub; cop/cup; hut/hot; some/psalm; shot/shut

    d. shock/shuck; hub/hob; pot/putt; cub/cob; fund/fond

3. The same nondistinctive error of nasalization is heard in [ɑ] as in the previous back vowel sounds in many people. Usually, if speakers nasalize several vowel sounds in one position of the mouth, they will nasalize most or all of the others. The problem is a dropping or relaxing of the soft palate which allows air to escape partially or totally through the nose. If you have problems with nasalizing this sound, check the suggestions given under [u] and [ʊ] in this chapter.

EXERCISES FOR PRACTICING [ɑ]

1. Contrast the following sounds by reading the IPA transcriptions aloud.

a. [ɑ]   [æ]   [ɔ]   [ɑ o]   [ɑ]   [ɔ]   [ɔ ɑ]   [ɑ]   [ɑ]   [ɑ ɔ ɑ]

b. [kɑ]   [ɑk]   [lɑ]   [ɑl]   [gɑ]   [ɑg]   [ɑm]   [mɑ]   [pɑm]

2. Translate the following IPA symbols into words. Pronounce the words aloud as you are doing so.

a. ['sɑkɚ] _____   ['kɑmli] _____   [gaɚd] _____

b. ['stɑkɪŋ] _____   [lɑkt] _____   [fɑn'du] _____

c. ['kɑviɑɚ] _____   ['rɑkstaɚ] _____   [pɑdz] _____

d. ['ɑdli] _____   [blɑnd] _____   ['tɑpɪŋ] _____

e. ['nɑti] _____   ['bɑtm̩] _____   ['maɚkɪt] _____

3. Transcribe the following words into IPA symbols, using General American Speech as your model for pronunciation. Include primary and secondary stress marks.

a. possibility _____   lots _____   cotton _____

b. zombi _____   opera _____   Oscar _____

c. hotly _____   Occidental _____   waffle _____

d. combination _____   vodka _____   modeling _____

e. bottles _____   bombadier _____   shocked _____

4. Determine the number of syllables and phonemes in each of the following words. Transcribe each word and circle the correct numbers.

Word	Transcription	Syllables	Phonemes
a. stockcar	[ ]	1 2 3 4 5	1 2 3 4 5 6 7 8 9
b. ominous	[ ]	1 2 3 4 5	1 2 3 4 5 6 7 8 9
c. honestly	[ ]	1 2 3 4 5	1 2 3 4 5 6 7 8 9
d. positive	[ ]	1 2 3 4 5	1 2 3 4 5 6 7 8 9
e. moccasin	[ ]	1 2 3 4 5	1 2 3 4 5 6 7 8 9

5. Read the following groups of words aloud. Be sure your tongue and lower jaw are relaxed as you read.

a. Archie followed armies; honest father occupied; positive guard argued; are smart artists; on palm farms

b. bomb obviously alarmed; spotted arguing sergeants; are guarding frogs; Don followed Art; hostile doll argued

c. arms probably started; Lonnie sobbed artificially; arson marred Olive's; wants Mark's arch; bottom marred spots

d. arcade target sounds; onyx upon hard; father's heart barred; ominous car started; calm arbor on

e. largest barn honored; odd schoolyard hopscotch; modern opera got; toxic cargo obligations; college omelets intoxicated

6. Practice reading the following sentences aloud, using the same inflections and fluency you would use in daily conversations. Do not try to prolong any of the vowel sounds excessively.

a. Our Yugoslavian soccer team got a colossal cheer when it conquered the team from Holland.

b. Arnold got an anonymous response from a reader who didn't believe in the Socratic method.

c. Polly's only option was to operate the college carillon without the intoxicated visiting artist.

d. His partner had charged the movie star far too much to park his car in the garage.

e. The modern art archives qualify for an alarm that will start ringing in response to any lock that is picked.

7. Practice Paragraphs

a. We all called Rodney the "hotshot rock jock" because the music he played constantly on our local station got progressively louder every night. He started his programs with a confident march which was regarded as his theme song. Thereafter, he played progressive rock, electronic bop, and percussive shock-rock. His knowledge about modern musicians and musical compositions was phenomenal. His confident philosophy, simply stated, was: "Rock solves all problems." That's why we were shocked when he dropped his profitable occupation last October, joined the Peace Corps, and left the continent.

b. We grew tired of the propaganda coming out of Congress regarding the free market economics which were supposed to solve all our problems. The economy hadn't gotten any better and it was obvious that our quality of living had dropped since the majority party had been seated. The farmers were complaining that democracy was making a mockery of free trade. The dollar was in the process of disintegrating and the consequences of this were uncertain. Confidence was disappearing in the stock market as profits plunged following an announcement of trade restrictions on the Continent. Congress had to listen to our objections.

c. The rocket was being charged at Cape Canaveral. Holly kept her binoculars constantly trained on it. She had never seen a blast-off in person, although she had watched many shots on television. Now she was in the process of writing an article for a geography magazine—a task that should bring her a small profit. Her chair was hard and the sun was hot, but she refused to move from her choice spot on top of her motel. She had armed herself with plenty of ice water because she heard delays were common. Also, she had stopped to get a box lunch at a small shop two blocks away and had made a little progress on a hot dog. An Arkansas used car salesman and a Utah state park ranger sat next to her. They watched the progress through shared opera glasses while drinking from huge bottles of orange soda pop.

8. Dialogues for Oral Practice (for two or three readers)

Announcer: Thoughtful people shop at Ross Murphy's Card Corner when they seek the finest in greeting cards and contemporary art supplies. Just in time for Father's Day, Ross Murphy has a fresh stock of cards and wrapping paper to express your warmest thoughts to Dad on his special day. Whether it's a nostalgic remembrance, a saucy saying, or a quiet thank-you—you want to send, you'll find it at the Card Corner. Moderate prices, quality merchandise, courteous service—all make Ross Murphy's Card Corner in Arbor Mall a favorite place of thoughtful shoppers.

Weather Reporter: Today's temperature ranged from a low of 65 degrees to a high of 74 degrees. The humidity is now at a pleasant 55 percent and winds are out of the northwest at 8 to 10 miles an hour. A high pressure area was about two hundred miles southwest of the city at 9 p.m. tonight and should bring us clear skies on Friday. Our studio rain gauge shows no precipitation in the past 24 hours. My forecast for the weekend: moderate temperatures, lots of sunshine, and no chance of rain until at least Sunday night. If you have a family picnic planned for the weekend—you will have *perfect* weather.

Sportscaster: It *wasn't* perfect, but it *was* a fast-paced game at Lawson Stadium tonight when our Washington High Polecats met the Carson City Eagles in their first football game of the season. Art Parker was high point man for the cats, in spite of an arm injury he suffered last week in practice session. In just a minute, I'll be back to give you all the exciting details.

*   *   *   *   *

Lucy: You always look so healthy, Tony, even with your busy schedule. How do you do it?

Tony: Oh, it's not a secret, Lucy. I try to eat balanced meals, get in at least an hour of walking every day, and take a Wallcott's Super Vitamin and Mineral capsule every morning.

Lucy: Why do you take a vitamin and mineral capsule, if you eat balanced meals? I thought they would supply you with all the nutrition you need.

Tony: They *should*. But you never know where your food is being grown, these days. For example, tomatoes could be grown in soil that doesn't have some of the important trace minerals our bodies need. Those tomatoes may look and taste great, but without those important elements, we could become deficient in important things such as manganese, chromium, or selenium.

Lucy: Ohhh, I see! So your supplement acts like a daily *guarantee* that you will get the minimum amount of everything you need to stay healthy.

Tony: That's a good way of putting it! *A daily nutrition guarantee.* The best thing is that Walcott's products are moderately priced to fit even our budgets.

Lucy: Really? Where can I get Wallcott's Super Vitamins and Minerals? I'd like to try them.

Tony: Oh, all the Cost-Cutter Drugstores carry a complete line of Wallcott supplements. Don't you have one in *your* neighborhood?

Lucy: Yes! Thanks Tony. In fact it's just a few blocks from here.

Tony: In *that* case, would you mind if I walked you home?

196

CHAPTER 15

GLIDED SOUNDS:
DIPHTHONGS [aɪ] [aʊ] [ɔɪ]

This is the final chapter devoted to phonemes which will be useful for you to know as you prepare to evaluate the oral presentations of your classmates. By now, you are familiar enough with IPA symbols to understand the ways in which these final phonemes, called diphthongs, are formed. The word "diphthong" is a difficult one for some students to spell and pronounce. It contains two "h" letters in close succession and is pronounced ['dɪfθɔŋ]. You already know that when two consonant sounds are blended together in the same syllable to produce an entirely new sound, the result is called an affricate. When two vowels are blended together in the same syllable to produce a new sound, the result is called a diphthong.

Diphthongs have the same basic characteristics of vowels: they are not nasalized and they have a relatively unobstructed passageway from the lungs through the lips. Generally, diphthongs will begin from a low tongue position and will move to a higher tongue position. Also, they will start with one lip position and move to a different one. However, since diphthongs are continuous blends of sounds, they can't be prolonged as blends. For example, say the words "eye" and "toy" aloud. Notice that the tongue must continue its movement from the first to the last sound, or an entirely different phoneme results. Now compare the diphthongs in "eye" and "toy" with the vowel sounds [u] or [i] by prolonging each of these sounds. Can you hear the difference between a stable vowel and a gliding diphthong?

Two vowels can appear side by side in a word without creating a diphthong if they are in different syllables. For example, the word "chaotic" contains adjacent [e] and [ɑ] sounds which are in different syllables. Therefore, the two adjacent vowels won't create a diphthong, no matter how quickly you say the sounds.

We will not attempt to describe all North American English diphthongs here. Various regional and subsidiary dialects contain many. You may hear some of these in your class as students give oral presentations. However, you may find a brief review of a few of the diphthongs we already have discussed helpful as you try to understand their complexity in English.

We have said the sounds [e] and [o] have diphthong counterparts of [eɪ] and [oʊ] which are difficult for most inexperienced listeners to distinguish. For this reason, this book doesn't use these diphthong symbols. We also indicated that when the schwa or schwa-r sounds are added to various vowels, diphthongized vowels are created which may be either diphthongs or double vowels, depending on how long each sound is held, how much blending occurs, and whether or not another syllable is created. Therefore, "mail" is pronounced as [mel] in General American Speech, but may be heard as ['meəl] in the Southern American dialect. General American speakers pronounce the word "four" with a blended [ɔɚ]; Southern dialectal speakers may pronounce it as either a blend, or as two separate syllables as in ['foə]. We also said that in some subsidiary dialects, [o] often becomes a diphthong when speakers add the [ɛ] to [o] as when the word "go" becomes [gɛo]. The blending of [ju] and [jʊ] is sometimes called a diphthong, although in this book we have classified [j] as a consonant. Likewise, the blend [ɪu] which many speakers use instead of [ju] in words such as "huge," and "few," may be viewed as a diphthong. You can begin to see how complex this category can become. Let's try to simplify it.

In this book, we will refer to only three glided vowel sounds as General American Speech diphthongs: [aɪ], [aʊ], and [ɔɪ]. **Even though two symbols are used, they count as only one phoneme.** Any other vowel combinations should be viewed as blends of two separate vowels. (A potential problem arises if we attempt to apply the generalization that the number of vowels and diphthongs in a word usually determines the number of syllables it will have, particularly in words containing a vowel and the schwa-r sound as in "parking, courtly, Pierce." However, we modified this generalization earlier when we indicated that syllabic consonants often replace vowels in General American Speech, but still create a syllable.) **If you remember that only three diphthongs will be used to describe General American Speech, then you always should have an accurate phoneme count in your transcription exercises.** Remember that you may hear other diphthongs in oral class exercises.

[aɪ]

(kind)

Technical Description:	Diphthong (Low, Back to High, Front Vowel Glide)
Physiological Description: How the Sound is Made	Vocal folds vibrating, central part of tongue begins in a low position as lower jaw is relaxed and the unrounded lips are widely parted, then gradually glides to a high front position while the tongue tip remains close to the lower front teeth and the blade and middle portions move upward and forward close to the gum ridge as the jaws close, soft palate is raised, tongue and lip muscles remain relaxed, voicing continues as both sounds blend into one sound
Common Spellings:	i in item, tides, bribe, hi y in flying, try, why, rhyme ie in pies, lie, die uy in buying, guy ei in Eiffel, heighten, sleight igh in higher, fight, thigh
Periodic Spellings:	ey in geyser oi in choirs ye in rye, lye ui in guidance eye in eye is in islands ais in aisle aye in aye ai in Cairo

The [ɑɪ] diphthong is one of the two sounds which most people characterize as most clearly distinguishing General American Speech from the Southern American dialect. (The other sound is the schwa-r.) In the Southern dialect, the words "high, white sky" would be said as [hɑ hwɑt skɑ], but in General American Speech they would be pronounced [hɑɪ hwɑɪt skɑɪ]. Therefore, you would transcribe this substitution in someone's speech as [ɑ-ɑɪ].

COMMON PROBLEMS

1. If you speak either an obvious Southern or Black American dialect, you may substitute [ɑ-ɑɪ] regularly in all positions of words. You may eliminate the [ɪ] ending of this diphthong entirely, or use an extremely short, unstressed version of it. The middle and back of your tongue don't glide upward and forward. If you have this problem, you should practice saying the two vowel components of the diphthong aloud in slow succession, then gradually connect them. Beginning with the first consonant sound in the alphabet, [b], add the [ɑ] sound to it, then add an ending which begins with [ɪ] to each combined sound. Prolong the [ɑ] and then quickly add the ending. Gradually speed up the rate of pronouncing each combination, but be sure your tongue continues to move up to [ɪ] in each combination. Work your way through the consonant sounds until you begin to feel relaxed in completing the necessary movement of the tongue. Some of these combinations will create words; some will be nonsense combinations. For example, here are some possible combinations:

[b] + [ɑɪd]	[b] + [ɑɪnd]	[b] + [ɑɪz]
[f] + [ɑɪd]	[f] + [ɑɪnd]	[f] + [ɑɪz]
[g] + [ɑɪd]	[g] + [ɑɪnd]	[g] + [ɑɪz]

Could you hear the words "bide, bind, buys, find, guide, guys" in your speeded up pronunciations?

Now contrast the two sounds by reading aloud the words in the following list to be sure you can continue making the distinctions clear.

WORD PAIRS FOR CONTRASTING [ɑɪ] AND [ɑ]

a. sighed/sod; bah/by; hi/ha; Roz/rise; rah/rye; slights/slots; hot/height
b. I'd/odd; right/rot; eyes/ahs; sot/sight; rod/ride; tide/Todd; cot/kite
c. sight/sot; shy/shah; pa/pie; not/night; ah/I; hide/hod; trod/tried
d. dime/Dom; ma/my; light/lot; pod/pied; like/lock; tight/tot; pa's/pies
e. tykes/tocks; Tom/time; Mike/mock; Bach/bike; ides/odds; died/Dodd; spa/spy

---

2. Some North Americans and many British speakers change the initial sound in [ɑɪ] to [ɔ]. When American actors and actresses play a part requiring a British cockney accent, this is a change which many incorporate in their speech. The back of the tongue is raised to the position of [ɔ] and the lips are rounded slightly to make this change. Both elements must be omitted to create a clear General American [ɑɪ].

199

3. Some people create a triphthong when they add the schwa to the end of [aɪ]. The triphthong lines up three vowel sounds next to each other in the same syllable, without an intervening break, as [aɪʌ]. This becomes most obvious in the final position of words such as "my, buy, sly, tie, guy, high, try, deny, rely, defy." However, it also is heard frequently before voiced continuants in the initial position of contracted words such as "I'll" and "I'm" and in the medial position of words such as "time, rhyme, smile, awhile." To remedy this problem, the back of the tongue must not be allowed to drop from its [ɪ] position to create the schwa sound. In the final position, this can be handled by eliminating the voicing and/or closing the lips as soon as the [ɪ] has been voiced.

4. Often, the diphthongs are nasalized by individuals who nasalize their vowel sounds. As described in previous chapters, the soft palate is allowed to relax and drop, opening up the nasal passages to escaping air. If you have this problem, choose words with this diphthong but without any nasal sounds. Hold the nostrils shut with your finger and thumb while pronouncing the words to force all of the air through the mouth. If necessary, yawn before each new list of words to feel the soft palate elevate and close off the nasal passages.

EXERCISES FOR PRACTICING [aɪ]

1. Read the following phonemes aloud, contrasting the sounds as you do so.

a. [aɪ] [a] [ɪ] [aɪ] [aɪ aɪ] [a] [a] [aɪ] [ɪ] [aɪ]

b. [zaɪ] [aɪz] [aɪt] [taɪ] [paɪ] [aɪp] [kaɪ] [aɪk]

2. Translate the following IPA transcriptions into words and write them on the lines provided.

a. [slaɪd] _____   ['aɪsi] _____   [taɪmz] _____

b. [baɪts] _____   [braɪdz] _____   ['saɪdɪd] _____

c. [taɪt] _____   ['maɪti] _____   ['haɪtn̩] _____

d. [naɪf] _____   [aɪst] _____   [di'faɪ] _____

e. [klaɪd] _____   [di'naɪd] _____   [raɪts] _____

3. Translate the following words into IPA symbols, using General American Speech as your model for pronunciation. Include accent marks in your transcriptions.

a. insight _____   trying _____   shy _____

b. climber _____   delighted _____   nine _____

c. chimes _____   trite _____   tithe _____

d. siphon _____   python _____   quite _____

e. stylish _____   child _____   trials _____

200

4. Determine the number of syllables and phonemes in each of the following words. Transcribe each word and circle the correct numbers.

Word	Transcription	Syllables	Phonemes
a. stylish	[ ]	1 2 3 4 5	1 2 3 4 5 6 7 8 9
b. enlightening	[ ]	1 2 3 4 5	1 2 3 4 5 6 7 8 9
c. kindliest	[ ]	1 2 3 4 5	1 2 3 4 5 6 7 8 9
d. silent	[ ]	1 2 3 4 5	1 2 3 4 5 6 7 8 9
e. childhood	[ ]	1 2 3 4 5	1 2 3 4 5 6 7 8 9

5. Read the following word combinations aloud. If you have problems with this diphthong, practice these words slowly at first and then speed up your rate of speaking.

a. Ike buys rye; hide Ida's pie; my ice shines; Issac's dyed kite; shy Mina's eye

b. why I'm guiding; Eiffel's tie hides; by nine items; why I'd slide; I've tried high

c. times I spy; guided Thai ideas; isolated five lies; thy wife idolizes; kind Iva try

d. iced tiles fly; bribes I'll die; island mice dry; idle spider fly; buy briar items

e. iron pipes vie; my idea surprised; butterfly isolated twice; spry beguiling Ina; try Ireland's prize

6. Read the following sentences aloud at a conversational rate. Do not try to prolong the diphthongs.

a. What time should I try to bake the pie for the ice cream social on Friday?

b. The beguiling bride came down the aisle with a smile that was twice the size of her father's.

c. He made a sign that it was time for Clyde to draw the diagram for the bilingual exercise.

d. Despite her diabetes, she tried to design the finest, most stylish line of clothing for her blind friends.

e. He tried to rhyme the final line of a poem which described his ride in a glider over Hawaii.

7. Practice Paragraphs

a. When the airline advertised special fare flights to Miami if we could leave on Friday, Ty and I decided to go. We were tired and needed some exercise to clear our minds for the next term. "The price is right; the sun is bright; we need it to survive," we said. We got a supply of sun tan lotion as soon as we arrived. Then we rented diving equipment, climbed in a boat and piloted ourselves to an offshore island. We divided our entire time between diving in the wide channel and lying on the white sandy beach. What a sight to watch the waves striking the high rocks beyond the island. The incoming tide finally guided us back to reality and we climbed into the boat and glided back to shore.

b. My junior high school required us to take a course called "Highlights of Science." Mike Cline hated science, even though he was the brightest guy in class. During class he would write notes to me, just out of the teacher's line of sight, like "How's your wife?" and "The teacher's all wet and science is dry." Often, I had to stifle my desire to laugh right out loud. He aspired to drive the teacher crazy with his innocent questions which were designed to guide her away from her topic. Because she liked him, she tried to show signs of great interest in his questions. Sometimes, the whole class recognized what Mike was doing and would smile and nod wisely as the teacher supplied us with a library of scientific information that never would appear on a test.

c. Inez stood outside the store looking at the prices posted on items in the window. In spite of her small salary as a library clerk, she had acquired enough money to buy one gift for her daughter this Christmas. She had already decided it must be something that her five-year-old Lida would like. A fine white linen dress caught her eye—the kind she had always dreamed of having as a child. The price was too high. It required more than she had saved. But it would be so nice to see her daughter's eyes brighten! She could picture Lida's bright smile as the light fabric slipped over her head. Perhaps a slightly different menu for their Christmas dinner could be devised to supply the needed amount.

[ɑʊ]

(owl)

Technical Description:	Diphthong (Low, Back to High, Back Vowel Glide)
Physiological Description: How the Sound is Made	Vocal folds vibrating, lower jaw is relaxed and dropped, lips begin in unrounded, lax position (not drawn up at the corners), soft palate is raised, tongue begins in a flat, relaxed position and then the back of the tongue moves upward towards the soft palate as the lower jaw closes and the lips round for [ʊ], voicing continues uninterrupted as both sounds blend into one sound
Common Spellings:	ou in our, bound, trout, thou ow in owl, towel, crown, endow
Periodic Spellings:	au in sauerkraut, pau, Maui ough in plough, bough ao in Maori, Taoism, Taos

Of the three diphthongs we are studying, this one tends to have the most variations in pronunciation throughout North American dialects. In its [ɑʊ] format, it begins as a full, relatively open and relaxed [ɑ] sound and moves to a more closed but still relaxed [ʊ] sound. In its variations of [æʊ] and [ɛʊ], it begins as a relatively tense, closed sound and continues to remain fairly closed and tense. The full [ɑʊ] diphthong is more resonant than its variations. However, these variations have embedded themselves in the speech habits of many young speakers, perhaps partially as a result of their common use among popular Country Western singers. If one wishes to be perceived as an authentic Country Western singer when singing the lyrics to music, if not in daily speech habits also, he or she must use one of these substitutions.

The mispronunciation of [ɑʊ] is not a unique problem of the current younger generation. In fact, for many years diction teachers required students to practice saying "How now brown cow?"

with round, full diphthongs. This is one of the sounds that Professor Higgins had Liza Doolittle work on in the musical comedy "My Fair Lady." If you ever lived near the Canadian/United States border where you could hear broadcasts from both countries, you may have noticed this was one of the few sound changes which indicated certain broadcasters were from Canada and not the United States.

COMMON PROBLEMS

1. One of the most common problems faced by speech improvement teachers who are trying to teach students to speak a General American Speech pattern is the substitution of either [æ] or [ɛ] for [ɑ] in the [ɑʊ] diphthong. In both substitutions, the tension in the tongue is too great as the sound begins and the lips are drawn up slightly at the corners. Since this is such a common substitution, you may need to go through a period of ear training as you try to distinguish which of these sounds is being said by a speaker. Your instructor may give you a listening exercise to see if you can hear the differences. Unless you can hear the differences, you probably won't be able to change your own substitutions if you are making them.

Place a thumb in the fleshy part under your chin and say [æ] and [ɑ]. Then say [ɛ] and [ɑ]. Notice that the thumb is pushed down for both [æ] and [ɛ], but not for [ɑ]. This is because the muscles under the tongue are relaxed for the initial sound in a good, full [ɑʊ] sound.

Hold onto the initial relaxed [ɑ] sound while dropping the jaw considerably. Be absolutely sure you aren't beginning with [æ], or you may glide through it and the correct diphthong, creating another triphthong. Gradually glide up to the [ʊ] sound as you say the following words: our, out, ounce, ouch, ourselves, outside, outer, outrageous, outstanding, outreach. At first, the dropping of the jaw should feel quite exaggerated if you have been unaccustomed to saying this diphthong correctly. With practice, you'll discover you can form the diphthong without this exaggerated position. When you can handle the sound correctly in the initial position, place it in the medial and final positions of words and see if you can continue to control the sound. The following initial phonemes may be blended with this diphthong in practice exercises.

LINKING INITIAL PHONEMES WITH THE [ɑʊ] DIPHTHONG

Begin with each of these phonemes:	**Add:**
a. [b], [f], [h], [m], [p], [r], [s], [w], [gr]	+ [ɑʊnd]
b. [p], [l], [pr], [kr]	+ [ɑʊdɚ]
c. [kr], [kl], [l], [v]	+ [ɑʊd]
d. [d], [g], [t], [br], [kr]	+ [ɑʊn]
e. [b], [k], [h], [n], [p], [v], [w]	+ [ɑʊ]
f. [b], [fl], [gl], [k], [p], [s], [t], [ʃ]	+ [ɑʊɚ]
g. [b], [fl], [p], [tr]	+ [ɑʊns]
h. [k], [m]	+ [ɑʊnt]

---

2. Because of its complete location at the back of the throat, this diphthong tends to be nasalized more often than the other two. The soft palate is allowed to relax and drop, and air flows through the nose. If you have this tendency, check previous sections of this book on nasalized vowel and diphthong sounds to receive help on correcting this problem.

3. Many people omit the [U] when this diphthong precedes the schwa-r in words such as "flower, tower, sour, power," and especially "our." They avoid any lip movement to complete the [U] sound. Say these combinations aloud to see if you have this tendency: our action, our only, our honest, our coffee.

EXERCISES FOR PRACTICING [ɑU]

1. Contrast the phonemes in the following transcription by reading each item aloud.

a. [ɑ]   [U]   [ɑU]   [æ]   [ɛ]   [ɑU]   [ɛ]   [ɑ]   [ɑU]   [ɑU ɑU]

b. [ɑUt]   [tɑU]   [mɑU]   [ɑUm]   [bɑU]   [ɑUb]   [vɑU]   [ɑUv]

2. Translate the following IPA transcriptions into words and write your answers on the lines provided.

a. ['brɑUnɪŋ] _____   [tɑUn] _____   [ə'mɑUnt] _____

b. ['kɑUnti] _____   [grɑUndz] _____   [pɑUnst] _____

c. [grɑUl] _____   [ə'bɑUt] _____   [drɑUnd] _____

d. [ɑUns] _____   [ɑUt'saɪd] _____   [kɑUtʃ] _____

e. [hɑUs] _____   [krɑUtʃ] _____   [bɑUns] _____

3. Transcribe the following words into IPA symbols, using General American Speech as your model for pronunciation. Include stress marks wherever appropriate.

a. crowded _____   Howard _____   shout _____

b. prowler _____   eyebrow _____   ours _____

c. chowder _____   towel _____   allow _____

d. mountain _____   boundary _____   power _____

e. allowance _____   clowns _____   astound _____

4. Determine the number of syllables and phonemes in each of the following words. Transcribe each word and circle the correct numbers.

Word	Transcription	Syllables	Phonemes
a. downtown	[ ]	1 2 3 4 5	1 2 3 4 5 6 7 8 9
b. amounting	[ ]	1 2 3 4 5	1 2 3 4 5 6 7 8 9

c. surrounding	[	]	1 2 3 4 5	1 2 3 4 5 6 7 8 9
d. outlaws	[	]	1 2 3 4 5	1 2 3 4 5 6 7 8 9
e. outlines	[	]	1 2 3 4 5	1 2 3 4 5 6 7 8 9

5. Read the following word groups aloud. Do not try to prolong the pronunciation of diphthongs in the words.

a. allow brownstones outside; crowded out now; how our couch; rowdy plow ousting; endow outdoor cloudiness

b. hours somehow mount; now brown owls; sow around outfits; outlaw's brow astounded; crown's tower outlet

c. ourselves jousting about; outcast cowboys vow; now output amounts; frown's outer power; mouse around ours

d. avow towel outlines; pow wow amounted; flowers allow ounces; Audi found out; how flounder outweighed

e. Gow announced outreach; allow thousands outside; doubt thou outlaw; shouted wow ourselves; sauerkraut bounced

6. Practice reading the following sentences aloud as you would say them in daily conversation.

a. We were confounded by the background of our only remaining farmhouse in the downtown area.

b. After an hour we found we pronounced the sound with rounded lips and a resounding loud "ow."

c. The crowded township was surrounded by an astounding mountain of brown sandstone.

d. The mayor announced all outcast hounds carousing around the town would be impounded.

e. She scowled when she found another gown just like hers on a clown in the ship's lounge.

7. Practice Paragraphs

a. Somehow, the downpour of mid-afternoon showers hadn't drowned out our welcoming party at the Maui airport. We found ourselves surrounded by smiling faces, fragrant flowers, and soft Hawaiian music. Everyone crowded around the baggage claim carousel, talking excitedly about the flight. It seemed strange to be standing outside in the middle of January, waiting for our luggage. Someone shouted, "Look up at the mountains. A double rainbow!" We all turned around. Sure enough, surmounting the crest and streaming into a shrouded valley was the most outstanding rainbow we had ever encountered. "Around here," our smiling host said, "That is very common."

b. For an hour, the scouts had worked on the foundation for a cabin. They never doubted their ability, after their scoutmaster showed them the layout in a diagram. After thousands of sweeps of their trowels over wet cement, their leader announced their first job was done. They closed the remaining bag of cement powder, bound it with a rope, and placed it next to the water fountain. Their leader said he was proud of their work and he doubted they would find any flaws when it was dry. The south wind and cloudless sky were good omens and would allow them to sleep outside that night as the cement cured.

    c. A housewife from Mountain View won first prize for her sour cherry pie at the county fair. She hadn't counted on even placing, so when her name was announced, she burst into tears. When she shook the judge's outstretched hand, she said, scarcely out loud, "I never won anything before. I am so proud." The judge replied, "Our contest sponsor found your pie so outstanding, it is offering you a thousand dollars if it can use your recipe on its bags of flour. Now what have you to say?" She finally found her voice, and murmured, "For that amount, they can print it on anything they please!"

[ɔɪ]

(coy)

Technical Description:	Diphthong (Mid, Back to High, Front Vowel Glide)
Physiological Description: How the Sound is Made	Vocal folds vibrating, back of tongue begins in a mid-high, relaxed position and moves forward to a high front [ɪ] position as lips move from a rounded to an unrounded position, the tongue muscles remain lax, the soft palate is raised, voicing continues uninterrupted as both sounds blend into one sound
Common Spellings:	oi in ointment, noise, poi oy in oyster, royal, annoy
Periodic Spellings:	eu in Freudian

    This final diphthong is different from the other two because it moves from a rounded lip sound [ɔ] to an unrounded lip sound. It is the sound which many people associate with Brooklynese and with early gangster movies. This substitution replaces the schwa-r sounds in a sentence such as: "She got noivous when she hoid the boid singing on the thoid (or toid) floor (or flaw)." Actors and actresses who play the stereotypical role of relatively uneducated, uncultured Brooklyn residents try to make these substitutions throughout their dialects.

206

COMMON PROBLEMS

1. The substitution of [ɔɪ-ɜˑ] or [ɔɪ-ɚ], which was mentioned above, actually is an error in the production of the schwa-r sounds. If you make this substitution, you will need to work on words which contain the schwa-r sounds in all positions of words. You will gain the most help by turning back to the chapter containing exercises for the schwa-r sounds. The middle portion of the tongue must be pulled up high and tensely toward the hard palate to produce good schwa-r sounds. Here are just a few words that may be helpful in your initial practice session: learn, turn, bird, certain, curtain, murder, word, verb, third, curve, nervous, service, Herbert, sherbet, curb, thirty, shirt, flirt, dirty, courteous.

2. Quite a few speakers of the Southern American dialect replace the [ɪ] sound with a schwa when saying this diphthong. In addition, some speakers also add the [w] or [j] sound so that a word such as "toil" sounds like ['tɔwəl]. Others omit the [ɪ] entirely without substituting anything, thus creating the [ɔ-ɔɪ] substitution. When these changes occur, quite a few semantic changes also occur. The following list indicates a few semantic changes which could result from these substitutions.

SEMANTIC CHANGES WHICH RESULT FROM SELECTIVE CHANGES IN [ɔɪ]

Word	If a schwa replaces [ɪ]:	If [w] and a schwa are substituted:	If the [ɪ] is omitted:
join	jaw on	jaw one/jaw won	
poise	paw's	paw was	paws
joys	jaw's	jaw was	jaws
boys	Baugh's	Baugh was	Baughs
coil	call		call
boil	ball		ball
rejoice	rejaws	rejaw was	
loin	law on	law won/law one	lawn
oil	awl	awe wool	all
soya			saw ya
noise	gnaws	gnaw was	gnaws
Roy's	raws/Roz	raw was	raws/Roz
joint		jaw want	jaunt

3. Occasionally, the diphthong [ɑɪ] is substituted for [ɔɪ] in North American speech. However, this is heard more often in Irish, Australian, and English dialects than in American dialects. When this change occurs, usually the lips are not rounded to begin the diphthong and the lower jaw has not been dropped to allow the tongue to move downward far enough. No distinction is made between "toil" and "tile."

4. Finally, because [ɔɪ] begins at the back of the throat, many people nasalize it when they allow the soft palate to relax and drop. If you nasalize this diphthong, you probably nasalize other vowels and diphthongs and should review the information given previously on eliminating nasality. Remember to practice with a list of words that contains no nasal sounds first.

EXERCISES FOR PRACTICING [ɔɪ]

1. Read the following IPA transcriptions aloud.

a. [ɔ]   [ɪ]   [ɔɪ]   [ɔ]   [ɔɪ]   [ɪ]   [ɔ]   [ɔɪ]   [ɔɪ ɔɪ]

b. [fɔɪ]   [ɔɪf]   [tɔɪ]   [ɔɪt]   [sɔɪ]   [ɔɪs]   [fɔɪst]

2. Translate the following IPA transcriptions into words. Write the words on the blanks provided.

a. [ˈvɔɪdɪd] _____   [ˈɔɪstɚ] _____   [ˈbrɔɪlɚ] _____

b. [ˈælɔɪ] _____   [ˈmɔɪsn̩] _____   [tɔɪd] _____

c. [tʃɔɪs] _____   [ˈnɔɪzɪz] _____   [sɔɪld] _____

d. [ˈlɔɪəl] _____   [ˈpɔɪzn̩] _____   [əˈnɔɪnt] _____

e. [dʒɔɪnd] _____   [ˈkɔɪnɪŋ] _____   [flɔɪd] _____

3. Transcribe the following words into IPA symbols, using General American Speech as your model. Include accent marks.

a. gargoyle _____   poised _____   envoy _____

b. cloister _____   convoy _____   voices _____

c. Troy _____   highboy _____   pointer _____

d. employee _____   disloyal _____   boyish _____

e. viceroy _____   typhoid _____   appoint _____

4. Determine the number of syllables and phonemes in each of the following words. Transcribe each word and circle the correct numbers.

Word	Transcription		Syllables	Phonemes
a. disappoint	[	]	1 2 3 4 5	1 2 3 4 5 6 7 8 9
b. employment	[	]	1 2 3 4 5	1 2 3 4 5 6 7 8 9
c. celluloid	[	]	1 2 3 4 5	1 2 3 4 5 6 7 8 9
d. ointment	[	]	1 2 3 4 5	1 2 3 4 5 6 7 8 9
e. soybean	[	]	1 2 3 4 5	1 2 3 4 5 6 7 8 9

5. Read the following groups of words aloud, as if they were part of a normal conversation.

a. destroy choice oilcans; adroit oyster decoy; avoids oily alloy; coy loyal oink

b. royal convoy oil; Savoy parboils oysters; enjoy soiled oilcloth; oiling annoying joint

c. employ Joy's ointment; deploy boy's noise; poisoned gargoyle ploy; adjoining envoy oiled

6. Read the following sentences aloud without exaggerating any of the sounds. Use the same fluency and inflections which would be heard in good conversational speech.

a. The soil was poisoned by the adjoining oil company, even though its employees tried to prevent it.

b. Edith Choi, his loyal appointment secretary, brought a choice poinsettia to the office for us to enjoy.

c. He toyed with the idea of broiling the chicken while basting it with soy sauce, in honor of the Chinese envoy.

d. Miss Doyle's voice was very poised as she removed the oyster from her chair, thus, foiling the boys' hopes of frightening her.

e. There was no noise within the cloister walls except the quiet dripping of moisture from overhanging trees.

7. Practice Paragraphs

a. People loitered about the decks, talking in boisterous voices. Some of the younger girls and boys were broiling in the sun. Joyce was embroidering a corduroy skirt during her voyage. She sat in her canvas deck chair, joyfully talking to her mother who was crocheting a doiley next to her. They didn't wish to destroy the noisy atmosphere surrounding them. They knew those people had toiled as long as they, to be able to afford to join this convoy of three ships. They all viewed this voyage as a joint venture in enjoyment.

b. "Let's have broiled sirloin steaks, medium rare—and some boiled potatoes for dinner," he said to his loyal cook as he uncoiled his legs from his desk chair—an annoying habit he had had since youth. "The fishing fleets still are boycotting the oyster beds, so there's no point in searching the market for any. It's very annoying, since they made their point several weeks ago." She nodded and left him to toil over stacks of invoices piled on his desk. Mr. Lloyd turned his boyish face momentarily towards the moistened windowpanes, wondering if he hadn't heard someone outside shout, "Ahoy!"

c. As children, Joyce and I always enjoyed watching the coin dealers as they set up their annual Detroit convention center display booths. Our father was employed there each June and we were allowed to go along and watch—if we avoided getting in his way. We sat coyly on a wooden bench covered with a piece of soiled oilcloth and whispered to each other, even though the dealers' noise would have allowed us to talk freely without disturbing anyone. Bright silver and gold coins were placed adroitly in glass cases, then hoisted upright. The choicest coins always stayed well behind the counters as a pointed reminder of their value. At times, we were annoyed that we couldn't see over the counters and we would make mental "appointments." That meant we would exploit our father's patience, at the end of each day, and ask to be hoisted on his shoulders to see the special coins hidden from our view.

8. Dialogue for Oral Practice (requires two readers)

Anchor 1: (To camera) On Friday night, the Neighborhood Council of Boynton Downs will sponsor its fourth annual Coffee and Ice Cream Fair. Most of the outdoor festivities will take place between 5 and 11 p.m. in the town square at the intersection of Royal Road and Knight Boulevard.

Anchor 2: (To camera) All of you who attended last year's fair will recall the **numerous** flavors of ice cream that were served at 49 different booths in the town square. I started with a dish of mountain berry and Boston chocolate ice cream, both made by the ninth graders at Horton High School. (To Anchor 1) Ummm, they were both sooo good!

Anchor 1: (To Anchor 2) And I started with Sophie's Choice Butterscotch ice cream on a slice of moist pound cake, made by the County Volunteer Fire Department! To top it off, I had a cup of freshly ground and freshly brewed Kyle Supreme coffee, served by the South Kyle Kiwanis Club. It was so fragrant. But tell me, could you stop at just one dish of ice cream?

Anchor 2: (To Anchor 1) Oh, not at all! Before the fair was over, I had also had some Mount Rushmore Red Raspberry, Sidewinder Coconut, and Black Boysenberry ice cream. And speaking of coffee—I had two cups of Lilac Mountain Grown Coffee, served by the Fountain Forks Boy Scout Troop. It was so good, I bought a pound bag to take home!

Anchor 1: (To Anchor 2) Well, now I can confess, too. I had a cup of Kona Haven Hawaiian coffee at the Orlando Civic Roundtable's booth, and dishes of Ida Cross Vanilla and Cajun Brown Sugar Praline ice cream before the evening ended. It was quite a challenge to choose from all the flavors offered, wasn't it?

Anchor 2: (To Anchor 1) Yes, it certainly was. My son's favorite flavor was Chocolate Chip Cookie, made by the Tidewater Hospital Auxiliary and he says he's going back this year to get more.

Anchor 1: (To camera) If **you** missed the Boynton Downs Coffee and Ice Cream Fair last year, be sure to put it on your calendar now. It will be this Friday, beginning at 5 p.m. in the town square. In case of inclement weather, it will be moved into the municipal auditorium behind the square.

Anchor 2: (To camera) And for you out-of-towners who will be driving in—you can take either Royal Road or Knight Boulevard. Plenty of free parking is available around the square and at the municipal auditorium. We'll see you there!

CHAPTER 16

DEVELOPING VARIETY IN PITCH AND INFLECTIONS

Probably you enjoy listening to some type of music. Music may serve as a background for the tasks you are doing, adding variety to many routine functions such as shopping, waiting for a dental appointment, or riding in an elevator. You may listen to music to hear the lyrics and/or to hear the melody. Even though you don't pay close attention to each selection, you may respond unconsciously to the soothing, interesting, or invigorating qualities of music.

You may enjoy certain music, such as rock, jazz, classical, country western, or blues music, more than other music because it "brings back memories" of past experiences or suggests goals you would like to attain. However, you also may like one type of music more than another because of its unique sound, melody, or rhythm. Without these variations, you would have exactly the same melodies and lyrics repeated over and over again.

In its simplest sense, music is the controlled arrangement of the four fundamental characteristics of sound: pitch, volume (loudness), rate (duration), and quality (resonance). This ordering can become extremely complex in musical selections and also may involve repetition and pausing. These are some of the same considerations you will be studying to create "vocal variety" in human speech. Three of these characteristics, pitch, loudness, and resonance, were incorporated by Dr. Lawrence Kersta at Bell Telephone Laboratories, into a recording technique called "voice-prints," which show the unique graphic patterns of any person's voice.

THE MUSIC OF THE HUMAN VOICE

Outstanding speakers have versatile, musical voices—voices which vary continually in pitch changes, intonations, or inflections. These pitch changes tell a great deal about the emotions, responses, and intended meanings of the speakers. They help to keep your interest in what is being said. They also help you to understand levels or degrees of meaning that written words, by themselves, are incapable of implying without attaching narrative or descriptive words to elaborate on them. For example, if you saw the following words in a book, how would you interpret them?

"Come and sit down."

Obviously, if these were the only words on a page, you would assume they were a directive to "stop standing and start sitting." However, if they were placed within the context of a story or play, you would need more information in order to know how those words were spoken, and how *you* should read them aloud to someone else.

If these same words were followed by "she said softly," you would know a *little* more about how to read the material aloud to someone else. However, the words continue to lack complete definition. If the following words were added after "softly," notice how they begin to require you

	FOUR CHARACTERISTICS OF SOUND IN RELATION TO VOICE	
PITCH	Vocal folds flutter or vibrate at a specific number of cycles per second. Both the mass (thickness) and length of vocal folds can affect pitch. Male vocal folds tend to be longer and thicker than the average female vocal folds. (As vocal folds become more tense, they vibrate at more cycles per second, creating a higher pitch.) Common musical descriptions of pitch ranges are: soprano, alto, tenor, baritone and bass.
VOLUME (Loudness)	The amount or degree of muscular pressure placed on exhaled air creates the basis for volume changes. Much of the pressure for speaking louder should come from the abdominal and diaphragmatic muscles rather than the throat (pharynx) and neck muscles. The terms ''projection'' (focusing the sound waves to specific locations in an audience or auditorium) and ''intensity'' or vocal stress (attack placed upon individual phonemes or words) may be considered variations of volume.
RATE (Duration)	The basis for determining one's rate of speaking usually is the number of words spoken per minute. Rate is influenced by the amount of time each phoneme is held (prolonged) and by the number and length of pauses used. When changing one's rate, care must be given NOT to create disfluent or poorly connected thought sequences (phrasing).
QUALITY (Resonance)	Voice quality depends heavily upon the nose, mouth, and throat (pharynx) cavities. As sound is modulated or modified by bouncing about in these cavities, it creates unique sound wave shapes or patterns which oscilloscopes can show graphically for each individual. Resonance is affected by the size, shape, number, and texture of resonating cavities through which sound passes. Tense cavity surfaces usually produce a harsher quality because they deflect, rather than absorb sound.

to manipulate your voice in order to attain different meanings:

1. ''she said softly, unemotionally and deliberately, without raising her eyes from her magazine.''

2. ''she said softly, caressing her vowel sounds lovingly as her voice oozed down the musical scale until she sounded as if she were sinking deeper and deeper into her huge, overstuffed chair and soon would disappear completely from my view, leaving behind only the lingering echo of her charming southern drawl.''

3. ''she said softly but brusquely, trying to control the breath which struggled to burst from her chest in violent anger and hurl him against the opposite wall.''

4. ''she said softly and coyly, as if she were teasing him, coaxing him—*daring* him to actually sit beside her on the loveseat.''

From these examples, you may be able to see that written words have severe limitations for describing exactly how a voice sounds. Words can only attempt to describe the voice but they cannot imitate its actual sounds. Only by reading the words aloud can you begin to understand the actual sound changes which are necessary for producing the desired effects. Usually, these sound changes are directly related to intonations or vocal inflections.

How Do Changes in Pitch Occur?

The term ''pitch'' refers to a specific note on the musical scale. From a technical viewpoint, pitch is determined by the frequency of vibrations or oscillations (usually referred to either as ''hertz'' or hz, or as ''cycles per second'' or cps), which occur at the source of any sound. Pitch goes up as the cycles per second increase and down as they decrease. For example, the strings on a violin may be composed of different materials and may vary in thickness, even though they all are of equal length. As they are released or tightened, the degree of tension placed on each string can change the number of times per second each string will vibrate when plucked or stroked, thus raising or lowering the musical notes being played.

When violinists tune their violins, they tighten each string to a specific musical note which is always produced by a specific number of vibrations per second. Middle C, for example, is produced by 256 vibrations per second. This action creates a different "tuned" pitch for each string. Then, by pressing a finger on a string to shorten or lengthen the portion which is vibrating at any particular moment, violinists change the number of times each second that a string vibrates as their bows move over it. Whenever any string is released, its original "tuned" note will be repeated, since the string will vibrate the same number of times as when it originally was tuned.

Creating Pitch Changes in the Human Voice

The vocal folds are similar to a violin string. They stretch or relax as air passes between them to produce more (higher pitch) or fewer (lower pitch) vibrations per second. Unlike standardized violin strings, your vocal folds will be slightly different in size, shape, and texture from anyone else's. However, these differences don't prevent you from attaining the same pitch as other voices (as you realize from your past experiences in singing the same musical notes other people are singing!) When the singers in a choral group sing exactly the same musical note, their vocal folds vibrate at the same frequency.

SOME IMPORTANT ASPECTS OF VOCAL PITCH

If you could record and tabulate all the musical notes you use in speaking during a month's time, you would find you consistently use a relatively small range of musical notes. This range is your **prevailing or habitual pitch range.** Your prevailing range may have more or fewer notes than your friends' prevailing ranges. Within this range, you also could find *one note which occurred most often.* This is your **pitch mode or modal pitch.** Notice that mode is not the same as a statistical average or "mean."

Modal and Optimum Pitch

Your modal pitch should be comfortable for you to produce—and pleasant for others to listen to in daily conversations. If this is true, you probably also are speaking at your **optimum pitch— the pitch at which you can speak your loudest and clearest with the least amount of physical strain on your throat and vocal folds.** On the other hand, your modal pitch may be above or below your optimum pitch and your voice may sound too harsh or strident, too raspy or guttural, too delicate or weak, too throaty or breathy, or may lack changes in inflections. In these cases, you may be speaking above or below your optimum pitch. If this is true, you may need to work to modify your modal pitch. Your instructor will be able to help you modify your prevailing pitch if it is unsatisfactory for you.

Usually, through maturation and experience, you learn that adult voices sound different from children's voices, and you adapt your pitch to copy the adult voices surrounding you. When the vocal folds stop growing, you find a slightly lower pitch is easier and more comfortable for you to make than your higher childhood modal pitch. Thus, you change your modal pitch as a normal, developmental step.

In some cases, however, individuals become so accustomed to using sounds in their prevailing childhood or early adolescent pitch range that when their vocal folds grow, the individuals increase their larynx and throat tension in order to retain the pitch they are accustomed to using. As a result, some adults ignore their optimum pitch and continue to speak with child-like voices.

Also, at times individuals emulate someone they admire or want to be like. Popular movie, radio, and television personalities, for example, have great potential for becoming speech models for children. If a potential model or "idol" has a very high or very low modal pitch, children and adolescents may attempt to copy this pitch, even if they have to strain their vocal folds to do so. This becomes especially obvious when teenage peer groups attempt to emulate a current idol's

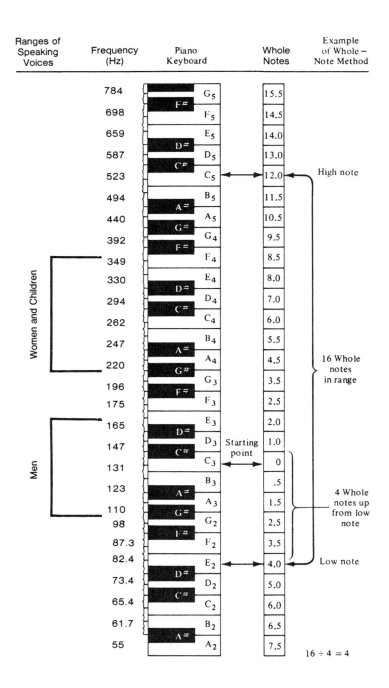

Figure 16-1 Chart for locating optimum pitch based on the Fairbanks method. The total number of notes vocalized, including falsetto, taken each time from a comfortable starting pitch (16 whole notes in the example on the chart). The sum (16) is divided by 4. Next, count up from the lowest note (E_3) 2 whole notes ($16 \div 4 = 4$) to find the estimated optimal pitch (C_3). Notice that any two adjacent keys (white-black/white-white) are *one-half* note or step apart. The numbers in the blocks under the column *Whole Notes* illustrate the proper counting for whole notes in the example. Also shown are the ranges of typical speaking voices. (Modified from Fig. 6-1 (p.67) in *Modifying Vocal Behavior* by John P. Moncur and Isaac P. Brackett. Copyright© by John P. Moncur and Isaac P. Brackett. By permission of Harper and Row, Publishers, Inc.)

214

faddish manner of speaking. Fortunately, most parents are able to convince their offspring that a comedian's or actor's contrived voice for a specific role is not an appropriate substitute for daily speaking.

As you begin to study how **pitch** influences inflections, remember that you probably are not an objective judge of your own pitch level. Many students believe their prevailing pitch is too high and that their voices are not as pleasant sounding as they should be. Voice and diction instructors are accustomed to hearing "I don't like the sound of my voice." Since you are hearing your voice through ears that are attached to your skull, not only are you closer to your voice than anyone else—but you also are aware of skull vibrations and slight pitch variations which no one else can detect.

How To Determine Your Optimum and Modal Pitches

In order to attain variety in vocal inflections, you need to be able to move your voice up and down the muscial scale without placing a great amount of strain on the vocal folds. By speaking with a relaxed voice, you avoid developing unpleasant vocal qualities and/or straining the larynx. If you must speak for extended periods of time as teachers, sportscasters, ministers, personnel supervisors, telephone operators, and receptionists do, you need to feel confident that you are using your optimum pitch while you are speaking. By becoming aware of your optimum pitch, you can learn to speak slightly above and below it, within a comfortable pitch range.

Several ways have been used by diction teachers to determine an individual's optimum pitch. One of the best methods which you can try by yourself requires the use of a piano or electronic keyboard. Take a deep breath, say "ah" in a relaxed voice, and sustain it until you find the exact note on the keyboard. Use the keyboard to find musical notes as you sing "ah" on successively lower musical notes until you reach a note at which clarity and audibility become unclear or difficult to sustain. This note marks the *bottom* of your range. Make a note of it, either by placing a piece of tape on the key, or if you read music, by writing the musical note you played.

Next, sing "ah" as you move up the scale to the highest note that you can sustain. This includes falsetto notes (if you can sing falsetto). This note marks the top of your pitch range. Make a note of this key as you did the lowest one. Now, counting every black and white key on the keyboard within your pitch range, add up the total number of keyboard keys (half tones or semitones) within your pitch range and divide by four. The resulting number indicates the note which probably is closest to your optimum pitch. It represents a comfortable fourth of your pitch range.

Using this resulting number, go back to the keyboard and play again the lowest note in your range. Then counting **every** black and white key, move up the scale until you reach the resulting number. That musical note should represent your optimum pitch. Now leave the keyboard, relax your throat by humming the easiest note for you to hum with your mouth closed. (Most people hum at their modal pitch level.) Take another breath, and hum by saying "ah" on one musical note. It probably will be the same musical note as before. Now, go back to the keyboard and find where that note is. It is your modal pitch. You now know where both your modal pitch and your optimum pitch are located on the keyboard.

Exercises for Working on Optimum Pitch

If you find a difference of more than two musical notes between your optimum and modal pitch, you should practice reading aloud by always beginning practice sessions at your optimum pitch. If necessary, tape record the piano note which represents that pitch and play it back every time you begin to practice. Read up two additional musical notes and down two more musical notes from your optimum pitch until you can feel and hear the pitch range you are using. Don't be concerned with sounding unnatural or "strange." As you develop greater competence in your new pitch range, you also will be able to develop more realistic or natural inflection patterns.

Here are several exercises for you to practice as you work to bring your modal and optimum pitch closer together.

EXERCISES FOR DEVELOPING OPTIMUM PITCH IN SPEAKING

1. Play your optimum pitch on a keyboard or tape recorder. Keeping your mouth closed, take a deep breath and hum this note as loudly and consistently as you can while sustaining it for ten seconds. This requires some control of the expulsion of air through your nose. You should be able to feel the bridge of your nose vibrating as this sound is intensified.

2. Play your optimum pitch again, take a deep breath, and sing "ah" at this pitch for five seconds and then gradually increase your volume for the next five seconds, all on the same breath.

3. When you can complete the first two exercises easily and accurately, read the following sentences at your optimum pitch. Do not deviate from one note. You will sound like you are chanting. Be aware of the sound that you create, but also keep your throat as relaxed as possible.

   a. I can beat anybody here playing dominoes.

   b. This is the last train to Boston.

   c. Who knows the answer to this question?

4. Begin each of the following sentences with your optimum pitch. Read each sentence aloud, first moving up the musical scale from your optimum pitch, one musical note for each new word, then moving down the musical scale one musical note for each word. Keep your throat relaxed and your volume level moderately loud.

   a. I can hear you.

   b. Who owns this car?

   c. You know one thing.

5. Play your optimum pitch on a piano or tape recorder. Hum that pitch, then using it for the first word of each of the following sentences, read them aloud. Stress the underlined word at a slightly higher pitch than your optimum pitch. Try to use as many different musical notes as you can in these sentences but strive to read them in a conversational manner.

   a. If I make <u>that</u> choice, I will lose my money.

   b. You said <u>Anne</u> could have it.

   c. Did you <u>know</u> he would be there?

   e. They live <u>miles</u> from our house.

   f. He only said he <u>thought</u> he could help.

216

GAINING VOCAL VARIETY THROUGH PITCH OR INFLECTIONAL CHANGES

Earlier in this chapter you read that outstanding speakers have musical voices. This "music" actually stems from the speakers' abilities to use a variety of patterned pitch changes, or **inflections,** in meaningful ways. Pitch change just for the sake of change is not very useful—and can be distracting if it detracts from the verbal message being conveyed. However, when changes in pitch **support** and **reinforce** verbal and nonverbal messages, they help to elaborate, clarify, focus, and delineate intended messages. Furthermore, listeners will report the message is of greater interest—and the speaker is more interesting—if these vocal changes occur than if no pitch changes occur. Inflections or patterned pitch changes occur regularly in English in specific situations which you may or may not know. A quick review of some of these occurrences may be useful before you read about common English inflections.

Pitch Changes in Polysyllabic Words

By now, you are aware that pitch changes occur regularly in all polysyllabic words. These pitch changes help to clarify stressed and unstressed syllables in words—and delineate syllables having a primary stress from syllables having a secondary stress. For example, say the word "Mississippi" aloud. You will notice it has at least three pitch changes because it contains a syllable with a primary stress, a syllable with a secondary stress, and two unstressed syllables. Thus, patterned pitch changes occur as adjuncts of stress when you distinguish accented from unaccented syllables in individual words.

Pitch Changes in Modes of Delivery

Pitch change "patterns" or inflections help you to understand in what mode a person is speaking. These modes allow you to determine, just by the sound of a person's inflections, whether a speaker is:

1. Asking a question (interrogative mode: Are you going home?)
2. Making a statement (declarative mode: Lionel paints well.)
3. Giving a command (imperative mode: Pick up that paper.)
4. Making an exclamation (exclamatory mode: It's beautiful!)

As you practice the exercises in this chapter, you should discover many words which take on entirely different meanings, when they are read with different inflections.

Pitch Changes to Delineate Thought Sequence and Importance

Pitch change patterns also occur regularly at the ends of thought sequences, such as phrases, one word interjections, and sentences, to indicate that an idea has or has not been completed. Besides normal end punctuation, such as question marks, exclamation points, and periods, other internal punctuation marks, including the comma, semicolon, colon, dash, and ellipsis occur in manuscripts. They indicate to an oral reader that a particular type of inflection should be used to let listeners, who can't see the manuscript, know that a thought sequence has or has not been completed. Listeners may become very confused at what a message means—or how it fits into the context of a paragraph, if these punctuation marks are ignored by the oral reader.

These pitch changes also help to establish an understanding of the priority of ideas in a thought sequence, such as a sentence or paragraph. For example, frequently you will want your listeners to understand that one idea is subordinate to a more important idea and you will drop your pitch and volume simultaneously to show this subordinated idea. This might occur in the sentence, "Carrie laughed hilariously at the joke, but Trudie sat quietly and frowned." At other times, you may want your listeners to realize that two ideas are of equal or coordinate value, so you will say the two things with approximately the same inflections and emphasis. This might occur in the sentence, "The clowns made funny faces at the children and the children clapped their hands in delight."

Pitch Changes in Connotative Meanings

Pitch changes also occur regularly as indicators of emotional responses to ideas. When a speaker's words say one thing but vocal inflections **imply** something quite different, as in sarcasm or double entendre, changes in vocal inflections become crucial factors for communicating ideas. Suggested or connotative meanings of words in oral communication depend upon vocal changes for their full impact, whereas denotative or dictionary meanings do not.

Superior oral readers and actors learn to use inflections so well that their listeners actually hear subtle changes in characterization, dialogue, attitude, plot development and setting as a consequence of those inflectional changes. These subtle vocal changes often give clues to changes in action, modifications in character, emotional climaxes, and unexpected endings—just as they do in daily life. People often are able to say, "When I heard her say . . . I had no idea she meant . . . ." After the fact, they discover subtle vocal clues were evident all along, but no one associated them with the action or results that ultimately occurred.

TYPES OF INFLECTIONS

Inflections may be used meaningfully in individual vowels, diphthongs, and voiced consonant continuants because they are capable of being prolonged and moved up or down the musical scale. For example, you can prolong [m], [o], or [z] while humming up or down the scale. You can't do this with voiceless consonants such as [s], [h], or [f] or to stop plosive sounds such as [p], [t], or [k] unless you add a vowel sound. At its simplest level then, inflections may occur at the phonemic level.

Read the following exercises to see if you can attach meaning to one phoneme simply by varying your inflections or pitch pattern in saying [m].

[m]: meaning "Oh, *now* I understand."

[m]: meaning "I'm a little suspicious of that."

[m]: meaning "That is delicious!"

[m]: meaning "Oh, oh, I made an error."

[m]: meaning "Yes."

[m]: meaning "I don't know that I want to do that."

[m]: meaning "I think that's very funny."

If you could do each of these, you already discovered that the **direction** of your pitch changes, as well as the **degree of sustained continuity of sound,** determined changes in meaning.

Sustained Continuity of Sound: Steps and Slides

Inflections may be classified according to the continuous or interrupted flow of sound required for using them. The easiest descriptive terms to use in describing continuity of sound are **slides** and **steps.** These terms describe the action of the pitch as it changes, and might be compared with the action of firemen who either slide down a pole or run down steps to get from the second floor to the first in their firehouse. A **SLIDE** is a **gradual** pitch change from one musical note to another, without an intervening pause within the thought sequence. Thus, if you start at a high pitch and gradually move or glide to a lower pitch while using the phoneme [o] without pausing between

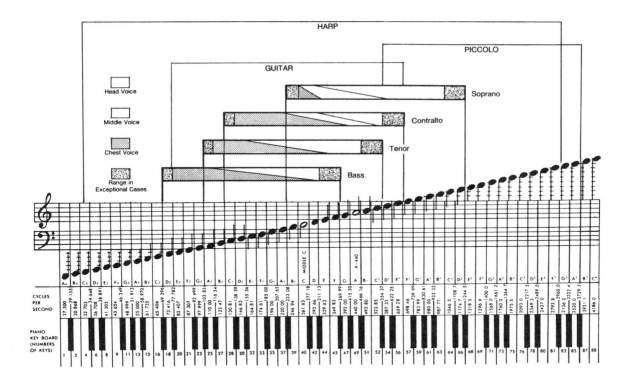

Figure 16-2 Pitch Chart showing the range of voices and the ranges of some musical instruments. Notice that a soprano voice extends up the high end into the range of a piccolo, whereas a human bass does not. Also interesting is the low range of a human voice which can actually go below that of a guitar. Cycles per second for each musical note remain the same, regardless of whether the note is sung by the human voice or played by a musical instrument. (Courtesy Bateman/Mason and Charles C. Thomas, Publisher)

these two musical notes, you will produce a gradual **falling** or descending slide. Likewise, if you begin reading a short sentence at a low musical note and gradually move up the musical scale to a higher note without pausing, you can create an ascending or **rising** slide.

A **STEP,** on the other hand, is an **abrupt** pitch change from one musical note to another with a short intervening pause between the two notes. If you use the phoneme [o] and drop abruptly from a high musical note to a lower one, or if you say a sentence in which you start at a high musical note and successively drop one musical note after each word, you create a pattern of steps.

Steps and slides usually convey slightly different messages to listeners. For example, read the following items aloud, first as slides down the musical scale and then as steps down the scale, to discover what different implications are created by each.

a. I am not going.

b. Take this to your mother.

c. What kind of person are you?

Can you hear the step pattern give more determination, authority, abruptness, assertion, or certainty to your responses?

219

In daily speaking you should attempt to use both vocal slides and steps. They will add variety to your speaking and will help you add more specificity to your messages.

Direction of Pitch Changes: Rising, Falling, Medial

Vocal inflections also may be classified according to the direction of their movement on the musical scale. They may be viewed as **rising** (moving from a low to a higher note on the musical scale), **falling** (moving from a high to a lower note), or **medial (circumflex)** (moving either from a high to a lower and back to a high note on the musical scale, or vice versa) inflections. When these directional inflections are linked with slides or steps, certain general meanings usually result.

A **RISING SLIDE** or inflection pattern usually suggests an incomplete idea, a questioning attitude, indecision or uncertainty. Questions (such as ''Did he call yet?'' or ''Shall we go now?'') which require only a ''yes'' or ''no'' response, usually end in a rising inflection. Frequently, incomplete thought sequences **within** a sentence (such as ''If I take this to him''), and listings of items (such as ''We thanked them for their advice, companionship, concern, and dedication''), end in rising steps to show that a sentence hasn't been completed yet. For example, notice how rising slides can help to suggest an incomplete (or continuing) description in the following sentence.

In her picnic basket were sandwiches, iced tea, frosted cookies, carrot and celery sticks, apples, and a huge bowl of potato salad.

A **RISING STEP** or inflection pattern also suggests an incomplete idea, progression toward a goal, a galloping or bouncing sense (particularly when reading iambic poetry), and a positive response in ''uh huh.'' (Novice readers of conventional poetry should be cautious that they don't read it aloud with such a regular, unchanging rising inflection pattern that listeners begin paying more attention to the meter than to the content of the poetry.) Most exclamations or interjections, such as ''Hurray!'' ''I know!'' and ''We won!'' are said with rising step inflections.

A **FALLING SLIDE** or inflection pattern usually suggests a demand, command, assertiveness, a definitive idea, or a completed idea. Questions which begin with interrogative words such as ''who, where, how, why'' normally end in a falling inflection. Usually, a direct statement or command, such as ''Darcy just arrived'' or ''Let me see that'' also will end in a falling inflection. Within a sentence the falling inflection may suggest the end of a phrase or thought sequence (as in ''She looked at her watch, wrinkled her brow, tilted her hat, and stepped into the shop.'') A **FALLING STEP** or inflection suggests approximately the same things, but with more abruptness, finality, or determination. For example, read aloud the statement ''I will not ride in that old wreck,'' first with a falling slide and then with a falling step pattern. The negative response of ''huh uh'' usually is a falling step.

A **MEDIAL SLIDE** changes in meaning depending on whether it starts at a high or a low musical note. As a result, it is capable of suggesting a variety of meanings which may range from sudden revelation or understanding (as in ''Ohhhhh!''), suspicion, added emphasis (as in ''If I have *my* way, he won't.''), capriciousness, to a whining attitude or a persecution complex (as in ''I don't want to spend my whole weekend in the library.''). A **MEDIAL STEP** may suggest emphasis or definition, determination, mimicry or echoing, capriciousness or incomplete thoughts. For example, read the following sentences aloud using an ascending and descending step inflection pattern. Stress the underlined word in each sentence as the most important and highest pitched word.

a. I am <u>not</u> going home.

b. This is the <u>last</u> time I'll call you.

c. We have <u>three</u> well qualified candidates.

a. I have no <u>intention</u> of always living here.

b. When she <u>arrives</u>, I will call.

c. Tom said he <u>would</u>—but not now.

SOME ADDITIONAL PITCH-RELATED PROBLEMS

Before turning to exercises for improving your facility for using pitch meaningfully, you should know about some problems that may be evident in your class or among your friends. These are common enough to warrant a few words regarding their occurrence. As you listen to in-class oral presentations you may observe one or more of these problems among your classmates.

A Lack of Inflectional Variation

Some people speak with little inflectional variation. Laypersons often refer to this as "talking in a monotone." It also could be called a monopitch. Technically, "mono" means **one**—but few normal people speak on only one musical note, so either reference is inaccurate. Nevertheless, speakers who lack inflectional variety usually suggest attitudes of general boredom or disinterest, coldness or insensitivity, numbness or shock, dullness or ignorance, mechanical or robotic response, depression, illness, or grief to listeners.

No easy answer exists to the question, "Why do people speak with little inflectional variation?" The individuals may have a personality or psychological problem, a hearing loss, or may be so accustomed to hearing themselves speak without much variation that they assume they sound just like everyone else. In fact, in many cases they may remain unconvinced that they have a problem until an instructor plays back a tape recording of their oral presentation and points out their lack of pitch or inflection variation. (Often, the instructor must make a direct comparison with another student's recorded reading, or read/say the same message aloud him or herself to reinforce this idea.)

If you have a very limited repertoire of inflections, you may feel you are exaggerating your reading when you begin to practice inflectional variations. This is a normal reaction. Don't let it prevent you from following your instructor's recommendations for increasing vocal inflections.

Melody Patterns

When speakers and readers use the same inflections repeatedly, without any regard for their appropriateness to specific ideas, situations or characters, they develop a singsong inflection, intonation, or melody pattern. This habit, which is distracting or irritating to most intelligent listeners, suggests that the speaker or reader has spent little time in determining which ideas are important and which ones are unimportant. It reminds many listeners of their grade school reading classes where some readers thought they could make everyone believe they understood what they were reading just by interspersing rising and falling inflection patterns regularly throughout their oral reading.

Even now, you may hear some adults read material aloud in a contrived manner, often allowing the pitch to rise regularly to the middle of every sentence, then drop regularly to the end of every sentence. Most of these readers don't *speak* in this manner, but they have come to believe that oral reading must be intoned or said differently from conversational speaking. When speakers or oral readers use a melody pattern and unvaried rate and/or volume, listeners normally report that the speakers are tedious, monotonous, or boring to listen to for any period of time.

Excessive Inflectional Variation

Occasionally, a student may have a good repertoire of inflections but may use excessive pitch changes within those inflections. Listeners tend to perceive this speaker as being "overly dramatic," "too emotional," "unnatural," or "too artificial" in speaking or reading aloud. Usually, the individual either is using too many slides, or slides and steps that continually sweep through the individual's total pitch range, sometimes including the falsetto range.

Earlier, you read that everyone has a prevailing pitch range. Except in moments of utter, unexpected amazement or surprise, normal people seldom "leap" from a pitch near the low end of their range to a pitch near the high end of their range for *one* inflection. Most listeners consider these vocal "leaps" excessive. Even though slides technically can glide through many musical notes, and steps can leap over many different pitches, in daily conversation and most public oral reading these inflectional movements will not be quite so startling or dramatic. If you discover your inflectional steps regularly jump six or eight full notes on the musical scale, you probably are using too great a pitch range. Two to four notes would sound much less exaggerated.

A REMINDER CONCERNING INFLECTIONS IN ORAL READINGS

Several of your oral presentations in class should be practiced readings. They help your instructor understand how well you can control both voice production and diction after periods of practice. The material that you chose should allow you to demonstrate care and versatility.

Some material, such as conventional poetry, may be lyrical, following a regular rhythmical pattern and requiring prolonged tones and a musical quality while condensed, intense images and situations are described. Other material, such as plays and short stories, may be more conversational and filled with highly emotional dialogue, descriptions, or action. Some material may be highly intellectual; other material, highly emotional.

In general, if a piece of literature contains major shifts in emotion or an expression of intense emotion, you will need to use more inflectional variations than if you use literature containing an intellectual discussion or an unemotional (objective) description. Radio and television newscasters probably use fewer inflectional variations during their script readings than news commentators and talk-show hosts, in order to maintain an element of "objectivity" in their reporting responsibilities.

Also, if your literature contains several different characters who are speaking to one another, you will need considerably more inflectional and general pitch variations to help your listeners understand who is speaking at any particular time than literature in which only one character speaks. If you read from a play script you must use your voice as the primary vehicle for setting the scene, delineating and maintaining different characterizations, creating mood or atmosphere, building to climaxes, and clarifying situations. In short stories and novels the author's descriptive and narrative passages place less burden on inflectional variation by focusing on specific images, traits, personalities, and situations, all of which are described in some detail by his or her carefully chosen words.

You might wish to keep these ideas in mind as you practice reading the following exercises aloud. Certainly, you should remember these things as you practice future readings for class presentation.

EXERCISES FOR PRACTICING INFLECTIONAL VARIATION

1. Read each of the following with rising inflection patterns. Then reread them with a falling and a medial inflection pattern. What differences in meaning become evident?

a. She was beautiful.

b. It is finished.

c. *This* is funny.

d. Have you made up your mind yet?

e. Undoubtedly, she knew her.

f. Who

g. Oh

h. Ah

i. No

j. Well

2. Read the following sentences aloud, using both rising and falling inflection patterns in each one.

a. I think there is nothing more entertaining than watching a monkey try to play the piano.

b. If the weather remains good and we have no difficulty with the car, we will drive to the lake tomorrow.

c. As I stood in line at the check-out counter I tried to shift the loaf of bread to my arm that was holding the stalk of celery.

d. We have no use for power over others, for we have not yet learned to use power over ourselves.

e. Without the support of my brother and sister I could not have found this place.

f. Whatever makes you happy will make me happy, and whatever disturbs you will disturb me.

g. We searched the city for our dog, checking alleys, side streets, yards, and entrances to old buildings.

h. Casual acquaintances are seldom adequate substitutes for old friends.

i. We heard the sad, soft bleating of the fog horn echoing across the bay.

j. How long will it take for us to travel from Paducah, Kentucky to Bluefield, Virginia by expressway?

k. We had hardly awakened before we heard a terrible squawking rising from the chicken farm next door.

l. We stood on the Great Wall of China, casting our eyes over hundreds of miles of rolling hills and mountains.

m. Obviously, there was no longer any need for our help at the end-of-the-year celebration.

3. Read the following sentences, stressing the underlined words in each sentence by raising your pitch slightly while increasing the volume or intensity for those words.

a. She told us she <u>definitely</u> was not going to the spring formal with <u>him</u> this year.

b. What ever <u>happened</u> to that little, white kitten that used to sit on your front railing and <u>spit</u> at every dog that passed by?

c. If you would take the <u>time</u> to look at the sky at <u>night</u> you might be <u>surprised</u> at what you would see.

d. <u>Other</u> people may <u>adore</u> chocolate chip cookies, but <u>I</u> don't.''

e. Whenever I visit the doctor in the <u>spring</u>, I know <u>exactly</u> what he is going to say.

f. The house had a <u>long</u> outside stairway that went <u>straight</u> up to the third floor.

g. <u>You</u> were the one who said, ''<u>Nothing</u> would prevent us from attending <u>this</u> year's conference.''

h. If I <u>thought</u> that, I <u>certainly</u> never <u>said</u> it.

i. As our <u>car</u> rounded the bend in the road, our <u>headlights</u> began to <u>flicker</u>.

j. <u>Look</u>, if you have enough <u>evidence</u> to place him at the scene of the crime, by <u>all</u> means <u>show</u> it to me.

4. The following selections contain dialogue. Practice reading the selections aloud until you are sure your vocal inflections remain consistent enough for each different character to allow listeners to follow which character is speaking.

a. Nelda had grown tired of her younger sister's idle chatter about all the boys who were interested in her. She closed her eyes and tried to imagine she was back at the ranch, riding her favorite horse. Still, her sister droned on, ''Now take Bret. He's a little too short for me . . . especially when I dress in high heels. Don't you agree?''

''Ummm, maybe.''

''He's always asking me to have lunch with him, or go to the ballgame, or go out walking. Never to go to the dance.''

''Maybe he doesn't like to dance.''

''And then there's George. Now, he's tall.''

''He sure is—about six feet seven!''

''And he likes to dance. But he's never on time and he never dresses up. Always in slacks and an open-necked shirt. I like someone with a little 'couth,' who knows how to treat me like a woman.''

She could feel the horse trotting softly through the field now, heading straight for the mountains.

"Ben dresses well. I think I like Ben's taste best of anyone's. He has good taste. His colors always match and he never wears brown shoes with navy blue trousers like George does."

"His father owns the shoe store."

"Ben also plans things better than most of the other boys I know."

She could feel the horse's mane, brushing gently against her hands—and the cool afternoon breeze, carrying the aroma of early spring wild flowers on the mountain slopes."

"Of course, Ben still is seeing Sally, and I've always said that I wanted a steady boyfriend—not a sometimes one."

"Sometimes is better than none at all."

"Oh, you know what I mean!"

b. Lisa stood on the ground, looking straight up the tree trunk to where her brother, Mel, was crouching. "Can you see her?" she shouted.

"No, not yet. The leaves are too thick up here."

"Remember, she likes to hide under thick branches where the shade is greatest."

"I know," he groaned and shimmied carefully up to the next branch. "Remind me to sell her the next time we have a good chance."

"Oh, Mel, you wouldn't—would you?"

"At this moment, I would give her away—if I could catch her."

Lisa stood on one foot, peering anxiously up at the tennis shoe and red sock that was the only remaining evidence of her disappearing brother.

"Be careful, Mel. You're getting awfully high."

"You're telling me? I can see Royerton from here."

"How much higher can you climb?"

"About eight more feet—then the branches get too small." He paused to catch his breath. The tough, black bark had bruised his elbows and he knew he would be covered with iodine tonight. A fly kept buzzing around his ears and the perspiration was trickling down the back of his neck. He had to hold on with both hands now. Otherwise, he would have taken out his red bandana handkerchief and wiped his steaming face.

"Oh, Mel! I see her. She's not in the tree at all. She's on the roof. She must have jumped off the limb overhanging the garage."

"Oh, fine! I'm halfway to heaven with sore knees and elbows—and now she's not even here!"

"Be careful sliding down. Take your time. She won't be able to get off the roof. I'll wait to hold the ladder for you."

c. Grandma frowned when she heard the front door slam. "Is that you, Jeff?"

"It's me, Gram."

She continued kneading the huge mass of dough at the kitchen table. "Why are you home from school so early?"

"We got time off for good behavior," came a muffled reply, accompanied by the thud of books being dumped on the dining room table.

A door opened upstairs and Jeff's mother called, "Jeff? Is that you Jeff?"

"I'm home, Mom."

"Why so early?"

"I just told Gram that we got off early for good behavior."

"Good behavior?" Footsteps hurried down from the second floor. "What in the world is that supposed to mean?"

"That's what I was wondering," muttered Grandma, still rolling and punching the dough. "I thought that was only for prisoners!"

Jeff strode into the kitchen, carrying an envelope in one hand and his lunch box in another. "Mmmmm, smells like cinnamon rolls, Gram. Are they for supper?"

"If they're ready by then. They have to rise yet."

Jeff's mother hurried into the kitchen, wiping her furniture-oil scented hands against her apron. "What do you mean 'time off for good behavior'? I never heard of such a thing!"

"No one else in our school district did either," said Jeff, placing his lunch box on the kitchen sink where it would wait for its nightly cleaning. "Not until this year."

His mother looked at him carefully—somewhat doubtfully. "And what's so special about this year?"

"That's exactly what I was going to ask," said Grandma, breaking the large doughball into three equal pieces. "Exactly!"

Jeff filled a plastic cup with cool water from the faucet, then took it to the kitchen table where he watched his grandmother rolling out the dough in preparation for the sprinkling of cinnamon and sugar. "The citation is in that envelope," he said to his mother, pointing at the envelope next to his lunch box.

"Citation!" Jeff's mother hurried to the sink, opened the envelope, and read aloud: "In recognition of exemplary behavior during the first grading period, the entire *8th* grade class is hereby released one hour early from school on this day. Signed, Buell M. Harris, Principal."

Grandma looked at her daughter, then at her grandson. "Well, I'll be. We have to hurry up these cinnamon rolls so we can celebrate tonight!"

d. "I can too!"

"No, you can't!"

"I said I *can*!"

The twins stood in front of the open iron gates, looking up the straight brick walk that ran like an arrow to the porch of the huge, Victorian mansion. They were identical in every respect. Even their parents had trouble telling them apart.

Myrna shifted her box of cookies to her aching left arm, out of the reach of her sister. "I can—and I *will*." She tossed her ponytail in one quick movement of her head and faced Clara. "You had your chance to sell her cookies last year. Now it's my chance."

Clara knew her sister was right. But she still fought for another chance to make a sale. Myrna already had sold three more boxes of Girl Scout cookies than she had. "You know Mrs. Henderson always buys two boxes. That will give you five more boxes than I've sold—and that's not fair."

Myrna smiled confidently. "Maybe she'll buy more this year. She has had lots of company this year. Besides, you will get a chance to sell her cookies next year."

Clara looked at her carton—then at her sister's. She just *had* to sell two more boxes tonight. "Will you walk with me down to Mrs. Gresham's afterward so I can try to sell her some cookies?" Clara asked, reluctantly. The Gresham home was a long four blocks away, but it seemed like a fair trade to Clara.

"Only if Mrs. Henderson buys two boxes from me," Myrna said, quickly. "This carton is too heavy to haul around town any more tonight. Remember, *I* carried my cookies all day in school today and you didn't."

Clara shifted her carton of cookies to *her* left arm, too. "Oh, all right. But walk slowly. My feet are aching and I don't want to have to run up those steps to the front porch."

The two ponytails walked slowly up the front walk, looking for all the world like private enterprise on the move—in duplicate.

5. Read the following excerpt of radio drama aloud in class. Remember, the audience will not see what is happening and your voice must suggest such aspects of character as size, sex, emotional response, age, and psychological state.

Narrator: The rain was falling hard now. The wind drove the drops against the casement windows with such fury—that it sounded like gravel was being thrown against them. Howard Cabot continued to read his newspaper in front of the fireplace while his wife crocheted a tablecloth in her rocking chair next to him.

Corrine: (Slowly, almost in rhythm with her rocking) Maria is getting the tea ready now, Howard. (She pauses but the rocking sound continues) It sounds like the storm is almost over us, now. Sounds like a bad one.

Howard: (Turning his paper) Ummm hmmm. Another big one.

Corrine: That's the only thing I dislike about Mountainview—the **awful** autumn storms. Seems like we just get over one, and another one begins—especially during September.

(A long roll of thunder occurs outside.)

Howard: I know dear. This just happens to be the area of the country that gets the heaviest Autumn storms.

Corrine: (Still rocking) Last week, the Albertsons lost their beautiful oak tree in front of their living room window because of heavy winds. All that lovely shade—gone. I know I'd miss the shade from **our** oak tree, if we were to lose it. The grandchildren love that tree as much as I do.

Howard: (Folding up the paper noisily) It has been there for three generations so it's like part of the family.

Corrine: Anything in the newspaper, tonight?

Howard: The Sox lost their final game last night—Shawnee Lodge is closing next week for the season—and, another prisoner escaped from the work crew yesterday morning over near Idabelle Springs.

Corrine: I hope the police will find this one sooner than the last one. I get so nervous when I hear about those escapes.

Howard: (Door opens) Ahhh, here's Maria with our tea!

Maria: This should help to cheer us up on a cold, wet afternoon. I made Aunt Corrine's favorite—spiced tea. (Places tray on table)

Corrine: Oh, thank you dear. I really need that today. It certainly smells good!

Maria: And some peanut butter cookies, fresh out of the oven, especially for you, Uncle Howard.

Howard: My favorite! Thank you, Maria.

Martin: (voice from the distance) Hello, where is everybody? (Door slams in the distance)

Maria: We're in the family room, Dad. Come on in. We're just about ready for tea.

Corrine: Martin is early, isn't he? I thought he was working until five tonight.

Maria: (Pouring tea into cups) Yes, he *is* early. It's only 4:15 so maybe he finished his work earlier than he expected.

Howard: Here, let me slide this chair a little closer to the fire. He's liable to be damp after tramping through that rain.

Martin: Well, well, well. I timed that just right. Hi, Mom and Dad. Mind if I join you for tea? I brought another cup and saucer from the kitchen. Ummm, that fire looks good.

Corrine: Your father just pulled up this chair for you, dear. Come and join us. Your daughter even made peanut butter cookies to spoil our appetites for the dinner that she's been cooking all afternoon.

Howard: Were the roads bad on your way home?

Martin: Countyline Road had a tree over it. I had to backtrack and come by way of Detroit Drive and Fourth Street. Looks like we may get some flooding from all this.

Maria: Let me have your cup, Dad.

Corrine: Really? Has **that** much rain fallen already?

Martin: We had a cloudburst in town! (Sound of cup being placed on saucer) Ahh, thank you Maria. It smells good.

Howard: Any more news about the escaped prisoner over at Idabelle Springs?

Martin: That's **one** reason I came home early. The Sheriff said he received word that the prisoner was spotted heading up the mountain on foot towards **your** place. When I heard another storm was brewing, I decided to bring my paperwork home—just to be sure you were secure. (Loud crack of thunder outside)

Corrine: Well, I'm **glad** you're home. (A loud knocking is heard at the front door.)

CHAPTER 17

INCREASING VOLUME AND INTENSITY

You are seated in the middle of a crowded restaurant with a friend, enjoying a pleasant meal, while a string quartet plays music softly near the front of the restaurant. The two of you have been so interested in your quiet conversation that you have been completely unaware of the conversations going on about you, even though some of the tables are quite close to yours.

Your friend excuses himself and goes to make a phone call. For the first time since entering the restaurant, you become aware of the couple next to you who have been involved in an agitated, quietly intense conversation. Although you can't hear *what* they are saying, you can tell from their facial expressions, strong gestures and bodily tension that the conversation must be about an *extremely* important matter. Simultaneously, you hear a slightly drunk patron at the far end of the room telling his waiter that he must have his check in a hurry because he already is late for an appointment with his stock broker who is leaving on vacation that afternoon.

In this hypothetical example, you have observed two aspects of voice production which commonly are confused by laypersons: intensity and volume. The neighboring, agitated couple, whose words were impossible to hear, were communicating quietly but with the element of intensity. The slightly drunk man, whose words could be heard easily across an entire restaurant, even above the quartet music, was using the element of volume. In this example, intensity carried with it a suggestion of quiet, selective control of force as breath was expelled whereas, volume carried a suggestion of **sustained,** overall loudness.

Volume and intensity are quite different forms of sound intensification. In general, volume is the more obvious, easier, and more frequently used method for stressing an idea; intensity is the more subtle, more difficult, and less frequently used method. They both are useful components in human communication provided that they are used at appropriate times and in the appropriate places.

VOLUME OR LOUDNESS

The terms "volume," "force," and "loudness" often are used interchangeably. This book prefers the term "volume" because it is short, commonly used in relation to mass media communications, and it is not associated with one end of the soft-to-loud continuum as is "loudness." Volume may be described generally as loud, soft, or moderate from the viewpoint of either a speaker or listener. It also may be thought of in relative degrees as existing on a continuum, much like the volume control on a radio or television set. From the speaker's viewpoint, volume is the intensity or energy required to force breath through the vocal folds, resonate it in the oral or nasal cavities, and expel it through the nose or mouth.

This same energy may be described from the listener's viewpoint as the audibility or decibel level, or as the strength of sounds perceived by the human ear and/or mechanical measuring equipment. The term "decibel" is a notation for an expression of ratios of sound wave intensity and is abbreviated as db. A decibel is equal to one-tenth of a **bel,** a term named after Alexander Graham Bell, inventor of the telephone. In daily speaking/listening situations, you probably conclude that a person is speaking too softly, too loudly, or at an appropriate volume level, depending on how well you can hear the sounds the individual is saying. (It is possible for an individual to be heard easily, but not be understood. In this case, the individual would have adequate volume control but faulty diction.)

How Is Volume Changed?

In the last chapter, you learned that you tend to hear your inflections and pitch differently from people who are listening to you, simply because you are closer to the source of your own sound. The same thing may be said of volume. You hear yourself as being *louder* than your listeners will, simply because your ears are closer to your mouth than any of your listeners' ears will be. If you are accustomed to speaking in a relatively quiet voice, you may think you are shouting when you begin to increase your volume level—but your classmates will report that you are speaking at a moderate volume level. You must learn to hear (and feel) the volume level changes that are necessary for you to be heard easily in public situations.

Among most college students, too little volume appears to be a problem in speech improvement classes more often than too much volume. The problem often results from conditioning and habitual use. In a society which finds people shoved closer and closer to other people in enclosed spaces, such as subways, classrooms, offices, condominiums, and restaurants, you have learned to "keep your voice down" so you won't disturb others. As a result, you may now perceive loud volume as representing an attitude labelled as impolite, stubborn, disruptive, defiant or "pushy."

Loud volume can imply any of the things mentioned above, depending upon the situation and place in which it occurs. However, it also can imply confidence, leadership, eagerness, and enthusiasm. If your instructor comments on your lack of adequate volume, you may need to reevaluate your own perceptions of the meaning of volume—at least in your classroom. One of the first steps in changing volume, then, is a psychological one. You must begin to view louder or softer volume levels from your instructor's and classmates' perspectives rather than from your own habituated responses. Develop a *genuine* interest in sharing your practiced material with your classmates, and a desire to be heard and understood easily.

In a beginning class of this nature, many technical considerations must be simplified (perhaps, at times, oversimplified) to introduce important ideas without confusing you with technical and scientific complexities of those ideas. Volume is one of those ideas. The physical properties of sound won't be discussed in detail and you will not be expected to understand the principles from mathematics and physics which relate to sound production or reception unless your instructor wishes to give you supplemental information on these technicalities.

Earlier in this book, you learned that pressure builds at the larynx as air from the lungs is restrained, then released at the glottis. By increasing the breath pressure at the glottis (by exerting the muscles involved in exhalation), you increase your opportunity for creating louder volume when your breath finally is released, resonated, and shaped. (If it is unvocalized, it may become simply a sudden, loud exhalation of air.) As the released air passes between the vocal folds, the folds begin to vibrate rapidly and the strength or amplitude of their vibration determines the loudness or softness of the resulting sound.

Since you can't see this process in action, perhaps an analogy would be easier to understand. If you have ever watched a drummer, you know that the loudness or softness of a drum is determined by the amount of pressure applied to the drum's membrane surfaces by sticks. A drummer must raise the sticks quite high in order to gain enough momentum to hit the membrane hard. When a bass drummer swings at the drum from quite a distance with all the strength and momentum he or she can muster, the membrane of the drum responds with a resounding, loud "boom." If you could see the surface of that drum's membrane, you would discover it is vibrating up and down, moving quickly through a space above and below its at-rest position. This space or total distance of vibratory movement indicates its amplitude. The amplitude becomes much greater as the momentum and force of the impact increases than when the drum is hit or tapped lightly with little momentum or force by sticks held at a close range.

This same principle is involved in vocal fold vibration. As greater force is applied beneath the folds, louder volume results from greater movement of the folds on various sounds. Since gross abdominal muscles give the best vocal support with the least amount of strain on the larynx and throat, they should become your primary concerns as you practice to increase volume. If you need to decrease your habitual volume level, you must decrease the force applied beneath the vocal folds by relaxing the abdominal muscles more.

Common Errors Made During Practice on Volume

A common error which you may make while working to increase an habitually soft volume level is to constrict your throat and larynx and contract your upper chest muscles while attempting to increase volume. By doing these things, you would increase the strain on your vocal folds and tense or narrow your oral cavity, creating a harsh, higher pitched voice quality. One general rule to remember whenever you practice exercises designed to increase volume is: keep most of your physical tension **below** the chest cage and keep the upper portion of your anatomy fairly relaxed. If you feel the upper chest and throat tightening, stop your practice a few minutes, yawn, stretch several times, and consciously relax all the muscles in your upper torso. Once you are relaxed, you can begin the exercises again.

Another common error made while working on increasing volume level is allowing the pitch to rise in conjunction with each increase in volume. If you have found your optimum pitch level, you should begin your volume exercises on that musical note and try to sustain it as you increase your volume. If you have not, close your lips and hum the easiest note you can without straining. It should be close to your optimum pitch and will serve as a useful place for beginning your practice sessions. A drastic rise in pitch from this note, during volume exercises, often indicates a tightening of the throat and larynx. This, in turn, frequently produces unpleasant vocal quality. Try to keep your practice of volume exercises in a range of a few notes above and below your optimum pitch level.

A third common error which occurs during practice sessions on volume is keeping the jaws too close together. Your oral cavity should be used as a resonator for sound—and resonation even may help to increase your overall volume level. However, if your lips are close together and your oral cavity is narrow, little room will be provided in which resonation can occur. Elocution teachers used to teach their students to think of their mouths as megaphones which could help to amplify and project sound. This idea still has some value. Don't be reluctant to drop the lower jaw and open your lips as you practice on increasing volume.

232

"Speak up! Speak up! How do you expect me to hear you?"

A final common error in regard to volume practice relates to the room in which you practice. Frequently, you may use a small dormitory room or home bedroom/study as your practice area. To be ready to speak to a classroom of students with adequate volume, you must become accustomed to how your muscles feel when they contract—and you must begin to hear the volume that is needed to fill your regular classroom. The only ways you can do that are to practice in a room that is approximately the same size as your classroom or to speak louder than is necessary in your small practice room because you recognize that it represents only a fraction of the space your voice must fill in the classroom.

Also, you should remember that human bodies, draperies, and acoustical ceiling tiles absorb sound quickly in a regular classroom. If you practice in a room without equivalent sound absorbing materials, you will tend to speak at a quieter level than will be needed in your regular classroom. You will need to compensate for the lack of sound absorbing materials by increasing your volume a little more than is needed for that particular room. If you can practice in a larger room or in the empty classroom, do it. You will feel more comfortable and confident during your oral presentation to the class knowing you have had adequate practice for your anticipated audience and room.

Gaining Variety in Use of Volume

You can turn the volume of a television or radio program up or down to compensate for outside noises, activities that you are doing as you listen, the general volume level of speakers on the media, other people who are talking in the room with you, or your own proximity to the source of sound. As a listener in a classroom, however, you don't have this same opportunity to turn the volume up or down. If a speaker's volume level is too soft to be heard easily, you may not receive important portions of the message being sent by the speaker or reader. If the speaker is too loud, you may only be able to cover your ears with your hands (which isn't exactly a polite thing to do in a public situation) or suffer through the barrage of noise.

As a speaker, you need to be flexible with your own volume control. Also, you should attempt to compensate for potential distractions in and outside the classroom while using enough variety

233

in volume to keep listeners interested in your presentation. *You* hold the "volume controls" for your presentation and you must be ready to increase or decrease your volume to compensate for potential distractions and disruptions. By remaining alert to these potential distractions you make the task of your listeners easier and more enjoyable.

An interesting voice is one that has variety. Volume is the most obvious way of attaining some variety. In fact, if you gave an unfamiliar manuscript to friends and asked them to read it aloud spontaneously, emphasizing the important ideas, you probably would find most of them depending upon volume for this emphasis. Volume is the easiest, though not always the best, method available for gaining attention.

Changes in volume can suggest mood changes, increasing and decreasing tension or mystery, your own emotional responses or those of the characters in a story, time and place changes, relative importance or unimportance of ideas and images, and a variety of other things. When you begin the practice exercises at the end of this chapter, be alert to the changes in meaning that result from variations in volume.

INTENSITY, EMPHASIS, STRESS, ACCENT AND PROJECTION

In earlier chapters on individual phonemes, you found that spoken English depends upon stressed and unstressed (or accented and unaccented) syllables for clarity of meaning. Improper stress or accent in words produces incorrectly pronounced words. All polysyllabic words have at least one syllable which is said with slightly more force or volume, a higher pitch, and/or longer duration than any of the others. It is called the primary stress syllable. Some polysyllabic words contain additional stressed syllables which are not produced with the same degree of force or volume, pitch, or duration as the primary stress. These are called secondary stress syllables. The slightly different *degrees of volume or force* applied to primary and secondary stress in syllables are simple forms of emphasis, stress, or accent which help to clarify the words being pronounced. By controlling breathing, particularly the release of air through the vocal folds, you can modify the degree of force on **individual** sounds (intensity, accent, or stress) as well as the **overall loudness level for longer segments** (volume) in spoken messages.

The Importance of Stress or Accent

Stress or accent often serves as a helpful key to pronunciation accuracy in a particular language. Although speakers of different dialects of the same language use the same words, they may use different stress patterns. Frequently, you can distinguish British from American speakers simply by the stress they use on different syllables when they say certain words. For example, when pronouncing the word "laboratory," most American speakers emphasize the first syllable, but British speakers emphasize the second one.

Stress or accent also is important for establishing accepted speech rhythms in specific dialects and/or languages. These rhythms may change only slightly from one dialect to another, but they become factors for identifying people who "belong" to specific national, ethnic, linguistic, and socioeconomic groups. Often, the terms "brogue," "melody," and "lilt" are used to describe regularly repeated stress patterns. Nonnative speakers of English often have difficulty mastering oral English communication skills because they don't hear any difference between their native speech stress pattern and the English system of stressed and unstressed sounds.

You need to know which syllables are stressed and unstressed when you read poetry aloud. Poetry is basically organized or systematized rhythmical patterns based partially on how words are pronounced in daily speech during a particular era. You might discover rhythmical changes occurring in poetry written in Dublin, Ireland and in Emporia, Kansas simply because words and phrases are stressed differently in these two places. Likewise, you might find the poetry of Henry Wadsworth Longfellow quite different in rhythmical structure from the poetry of Theodore Roethke because common English speech patterns have changed during the century.

When reading poetry aloud you also need to know which words require the greatest emphasis in every line of poetry. You can easily disrupt a very regular rhythmical pattern of a line of poetry by not knowing which words to stress. On the other hand, you can destroy the mood, impact, and message of a poem by overemphasizing the unvarying line-by-line **metrical** pattern (such as iambic pentameter—which should serve primarily as the hidden "skeleton" upon which a poet builds a poem) rather than emphasizing the primary rhythm of the poem. If one of your class presentations will be a reading from a poem, be sure you don't allow the regularity of the meter to "control" your oral presentation. If you emphasize the meter as you read poetry aloud, you could sound like you are galloping on a horse or walking on a wooden floor with squeaky shoes.

What Is Intensity?

By expanding this idea of stress beyond individual syllables—to words and groups of words— you begin to develop the concept of **intensity.** Intensity is the degree of force applied to individual sounds occurring in thought sequences such as phrases, clauses, sentences, and paragraphs. By controlling the degree of intensity used in thought sequences, you suggest to listeners that a specific vocal message—or a certain component of a vocal message—is extremely significant, **no matter how quietly the message is said.** Intensity, then, should not be confused with overall loudness or volume.

As you speak or read aloud, you must decide when and where to use selectively sustained force to enhance the meaning of ideas. If you decide that certain ideas are central to the understanding of a sentence or paragraph, you can use vocal intensity to emphasize those ideas. This "vocal attack" becomes very important for clarifying meaning by helping to show forcefulness, emphasis, or great feeling. Printed material which is underlined, capitalized, italicized, or placed in boldfaced type tries to represent oral techniques used for indicating emphasis, stress, or intensity. Intensity, then, is a useful vocal technique for indicating comparisons and contrasts, subordinated (unequal) and coordinated (equal) ideas, and strong feeling in oral messages.

If you are reading aloud, "I told him once and for all, I <u>will not</u> accept financial help from <u>anyone</u>," your greatest intensity would come on the two underlined thought units: "will not" and "anyone." However, if the statement were emphasized as the words are underlined in "I told him <u>once and for all</u>, I will <u>not accept financial help from anyone</u>," the meaning changes. Now, suppose the entire sentence is underlined and appears in a paragraph where nothing else is underlined. Suddenly, the entire sentence becomes an emphatic thought sequence when seen in context with the rest of the paragraph. You *could* read the entire statement in a louder voice. This change in volume would indicate to listeners that this thought sequence is different from adjacent ones. However, an even more effective technique would be to stress or vocally "punch" *each* word within this thought sequence to underscore the significance of this entire thought sequence over adjacent ones.

The element of intensity allows you to suggest strong emotional reactions such as seething anger, subtle sarcasm, sudden surprise, determination, burning passion, or utter terror with or without loudness.

Read the following sentences aloud quietly, but with great, passionate control. Imagine you are saying these words emphatically to someone who is seated directly across a small table from you, but you don't want other people to hear what you are saying. Feel the muscles of your abdomen contract as you control the forceful flow of air through the larynx. Use plenty of energy to say the words, but at the same time, avoid expelling a great amount of air or using loud volume while reading them. Decide which words will have the greatest and least emphasis in each sentence.

     a. His actions are despicable, and his ideas are revolting!

     b. We have little chance of succeeding, but we are determined to spend every dollar we have to fight this law.

     c. She is absolutely gorgeous!

     d. He told you what?

     e. They wouldn't do such a thing.

     f. We simply can't understand what this article means.

     g. That is absolutely the last straw!

     h. She should be ashamed of how she treats her family.

     i. You are not the only person I have ever loved.

     j. I have tried to help you, but you won't let me.

     k. Take my advice. Leave it alone!

Intensity requires sustained control of the breathing process throughout any emphasized thought sequence. In fact, we might simplify the idea of intensity by calling it sustained periods of increased stress. If you intend to say only a few words with great force, your abdominal muscles and diaphragm must prepare for those words by contracting, just as they would contract if someone playfully threatened to punch you in the "stomach" with a fist. Simultaneously, you must *control* the expulsion of breath through the vocal folds as the words are said. Intensity should make you feel like you are "punching" or stressing each individual syllable in several words for the sake of emphasizing those specific words, while simultaneously controlling, holding back, or holding in reserve your ultimate volume level. Volume, on the other hand, should produce a physical reaction which makes you feel like you are exerting a sustained physical effort to maintain a specific level of loudness *throughout* an entire speech or oral reading. Listeners frequently perceive individuals who depend primarily upon volume to get their points across as aggressive—and individuals who depend primarily upon intensity, as assertive.

Now let's check your ability to handle stress and intensity, as contrasted with overall volume, (and also add an element of comic relief). Read the following classical diction exercise concerning a man named Esau Wood who loved to saw wood. Read it aloud in a normal, conversational voice. Stress the words that are necessary for clarifying the meaning of each sentence to a listener. Take time to determine the meaning of each sentence, since some of the sentences can become confusing without proper stress.

236

ESAU WOOD AND HIS WONDERFUL WOOD SAW

Esau Wood sawed wood. Esau Wood would saw wood. All the wood Esau Wood saw Esau Wood would saw. In other words, all the wood Esau saw to saw Esau sought to saw. Oh, the wood Wood would saw! And oh, the wood-saw with which Wood would saw wood. But one day Wood's wood-saw would saw no wood, and thus the wood Wood sawed was not the wood Wood would saw if Wood's wood-saw would saw wood. Now, Wood would saw if Wood's wood-saw would saw wood. Now, Wood would saw wood with a wood-saw that would saw wood, so Esau sought a saw that would saw wood. One day Esau saw a saw saw wood as no other wood-saw Wood saw would saw wood. In fact, of all the wood-saws Wood ever saw saw wood Wood never saw a wood-saw that would saw wood as the wood-saw Wood saw saw wood would saw wood, and I never saw a wood-saw that would saw as the wood-saw Wood saw would saw until I saw Esau saw wood with the wood-saw Wood saw saw wood. Now Wood saws wood with the wood-saw Wood saw saw wood.

Author Unknown

Projection

Perhaps you have heard the term "projection" used in reference to sound production. Often, it is used to mean the ability to "throw" or project the voice over a relatively long distance. The term may be used in reference to a consistently loud volume level (the ability to be heard by everyone in a large room) or to focusing the direction of the voice toward one particular area, such as the back corners of a room.

Before public address systems were invented, people depended upon training in projection to help them gain proficiency in speaking to large groups. This experience included breathing and speaking exercises to: increase lung capacity, support sound production with adequate abdominal and diaphragmatic control, and sustain sound through controlled exhalation of breath. The oral cavity often was compared to a megaphone which could be used to project the voice over great distances with the proper training.

Projection of sound also involved the careful formation of sounds. By making their sounds distinct, crisp and clear, early speakers could project them over long distances without causing listeners to confuse them with similar sounds. American elocution teachers of the late 1800s and early 1900s took great pride in producing eloquent speakers who had loud, flexible voices and accurate diction.

Today, the term "projection" probably is heard most often among theater instructors who are trying to get their students to speak louder so that they will be heard easily in an auditorium which has no (or a poor) public address system. Some still use the analogy or physical pantomime of throwing an object to the far reaches of the auditorium and then vocally "throwing" the voice after it by controlling the forceful expulsion of air with abdominal muscles.

When the term "projection" is used today in movies, radio, and television (where public address systems and close-up microphones are standard equipment), it usually refers to the physical ability to create and sustain vocal and nonverbal attributes of a specific character in order to make the individual consistently believable for an audience. In this respect, it also involves psychological considerations regarding the character. Presumably, if you have strong mental images of what your character looks, acts, and talks like, and you understand the character's motivations for responding, you will be able to make the character more believable for an audience. The term, in this context, has more to do with intensifying or clarifying a character's identifying traits than with voice amplification.

Saturday Evening Post

"Let's hear about the Democrats again —you get more expression into it!"

EXERCISES FOR PRACTICING VOLUME AND INTENSITY

Since you are working to increase volume above your ordinary conversational level, you should find a place to practice the following exercises where you won't disturb other people. You will be less self-conscious in a relatively isolated area where your voice can reverberate throughout the room. Remember to take time out to relax periodically if your chest and throat muscles begin to feel tense. Space your practice over several periods rather than trying to accomplish everything in one sitting. Keep your muscular tension **below** the larynx, primarily in the abdominal area—not in the throat or pharynx.

1. Stand in a relaxed position with your hands placed on either side of your hips, just below the rib cage, and your fingers pointed toward your navel. Inhale slowly through your nose. Fill your lungs without elevating your rib cage. Feel your waist gradually expand outward as your lungs push the abdominal area down and out. Hold your breath for five seconds, then slowly exhale it without making a sound. Feel the abdominal muscles contract. Just before you run out of breath, exert a slightly greater pressure with a slight vocalized "grunt" to push the remaining air out of the lungs. The abdominal muscles should be tightly contracted at this point. Be sure to keep your mouth closed throughout this exercise. Relax and breathe naturally. Repeat this exercise until you are sure you can complete it without lifting the rib cage.

238

2. Use the same steps in item 1 above to fill the lungs, but when you exhale, open the lips and round them slightly as you **silently** blow the air from your mouth (rather than from the nose). See how long you can prolong a strong, steady flow of exhaled air. Repeat this exercise three times. Next, repeat it three more times, but when you exhale, produce a prolonged, moderately loud [u] sound. See if you can sustain the sound as long as you sustained the silent exhalation of breath.

3. Close your lips and hum the easiest note for you to make with the least effort. Hold that note and open your mouth to prolong "ah." This should be approximately at your optimum pitch. Now take another full breath (without expanding your rib cage) and starting each word with this same musical note, quietly and slowly begin pronouncing the months of the year, beginning with January. Don't rush their pronunciation. Gradually increase the volume level until you must pause for breath. Pause, take another breath, hum, say "ah" and begin the process again. Try to increase your volume without raising your pitch.

4. In this exercise, you will attempt to increase and decrease your volume level continuously as you count at a moderate rate of speed. You may allow your pitch to vary as you count, but try to keep it in a range close to your optimum pitch level. Begin by counting to five while gradually increasing your volume with each number, then gradually decrease your volume until you reach ten. Continue this until you reach thirty. Pause to take breaths whenever you need them. Be sure the abdominal muscles support your increased volume.

5. Try to pitch or project your voice towards the two corners of the room farthest from you. If you are outside, try to project your voice towards certain definite spots or objects. You will need to release your breath suddenly, contracting the abdominal muscles quickly as you do so. Allow your lower jaw to drop sufficiently to have plenty of room in your mouth and throat to articulate the vowel sounds in each of the following word groups. If necessary, visualize the first word as the "wind up" and the second word as the "pitch."

a. You what?   e. Oh no!   i. Too late!

b. I am!   f. You know!   j. So long!

c. Now one!   g. My home!   k. Who knows?

d. Ah, so!   h. I will?   l. Come on!

6. Read the following sentences aloud, stressing the underlined words with more energy than words that are not underlined. First read each sentence with quiet intensity. Then read it with loud volume. Remember, even with loud volume you must be able to stress the underlined terms.

a. Monday <u>always</u> seems like the <u>worst</u> day of the week.

b. Is <u>this</u> your idea of a <u>joke</u>?

c. Come on in—the water's <u>warm</u>!

d. You are <u>not</u> in <u>charge</u> here.

e. Why don't you go <u>help</u> her?

f. If you <u>take</u> your <u>time</u>, you'll do just <u>fine</u>.

g. <u>Call</u> me tonight if you <u>can</u>.

h. He wouldn't even <u>look</u> at me.

i. Bring me a <u>double cheese pizza</u> when you come back.

j. I told her I <u>can't</u> accept the nomination.

k. While <u>you</u> were <u>playing</u>, <u>I</u> was <u>studying</u>.

l. Don't turn <u>left</u> at the sign, turn <u>right</u>.

m. All I want is <u>five minutes</u> of your time.

n. <u>Please</u>—<u>try</u> to come to my party.

o. <u>Where</u> did all the children <u>come</u> from?

p. If <u>that</u> isn't <u>Pat</u> I'll <u>eat</u> my <u>hat</u>.

7. Read the following sentences aloud several times, stressing a different word each time. Does meaning change?

a. I really like your brother.

b. If I knew, I'd tell you.

c. His music is different.

d. She was my friend.

e. This house is old.

f. Two men hit him.

8. Selections for Practicing Volume and Intensity

a. The police officer had stood in the blazing sun directing holiday traffic for two hours. It was obvious she was irritated by the motorist who kept tooting his horn to indicate he thought it was time for his lane of traffic to go on. Finally she blew her whistle, motioned the moving cars to continue through the intersection, and marched over to his waiting car. She leaned heavily against the car with both hands, stared directly at the young, redheaded driver, and said, "You seem to be having a lot of trouble with your horn, Mister. So far, it hasn't gotten you very far. But let me tell you something. If it toots one more time, it will get you a bright blue traffic citation that will almost match the color of your eyes. And that, sir, will cost you fifty dollars! Now think about it while I go back and try to help everyone get home safely tonight." Then she straightened up, whirled around and marched back to the center of the intersection.

b. The little boy stuck out his tongue at his older sister. She ignored him.

"I'm going to tell Mama that you wouldn't help me!" he shouted angrily, watching her face for some sign of fear.

"You go right ahead," she said, feigning disinterest while staring off into space.

"She won't let you go to the dance tonight!" he added as an additional warning.

240

She smiled at his childish response and began humming softly to herself. She remembered when she used the same types of arguments.

"And you won't be able to leave the house all this weekend!"

He didn't like her all-knowing smile and her superior attitude, even if she was eight years older than he was. After all, *she* was supposed to be taking *care* of him—and to him, that meant doing the things *he* wanted to do. Why should he have to color all the pictures in his coloring book all by himself when she was right there, doing *nothing*?

"You *promised* you'd help me color in my book the next time I colored."

Rebecca watched two boys as they pushed their old car down a small hill a block away. They were trying to get it started, but were not having much luck.

"I never did," she said with a mixture of patience and utter boredom. "You must have dreamed it."

"I *didn't* dream it! I *didn't!*" He threw his black crayon down on the porch floor where it broke into several small pieces, ran into the house, and slammed the screen door.

The two boys were shouting directions to the driver now as a little puff of smoke came out of the exhaust pipe. The car gave a tentative lurch forward, then began whining and coughing. Her ride to the dance tonight was beginning to look more promising by the moment.

"Little brothers *really* can be trying at times," she mumbled to herself. She bent over to pick up the pieces of black crayon before anyone stepped on them.

    c. Thea and Kirby Taylor were excited! They hadn't seen Uncle Tim and Aunt Della for two years. Now they were arriving on a huge jet plane from their latest jobs in South America. They would be staying with the Taylors for a week before they resettled in St. Louis, Missouri.

"There it is!" Thea said, pointing at the sky from the airport waiting room window. "See, over there—you can just see the plane coming out of the clouds."

"I see it!" said Kirby with less intensity than his sister. "It is beautiful! Look how easy it's coming down—almost like a huge eagle gliding on a breeze."

A quiet, lilting voice on the public address system was saying, "This is to announce the arrival of flight 784 from San Juan. Passengers will be deplaning at gate B–7 in the Green Concourse."

"They're here!" squealed Thea, tugging at her older brother's arm as the wheels touched down on the long stretch of white runway. "I can't wait to hear about their adventures during the last two years. Just think, they have lived in three different countries in the past two years. Come on! Let's get closer to the door where we can see them when they get off the plane."

"It will be several more minutes before the plane gets to the terminal. Don't rush," said Kirby calmly. He smiled at his sister's unbridled anticipation. Although he felt some of the same anticipation, he kept his emotions well concealed. "Besides, Mom and Dad are already over there waiting for them. I can see them from here. There's plenty of room for us."

"I wish we could go on the plane and see what it looks like," Thea said as they walked across the long reception area. "Those planes look so big from the outside but Dad said they are much smaller inside. I'd like to be able to go aboard just one."

"In another few years, we'll probably have many chances to travel on a jet," Kirby said. "Just keep saving your money! You know, if you go away to college, you'll probably have to fly there."

"Wouldn't that be great!" Thea's eyes lit up as she thought about the possibility. "Every vacation, I could come home on a big jet, just like this one!"

Just then, the hissing and whining of the jet engines could be heard outside the blue door with a huge, white "B–7" printed on it. The giant ramp began to rumble as it moved out to meet the plane.

d. Our ship was at anchor in the small port of Beira, Mozambique, waiting for space at the dock to unload grain from the holds. It was Christmas, a time of year when most of the Western World celebrates with music, lights, gifts, and food.

On this night, while sitting on the top deck facing the small city, I was struck with the lack of *all* these things in this small port. Even the few highrise buildings hanging onto the side of a rather steep hill, were dark and ominous. Only a few lights were evident *anywhere* in the city. An occasional pair of truck headlights wandered about in the hills. Otherwise, no evidence of human movement could be seen or heard.

A mild, pleasant evening breeze blew down from the hills. However, it carried no sounds of laughter or music. No colored lights, except those on our small artificial tree in the freighter's dining area, were glowing this evening. It was a holiday without cheer. It was a time to celebrate, but where were the celebrants? If there were joy on earth, it was not evident *here*, tonight. What an eerie sensation!

I wondered if the rumors that I had heard among the crew were true. Was poverty as widespread as they had said? Did the dock workers exist on meager incomes, live in cardboard shanties, and come to work hungry? What about the children? Did they have little hope for their futures? What would Christmas mean to them? Had they *ever* seen a lighted Christmas tree? Or heard any Christmas music? If they were looking out their windows tonight and down on us in the bay, what were they thinking about as they saw our ship's lights?

Then *I* thought of something! I had a small battery operated tape recorder and a casette of holiday music. If I played it out on deck this night for my *own* enjoyment, certainly no foreign government could criticize my action. Who else might become a listening companion? That would depend on who was still awake—and how much sound would carry across the water. What dreams might be stirred by the soft, sweet notes of alien choirs and orchestras echoing "Hallelujah" and "Santa Claus is coming to town"?

Even now, I sometimes wonder if I was the sole listener to those melodies on a dark ship deck in a small Mozambique port in December.

CHAPTER 18

PAUSING FOR BREATHING AND MEANING

Many listeners think of pauses in vocal messages as vocal punctuation marks which break long sequences of ideas into smaller ideas. If you always could have a printed copy of a speaker's speech or reading, you would have no difficulty identifying ends of phrases, sentences, paragraphs, or other thought sequences. Without this visual assistance, you must depend upon the vocal cues given by the speaker or reader to tell you when you should get ready for a mental shift in scene, character, emotion, or idea.

Two types of pauses occur regularly in oral communication: meaningful pauses and vocalized pauses. Both serve as forms of oral punctuation, as well as a time for catching your breath while you are speaking. Meaningful pauses mark ends of thought sequences, help to make transitions clear, serve as means for emphasizing ideas, help to establish mood or atmosphere, and indicate changes in time, place, and characters. Vocalized pauses are meaningless vocalizations, such as "uhm, ah, er," which occur within or between thought sequences. Words that could have meaning in other contexts (but have none in the thoughts being expressed) also can be vocalized pauses. The words "well," "you know," and "man," have all been used as vocalized pauses. Vocalized pauses often serve as "vocal markers" to let listeners know the speaker or reader hasn't finished speaking yet.

PROBLEMS CAUSED BY LACK OF PAUSES

Perhaps you have heard speakers and readers who use few pauses during their oral presentations. These individuals are quite difficult to follow. Most of their ideas seem to run together. You have to sort out or organize their ideas while additional ones are being spoken. If you think a speaker still is developing one idea, and then discover a little later that the idea was concluded some time previously, you have to make some quick mental adjustments. You try to determine when a previous idea ended and the current one began. Momentarily, you try to "make sense" out of what you **thought** was happening and what **actually** happened in the verbal message.

If the speaker has given enough other vocal cues, such as changes in rate, inflection, and duration, you may have concluded earlier that one idea **probably** ended at a certain spot in the presentation. However, if the individual speaks rapidly, with little inflectional variety, you may be too busy trying to decode the flow of words to realize that a new idea is being introduced. When these periods of confusion occur regularly in a speech or reading, you could become so discouraged at trying to "make sense" out of the message that you stop trying to follow the development of plot or major ideas. Communication breakdowns can occur between speakers and listeners because pausing is not used—or is not used effectively.

Speakers and oral readers also may eliminate pauses when they begin to run out of breath. If they haven't completed an idea, they may try to talk faster, or with less intensity, in an effort to complete their idea before pausing for a breath (even though the content of the concluding idea should require **more intensity** or a **slower rate**). They also may stop in the middle of an idea to "catch their breath," thus, breaking thought units. Speakers should *not* try to get rid of all their breath before pausing for the next breath in speaking or reading aloud. Speakers who do this usually end up "gasping for breath." A small reserve of air always should be available in the lungs when a new breath is taken. This habit helps to eliminate breathiness, and throat and upper chest tension.

VOCALIZED PAUSES

Most people develop an ability to modify their oral language habits as they mature. They learn that juvenile vocabularies, trite expressions, and faulty grammar give people who don't know them well the wrong impressions. They develop varied vocabularies which allow them to move easily among many groups of people. They can modify their language to talk with children or with adults, with well educated or poorly educated people, and with subordinates or superiors. This adaptability helps them to move up or down the socio-economic ladder, from one geographical location to another, and among a variety of groups of people with ease and confidence.

Periodically, however, some speaking habits become so firmly ingrained that speakers are unaware of their obviousness and/or tediousness. Vocalized pausing is one of these habits. It occurs frequently in informal situations, among friends who tend to be accepting, patient, and uncritical. Speakers become unaware of the number of times they are using vocalized pauses. In a few cases, the speakers are convinced that the overworked terms help to establish their casual identity with a certain "in-group." Depending upon the era, and the speaking fads of that era, the speaker may believe using the terms helps to make him or her "cool," "keen," "part of the gang," "in," or "with it."

Vocalized pauses can be very distracting when they are used repeatedly. Read the following examples aloud and see how vocalized pauses disrupt ideas without making meaningful contributions to them:

We were standing on the corner, you know, when up walks this kid, you know, who has this ugly dog—you know—in his arms? He looks around, you know, like—you know, he expected me to say something—you know, like "That's sure an ugly dog!" You know!

Man, I know him! I mean, man, we met in kindergarten. He's only a year older than me, man. But let me tell you something, man. I mean, when he shoots a basket from the centerline, man—it goes in! No kidding. I mean—man—it doesn't even touch the rim!

Uhm, I'd like to, uh, to say, uh,—there's nothing—uhm, nothing like, uh, a diesel car for, uhm, getting good mileage—uhm, on the—uh, open road. Uh—it would be—uh—my first choice if, uh, if I could go out today—uhm, and buy a car.

When you read these three examples silently, your eye catches the vocalized pauses quickly. Your immediate reaction probably is "That's unreal. People don't actually talk like that!" However, if you tried to keep a transcript of the comments of many individuals during casual conversation, you would discover these are relatively mild examples of the misuse of vocalized pausing.

244

Vocalized Pauses and Disfluency

The three examples given above should help you understand what the term **disfluency** means. When thought sequences are continuously broken by meaningless sounds, or by silence, the flow of sound (the vocal message) and the continuity of words (the verbal message) become erratic or choppy and disfluency results. Disfluent speech implies uncertainty, difficult reading material, disorientation, lack of confidence, poor spontaneous reading ability, or inadequate preparation to listeners.

If you know someone who has a bad habit of using vocalized pauses, keep a tally sheet over a short period of time to see how often he or she uses these meaningless vocalizations. You may be surprised to see how quickly your paper fills with marks. If you know the individual fairly well, you may be so accustomed to hearing these vocalized pauses that you pay little attention to them. However, if you are listening to an uninteresting speaker who uses many vocalized pauses—or if you are meeting a person for the first time, you may become acutely aware of their use of vocalized pauses.

Probably you will give more **practiced readings** in your class than spontaneous speeches. As a result, you may not use vocalized pauses in class as often as you do in daily speaking, since you will not be searching for words as you give your presentations. Your instructor may comment on vocalized pauses which occur during your unrehearsed introduction to a presentation, an extemporaneous speaking assignment, or during class discussions.

Eliminating Vocalized Pauses

If your instructor indicates vocalized pausing is one of your speaking problems, you will need to raise your own consciousness level to begin hearing them as they occur in your daily speech. A good friend may be willing to give you a signal, such as saying "no," pointing a finger at you, or frowning each time you use a vocalized pause during conversations, to help bring it to your attention. Some students agree to cooperate in giving each other subtle nonverbal cues to help them recognize when they are using vocalized pauses in social groups. Other people never need to be aware of the cues that are being given.

Your instructor may tape record your presentations and ask you to listen to your recording so you will hear the frequency with which vocalized pauses occur. Since you will be listening to yourself at a time when you are not engrossed in completing the oral assignment, you will be able to concentrate on the vocalized pauses. If your instructor doesn't do this, you may wish to have a friend tape record your class presentation.

Once you become aware of how often you use vocalized pauses, you must work to eliminate them. Usually, you can eliminate the vocalized pause simply by remaining silent during the time that you would be saying "uhm" or "er." This will seem awkward to you at first, since you are not accustomed to the moments of silence. These pauses may seem excessively long to you. Keep in mind that adopting new habits always involves a short period of self-consciousness. As you become accustomed to using silence meaningfully, you will find it less intimidating. Pausing can become another tool for developing your vocal versatility.

MEANINGFUL PAUSES

The number, length, and location of pauses affect the rhythm, fluency, rate and meaning in oral communication, regardless of whether they occur in informal conversation between friends in a coffee shop, or a formal lecture to strangers in a learned society. When a message is relatively unimportant, or very simple, pausing may not be a crucial consideration for listeners to understand what is being said. However, as the message grows in complexity and importance, pauses become very important. Sensitive speakers who recognize the importance of pausing, purposely use them in certain spots for emphasis or dramatic effect. They realize pauses can enhance emotional impact and help an audience focus upon certain ideas. Effective public speakers, readers, and actors often rehearse their pauses as carefully as they practice their inflections.

Number of Pauses

You already recognize that fluency or smoothness of speaking can be disrupted by too many pauses—particularly if these pauses continually break into thought sequences. Many novice speakers believe that they should pause after every thought sequence. They view pauses literally as oral punctuation marks. However, listeners often find an oral presentation "labored" or "slow" if a speaker uses too many pauses. In fact, one of the determinants of any speaker's **rate of speaking** is pausing. If a speaker uses too many pauses, he or she will be perceived as a slow, hesitant speaker.

Punctuation in manuscripts can give important clues to an oral reader on when to pause. For example, **end punctuation** marks (periods, question marks, exclamation marks) which mark the ends of sentences or primary thoughts, *always* require pauses. They indicate the completion of a thought, even when only one word occurs such as "No!" "Who?" and "Maybe." End punctuation marks also occur between sentences and paragraphs and help to keep larger sequences of ideas together.

Internal punctuation, or punctuation which occurs within sentences, may or may not require pauses. Colons, long spaces, and semicolons *usually* require pauses. However, commas, dashes, and ellipses are not always predictable, since the ideas following them may be indicated by changes in inflection, rate, duration, and/or pitch. You must determine the meaning suggested by internal punctuation marks—and the meaning *you* wish to convey to listeners (your interpretation)—rather than deciding you will pause after every comma or dash. The relationship of words and groups of words may be made clearer by determining during your preparation sessions where pauses should occur. If you leave pausing to chance and the inspiration of the moment, your class presentations could have too many or too few pauses.

If you are giving practiced or unpracticed speeches, as well as readings in your class, you also need to be aware of the pauses *you* are using. Although you will have no manuscript to guide you, you should recognize the value of clarifying or simplifying ideas by using pauses. Pauses shouldn't suggest more than they deliver. If they suggest that ideas are complete, and then you continue with those ideas, your audience will begin to distrust you. If your pauses become excessive, your audience could become irritated by your disfluency. Your listeners may suspect you don't know what you're talking about. The number of pauses you use can be important for gaining the confidence of your listeners.

Length of Pauses

If you read music, you realize that pauses are counted with the same regular beats that musical notes are. Sound and silence combine to create rhythmical patterns in music. Musical notes or sound can be prolonged. So can pauses. This is true in speaking and oral reading as well in music.

Pauses are varying lengths of silence. If you think of them as oral punctuation marks, you realize that you can equate their various lengths with different printed punctuation marks. If you are reading a script aloud, you will discover that end punctuation marks usually indicate longer pauses than internal punctuation marks. Therefore, you would pause slightly longer for periods or exclamation points than for commas or semicolons.

Novice oral readers frequently find they can apply this idea best if they begin with a mechanical means for determining the length of pauses. They try to use some method that will be similar to watching the sweep second hand on a watch—(without actually having to look at a watch). One method is to count silently while pausing; another, is to tap the toe or foot (as many musicians do) to measure the elapsing time for varied lengths of pause. Eventually, you can eliminate these mechanical means as you develop a sense of time which allows you to hear approximately how long you are pausing.

In addition to equating length of pauses with printed punctuation marks, you also should consider their importance in implying meanings within the context of your message. Long (dramatic) pauses may be useful in certain portions of a speech or reading for building suspense, slowing down action, showing the passage of time, or suggesting extreme reluctance, laziness, or caution. The length of a pause often shows listeners which ideas are of greatest importance in your presentation. When you give an audience a longer time to think about images, emotions, and ideas, you are implying that they are particularly important. Short pauses, on the other hand, may help to speed up action, suggest confusion, urgency, turbulence, or add syncopation and comic relief to ideas.

Location of Pauses

The final component of meaningful pauses relates to where they are located in an oral presentation. If you give an introduction to your class presentation, one of the pauses should occur between your introduction and the first line of your speech or reading. This pause helps listeners make the transition from your introductory informational comments to the content and/or mood of your speech or reading. A common error made by students in beginning speech improvement classes is to rush directly into a practiced reading without letting the listeners know they have stopped speaking and another person (such as a character in a story, an observer, or the author) is beginning to speak. This initial pause should be long enough to let the listeners absorb introductory comments and get ready to hear the presentation.

Furthermore, this pause should allow you to get a good breath before you begin your oral presentation and concentrate on the first idea or emotion you wish to convey to your listeners. If you continue to speak on the air remaining in your lungs after you conclude your introduction, you may discover you can't complete the initial lines of your presentation without running out of breath.

Meaningful pauses also occur at the ends of completed points in speeches. If you write an outline of your speech, you should be aware that a pause becomes especially important each time all the supporting contentions and evidence for major points in your speech are completed. In a conventional outline, this would mean your pause would come just before you move from the last piece of information under Roman numeral I (your first major idea) to the first piece of information under Roman numeral II (your second major idea). If you don't outline your speech, you would plan to pause between the two or three major points in your speech. Since the ideas in an original speech are your own, you will know which ones are most important to you.

Meaningful pauses also may be used to introduce quoted material. The pauses suggest that the ideas which you are about to express come from another person or source—or are your own. Often, you don't need to use ''quote'' and ''unquote'' if your pauses are adequate for suggesting that you are moving away from, or back into your own comments.

In practiced readings, frequently you will find no clear indication of all the ideas that are more important than others in a particular selection. You must use your own interpretation to make these decisions. Having made your decisions, you then must make them clear to your listeners.

Generally, you can begin to do this by pausing just before changes occur in time, scene, character development, point of view (the individual telling the story), mood or atmosphere.

When you are reading dialogue between two or more characters, regardless of whether it is in prose, poetry, or drama, you should realize that you will use short pauses frequently between different characters (except in fast-paced scenes such as angry confrontations, or quick, comical interrupted bantering) in order to let your listeners know when different characters are talking. Drama usually has no narrator and depends totally on vocal changes to indicate shifts in character. Prose and poetry often contain descriptive or narrative sequences, such as "she said playfully," before, during, or after dialogue to remind the listener which character is speaking at a given moment. (These narrative or descriptive sequences would be spoken by the narrator—and would require some vocal changes to remind the audience of this fact.)

In all of these cases, your vocal versatility will help determine where your pauses must occur to let your listeners know who is speaking at a particular time. If you use many inflection, rate, or quality changes well to delineate various characters, you will need fewer obvious pauses than if you have few of these delineating vocal changes.

USING VISUAL MARKERS FOR PAUSES

When you hear an excellent speaker or oral reader give a public presentation, you probably never wonder what preparation went into that presentation. You might be surprised to discover that the manuscript, outline, or notes of the individual gave him or her continual visual reminders of what to do, or how to say certain things. In this class, you may wish to do the same thing. If you are expected to submit a copy of your practiced reading, notes, or outline to your instructor, check to see if you can mark up the script with visual markers. Instructors often are happy to see these indications of your practice—particularly if you follow through on your intentions during your public presentation.

Probably the most common visual reminder used for indicating places where pauses should occur in readings and speeches is the slash mark (/) placed between words or at the ends of paragraphs. Some speakers use varying numbers of slash marks (//, ///, etc.) to indicate longer or shorter pauses for certain ideas. The following selection illustrates these varying lengths of pauses:

Kay knew,/ without the slightest hesitation,/ that her fingers had just located the long-sought jewel inside the lining of the used purse. //She continued to chatter aimlessly / while watching the old woman's face—//searching for some sign that the woman knew of its presence.///The woman's expression never varied.// "One dollah! /Fo' you—// I mek gooood price!"/ she cooed.

The slash marks may be typed in the actual manuscript or drawn in with pen or colored pencil after the manuscript is complete. Usually, colored pencil marks are better to use in a typed or written manuscript. You can change the marks during your practice sessions if you find they don't "fit" the idea, or slow down your pace too much.

If you discover a page of your manuscript is "bleeding to death" from all the colored slash marks, you can *see* that you probably are including too many pauses. On the other hand, if only a few slash marks appear on a page, you will see that you have too few pauses.

You may want to try marking some of the passages in the practice section of this chapter before you begin to read them aloud. The logical pauses—which help listeners to understand the phrasing, structure, or syntax of word groups—will be fairly easy to locate. Your understanding of the English language and punctuation will help you find logical pauses. The emotional pauses—which emphasize or suggest atmosphere, mood, character attitudes, or author's attitude—will be more difficult to determine. When you make your own cuttings from published material, your emotional pauses will depend upon your familiarity with the total theme or plot of the material for their meaning, since they reflect your interpretation of what is being said. Therefore, the more you know about the material you are reading (and perhaps, about the author who wrote this material), the better you will be able to place meaningful, emotional pauses in the most appropriate places.

In the original selections which follow, you must work with incomplete compositions which give you little information about what happened before, or will happen after the incident cited. You must base your interpretation of emotional pauses upon only the material given.

SELECTIONS FOR PRACTICE

1. Read the following sentences aloud. Experiment with the number and length of pauses you can use to enhance meaning.

a. Around the corner, less than half a block from the white brick store, stood a large, black car with its windows rolled up—and its engine idling.

b. There was no sound—no human voices—no clock ticking—no radio playing—not even a dog barking.

c. She counted the items again: three bars of soap, a box of crackers, two frozen dinners, a pound of coffee, a package of cheese, two boxes of cereal—but there was no sugar . . . and she remembered seeing the clerk put it in the bottom of the sack.

d. Murphy checks the runner at third base, adjusts his cap, nods at the catcher, winds up, and pitches to Eddie Mertz.

e. They had been climbing up the steep incline for ten minutes, being careful not to knock their knapsacks containing the precious pheasant eggs against the jutting pieces of rock, when suddenly, without warning, Josh gave a cry of pain and dropped to his knees.

f. The temperature in Moosejaw is 62 degrees and cloudy; in Calgary, it's 58 degrees and overcast; and in Vancouver, it's a delightful 70 degrees and sunny.

g. Craig called, "Betsy?" but heard nothing—so he placed the package on the wooden lawn-chair, took a red bandana from his shirt pocket, wiped the perspiration from his forehead, and started around the house to look for her.

h. The prosecutor's office had no comment when asked why Bert Crawley had been released—but an observer, who did not wish to be identified, told us that Crawley's father had posted the $50,000 bond.

i. Kitty knew that look: cold, calculating, and secretly gloating; she had seen it at least a dozen times before, all immediately before Vance disappeared for several weeks.

j. And if this was the end—if there were no last minute "turn-of-events" as happens in the soap operas—then this would mean Julie would . . . but surely, that couldn't happen!

k. Three bounces of the basketball . . . two to three quick steps . . . a twist of the shoulders . . . and Merle was under the basket again, raising his arm in a long, fast sweep, but never looking directly at the basket.

l. Laverne scrubbed the carrots with a small, firm brush; Christy filled the copper kettle with water from the well, lifted it to the hook overhanging the campfire, and fastened it in place.

m. When he said, "I'll stop for Luther on my way back from the office," she nodded, knowing that he would have to hurry now to catch his train.

n. She ran her finger slowly down the list of typed names, murmuring softly to herself: Trayner, Troy, Tuttle, Ulrich, Upton, Utting—ah, there it was—Utting—Leonard Utting, 1225 Bostwick Circle!

o. She spotted her grandfather, a short, slight, white haired man with light green eyes, sitting on a park bench near the oak tree she had played in when she was a child.

p. He stood in the rain, bareheaded, without a job or a place to stay, and with only two dollars in his pockets.

q. At the International Conference on Arms Limitation in Paris this morning, Secretary of State Bradley announced that the United States is ready to accept yesterday's general agreement on nuclear arms disposal.

r. Twice he checked his pockets, but each time he found them empty—utterly, completely empty.

s. Beyond the crossroads, just behind the large billboard sign advertising Crossfire Gasoline, was a tiny house, just big enough for two people.

t. Prunes—that was what he was to get—and he had almost passed them on his quick trip down the supermarket aisle, as he headed for the check-out counter.

u. Mayor Delaney spoke to the City Club at noon today on the proposed mass transportation system which will link Chester and North Burton.

v. I thought, "If I can wait an hour, I can have lunch with Vern at the new restaurant that just opened . . . and that would give both of us a chance to talk about our summer plans."

w. Many times during the past hour I have been ready to pack up my briefcase and leave, knowing full well that you probably wouldn't even be aware of my departure!

x. The candle was burning low now, and Sybil knew that—unless someone arrived with supplies from the mainland—the lighthouse would soon be *completely* dark.

y. "It could have been the radishes . . . since radishes do upset my stomach periodically . . . but I really believe it was the tunafish that gave me indigestion this time," Mrs. Mitchell said, shifting sideways in her chair so she could see the doctor better.

z. Looking at the market indicators at noon: the Dow Jones Average stands at 1287, down six points; gold is off fifty cents, at $387 an ounce; and silver is up one cent, at $7.12 an ounce.

2. Longer Selections for Practice

A. By standing on her toes and resting her chin on the high windowsill, Marilyn could see the mountains from her bedroom windows. She loved those mountains! They reminded her of accomplishment, eternity, and greatness. Oh, yes—she realized she was very romantic about mountains. She had been in them enough times to realize they were not always glamorous—or even trustworthy. But they were always there! Even when the fog rolled in from the coast and made them invisible, she knew they were permanent. In this respect, they were unlike so many things in her life in recent years. Her marriage . . . her career in the movies . . . her friends . . . and now her health.

Marilyn gazed at the mountains, wishing she could be in them at this moment. Oh yes, it was only an hour's drive by expressway. But the doctor had warned her not to drive for at least three more weeks. She still could have a sudden reaction to the drugs she was taking—those never-ending pain killers—and the doctor didn't want her behind the wheel. But the lure of those mountains was powerful—so powerful, that she lost all sense of time . . . until the tendons in her legs warned her that she had been standing on her toes long enough.

Reluctantly, she drew away from the windows and returned to her tiny living room. The newspaper still was unopened on the coffee table, and her lukewarm cup of tea had not been tasted. Three more weeks of imprisonment in her apartment! Could she stand them?

A year ago, her phone would have rung seven times by now with friends wishing her well in her next performance . . . complimenting her on her recent performance . . . asking her advice about some matter . . . or just calling to say they were thinking of her. Wasn't it strange how quickly they had disappeared when they heard of her pending divorce! Her few remaining friends: Berta, Wade, and Marcie had called periodically until she entered the hospital. Then they stopped calling too.

She hadn't really cared—or even noticed when she was in intensive care because she was too tired—and too sick to care. But those two months of hospital recuperation without a card . . . or a telephone call . . . or a note from anyone . . . that was difficult to take! She had read about several of them in newspapers the aides would bring her, so she knew they were in the city—but she didn't know why they never attempted to contact her.

If it hadn't been for her panorama view of the mountains—she was sure she would have given up hope of ever coming home. But those mountains remained her friends and she promised *she* wouldn't let *them* down. She would get well enough to walk on them again.

B. "Three tablespoons of cocoa."

"And a teaspoon of vanilla."

"One teaspoon of vanilla. O.K. And that's all?"

Sidney nodded. "You should be ready to blend it now until it's a smooth paste. While you do that, I'll grease a couple of cake tins."

"This isn't as bad as I thought it would be! When I tried to read the recipe by myself, I got very confused. But having you read it aloud while I added the ingredients simplified the whole thing. Thanks Sid."

Clara was telling the truth. She had done so little of her own cooking and baking that she hardly knew where to begin. A "recipe" usually meant adding two cups of milk to the contents of a box. That, to Clara, was making a cake from "scratch." Actually following a recipe, step by step, was a quaint relic from the past—a custom that may have been used by early settlers and the Pilgrims—but not by modern housewives!

She had been surprised when Sid insisted that she bake his favorite cake "from scratch" for his birthday—using a secret recipe that had been in his family for six generations. She also had been surprised when she found herself agreeing to do so—on condition, of course, that he help her!

Sid took a paper towel, dipped it in a can of pure white shortening, and carefully greased the sides and bottoms of two round cake tins. He had watched his mother and sisters do this often—so he knew the procedure well, even though he had never done it himself. His jobs had always been in the yard or garage—never in the kitchen. That was why he was amazed to discover that Clara knew very little about baking cakes. He thought all women had had the same experiences his sisters learned early in life.

"Do you have a little flour left?" Sid asked over the noise of the electric beater.

Clara looked up from her task. "Do you think the cake needs more flour?" she asked.

"No, the batter looks fine. I need a little flour for the bottom of the tins." He pointed at the cake tin he was holding. "It helps to keep the cake from sticking to the tins."

Clara's eyes widened. "It does! I never knew that. No wonder my other cakes were hard to get out ot the pan. Yes, there's some flour in the cannister next to the stove." She nodded toward a round, yellow container. "Use it all, if you want. I have another package of flour in the cupboard."

Sidney looked inside. "Oh, there's *more* than enough here. All I need is a little to sprinkle on the bottom."

C. The town was named after Lucius Lyons, an early Michigan politician, who probably never realized that his namesake would spread along two sides of the river. But it did, and that created an interesting puzzle.

During the early 1940s, the main part of Lyons, including the business district, most of the homes, and the Methodist and Baptist churches, were on one side of the river. The business section consisted of a main street and one cross street on whose corners were located a sturdy but vacant red sandstone bank building, a tall, gray brick hotel, the newly opened and painted Park's Red and White Store, and a tavern that still had a hitching area for horses outside—though horses seldom came into the business district any more. The main street consisted of two blocks of adjacent stores and shops—and the remains of a casket factory. It ran straight down to the tall metal bridge which crossed the river.

On the other side of the river were a few scattered houses, a large, vacant commercial building, a feed and grain store, and the town's only school. This two story, red brick building, almost hidden from the rest of the town down a gravel road—next to a field that was planted each spring with various grains and harvested each fall—was a part of the puzzle. The school children benefitted from this puzzle practically every year.

Lyons was hardly a prosperous community during the 1940s. It was far enough away from the former automobile (and now defense) factories in Lansing to be "safe" from potential enemy attack, but close enough to allow many of its citizens employment there on one of its twenty-four hour shifts. (It also was small enough to allow instant recognition of potential intruders. However, with gas rationing "for the duration" and a scarcity of tires, no one seemed interested in intruding on this town's isolation.)

The puzzle regarding the school was this: why was the school built on the opposite side of the river from the main part of town?

That doesn't seem strange to you? It might if you realized that practically every spring the

252

river would overflow its banks, making travel across the bridge risky—and guaranteeing the school children a period of time away from school.

Spring thaws were eagerly awaited by the children. As great chunks of ice began drifting down the river, the children watched the rising waters with great anticipation. Dynamite explosions up the river were omens that ice was beginning to collect and soon might not be able to pass over the dam just above the bridge. A sudden thaw would add much additional water to the run-off from snow melting. Worried adult eyes watched the warning signs of a pending flood; unworried children's eyes considered the opportunities of a few extra days of vacation—due to an act of God.

Certainly, this annual flooding season was not new. The townfathers and mothers must have recognized the dangers involved in placing a school on the other side of the river. If the main bridge ever washed away, how would the children get across the river to attend school?

The bridge didn't wash away (although it was later replaced—but the floods occurred regularly. Today, no one worries about this puzzle any more. The old, red school has been closed for many years. Today, the children are transported in sturdy buses to the neighboring town of Muir, across a different bridge!

D. Once we became "permanent party" in the army, we acquired half a day each week for doing some type of physical training—or "PT" as it was more commonly known. We were not restricted in the type of activity, as long as it was something active. Calisthenics was among the least popular—since that had been required in basic training. Swimming, golf, and tennis were among the most popular in our portion of the base.

The rationale for physical training was that every soldier was to "keep in shape." Even though some soldiers had office, kitchen, or teaching jobs, they were not expected to become overweight, lazy, or weak. (This was difficult to understand in our unit, where most of the career soldier sergeants had ample waistlines and could barely walk up a flight of stairs in the barracks without breaking out in a cold sweat. Most of them preferred to bellow their commands from the ground floor—or better yet, go to the orderly room and use the public address system.) We were to be ready to move into the field at a moment's notice—though most of us hoped it would not be the same type of field we were in during basic training bivouac!

It was not too long before we realized that PT was not an enforced requirement. If you had a job that you really enjoyed doing, you could stay on duty during your regular PT day and allow someone else to take their PT.

Few of the permanent party staff in my unit passed up their weekly afternoon-off! Even if we decided to hit a few tennis balls back and forth across a net (and often over the backstop, giving us additional physical training in having to go and search for the balls), we could then carry our rackets around for the rest of the afternoon while we strolled leisurely about. This allowed us to claim that we were going to, or returning from, an active game of tennis, should anyone inquire about our intent (which they never did).

An even more enjoyable way of PTing was to go to one of the pools, paddle around a little to get wet, and then sprawl on a white, army-issue towel for the rest of the afternoon and enjoy the sunshine. On particularly cool days at the beginning or end of the pool season, we would find a protected area where the breeze wouldn't raise goosebumps on our arms, and stay there all afternoon—without ever sticking a toe in the water.

Those of us who were draftees had to watch our weight so we wouldn't outgrow our two-year-issue of clothing. Otherwise, we would have to buy new clothing—and that would be a waste

253

of our miniscule pay. Fortunately, the only food that might have challenged us to gain weight quickly was the chocolate sundaes which we bought at the service club one night a week when old, canned C-rations were served in the messhalls. We were not opposed to helping the army get rid of some of its stockpiles of C-rations. However, we found the same menu every week was more than our stomachs could take and we gratefully spent our own money once a week for a sandwich and a sundae with lots of chocolate and marshmallow topping. That was always a good time to discuss what we would do on our *next* afternoon of PT.

3. Dialogue for Oral Practice (for two readers)

Speaker 1: When you first moved to California, were you surprised at the heavy traffic on the freeways?

Speaker 2: Yes, I was! I had heard jokes about California traffic, especially around Los Angeles, but I had **no idea** what "heavy traffic" meant until I settled here.

Speaker 1: Had you lived all your life in Canada before coming here last year?

Speaker 2: Yes, all of it. In fact, the largest city I had ever visited was Regina. I sang in our school choir for three years and in my final year, we were asked to sing in a large auditorium in Regina. We stayed overnight in a hotel and it was my first experience in one. You can tell that I lived a very protected life in what you Americans often refer to as the "boondocks."

Speaker 1: Is it true that you were "discovered" while singing in Regina? I read that a talent scout was in the audience there and heard you sing a solo.

Speaker 2: Actually, she was looking at the auditorium while we were practicing—the night **before** our concert. She—that's Susan Duffey—was looking at the sound equipment while I was doing my solo. I didn't see her because the stage lights were on and she was in the auditorium with a friend. After we finished our rehearsal, she came backstage and talked with our choral director, then talked with me. I thought she was just being kind when she said she would like to hear me sing *without* a choral background. My teacher played the piano and I sang a popular ballad while my classmates left to have pizza.

Speaker 1: And evidently, your solo impressed Ms. Duffey.

Speaker 2: Well, she went out and bought a ticket to our performance immediately and said she wanted to talk with me after the concert.

Speaker 1: Had you sung commercially—or with any entertainment group—before that?

Speaker 2: No. My town only has a population of 2400, so we don't have nightclubs or lounges. I sang in my church choir—that's all.

Speaker 1: And now you have the most popular record in North America, a recording contract for an album, and concerts scheduled in New York, Toronto, and London!

Speaker 2: Yes. It's really amazing how quickly things happened. I recorded my current record the last week I was in high school, then went off on a vacation to Jasper. The record was released in August and by February, I was moving to Los Angeles.

Speaker 1: Well, folks, that's a quick summary of the events which led to this week's biggest hit—and for the fourth straight week—the largest selling single on three continents, "When I Can Understand." And here is that record!

CHAPTER 19

USING RATE TO INFLUENCE MEANING

You are aware of the "fast talking" salesperson who immediately puts you on the defensive. Regardless of whether the individual calls you on the telephone, buttonholes you on the used car lot, gives a "fast pitch" to sell the buy-of-a-lifetime on television or radio, or calls at your front door, if his or her rate is very fast, your common sense tells you, "Be careful! I'm being pushed too fast. There must be a catch somewhere if I have to make a decision right now!" You don't want to be rushed into making a decision you will regret later on.

On the other hand, the slow talking "good old boy" who seems to be in no hurry at all, may aggravate you with a ponderous rate if you have to complete a transaction quickly and get back to work, school, or another appointment. This individual seems capable of prolonging a short story until it is as long as a novel. In some situations, you may feel an individual is humoring you, stringing you along, or talking down to you because of a slow, methodical rate of speaking. Undoubtedly, you will feel this turtle-like rate is tedious or monotonous.

Rate of speaking usually is associated with terms such as time, speed, pacing, tempo, and timing. Rate consists of two basic components: the number of words or syllables pronounced in a specified amount of time (speed of phonation), and the length of pauses used between words. It may include the concerns for pausing which were discussed in the last chapter, as well as concerns for duration (time used in producing individual sounds), rhythm (the repetition of any discernible factor), and speed of blending (assimilating) sounds within thought units to create fluent speech. Rate becomes a significant factor to listeners who are evaluating intelligibility and effectiveness of verbal messages. In general, you will find that speakers of the Southern Dialect use a slower rate than speakers of the Eastern or General American Dialects. Also, people who live in large cities tend to speak faster than people in small towns and rural areas.

THE RELATIVE NATURE OF RATE IN HUMAN SPEECH

Listeners will perceive rate as long or short depending on their own emotional involvement and interest in the topic, environmental conditions surrounding the speaker (including factors such as comfortable seating, room temperature, and competing noise), immediate demands on the listeners' time, and influences of the particular occasion (such as the close camaraderie that results from a major business accomplishment or the joy that is shared at a family wedding). Inevitably, rate of speaking becomes a *relative* factor in each individual's oral presentation. This relativity also may be based on one or more of the following comparative considerations.

1. Speakers may speak slower or faster than they usually speak. In this case, the rate is relative to the known habituated patterns of each person over a period of time. For example, as a child, you learned when a member of your family was tired, joking, determined, or excited partially by that person's speaking rate, when contrasted with his or her "normal" speaking rate. In new situations, where a speaker *isn't* known, an audience has no basis for determining this relativity.

2. Speakers may speak slower or faster than they just spoke. The rate being used at the moment is compared to the rate used a few moments before. Changes in emotion or mood frequently are indicated by sudden rate changes within the same sentence. For example, you can read the first part of the following sentences slowly and the second part quickly to emphasize contrasting ideas and emotions:

    a. I have had a splitting headache all afternoon—but I've wanted to see this movie for so long, that I'll go with you.

    b. He made a long, smooth, gliding "S" turn down the slope, then suddenly flicked his skis, made a ninety degree turn, and flashed past the finish line.

    c. She resolved to give him one more chance, but that was all.

    d. At first, she was reluctant to say *anything,* but when the detective assured her that her comments would be confidential, she began rattling off names of all the people who had pawned valuable items in the past six days.

3. Speakers may speak slower or faster than other speakers in a particular situation or environment. When comparing a speaker with other people in a given situation, you might conclude that the person speaks at an habitually slower rate than anyone else. In this case, you are making a judgment based on your observations of specific people. Your judgment may be based on a quick generalization (such as you might make at a party) or on careful observation over a period of time (such as you might make in a class or office where you spend considerable time).

4. Speakers may speak slower or faster than a stated norm or criterion such as the number of syllables or words spoken per minute. For example, approximately 150–160 words-per-minute is viewed as an average rate used in normal impromptu speaking. In normal daily conversation, the average rate may be slightly faster than this in the United States. The average oral reading rate will be slightly faster than the rate used in conversational speech, depending on the type of material being read. Probably a reader of oral prose would use a rate of 140 to 180 words per minute.

If you usually speak **much slower** than these speeds, your listeners may perceive you as being lethargic, lazy, ponderous, tired, insensitive, hesitant, ill, unprepared, monotonous, reluctant, or lacking in self-confidence. If you generally speak **much faster** than these speeds, listeners may perceive you as being excited, insecure, aggressive, insensitive, "pushy," exhilarated, breathless, eager, glib, confident, mechanical, or defensive. Keep in mind, however, that other factors such as noise, competing messages, inflectional variety, intensity, and clarity of diction all can influence listeners' perceptions too.

You may never have timed your speaking rate before. The selection below will help you make an estimate of how fast you **read** aloud. Using a watch with a sweep second hand or a digital counter, read the selection aloud as if you are telling the incident to someone. After one minute, pause and mark the word you were reading when you reached one minute. Repeat this process several more times, marking the ending word each time. When you see approximately where you are ending, count the total number of words and you will have a general idea of your oral reading speed. (Slash marks have been used after each twenty-fifth word to help you in your tabulations.)

Remember, your oral reading speed probably will be slightly faster than your conversational speaking speed. If you read slower than 140 words per minute, you probably are reading too slowly. If you complete the reading before the end of one minute, you probably are reading too fast. Try to control your rate to see if you can read 150 to 160 words per minute.

PASSAGE FOR ESTIMATING ORAL READING RATE

When Delbert arrived home from college during his first winter vacation, he was unprepared for the reception he received. His younger brother actually sat down // and talked with him, instead of rushing off to play with his gang. His mother baked his favorite dessert, pecan pie, and insisted that he // eat a second piece at the evening meal—something that happened only once before, at his last birthday party before leaving for college. His two // sisters escorted their girlfriends to the house to admire their brother who was a "real college freshman." His father gave him the keys to the // family Oldsmobile and said he wouldn't be needing the car all weekend, so Delbert should feel free to use it— if he wanted it. Even // Tate, the ancient family dog, curled up at his feet while Delbert sat in the wooden rocking chair. Usually, Tate would have wandered off to // the kitchen to find peace and security under the kitchen table. Everything seemed friendlier and considerably more relaxed than when he was living at home. // Without a doubt, this vacation would be wonderful!

5. Speakers may speak slower or faster than they can handle effectively. Usually this relative judgment is made in relation to an important criterion commonly used by voice and diction instructors—accuracy of sound production. If a person's diction becomes indistinct or inaccurate because of rate of speaking, a student should change his or her rate of speaking until clarity is no longer a problem. This factor of sound accuracy often is an obvious one among fast speakers. You may have no difficulty understanding one fast speaker—but a great amount of difficulty understanding another speaker who speaks at exactly the same rate.

Individuals who are unaccustomed to speaking rapidly, usually have difficulty moving the tongue, lips, and jaw quickly enough to form sounds distinctly when they attempt to increase their rate in initial practice sessions. They blend and blur sounds, creating indistinctly pronounced words. (Comedians who make these diction errors as they increase their speaking rate, excuse themselves by claiming their tongue gets in front of their eye teeth so they can't see what they're saying!)

High school and college interscholastic debaters often are criticized for their use of an inarticulate, rapid rate of speaking during their presentation of debate cases. Many of the students ignore diction and place their total attention on a fast rate of speaking which allows them to present all their ideas within the strict time limits. They become accustomed to hearing other debaters repeating the same ideas in fast, "machinegun rapidity," (often in a verbal shorthand style which is meaningful only to debaters), in debate after debate. They can't understand why non-debaters and first time listeners are appalled by the experience! This rapidity usually destroys their communication effectiveness with judges and listeners.

When rate of speaking destroys clarity of diction (usually because it is too fast) or becomes tedious for listeners (usually because it is too slow), it becomes a major barrier to good communication. Probably more voice and diction instructors criticize fast speaking rate than slow speaking rate.

Nonnative speakers of English who have distinctive, obvious accents need to speak at a fairly slow rate until their associates' ears become attuned to their common phonemic changes. They must form their English sounds carefully if the sounds don't occur in their native language. When nonnative students become accustomed to changing their articulators to produce accurate, clear sounds, they may *then* begin to increase their rate of speaking. This same advice may be given to native American speakers with distinctive regional or subsidiary dialects when they communicate with speakers of other English dialects—or with nonnative speakers of English!

If you know you have an obvious dialect, you probably will need to speak slowly—or you will increase your chances of being misunderstood. Regardless of how fast you normally speak at home, if you can't be understood among strangers, you probably are speaking too fast.

DURATION OR QUANTITY OF SOUND

Duration or quantity of sound relates to the amount of time used by a speaker to say individual sounds. As you studied the IPA, you learned that certain sounds are difficult to sustain because they stop and start quickly. The **stop** or **plosive** sounds [p], [b], [t], [d], [k], and [g] are very difficult to prolong by themselves. Therefore, words which contain several stop sounds will seem short, clipped, or abrupt when compared to words without any stop sounds. Words which contain only continuant sounds can be sustained over a long period of time.

Pronounce the words in the following two lists aloud to hear the difference in duration between stopped and continuant sounds. Notice that you can prolong diphthong and vowel sounds before and after stopped sounds—but you can't prolong the stops.

Stopped	# of stops	# of syllables	Continuant	# of stops	# of syllables
feet	1	1	owns	0	1
patted	3	2	rowing	0	2
debated	4	3	remaining	0	3
totality	3	4	inferences	0	4
decapitated	6	5	unmercifully	0	5

Words which contain stop sounds but begin or end with **two** adjacent continuant sounds, such as "roast," "grow," and "entitles," may be prolonged for moderately long periods of time. Words which contain **no** stop sounds, as indicated in the list above may be prolonged for very long periods of time. As you can begin to see, words have varying capacities for being prolonged.

You should not confuse a word's capacity with its actual prolongation in oral presentations. Some speakers and oral readers ignore the opportunities that exist within a word for prolonging sounds. They use little variation in duration of sound for saying most sounds. They may say the word distinctly so listeners understand the dictionary (denotative) meaning of the word, but force their listeners to derive their own subjective (connotative) meaning from it. This may be a desirable quality in factual news reporting where total objectivity is required. However, in most other forms

258

of speaking, it becomes a serious limitation. Listeners who are unfamiliar with material being presented by a speaker or oral reader, need to know the emotional as well as the logical content of the message. Changes in duration can help a speaker suggest a variety of emotional responses.

This element of duration may be demonstrated in the following sentences. Say each sentence as if it is a simple statement of fact. Then, read the sentence again but stress the underlined word by holding it twice as long as you did the first time. Finally, read the sentence a third time, but this time hold the underlined word twice as long as you did during the second reading. Notice the different shades of meanings that can be suggested with these changes.

a. He took a <u>long</u> time before he replied.

b. The student pilot made a <u>smooth</u> landing.

c. The teacher raised her eyebrows, then said <u>"Oh?"</u>

d. She had waited <u>so long</u> for this letter.

e. A <u>cool</u> wind blew down from the mountains.

f. Grandma Tyler gave each of her grandchildren a <u>warm</u> hug.

g. The workmen moved the priceless ceramic statue <u>very</u> carefully.

h. She knew her father was going <u>far</u> away and would be gone for <u>three</u> years.

As you begin to examine the opportunities for changing duration in various words, you will discover certain words can be shortened or lengthened to suggest, define or elaborate upon actions or emotions. The meaning that you intend to give (your interpretation) can be enhanced or clarified by prolonging or shortening sounds in words. Some of these words may attempt to imitate the actual sound (which is called onomatopoeia), as in the words "splash," "scratch," "zipped," and "hoot." Other words may represent a specific action, such as "cut," "crush," "hit," "soothes," "clawed," "scream," or a specific emotion or image such as "fighting mad," "lonely," "determined," "ghostly," "beautiful," "rich," "delicious," and "expensive." When other vocal considerations, such as vocal quality and inflection, are added to duration, you will find you are able to make fine distinctions in your oral presentations which will help your listeners gain a quicker, more complete understanding of your message.

During your class presentations, you should begin to look carefully at words in your manuscript readings to see what opportunities they allow for enhancing meaning through the use of duration. All words are not of equal importance. Some should be treated like royalty! It is part of your job as an oral reader to determine which words deserve this treatment. Once you become accustomed to varying the duration of words in oral readings, you will feel more secure about carrying this practice over to daily speaking situations. By adding rate variation to your repertoire of speaking skills, you increase your speaking versatility and your potential for becoming an effective communicator.

THE SUBJECTIVE NATURE OF RATE IN HUMAN SPEECH

Rate is difficult to evaluate in a totally objective manner. Listeners unconsciously evaluate rate of speaking on such subjective continuums as effectiveness, emotional control, understandability, and enthusiasm. These evaluations often are influenced by a speaker's emotional reactions to material being presented, the situation in which a thing is being said, and the speaker's motivations and drives.

Rate as a Practiced Response

If, as a listener, you are influenced by the same emotions, drives and/or motivations as the speaker, you may not be aware of how or when rate modifications influence you. Instead, you may be "swept away" by the emotional impact of a message without realizing (at least, until later) that changes in the speed of a message helped to create your feeling of urgency, compulsion, or eagerness.

Planners of group events who recognize the psychological value of rate changes in speaking or in nonverbal communication, may deliberately "set the stage" for them in advance. A speaker may be encouraged to begin "picking up momentum" or "increasing the rhythm" of an oral presentation in order to take advantage of audience responses which *probably* will occur as a result of certain incidents, statements, or behaviors. If the same presentation has been given several times to similar audiences, the influence of certain vocal elements becomes fairly predictable. Rate changes become a part of the "staging" or "choreographing" of group events, such as political addresses, public revivals, and public action rallies.

Rate as an Habituated Response

In your daily conversations, do you use the same speaking rate with:

Males as you use with females?

People your own age as you use with older or younger people?

People in authority as opposed to your subordinates?

Members of your family as compared with nonmembers?

You may discover that you have a relative consistency in your speed of speaking that remains, regardless of the individual to whom you are speaking. You may vary ten or fifteen words per minute, but your average rate of speaking probably remains quite regular. On the other hand, your rate may vary considerably as you move from one group to another. How and when did you learn to speak at the rate you use during your daily conversations with others?

Just as certain people move at different rates and react to the same stimuli at differing rates, they also talk at different rates. To discover the original reasons for these rates would be a challenge. Often, the reasons existed in early childhood: childhood idols who were copied, numbers of individuals in a family, emotional experiences, environmental influences, physical health, rewards and punishments for specific behaviors, and so on. Those reasons may have been forgotten over the years while the behavior continued, unmodified, to the present day.

Rate of speaking becomes a component of your daily speaking behaviors. Your associates, in turn, view your speaking behaviors as part of your "personality." You can begin to see how your rate becomes a part of the "you" that other people have come to accept and expect.

The Misuse of Rate as a Gimmick

Unfortunately, some business firms lead salespersons and public relations representatives to believe that increased rate is the chief element (if not the *only* element) in enthusiasm. In their

260

attempt to train inexperienced speakers quickly and efficiently, some firms emphasize a particular component, such as fast rate or increased volume, out of the total complex of effective speaking attributes. They stress this component as an essential sales "gimmick" because it "gets results." (The results actually may be coming from something entirely unrelated to the gimmick—but the trainers don't recognize this.)

Unfortunately, many aspiring politicians also receive the same type of "crash training" in speaking. They fit their verbal message into a set vocal pattern (often using rate as one of the primary features of the pattern) without giving any thought to changing rate to fit the circumstances of each unique audience and situation. They use a formula—a set approach to speaking—and seldom deviate from it. As a result, many audience members feel they are being talked to as if they are inexperienced seventh grade school-dropouts.

The simple combination of fast rate and loud volume might be viewed as a form of "verbal bludgeoning" which attempts to beat listeners over the head with words until they can't forget the message! The technique is used often by local television advertisers—usually in an attempt to be humorous—and usually in the guise of a simple, uncouth huckster.

Overly simplistic approaches to coaching speakers smacks of shysterism and encourages innocent individuals to develop a fast-talking style because their trainers (who are presumed to be authorities) claim it works. Many telephone salespersons, for example, are taught to say as much as possible in the first few moments of contact to keep a potential customer listening and wondering what the message is all about. Politicians are advised to appeal to as many different interest groups as possible in the early moments of a speech.

This gross oversimplification and overgeneralization of effective speaking style is only one step above the training received by fast-talking sideshow barkers and purveyors of marvelous snake oil remedies of traveling tentshows in past years! The naive sales trainees often are unaware of how transparent their efforts are to individuals who have had academic courses in public speaking, oral reading, voice and diction, and interpersonal communication.

Intelligent, perceptive people can spot the fast talker who is using a practiced script or a memorized (canned) "pitch" almost immediately. They can show their disdain for the salesperson's insensitivity to, or disregard for, effective human communication training by hanging up, walking out, closing the door, turning to another station, or simply rejecting the message and product because of its lack of honesty and sincerity.

RATE CHANGES IN ORAL READINGS

As you prepare your oral presentations, you may wonder when changes in rate may be best used. Are there specific indicators, for example, in manuscripts that tell you when to change your speaking rate?

Whenever descriptive or narrative terms are used to indicate speaking speed, they should be reflected in the actual speed used in reading material. Frequently, these descriptions **follow** a quotation or piece of dialogue. If you don't look ahead at material you're reading aloud for the first time, you may not realize the rate should be changed until after you have read the quotation—and then it's too late. For example, read the following sentences silently to understand the rate called for, then read them aloud, using the described rate.

a. "Whatever gave you *that* idea?" she snapped.

b. "I can say, without the least hesitation, that you are the nicest person I have ever known," she drawled in her oozing southern Alabama style.

261

   c. "My mind is made up," she said without hesitation, "And I fully intend to take the witness stand tomorrow unless . . ." and here, she paused for several moments, then continued with quiet determination, ". . . . unless *you* take it instead!"

   d. "Mama," the child called in a long, low voice like an echo from a tomb, "Mama, I . . . I love you."

   e. The supervisor turned on her heels to face the smiling mass of freckles behind her which was saying, "Your old man wears bunny slippers," in such a slow, dry manner that she knew he must be the kid everyone had told her about.

If you are reading from a playscript, the descriptive terms usually will be placed in parentheses either before or after the character's lines. You are not expected to read the descriptive terms aloud since they are intended to be used as instructions to the actor or actress. For example, the following excerpt shows you how these descriptive terms indicate changes in rate.

MAUDE (With quiet, slow dignity). The world holds no mystery for me any more. I have been around the world twice, had dinner with kings and princes, appeared on the stage in sixty different countries, and (pausing to adjust her spectacles) and I am now seventy-five years old.

CLARENCE (Impatiently). But you once told me that you would never forsake the theatre. (Then, realizing he may have spoken too hastily) You do remember that day, don't you?

MAUDE (Sighing). Yes. Yes, I remember. You must have been all of six years old then.

CLARENCE. Seven. It was the year father bought me the blue wagon.

MAUDE (Smiling slightly in tired recognition of her own failing memory). Seven. Yes, it was. (Then, with great patience) But Clarence, you were just leaving the world of make-believe . . . just beginning to trust the world of reality for its rewards and . . .

CLARENCE (Quickly). And distrust it for its punishments!

MAUDE. (Leaning back in her chair) Reality is such a difficult thing to accept. (She turns her face and looks directly at him.) But *you succeeded,* Clarence. Even with all your ideals and imagination, you succeeded. (Slowly, as if underscoring every word) And that is more important to me than all my past loyalty to the theatre. Can you understand that?

If you are reading material with two or more characters who are speaking to each other, you will find that rate of speaking will be a useful vocal characteristic for delineating one character from another. Even though the manuscript may contain no indication of rate changes, you may decide that certain physical and emotional characteristics can be emphasized by slower or faster rates of speaking. Often, for example, older characters can be distinguished from younger ones by using a slower rate to show progressively older characters. By using contrasting rates, you help your listeners understand who is speaking at a particular time. These decisions regarding rate of speaking become part of your interpretation of each character's personality.

A manuscript also may give contrasting (dissimilar) ideas, emotions, situations, environments, and characters. These contrasts may suggest one thing is bigger, more important, better looking, easier to find, more intelligent, faster, more dependable, more pleasant, tastier, more relaxed, etc., than something or someone else. Changes in rate of speaking can be useful for designating or emphasizing these contrasts.

When a piece of literature is building to a climax or a conclusion, rate often becomes an important element for suggesting this progressive intensification of emotion. Mysteries, for example, may use a slower pacing to develop suspense, fear, and a feeling of impending disaster. They may use a faster pace for conflict, terror, lack of control, and increasing action. When you are selecting material to read aloud, you may discover that individual chapters in novels often end at a slightly faster pace than when they began. However, the episodes of action which occur within a chapter may contain faster rates than the ending. In general, your rate of speaking will increase as the intensity of conflict or suspense increases.

Often, the passage of time in a piece of literature may be suggested by your rate of speaking. If you hold onto sounds and use long pauses, you can suggest to your listeners that an event is taking place over an extended period of time. If you clip your sounds and shorten or eliminate pauses, you can suggest the quick passage of time. Some manuscripts actually **squeezewordsto-gether** without spaces in order to suggest an increased rate—and use **long   spaces   between words** (or letters within words) to show a much s-l-o-w-e-r rate. These typographical arrangements should give you a clue to how the author intends you to read the material.

RATE CHANGES IN SPEAKING

In the preceding paragraphs, you have learned some of the ways in which manuscripts may indicate the advisability of using rate changes. If you remember that literature attempts to translate speech and action into **words,** you will be able to reverse this process after practicing your oral readings for class. By becoming aware of the opportunities for effective use of rate changes in literature, you may then apply these principles to prepared public speeches and, ultimately, to your own daily speaking habits. By doing this, you will be translating words into **speech and action.** The purpose of in-class readings is to increase your awareness of ways for attaining vocal variety and to give you practiced experiences in using these strategies—not to make you superior oral readers. It is important that you not view the procedures or "means to an end" as the end result. Rate is an important element for attaining vocal versatility. When it is used in conjunction with other vocal elements (pause, pitch, inflection, quality, rhythm), it assists you to say what you mean efficiently and effectively in a variety of settings and situations.

PRACTICE EXERCISES

1. Use changes in rate to indicate contrasting ideas in the following sentences. Read them aloud to hear the distinctions being made.

a. Connie was slow, determined, and very cautious; Carla was quick, disorganized, always at "loose ends."

b. The children scrambled to the top of the hill, pushing and shouting while their cabin counselor casually strolled to the top, viewing the scenery as he climbed.

c. There is no purpose, no goal, no ultimate objective of this group—only lengthy delusion, drawn-out negotiations, and self-serving political maneuverings.

d. What? No ice? I asked for ice! Surely, the management knows the consequences of this oversight!

e. The long, winding road goes slowly through the forrest until it hits the barren plateau, then drops abruptly to the ocean.

f. The rotten stench of the garbage dump was a stark contrast to the sweet, delicious aroma of cherry pies resting on the windowsill.

g. Icy cold glasses of homemade root beer complemented the crisp, hot, taco corn chips and spicy dip.

h. She leisurely rolled down the window of her blue Chevrolet, then beat a quick rat-a-tat rhythm on the top of the car with her sharp fingernails.

i. Subtle, he was not; but suave—ah, yes, he indeed was suave.

j. Left, right, left and left again, then snap—and he was falling through space with the noise of the boxing ring growing---- fainter-------and------------f-a-i-n-t-e-r.

k. "Whoooooo are youuuuuu?" came the voice from the cellar, but Irmgard, determined that she never would talk to a ghost, bolted the door and flicked on the light.

2. Try to determine the atmosphere or mood required in each of the following selections. Read the selections aloud, using rate changes to support the prevailing mood.

a. It was illogical. That was all there was to it! Nobody spent $20,000 for a sailboat and then set it adrift on an open bay to test its durability in a storm. What if Jack *had* tried to leave the country once before. It was no reason to believe he would do it again. Certainly Jack wouldn't have left an investment like this behind. If he really wanted to disappear—he would have sailed to Haiti on his boat. He definitely wouldn't have left it untended. The missing anchor *must* be the clue. Where was the anchor? And why was there no note where he had promised to leave it?

b. "I'll bet you five bucks, you can't!" he quipped, with a wide smirk washing over his face. He was confident that Cal would take the bet, simply because Cal hated that smirk. It always goaded him into doing the wrong thing for the right reason.

Cal's jaw quivered slightly. The color was rising in his neck and would soon turn his ears bright red. That *always* happened when he was furious. He tried to control his voice by keeping it very low in pitch—and *very* quiet. That was another of his problems. He couldn't get furious and loud. He always became furious and quiet. He was sure that had come from his granddaddy who considered loudness a sign of weakness.

"Well, what do ya say?" Martin leaned over the table where Cal was eating, holding out his claw-like hand. "Deal?"

Cal slowly put down the fork he was holding, wiped his mouth carefully with the paper napkin that had come with his quick lunch, looked sideways at his wife who had been sitting silently, watching the whole episode with growing dismay, then raised his sunburned hand—and—gently—shoved Martin's hand to one side.

"No deal," Cal said in his Texas drawl. "Back home, we'd call that a pig-in-a-poke."

Martin was so startled by this simple action that he almost fell over backwards. He gripped the back of the chair he had been leaning over, took a halfstep backwards, blinked his eyes twice, then shut his mouth with a click that made Charlene glance up from her salad.

"And now, if ya'll will excuse us, my wife and I would like to finish our lunch." With this, Cal took up his fork again, dug into a large piece of lettuce, put it in his mouth, and began to munch on it with a certain amount of delight he had never felt before.

c. She usually went to town to shop on Tuesdays. But today was too beautiful to waste on pushing a cart through aisles of cans and boxes. The bright sunshine and the pleasant breeze had changed her mind as soon as she opened her front door that morning. So, instead, she was planting the flower garden she had postponed for so long.

"Hup, two, three, four . . . hup, two three, four"

She could hear the trainees practicing their close order marching down at the parade grounds, about a block away. She had become so accustomed to the sounds of the drill sergeant, that they almost were like background music to her now. When she had first arrived at the base, those sounds had interrupted her thoughts daily. She would be in the middle of reading a book, sewing on a button, or fixing supper for Jerry when those drill sounds would disrupt her concentration. They had been like darts puncturing her serenity.

"Hup, two, three, four . . . . .Company . . . halt!"

Having never lived near a military base before, she had been completely unaccustomed to the sights and sounds of military life. Jerry had warned her that once they were married, she would have a period of adjustment to go through. But he had promised that she would really enjoy being a career soldier's wife, once this period of adjustment was over.

"Parade rest!"

She tore open a package of petunia seeds and carefully dropped them into the trench she had dug in the warm soil. Jerry had been right. She really did enjoy being a military wife, now. The security of the base . . . the opportunities for travel . . . Jerry's opportunities for advancement . . . and the companionship of other military wives who had become her good friends . . . yes, this was much better than living back in the mountains of West Virginia with the generations of her Anderson family.

"Company . . . .a--tten----tion!"

Her older sister, Betsy, had written her several times about the same people, the same activities, and the same general level of poverty that never seemed to go away. She was struck with the fact that nothing ever changed back home. Perhaps *that* was the thing that had made her even consider Jerry's request for a date on his first leave at home. He had been experiencing so many new things after his graduation from high school that she found his stories difficult to believe. Even though he had been a relatively average high school student, he seemed to be doing very well in the army—and that impressed her.

"Aboooout Face."

Her parents had cautioned her about getting too interested in Jerry. After all, he was two years older than she was. He might never return to the mountains of West Virginia now that he was a career military man. He wasn't too smart. And she was the reigning homecoming queen! That meant she would be the most popular girl in school for the entire year.

"Forwarrrrd . . . march!"

But she had decided that there must be something in that old saying "Beauty is only skin deep" if it had been around so long. None of the other boys in her school were inclined to get away from the community. If she didn't accept Jerry's proposal, he might go away and forget all about her. She couldn't plan on his asking her again. So she had accepted. Two days after graduation from high school, she was married—and three days later they were on their way to Colorado.

"Hup, two, three, four . . . hup, two three four."

And it had been just like Jerry had said. A period of adjustment, when she missed her old friends and all the old sights at home. A period of loneliness when she had cried for several days. And now, new friends, new opportunities, and new hope. She covered the seeds carefully and patted the warm earth gently.

DIALOGUE FOR ORAL PRACTICE (requires four readers)

Commercial 1: Are you thinking of taking a winter vacation this year? Renaldo's Travel Service at 215 Simpson Drive would like to remind you that it's not too early to make your reservations. December or January cruises to Jamaica; Cancun, Mexico; the Netherland Antilles, and Puerto Rico are available now. For modest prices, starting at $1200 per person, double occupancy, you will relax for two glorious weeks. You will enjoy leisurely strolls on deck, warm breezes, sumptuous buffet dinners, cool dips in two fresh water pools, shore visits to enchanting fishing villages, colorful markets, and first-rate evening entertainment every night. Free roundtrip airfare from major gateway cities to Port Everglades or Tampa, Florida is included. For more information, stop in to see Rodney or Lynn at Renaldo's Travel Service today—or call them at 625–9898.

C.D.: The weather this evening will remain cool, windy and dry. Tonight's low will be 52 degrees but the windchill factor will make it feel more like 46 degrees. Sunrise tomorrow morning will be at 6:52. The forecast for Wednesday is for more cool, dry weather. The temperature should rise to a high of 71 degrees by mid-afternoon. The wind will continue out of the northwest at from 8 to 10 miles per hour throughout most of the day. So, Elise, it would be a good idea to get out your sweater and keep it handy tomorrow morning.

Elise: Thanks C.D.! I'll take your advice. In fact, I brought one with me tonight. Now, here's Ralph with a quick wrapup of local sports news.

Ralph: Well, Elise, Sid Devrett has decided to leave Alabama State at the end of the season to play professional basketball in Japan. He claims he received an offer that was too good to refuse. He'll have more to say about this on tomorrow night's broadcast. And Jo Jo Martinez, local boxing sensation, says he will fight Bantamweight title holder, Art Crenshaw in November. Jo Jo hasn't lost a fight in his last ten bouts. Lucy Thompson, last year's indoor tennis state champion, is giving an exhibition at the Greeley Country Club this weekend. All proceeds will be donated to the Muscular Dystrophy Foundation. And this weekend, it will be football, football, football! Local high schools will be winding up their seasons—and all will be playing on their home fields. More tomorrow night.

Elise: Thanks, Ralph. It sounds like an exciting weekend. Finally, if you've been wondering what all those bright green trucks are doing along Memorial Boulevard, here's the answer. It seems that seventy-five year old water lines have begun to leak and need to be replaced. Those trucks are from the City Utilities Department. They are trying to locate the worst pipes before they develop major breaks. Clyde Fusilla, Director of City Utilities, says all the pipes are to be replaced along Memorial during the coming year. He apologizes for any delay they are causing you motorists, and is trying to finish most of the work after rush hours. So be patient during the next few weeks. And that's the ten o'clock news for tonight. "Driving On" is next. Thanks for joining us! Goodnight.

DEVELOPING A PLEASANT VOICE QUALITY

Your voice quality is your unique vocal "identification tag" which pervades everything you say. Even in a family of several children, all of whom are close in ages, members have little difficulty distinguishing one family member's voice from another. They recognize identifying vocal qualities in each voice.

Voice quality can't be completely isolated from other distinguishing features of voice, such as volume, pitch, pause, duration, inflection, rate, and rhythm, since all of these help to create your recognizable speech characteristics. However, the final "sound" which others **identify with you** involves the origin, resonation, and emission or radiation of your **unique sound waves,** often referred to as **voice quality.**

Voice quality begins with the completeness of contact made between your vocal folds, degree of tension placed on your larynx as this sound is initiated, and force with which this sound is released. (Throughout this chapter, you will find that the tension and relaxation of your body and the degree of force or loudness will become primary factors for modifying most qualities of the voice.) As the sound travels upward through a series of chambers and their interconnecting passageways, it gains overtones, timbre, or resonance by reverberating in the throat, nose, mouth and connecting passages. Some features of the original sound are reduced (damped) and some are enhanced (resonated). This process is similar to the sound changes which occur when you sing in a large open room, in a tile shower, and then in an echo chamber. In each location, the same musical note will sound slightly different.

CONTROLLING TENSION

Frequently, you may not be aware of the changes in tension that are occurring in your body during particular situations. For example, during your oral presentations in class you may be concentrating so hard on accomplishing a particular goal (such as saying certain phonemes correctly or conveying a particular emotional message to your listeners) that you aren't conscious of the growing tension in the muscles of your neck and shoulders. These muscles, in turn, may affect your throat, larynx, and lungs—all of which are important components in vocal quality.

Muscular tension and relaxation have considerable influence over vocal quality. They can control the size of tubes through which sound is flowing, influence the density of the walls surrounding vibrating sound waves, and even assist to make individual musical notes steady or unsteady. They are extremely important considerations for anyone wishing to modify vocal quality.

As you read about voice qualities in this chapter, you will discover you intentionally can create different vocal qualities in manipulating certain muscles of your speaking mechanism. For a particular oral reading, you may decide to use one or more vocal qualities, other than your own normal quality, to distinguish characters from each other, or delineate conflicting emotions for your listeners—even though you recognize those qualities are not needed in your daily conversation. By doing this, you will begin to become aware of physical changes in tension and relaxation which must occur in order for you to produce another vocal quality. You may be able to help your friends and family members who have difficulty with certain unpleasant vocal qualities, once you understand what they probably are doing to create those qualities.

If you have problems with voice quality, you may wish to begin your practice sessions with relaxation and tension exercises. They are intended to familiarize you with both the **feeling** of tension and the **sound** that results from it. Here are some suggestions to help you get started.

1. Sit upright in a straightback chair with both feet on the floor and your chin lifted so you can look directly across the room. Allow your arms to dangle loosely at the sides of the chair. Your fingers should be completely relaxed and slightly curved inward toward the palms. Close your eyes and allow the complete relaxation of your fingers to move up your arms and across your shoulders. When you can feel that your shoulders are completely relaxed, open your eyes and look across the room, without focusing on any particular object (much as you might do if you were daydreaming). Take in a long, deep breath slowly without elevating your shoulders, and while your arms and fingers still are completely relaxed—release it quickly and effortlessly. Close your eyes and repeat this process again, but this time, allow your head to drop forward effortlessly until your chin touches your chest when you exhale. Your upper torso should be completely relaxed.

2. Beginning the second exercise from your previous relaxed position, close your eyes and slowly roll your head from side to side without tensing any of your neck or shoulder muscles. Each time you come to the middle of your head roll, allow the head to dangle forward and pause (with the chin on your chest) before rolling to the next side. Begin by moving the head only a few inches to either side. Gradually increase the distance until you can roll your head slowly and completely from one shoulder to the other one without any muscle pull in your neck. Your chin will elevate as your head rolls. Try to keep your shoulders relaxed and unelevated. Breathe normally as you conduct these head rolls.

3. Sit in your chair in an upright, relaxed position with your chin raised so you can look straight ahead. Your hands should rest easily on your lap. Begin counting silently to yourself as you take a slow, long, deep breath. Feel your abdominal muscles expand as your lungs push downward, but be sure your shoulders don't elevate. When your lungs are full, close your eyes, slowly let your head drop forward, and release your breath by saying "mmmmmm" with an audible but relaxed sigh. At the end of the sigh, hold your position for a moment and consciously become aware of what your throat feels like when it is relaxed. Repeat this exercise again, this time parting your lips slightly and saying "ahhh." Be sure to keep your throat and neck muscles relaxed.

4. Stand up with your feet spread approximately eight inches apart, one foot slightly farther forward than the other one, and with your weight distributed equally on the balls of both feet. Allow your hands to dangle at your sides. Beginning with your toes, gradually tense the muscles in your feet, calves, thighs, abdomen, hands, arms, chest, shoulders, neck, and mouth. Feel the tension as it works its way up through your body and then say "Ha!" with a sudden forceful explosion of breath. Notice the vocal quality as you do this. Relax the body suddenly and feel the contrasting absence of tension.

268

5. Do exercise # 4 again, but then use the word "Go!" as your final exclamation. This time, instead of relaxing the body completely and suddenly, allow it to relax gradually, beginning with the lips, throat, neck and moving down to the toes. Repeat this exercise until you have complete, conscious control over progressive muscle relaxation. When you have relaxed completely, say "Go!" with the same amount of force you used at the beginning of this exercise. Listen for a difference in voice quality. If you can do this exercise at will, you have learned to control physical tension whenever you consciously tell yourself to do so. It will be a useful technique to use in your oral presentations to the class—and in all public speaking situations in the future. Only you will be conscious of what is occurring in your body but an audience may be able to tell that your voice quality has improved significantly.

WHAT CREATES UNIQUE VOCAL QUALITIES?

In the chapter on voice production and modulation, you learned that the size, shape, and composition of your resonating chambers influence vocal quality by enriching intensity of sound without actually adding energy to the sound. Now it is time to look more closely at voice quality as it relates to your use of changes in it during class presentations and in daily speaking habits.

A question regularly asked by beginning students in voice and diction classes is, "Why are voices so different if they all have the same basic components?" The answer is that these basic components aren't *exactly* the same in size, shape, or connections (coupling). The following analogy may help you understand this better.

Two expensive violins may be constructed of the same parts. However, these parts will be made from different pieces of wood which will vary slightly in composition and thickness. The glue that holds the wood together also may be different. The final shapes of the violins may have small variations (such as indentations or less distinct curves in certain places). Even though the violins may look exactly the same to the inexperienced eye, they will be found to be quite different if someone analyzes their components carefully. As a result, when the two instruments play exactly the same musical notes simultaneously, discerning listeners will hear slightly different qualities,

"It's a small voice—

but very unpleasant."

Saturday Evening Post

269

harmonics, or overtones. The vibrating strings of each instrument will vibrate at the *same number of cycles per second* (cps) for the *same notes*. However, the space inside each violin, acting as a resonating chamber, will respond differently to its surrounding vibrating wood. The original identical vibrations (sound waves) will change slightly, adding harmonics and overtones as a result of the two different resonating chambers. You may describe the sounds of one violin as "mellower," or "thinner," or "richer" than those of the other violin.

If you were to analyze those sounds with modern acoustical equipment, you would discover that the resulting sound waves are, indeed, different in composition. Thus, even though you are using subjective judgment and unscientific terminology for describing the sounds you are hearing, anyone with the equipment, knowledge, and patience who wishes to measure the actual physical components of sound coming from the two instruments could do so.

Approximately the same thing occurs in human voice quality. Suppose you and a friend say [o] on *exactly the same note of the musical scale, with the same degree of intensity, for the same length of time.* (Remember that the same musical note vibrates the same number of cycles per second, regardless of whether it is played on a musical instrument or is spoken aloud.) This original sound wave floats, flutters, bounces, and slides around various obstacles (such as tonsils, tongue, and teeth), and finally exits through the mouth and/or nose.

During this journey, parts of the sound wave may be absorbed or enhanced by the size, shapes and tension of tissue and bone walls surrounding it. If your friend had his adenoids and tonsils removed at an early age but you did not, he may have fewer nasal blockages to absorb or block the sound. If your oral cavity is smaller than his, your voice will have less room in which to resonate before exiting through the mouth. If your hard palate doesn't extend as far back at the roof of the mouth as his does, more of your sound may be absorbed by the soft, fleshy tissue than his. Even if some of your back teeth are missing, you will have a different shaped oral cavity in which sound can bounce around than he does. These, and many other factors can influence resulting differences in voice quality since all of them help to change the original fundamental sound wave each of you produced for the identical musical note.

The length, shape, or tension of *your* resonating tubes and chambers may complement certain frequencies in the original fundmental tone better than your friend's vocal equipment, and will enhance or liberate more energy associated with those frequencies. Thus, some relatively weak characteristics of an original tone may gain greater prominence (or even, dominance) as they find favorable conditions for resonance in your (as contrasted with your friend's) resonators. Do you begin to see how sound quality is modified by one's resonating equipment?

One other factor may be helpful to understand. You seldom will try to communicate significant ideas on only one musical note. Instead, you will move from one note to another, and from one phoneme to another to produce meaningful words and effective speech. This means the shape, tension, and size of the resonating chambers will be constantly changing. Even when you try to produce one steady musical note, you will have slight, uncontrollable waverings in your resulting sound. These continuous changes will affect your sound quality and will not be totally predictable. However, clusters of recognizable sound patterns within your daily speech habits may become easily identified with *your* voice quality. Thus, even within the continuous sound changes which are occurring, these "markers" will help to identify your unique voice quality. If you call someone on the telephone who recognizes these identifying markers, you won't have to identify who you are. The longer you associate with the same people, the easier it becomes for them to identify these vocal markers on a conscious or unconscious level.

FINDING LABELS FOR VOICE QUALITY

Have you ever heard individuals try to describe another person's voice quality? Often, they make subjective judgments about it, calling it "pleasant," "empty," "unique," "resonant," "strange," "funny," "unusual," "beautiful," or "different." They find it difficult to describe specific features of the voice. Instead, they may attempt to associate it with other sounds to create an analogy, such as "It's foggy," "It's like a child's voice," "It sounds like a prolonged sigh," or "It's brittle or metallic sounding." If a well-known individual has a voice quality that is similar, individuals may try to associate the speaker's voice quality with the well-known individual's voice.

In the late 1800s and early 1900s, American elocutionists, predecessors of today's oral interpretation, and voice and diction teachers, attempted to find terms which could be used to describe and classify specific voice qualities. Some of these terms continue to be used today. However, voice and diction teachers today still don't agree on uniform terms for describing human voice quality. Frequently, instructors will use a well known descriptor, such as "breathy" in conjunction with a subjective or evaluative term such as "unpleasant" or "immature."

At the outset of this discussion on voice qualities, one thing should be emphasized. Certain voice qualities which are labelled as improper, unpleasant, or inadequate in one situation may be very acceptable (or even preferred) in another siuation. For example, many radio and television commercials, popular songs, and character roles depend upon distinctively unique voices and sounds for their impact. A "brassy" voice may be unpleasant in daily conversation, but highly desirable for musical comedy. A "whining" voice may be irritating in interpersonal communication, but effective in a television commercial featuring the stereotypical overworked, unrewarded housewife.

In oral reading and acting, changes in vocal quality can be used to increase vocal versatility, which in turn, makes the resulting presentation easier for listeners to grasp. Children, for example, find that changes in voice quality help them "see" and "experience" people, places, emotions and things when someone is reading a story to them. They want the wicked witch's voice to have a scary quality and the good fairy godmother's voice to have a pleasant quality because they can associate voice quality with personality and can follow the action and the dialogue easier with these distinguishing qualities. Children are relatively discerning listeners and may not be at all shy about telling you that you don't tell stories as well as their mother, brother, or some other reader.

Adults don't lose this preference for vocal variety. They may, however, prefer fewer **gross** vocal exaggerations for distinguishing one character from another than are used for telling children stories. Usually, adults want oral readers merely to suggest changes in vocal qualities between two or more characters to establish and reinforce their different personalities and emotions. Clear character distinctions may be based upon suggested or figurative rather than definitive or literal "good" and "bad," or "old" and "young" vocal qualities for characters. (The degree of vocal exaggeration often increases significantly when someone assumes the role of a character in a play than when he or she reads the same role aloud.)

Appropriateness of vocal quality is related to particular situations and personal and professional goals. Most people want to have a "pleasant" voice quality which will not call attention to itself in daily speaking situations. Some voice qualities are distracting, irritating, or inappropriate for continuous daily use. This chapter will help you to identify some of these qualities. As you listen to your fellow classmates, you may begin to hear these qualities in parts of their presentations and you will be able to tell what those individuals are doing incorrectly—and what they should do to improve.

Guttural, Harsh, and Vocal Fry Qualities

When your pitch and volume drop simultaneously at the ends of thought sequences including sentences and paragraphs, you may have a tendency to use vocal fry. It is a fairly common noisy vocal occurrence which is not pleasant to hear. Vocal fry is a crackling, guttural quality similar to the sound that occurs when you gargle. It acquires its name "fry" from the sound that is made by something frying on a hot surface (such as bacon) and suggests a type of sizzling or irregular bubbling noise. (It might even be compared with quietly pronounced schwa-r sounds.) Usually, the vocal folds are quite tense and compressed during vocal fry and little air flows through the glottis as they vibrate.

If you tend to have extensive vocal fry characteristics in your voice quality, you may need to check both your optimum pitch range and your breathing habits to see if they are compounding your problem. Frequently, you can eliminate vocal fry by raising your modal pitch slightly higher than you use now and by completing thought sequences *before* you run out of breath. If you are speaking near the bottom of your pitch range, you may be putting too much strain on your larnyx. You also may discover that neck and throat relaxation exercises will assist you to feel when you are tensing your throat excessively.

During your practice sessions, you should listen for vocal fry at the ends of phrases and sentences. If you hear it, stop your reading and hum down the scale (or take a deep breath and prolong a sigh) until your voice ends on a comfortable, loud musical note. Try to read several sentences, using this note as a nucleus for your rising and falling inflections. It probably represents an easy or optimum note for you to say without straining your throat or larynx. Yawn several times to relax your throat, and if necessary, let your head drop forward and roll easily from one side to the other until you feel quite relaxed. Then take a full breath and begin reading again. Each time you pause, avoid letting your pitch drop far below your "nucleus note."

Initially, you may find it helpful to mark your manuscript in places where you will pause for breath and drop your pitch simultaneously. These marks will remind you in advance to prepare for places in your oral presentation where vocal fry is most likely to occur. Be especially alert for the occurrence of vocal fry on or immediately after back-of-the-throat vowel and diphthong sounds and schwa-r sounds.

In some cases, a consistently guttural (harsh, gravelly) voice quality, which sounds like you have contracted your neck and throat muscles tensely and are forcing your breath through very tight vocal folds, may be indicative of physical or psychological problems which should be handled by a physician or psychologist. Subconscious anger and/or tension can influence your vocal quality significantly. A guttural voice quality usually results from an extremely tense throat and larnyx. (In oral readings which require this type of latent or smoldering anger, a guttural quality may be quite appropriate.) Constant tension on the larynx and throat can lead to severe physical problems, including laryngitis from inflamed vocal folds. If relaxation exercises or changes in pitch and breath control have no influence on your vocal quality, you may wish to secure professional assistance from your speech pathologist or communicologist.

Nasal and Denasal Qualities

In the chapters which dealt with nasal sounds, you learned that the soft palate (velum) acts as a barrier to the nasal passageways. It is similar to a curtain that can be raised or lowered. When it is raised, air is prevented from entering the nasal cavities and is forced out through the mouth. When it is dropped, some or all of the escaping air may go into the nasal cavities. The

272

quality of sound changes considerably when it is resonated in the oral cavity and when it is resonated in the nasal cavity.

You also have learned that only three sounds are nasalized in English: [m], [n], and [ŋ]. Vowels and dipthongs should not be nasalized. When **non-nasal** sounds *are* nasalized, a speaker's voice quality is called "nasal." When **nasal** sounds are *not* nasalized, a speaker's voice is called "denasal." These changes are fairly clear-cut.

However, in practice, you may discover that you aren't aware of the action of your soft palate. If you are accustomed to nasalizing some of your non-nasal sounds, you probably don't hear the difference between how *you* say the sounds and how others say them. Unless someone calls your attention to your diction habits, you will assume you make your sounds like everyone else. (Indeed, you may make the sounds like everyone in your specific home or locality—but everyone makes them inaccurately! This becomes a way in which subsidiary dialects originate within a regional dialect.)

Probably more people in North America have difficulty with excessive nasality than with denasality. Often, this occurs because their vowels or diphthongs which precede or follow a nasal sound "borrow" part of the acceptable nasal sound. In other words, nasalization spills over to denasal sounds. The soft palate doesn't move quickly enough to prevent this "overflow" of nasalization. As a result, people develop nasal quality voices which may suggest a lazy or backwoods characterization. Since the aspects of nasal and denasal sounds have been discussed previously in this book, further elaborations shouldn't be necessary here. If you have problems with nasal or denasal voice quality, you should review the discussion of nasal sounds in chapters 7, 12, and 13 and the exercises in those chapters.

Breathy Quality

The breathy voice quality results from an incomplete closure of the vocal folds, an inadequate supply of air to support voice production, or a contrived manipulation of expelled air to intentionally prolong escaping air. Usually, breathiness springs from an inefficient use of air escaping through the vocal folds for sounds (particularly vowels and diphthongs) produced by a speaker. If you have just completed strenuous exercising and you try to speak before you "catch your breath" you will have a gasping, breathy voice. Frequently, it carries some of the same qualities of the whispered voice, particularly at the beginning and ending of each word. In modern movies, the breathy voice has been associated with sexy, relatively fragile or helpless characters—particularly, females.

You may be able to reduce or eliminate excessive breathiness by doing two things. You can increase your volume level slightly. This strengthening of vocal power can bring your vocal folds together with slightly greater force which, in turn, will eliminate the relaxed fluttering of vocal folds that occurs in breathiness. Also, by raising your modal pitch slightly, you can eliminate the **shortening** of the vocal folds which occurs at the lower end of your pitch range and your vocal folds will vibrate in a normal manner.

General breathiness may be compounded if you also sustain voiceless consonant sounds excessively. In an earlier chapter, you learned, for example, that many people prolong the [s] sound in all positions of words. As a result, their speech is characterized by a great amount of hissing or extra-sibilance. The same thing may happen on other voiceless consonant sounds such as [f], [p], and [k]. If you do this, you literally are wasting your breath. Try to stress the vowels and diphthongs and deemphasize the voiceless consonants in words as you practice to eliminate breathiness. Also, when voiceless consonants appear in the final position of words, shorten the sounds by closing your lips or stopping your flow of breath quicker at the larynx.

One other form of breathiness occurs in some speakers at the ends of sentences or paragraphs. Usually, this is due to inadequate breathing patterns, nervousness, or undue tension. By learning to use the abdominal and diaphragmatic muscles rather than the upper chest muscles, you can gain better control of your breath supply and your exhalation patterns. This, in turn, may help you to relax more when you speak before groups.

You shouldn't expect better breathing habits to occur spontaneously in the classroom if you haven't practiced breathing correctly during your oral practice sessions. You need to know *how* to breathe correctly. You also need to know *when* to breathe during your oral practice. If you are unsure how to do these things, you should review the information on breathing and marking your manuscript in this book.

Thin Quality

If you have seen old Popeye or Betty Boop movies, you have heard the female characters Olive and Betty using thin voice quality to portray their weak or tiny, helpless images. You also may hear adults using a type of "baby talk" as they play with little children which incorporates this thin quality. It is commonly used for caricature voices in television cartoons for stereotypes of "delicate, adorable but somewhat scatterbrained" women or for meek, submissive, or hen-pecked men. Children who are "teasing" parents to get what they want often use this vocal quality to suggest their own helplessness.

The thin voice usually is high in pitch, immature or childlike, and light or lacking in full resonance. It isn't considered an appropriate vocal quality for mature, intelligent adult conversation. Normally, it is produced by raising the pitch slightly above the optimum pitch level and by pushing the tongue upward and forward in the oral cavity for all sounds, but particularly for vowels and diphthongs. As these sounds are "squeezed" close to the front of the mouth (between the tongue and alveolar ridge) they lose some of their distinctive full resonance. The size of the oral cavity used for resonating sounds is diminished significantly by this action and sounds become small, weak, or delicate. If the speaker also smiles and keeps the lips close together while speaking with a thin voice, an even greater exaggeration of immaturity results.

If you have a thin voice, you will need to work on dropping the lower jaw and tongue more while pulling your tongue back from its frontal movement. This action should help you by creating more room in your mouth for resonating sounds. Use adequate lip rounding for vowels and diphthongs which require it to create their distinctive sounds. You probably will have your greatest success by starting with middle and back of the mouth vowel sounds. If necessary, exaggerate the drawing back and dropping of the back of your tongue in words such as "hound, crowd, home, go."

You also need to determine if you are using your optimum pitch range. If you discover your pitch is too high, you will need to review some of the exercises in the chapter on Pitch. Finally, you should see if greater volume can be used to eliminate some of the delicate quality. You may discover that you can gain a stronger, more mature voice quality simply by using your abdominal muscles with greater force as you exhale, to create greater vocal support.

Strident, Tense, Metallic Quality

Unlike the thin voice, which is relatively relaxed, the strident voice is very tense. It also is fairly high in pitch and, to many people, is as irritating as fingernails that are scratched on a blackboard. The strident vocal quality is piercing, shrill, and unpleasant. It often is referred to in such metallic terms as "brassy" and "tinny." It is the vocal quality used by many actresses who play the part of a shrew, witch, or street urchin and by many actors who play the part of the boisterous wheeler-dealer, shyster, or carnival "pitch man."

Some speakers demonstrate strident vocal quality when they are under extreme tension. They may not be aware of the fact that their voice quality has changed, but colleagues who work with them on a daily basis can hear it. It often is the quality which warns a housewife to keep the children away from father until he has time to "unwind." Voice and diction teachers hear this quality in students who haven't practiced their presentations adquately and are extremely nervous or ill-at-ease during in-class readings or speeches.

A strident voice usually is caused by extreme tension of the muscles that encircle the throat (pharynx). This action decreases the size of the throat. The throat actually serves as a tube between the larynx and the oral cavity. When a tube is narrowed in size, it resonates high frequency sounds better than low frequency sounds. As a result, the high frequency sounds are enriched or intensified to a point of becoming disturbing and unpleasant to listeners in small areas. (However, you will remember that the musical comedy star who must "fill" a large auditorium with song, often is admired for this type of voice. If this star can control the brassy quality in small groups, he or she will have both admirers and close friends!)

If you have difficulty with a strident voice quality, you will need to practice relaxing the muscles of the neck and throat, beginning with such things as the relaxed head roll from side to side, the silent yawn, and progressive tensing and relaxing of the hands, arms, shoulders, and neck. Do this until you can consciously control the tension in your throat whenever it begins to build.

Also, you can practice repeating and prolonging vowels and diphthongs evenly and distinctly. Begin by saying a vowel with only a little volume, and then gradually increase the volume **without** increasing throat tension. (The tension should be kept in your abdominal muscles.) Listen to the difference in tense and relaxed vowel sounds. Feel the changes that occur in the throat and under the chin as you move from a tense to a lax, and then back to a tense vowel. When you can feel these differences, choose a series of one syllable words containing a variety of back vowel and diphthong sounds (such as soul, pull, now, toy, news, psalm, Shawn) and read them aloud. Purposely alternate between a relaxed and strident production of these words in order to hear and feel the differences which occur.

Throaty Quality

Some speakers pull the tongue back and up too far, sometimes pulling the chin *down* towards the chest or *back* towards the neck simultaneously. A constriction or barrier is formed by the tongue near the back of the throat which impedes or stops high frequency sounds (sounds with short wave lengths) while allowing low frequency sounds to pass by. As a result, a throaty or cavernous vocal quality is produced which often is associated with "ghostly" or "tomb-like" voices. Front and middle vowels tend to be "pulled" back in the throat and lose some of their distinctive features. In some cases, a speaker with a throaty voice quality actually misarticulates many vowels and diphthongs which require the tongue to be humped near the front or middle portion of the mouth.

Another contributing factor to throaty voice quality may be an habitual pitch level that is too low for the speaker. This should be one of the first things you check if you are accused of having a throaty voice quality. You may have decided, sometime ago, that a lower pitch was important for establishing your image as a mature, controlled individual. This may have been during early adolescence when your vocal folds had not yet matured. If you had to strain to bring your pitch down, you may have sacrificed a pleasant voice quality for this lower pitch by pulling the chin down and elevating the back of the tongue. (Now your pitch may be naturally lower, but you have grown accustomed to this process and continue to strive to keep your pitch lower than it needs to be.) This habit may intensify your throaty vocal quality (which often is associated with the stereotypical big, dumb boxer or the fat, pompous, sleezy business tycoon).

If you need to work to eliminate throaty quality, you should begin by relaxing the muscles under the chin. Pull the chin and head up, and concentrate on moving your tongue closer to the *front* of the mouth for front and middle vowel sounds. Choose one syllable words with front consonant and vowel sounds (such as team, dim, meek, pill, day, base, ten) and practice saying them aloud several times in quick succession. You should feel the tongue moving forward for these words. You should also hear a "brighter" tone or sound than you have been making in the back of your throat.

Hoarse Quality

Most people have experienced a hoarse voice, either as the result of a cold or too much cheering at a public gathering. Periodic hoarseness is not our major concern here, since it usually goes away as soon as inflamed vocal folds regain their healthy status. We would advise you to be cautious in your cheering so you don't become hoarse. Also, if your vocal folds have been abused, avoid talking, whispering, and smoking until they have healed, to prevent further (and more serious) problems.

If you have a "naturally" hoarse voice that never disappears, you may have a potential problem. When growths or nodes occur on the vocal folds, they can cause a consistent huskiness or hoarseness. Although these growths may prove to be benign, they should be checked by a physician for your own peace of mind. Serious difficulty can result from growths that are left unchecked.

If you find you have nothing organically wrong, then you may wish to see if you can eliminate some of the hoarseness by: (1) gaining better breath support for your voice, (2) relieving the strain on your larynx, and/or (3) placing more of your sounds closer to the front lips. You may wish to review the material in this book on sound production, volume, and breathing, since incorrect breathing and incorrect projection habits could be at the root of your problem.

In dealing with better projection habits, you should attempt to focus your sounds toward the front of the mouth rather than the back, in order to remove some of the strain from your larynx and throat. If your neck and throat muscles feel very tense after you have spoken for a short period of time, you probably should do progressive relaxation exercises suggested previously in this chapter until you can feel the difference between a tense and lax throat. You should learn consciously to relax the throat, chest, and neck muscles as you talk. You also should feel the physical changes that occur when you use your abdominal muscles rather than your upper chest muscles for breathing.

CONFIRMING AND CONTRADICTORY MESSAGES

Vocal quality has the capability for confirming or contradicting words that are being said. All spoken messages have levels of meaning which are associated with both literal and figurative, logical and emotional meanings. Even though your words may say, "I am confident of my abilities," your vocal quality may say "You'd better not believe what I'm telling you." In this situation, your vocal quality contradicts your verbal message. Listeners may accept your total message as being a joke, or being unreliable.

Unless it is your intention to mislead your listeners (which happens in daily life when white or darker lies are being told—or in oral readings when you wish to keep the solution to a mystery secret), you need to be sure your vocal and verbal messages agree. Just by listening to strangers in public places, you frequently decide you would or wouldn't trust them—would or wouldn't like to have them as your friends, colleagues, or neighbors—would or wouldn't buy a product or service from them.

Even though you must be cautious of making a quick judgment about people on the basis of only one brief encounter, at times your personal safety, property, and welfare may depend upon just such a judgment. Vocal quality becomes an important consideration in making decisions about people. It is in your best interests to be sure your vocal quality says what you want it to say, when you want it to say it. By being aware of confirming and contradicting vocal qualities in yourself, as well as in others, you become better able to deal with daily events successfully. Vocal quality can serve as a fairly accurate barometer of personal relaxation, comfort, happiness, security, and confidence.

CHANGING VOICE QUALITY IS A MATTER OF PRACTICE

Some people are born with ideal bodily parts and proportions for creating a pleasant voice. The length and texture of their vocal folds complements the size, shape, and texture of their resonating cavities. They don't have to "work" to create and sustain a clear, resonant voice. They are reared in a relatively unstressful, accepting environment and don't learn to restrict their "natural" vocal functions. Their voices serve as ideal models for vocal quality for us.

Unfortunately, most of us aren't born with these ideal qualities and conditions. Furthermore, we must cope with varying degrees of tension throughout our lives. We become tense, cautious, and protective and even our breathing becomes labored and restricted. If no one gives us formal instruction in speaking, we develop vocal qualities which reflect our environment, our psychological state, and our physical health. Often, our initial development of voice is influenced by voices of people we love, respect, or idolize. Over the years, we are influenced by people we associate with on a regular basis (including radio, record, television, and movie personalities), even though we usually are unaware of their influence. When we are well, happy, contented, at ease, and relaxed, our voice qualities tend to be at their best (even though "best" may be far from **ideal**). Our voice qualities become almost as automatic as reflex responses, making them difficult to change without **considerable** practice.

From the moment the vocal folds begin their first vibrations as released air sets them in motion, vocal quality begins. Sound waves are modulated or changed by the intensity with which air is released, the chambers the impulses pass through, and the surfaces they hit. These modulations become **conscious** considerations which we pay attention to so that we can **feel** and **hear** the desired quality changes. (If our hearing is faulty, someone else will have to tell us when our quality is improving.) Once we can hear and feel the best way to produce sound (often after extensive, tedious oral drills), we must practice the vocal quality until it becomes an unconscious habit. During this period, the greatest barrier probably will be physical and psychological control of **tension.**

We *can* gain control over sound production by making our muscles respond the way we want them to respond, rather than the way we have been accustomed to having them respond. However, this requires time and practice.

CHAPTER 21

INTEGRATING IMPROVED SPEECH HABITS INTO DAILY LIFE

One of the goals of a beginning voice and diction or speech improvement course is to increase each student's level of perception regarding human speaking habits. Often, we can see and hear errors in other people before we recognize them in ourselves. It may be that this was the point at which you began your development of better voice and diction perception for this class. By listening to your classmates, other people on campus, and speakers on radio and television, you may have become aware of sound substitutions and additions, disfluencies, meaningful inflections, meaningful pauses, and distracting vocal qualities. If you learned the terminology used in the text and in classroom lectures, you also found yourself able to describe what you were seeing and hearing with a good degree of accuracy. That is an accomplishment!

PRACTICING TO "MAKE PERFECT"

One of the concerns of any speech/communication instructor who is teaching the pragmatics or application of speaking skills is that his or her students should practice extensively before they give their presentations to the class. Earlier in this book you learned that this was an expectation of the course. The old maxim, "Practice makes perfect" may not *always* be true but it will help to change habituated speaking patterns. If pursued carefully and over spaced periods of time, practice can help make your new speaking skills permanent, too.

In the final weeks of voice and diction courses, normally students are expected to give several practiced presentations to demonstrate their increasing ability to **control** their unique voice and diction errors and problems. At this point, practical application is emphasized more than theory. You may be asked to prepare specific oral readings from certain types of literature or to prepare speeches in order to demonstrate your vocal control.

For instance, you may be asked to read a descriptive selection aloud to demonstrate your ability to present relatively non-emotional and non-conversational material with good vocal distinctions in inflections, changes in rate, volume and duration. The reading may be for the primary purpose of demonstrating your control of technical aspects of voice. Your next assignment may require the selection of a piece of literature containing dialogue between two persons. This assignment would require you to delineate one character from another through vocal changes and also would require you to consider how differently conversation and description sound. Another assignment may require you to deal with a specific atmosphere or emotion by selecting a serious selection or a humorous one. Part of your instructor's evaluation is based on your ability to find and cut material that will allow you to demonstrate your vocal versatility and correctness while keeping your listeners interested.

278

If you are asked to present a portion of a speech to your class, you may be expected to find a speech from an anthology of speeches or from a publication such as **Vital Speeches of the Day** and present it as if it were your own words. Again, the emphasis may be upon technical considerations of voice production and diction accuracy, but within the framework of an actual spoken message, rather than a written message which also may be read aloud. A later assignment may require you to write your own speech, based on topics assigned by the instructor, and present it within a short time span. At this point, your instructor may be evaluating your ability to organize and present interesting ideas in a heightened conversational style while maintaining an accurate control of voice and diction.

Regardless of whether you are reading or speaking aloud, you are expected to find material which will interest your audience. You should give this element serious consideration. Be cautious of selecting something that you happen to have easily available in your dormitory room or from another class because the identical material may be in many other dormitory rooms and selected by several other students. (The element of originality or uniqueness gives any speaker or oral reader an advantage, whether the presentation is given in class or in a public situation.) Be careful of choosing a speech topic that is the "current hot issue" because several other students probably are considering the same topic.

As you consider material for oral presentation, you may be wise to choose material that you will be proud you chose several years from now. Consider the "ageless" and "timeless" quality of the topic or material. Avoid overly simple, trite, and easy topics or literature. Remember, during your class presentations you are indulging in both a technical endeavor (controlling voice and diction) and an intellectual and emotional endeavor (keeping an audience interested and involved in what you're saying) before a group of intelligent, sophisticated listeners. Since you are going to spend time in practicing, find material that is worth practicing.

MAKING YOU A MORE DISCERNING CONSUMER OF ORAL MESSAGES

This book was designed to help you understand and use a practical system for diagnosing and describing what you hear in human speech by using the International Phonetic Alphabet and specific terms related to voice production. Having familiarized yourself with these diagnostic and descriptive tools, you should now be able to "speak the same language" as your associates in this class, and understand what your instructor means in critiques of classroom presentations. You may never take another speech or communication course again, but for the rest of your life you will be aware of factors of human communication that many of your friends and family will not see or hear. These factors may affect you in a variety of ways.

You may become uncomfortable in having to sit through long college lectures in which the instructor has no inflectional or energy changes to keep the class interesting. Your awareness of various features of sound may help you teach your own children to speak without major speaking errors or dialects. You may discover you are hearing elements of a special television or radio program on an entirely different level of meaning than your family or friends. As a result, you will be less gullible, less susceptible to vocal tricks, and more discerning in what you are willing to label "excellent" entertainment.

You may hear the underlying tension in your spouse's voice and be able to avoid an unnecessary confrontation. You may be aware of a stranger's slight dialect and realize he or she should be given more of your time than the usual "local" questioner. You may be able to identify specific vocal changes a friend or acquaintance can make to improve his or her chances of getting a job, getting an interview, getting a promotion, running for public office, or any number of other goals which depend heavily upon oral proficiency. You may find you can help a loved one who had a stroke and lost the ability to speak to regain this critical ability through daily listening and speaking "patterning" exercises. These are just a few of the things you should be able to do better as a result of your increased awareness of voice and diction.

MAKING YOU A BETTER CREATOR OF ORAL MESSAGES

This course also attempts to help you understand your own speaking skills, and what you need to do to improve those skills that will be useful in your own personal and professional speaking habits. By learning what usually is considered to be acceptable and unacceptable, desirable and undesirable, appropriate and inappropriate in voice production and diction, you are now in a position to make decisions regarding what you will do about your current speaking skills. In many cases, you may have concluded that your errors were not *that* obvious or important—and you haven't worked to eliminate them.

You may be fairly comfortable with your fluency in conversational speaking, but you know you have a problem with fluency in oral reading. If your future will involve the delivery of written papers, presentation of verbatim reports, reading from radio or television scripts, or reading literature aloud, then you know this is an area you must continue to work on with great care. Your in-class oral presentations should be helping you to understand how adequate you are in preparing and presenting practiced material aloud.

If you have a strong regional dialect and you know you probably will have to move away from your region to gain future promotions, you may need to spend additional time on developing your spontaneous use of General American Speech. You may be able to control your regional or subsidiary dialect fairly well in short, practiced readings required in this class. This is a major accomplishment for many students in an introductory speech improvement course. However, this is just the first step for giving you conscious (or unconscious) **automatic** control of your dialect in **spontaneous** situations such as business conversations and conferences, social "smalltalk" at parties and luncheons, unexpected presentations in small groups, greetings and introductions, telephone conversations, and so on.

Unfortunately, a beginning course is limited in its ability to give everyone the amount and types of practice they need for their unique problems and goals. Usually, a major shortcoming is the need to continue practiced readings until almost the end of the course, which leaves little time for unpracticed presentations (including impromptu speaking assignments and conversations). If your future career depends upon your ability to use General American Speech with ease in a variety of spontaneous speaking situations, you should recognize that a one-semester course may be inadequate for changing a lifetime of habituated speaking patterns. When you leave this class, your continued progress rests entirely in your hands. We hope you have enough information, motivation, and inspiration for extending the gains you have made.

BEING CORRECT AND BEING FLEXIBLE

Humankind learns by doing—but it also learns by undoing and redoing, again and again. By gaining more information and diverse experiences in "higher" education, college students hope to avoid repeating the mistakes made by past generations. One of the strange things about human beings is that they often *know* what to do, but they fail to do it. This applies to human communication as frequently as to any other area of our lives. When the Creator gave human beings the right to make decisions, it was not with the condition that we must always make the *right* decisions! Often, it is only after we have made a decision that we discover it was the wrong one.

There are correct ways of saying things and incorrect ways. Being correct, however, isn't always the *only* standard to be used in effective human communication. At times, your speech will be absolutely correct, from a technical or theoretical viewpoint, but unsuitable for the time, place, situation, or listeners involved. For example, if your job requires you to complete a house-to-house survey in a poor, relatively uneducated community, you may not be able to do an effective job or obtain valid responses if you use technical terms, or overly precise diction. These may suggest to your respondents that you are "talking down to them" or that you "don't understand them because you're an outsider—and outsiders can't be trusted."

During this course you have learned that words which end in "ing" such as "running, jumping, singing, doing" do not end in [n]. However, this is a common substitution in many regions of North America. In informal, casual gatherings where everyone is involved in quick bantering and good humor, you may find your diction is less obvious or pedantic if you substitute an [n] periodically. This can be particularly important when you go home from college and you don't want to be ostracized by your family and friends because you suddenly have "gained culture" at college. You may wish to continue using your regional or subsidiary dialect in certain situations and then switch back to a General American Speech pattern when you return to college. This process, referred to as "code switching" by communications researchers, is quite common among bilingual speakers. It is useful for anyone who works in one ethnic or socio-economic community but lives in an entirely different one. After you leave college and establish yourself in the professional world, you may find it advantageous to do the same thing.

When reading a dialectal story, telling a local color joke, or relating a personal incident, you may underscore the "flavor" of the tale by incorporating some of the things you've been working to eliminate (dialectal changes, sound substitutions, and poor voice quality) in your oral rendition. When you do this, however, you must remember that a joke may backfire on you if members of your audience feel you are making fun of their manner of speaking.

Many times in your future speaking experiences you will find "exceptions to the rules" must be made on the spur-of-the-moment. If you have developed a repertoire of speaking alternatives, you will be in a good position to make the right decision. An intelligent (smart) person knows how to do the right thing without being told. A wise person knows how to do the right thing *at the right moment* without being told! The longer you live, the more you will come to realize there is no substitute for "good common sense" in situations involving human communication. By being well informed (which includes knowing the right answers), perceptive, sensitive, and practiced, you hope to make those right decisions regarding your personal speaking habits when the need arises. (If you make the wrong decision, you *may* be fortunate to have another chance at another time.)

One of the essential ingredients of effective speech is its ability to adapt to different situations, occasions, and audiences. Although you are gaining useful, practical experiences in speaking in your class presentations, you shouldn't consider them typical of what you will do before other groups. Your classroom audience consists mainly of your peer group: relatively young, attentive, intelligent, and motivated individuals. An older audience with less hearing acuity might respond to your volume level or your clarity of diction in quite a different manner. Your class is a "captive audience" and probably won't walk out on you. Furthermore, everyone in the class is fulfilling the same requirements you are. They recognize the difficulties you may have encountered in preparing for your presentation. As a result, if they can tell you have practiced your material well, they will have patience and understanding as you struggle to control and eliminate your speaking problems.

A different audience—one which isn't familiar with you or your speech development process—which is free to come and go as it pleases, may have an entirely different reaction to your speaking habits. It may be unwilling to sit politely through an uninteresting reading selection, mumbled or mispronounced words, a disfluent presentation, or a repetitive, monotonous intonation of words. It may get up and walk out, talk while you are talking, or give you nonverbal signals (reading papers, passing notes, sleeping) to indicate your presentation isn't interesting or important.

In any public speaking situation, whether it involves reading or speaking, you have two basic responsibilities. First, you should make your presentation as distinct or clear as you can without overexaggerating sounds. Second, you should use vocal and physical variety, within the constraints of your material and the situation in which you are giving your presentation, to make your presentation interesting for your listeners. These responsibilities require *considerable* planning and practice.

Probably you realize that "considerable" is a relative term to different students in this class. You may be able to accomplish your tasks and overcome your speaking problems in half the time that it takes your roommate or friend. On the other hand, you may need to practice three times as much as anyone else in your class, just to give an *average* presentation. The elements of determination and motivation are particularly important when this is true. However, even though you need a longer time to accomplish your assigned tasks, if you persist in your regular practice, you can accomplish your ultimate classroom goals.

SUGGESTIONS FOR CARRYING IMPROVEMENT INTO DAILY SPEAKING

Perhaps you are working on several different speech problems during your daily practice sessions. However, you find you can't pay attention to *all* of these problems in normal, daily conversations. When you try to do so, you lose track of what you're trying to say! Also, you become very disfluent in your responses because you're trying to handle too many items at once. As a result, your progress seems evident only in your class presentations. How can you gain any carryover value to your daily speaking habits?

Setting Short Term Goals

Developing better speaking habits is somewhat like creating a statue out of a beautiful block of marble. You have to approach the task methodically, with a definite plan in mind. Although you may have a basic idea of the result you hope to attain, you must begin by chipping away unwanted pieces of marble without being able to see any immediate artistic results. You should focus on a couple of problems which seem to give you the most difficulty and forget about the others until you have developed accuracy in changing the two most prominent problems. (Don't eliminate your emphasis upon all the problems during your regular practice sessions. You should be able to deal with several different speech problems simultaneously on short, prepared readings.)

No matter whether you are chatting with friends at the snackbar, answering a question in one of your classes, asking for information from a librarian, or dealing with a customer at your parttime

282

job, you can use this procedure of setting short term goals (chipping away that marble) for improving your speech.

Some students decide on a speech improvement goal for a specific time period and then evaluate their results at the end of that period. For instance, if you have problems with a nasal voice, you may decide to practice elevating your soft palate and saying your vowels and diphthongs very carefully in all your conversations at breakfast for the first fifteen minutes, every morning for two weeks. This allows you to chat with friends for the rest of your breakfast time without being quite so sensitive to your nasality. You should be rested that early in the morning (unless you spent the whole night reviewing your speech improvement notes) and able to control your soft palate better than at the end of the day. By following through on this short term goal, you will be able to make an evaluation of your efforts at the end of the two weeks and decide whether you are making the progress you wanted.

Extending Your Progress Beyond This Course

If you are taking this course because you genuinely want to modify your current speaking habits, you won't be completely satisfied with your progress until you hear improvements in your daily speaking. You will appreciate the positive comments your instructor and classmates give you about your class presentations. However, you recognize your progress in these presentations is based upon specific, *practiced* assignments. Demonstrating your competency in this class is important for meeting course expectations. Of even greater importance is whether or not you are able to demonstrate the same progress away from the scrutiny of a voice and diction instructor— and the temporary pressure (or reward) of a grade. Assuming for the moment that you are making the in-class progress you desire, how will you carry this progress over to daily activities after you leave the class—after the instructor stops challenging you to do something else to improve?

First, you need to remember most people won't know you are trying to work on specific voice and/or diction problems unless *you* call it to their attention. Of course, you can do this with a verbal remark such as ''Oops, that was wrong!'' or by nonverbal cues such as making a face or shaking your head after making an error. However, this isn't an appropriate way of participating in daily speaking activities unless your associates were members of your class who are all still trying to raise their errors to a level of conscious recognition.

Instead, you should attempt to recognize each obvious diction error you make each time you make one. If the error is a substituted sound, such as [u-ʊ] in the word ''would,'' you should say a different word containing the same sound as part of your regular conversation **as soon after your error as possible, being sure you pronounce the sound correctly.** Thus, you might say a sentence with ''should'' or ''could'' as a follow-up to your error, making a deliberate effort to produce [ʊ] correctly. Often, if you are in the middle of an idea, you can use this technique to complete the sentence you are saying. If your listeners noticed your first error, they may assume you simply misspoke yourself the first time because you said the sound correctly the second time. By using this technique, you recognize the error immediately after making it (or even as you are making it) and then correct it quickly, rather than promising yourself you will do better ''in the future.'' As your awareness grows, you should find yourself catching your error the split-second before you say it and you will be able to make a quick shift in your articulators and say the word correctly.

If you have problems with voice more than with diction, you can use the same procedure. For example, if you tend to use vocal fry at the ends of sentences, you may hear fry occurring at the end of a sentence. Either immediately after hearing it, or when your turn comes to respond again, you purposely will avoid allowing your pitch and volume to drop simultaneously at the end of your *next* sentence. You will prepare, physiologically, for this specific task while you continue to participate in your listening and responding responsibilities. Your corrections always will be made in the context of what is being talked about—regardless of whether it is something serious or something light. If you make the error again, you promise yourself to eliminate it the *next* time—and the next time! By raising your errors to this level of consciousness, you try to reach a point in your daily, informal speaking when you can catch your errors *before* they emerge. This is the last step before you begin making the correction automatically and spontaneously.

"Look, buster, don't take that let's-see your-driver's-license tone of voice with *me*!"

HUMAN SPEECH AND HUMAN PRIDE

Periodically, we have a student who believes the instructor's criticisms of his or her speech habits are unjustified, "picky," or unrealistic for our casual, accepting society. The student can point to dozens of well educated, wealthy, influential individuals who have worse diction and/or voices than his or hers. All of them appear to be successful, in spite of their speech problems. The student wonders whether voice and diction errors really make that much difference in one's future success.

Some individuals who complete a course in speech improvement believe the course information and tasks are relatively unimportant to their immediate concerns. They are convinced that they have no major problems in being understood by their peers. All of their friends have similar (or worse) speaking problems, so they are in good company.

This textbook and your instructor would be wrong to imply that your current speaking limitations will prevent you from accomplishing great things in your lifetime. Voice and diction problems *could* be barriers in certain situations. However, if you have enough motivation, drive, talent, and patience, you can compensate for many barriers. If you know many influential people, inherit a fortune, patent a new product or process, or step into your parents' thriving business, you also can overcome many barriers.

Today, influential people are actively engaged in all career-oriented areas where they are called "successful." Some of these people know they have a specific communication problem they never overcame. They accept the idea that they will have to live with the problem the rest of their lives. The star football player who can't read—the president of the national conglomerate who can't spell—the award winning scientist who can't organize thoughts spontaneously—and the internationally acclaimed artist whose diction is impoverished—all share the mantle of success—and a secret involving an aspect of human communication which they try to keep well hidden. Often, they are so busy that they don't have time to do something about their problem. Some are too ashamed to try to remedy it now that they are perceived as being successful. They are all proud of their accomplishments in their particular fields—but they also may be afraid someone will discover their secret deficiency. Would it surprise you to discover that these individuals envy you because you have time, or are taking time now to improve your communication skills?

Humankind continues to make major strides toward equality in employment for all persons, regardless of sex, race, nationality, or parental attainment. These strides are easiest to make where two different individuals have equal education or training, abilities, skills, and talents. The ability to speak distinctly, fluently, without major dialectal errors, and with good inflectional variety is an important delineating factor in the job market today. A pleasantly pitched, well modulated voice can open doors for you—and once those doors are opened, your voice can help you obtain employment, promotions, status, friends, and yes, even wealth.

At the beginning of this text you read that "individual initiative and personal choice are two opportunities that you have right now." Even as you come to the end of this course, you still have these opportunities! However, now you also have more knowledge and experience for making your decisions regarding your current speaking habits and your future professional and personal goals. You know what you have done in this class to help you accomplish your objectives—and you know what remains to be done.

Ten, twenty, or forty years from now, we hope this class will have made a difference both in your awareness of voice and diction in yourself and others, and in your application of these important communication elements to major moments in your life. Even more, we hope you will have reason to be proud of your vocal accomplishments wherever you go, for as long as you live!

WORD LIST FOR GENERAL AMERICAN DICTION

Word	General American	Deviation
1. amish	[ˈɑm ɪʃ]	[ˈe mɪʃ]
2. asked	[æskt]	[ækst], [ˈæsk ɪd]
3. audience	[ˈɔd i ɛns]	[ˈɑd i ɛns]
4. barbarous	[ˈbɑɚ bɚ əs]	[bɑɚ ˈbɛɚ i əs]
5. bath	[bæθ]	[bɑθ], [bɔθ]
6. belles lettres	[bɛl ˈlɛt rə]	[bɛls ˈlɛtɚz]
7. cavalry	[ˈkæv l̩ ri]	[ˈkæl və ri]
8. chasm	[ˈkæz m̩]	[ˈtʃæz əm]
9. couldn't	[ˈkʊd n̩t]	[ˈkʊ tɪnt], [ˈku dɪnt]
10. demise	[dɪ ˈmɑɪz]	[dɪ ˈmɑɪs], [di ˈmiz], [ˈdɛm ɪs]
11. discretionary	[dɪs ˈkrɛʃ n̩ ˌɛɚ i]	[dɪs ˈkri ʃən ˌɛ ri]
12. docile	[ˈdɑ sl̩]	[ˈdo sɑɪl], [ˈdɑ sɑɪl]
13. enclose	[ɪn ˈkloz]	[ɪŋ ˈkloz]
14. enough	[əˈnʌf], [ɪˈnʌf]	[iˈnʌf]
15. epoch	[ˈɛp ək]	[ˈi pok], [i ˈpotʃ]
16. especially	[ɛ ˈspɛʃ əl i]	[ɛk ˈspɛʃ li]
17. facile	[ˈfæs l̩]	[ˈfæs ɑɪl], [fə ˈsil]
18. farther	[ˈfɑɚ ðɚ]	[ˈfɑɚ dɚ], [ˈfɑɚ θɚ]

19. finger	['fɪŋ gɚ]	['fɪŋ ɚ]
20. geisha	['ge ʃə]	['gi ʃə]
21. gesturing	['dʒɛs tʃɚ ɪŋ]	['gɛs tʃɚ ɪŋ], ['gɛs tʃɚ ɪn]
22. goblet	['gɑb lɛt]	['gɑb ə lɛt]
23. government	['gʌv ɚn mɛnt]	['gʌvɚ mənt]
24. hasn't	['hæz n̩t]	['hæs n̩t], ['hæs ɪnt]
25. heinous	['he nəs]	['hɑɪ nəs], ['hi nəs]
26. hindrance	['hɪn drəns]	['hɪn dɚ ənts]
27. immobile	[ɪ 'mo bl̩]	[ɪ 'mo bɑɪl]
28. impotence	['ɪm pə təns]	[ɪm 'po tɛns]
29. indigenous	[ɪn 'dɪdʒ ən əs]	[ˌɪn dɪ 'dʒin əs]
30. judgment	['dʒʌdʒ mɛnt]	['dʒʌdʒ ə mɛnt], ['dʒʌdʒ mɪnt]
31. kindergarten	['kɪn dɚ ˌgɑɚ tn̩]	['kɪn i ˌgɑɚ tɛn]
32. larynx	['læɚ ɪŋks]	['lɑɚ nɪks]
33. lecithin	['lɛs ə θɪn]	['lɛk tə θɪn]
34. length	[lɛŋθ]	[lɛnθ]
35. library	['lɑɪ brɛɚ i]	['lɑɪ bɛɚ i]
36. maintenance	['men tən əns]	[men 'ten əns]
37. measure	['mɛʒ ɚ]	['mɛz ɚ], ['me ʒɚ]
38. men's	[mɛnz]	[mɪnz], [mɪns]
39. miserable	['mɪz ɚ ə bl̩]	['mɪz rə bl̩]
40. missile	['mɪs l̩]	['mɪs ɑɪl]

41. nuclear	['nu kli ɚ]	['nuk ə lɚ], ['nuk jə lɚ]
42. numerous	['nu mɚ əs]	['num rəs]
43. nuptial	['nʌp ʃəl]	['nup ʃəl]
44. o'clock	[ə 'klɑk]	[o 'klɑk]
45. ought	[ɔt]	[ɑt], ['o ət]
46. overcharge	[ˌo vɚ 'tʃɑɹdʒ]	['ov ə tʃɑdʒ]
47. papyrus	[pə 'paɪ rəs]	['pæ prɪs]
48. perhaps	[pɚ 'hæps]	[pri 'hæps], ['præps]
49. pretend	[prɪ 'tɛnd]	[pɚ 'tɛnd], [pɚ 'tɪnd]
50. prostate	['prɑs tet]	['prɑs tret]
51. quarter	['kwɔɹ tɚ]	['kwɔ tə]
52. raspberry	['ræz bɛɚ i]	['ræs bɛ ri]
53. ravenous	['ræv ən əs]	['rev ən əs]
54. recognize	['rɛk əg naɪz]	['rɛk ən aɪz]
55. register	['rɛdʒ ɪs tɚ]	['rɛd ɪʃ tɚ]
56. registrar	['rɛdʒ ɪs trɑɚ]	['rɛd ɪʃ trɑɚ]
57. secretary	['sɛk rə ˌtɛɚ i]	['sɛk jə ˌtɛɚ i]
58. secular	['sɛk jə lɚ]	['sɛk ə lɚ]
59. sepulcher	['sɛp l̩ kɚ]	['sɛp lə kɚ]
60. similar	['sɪm ə lɚ]	['sɪm jə lɚ], ['sɪm ju lɚ]
61. solace	['sɑ lɪs]	['so lɪs]
62. statistics	[stə 'tɪs tɪks]	[stə 'stɪs tɪks]

63. sustain	[sə 'sten]	[səb 'sten]
64. tactile	['tæk tl̩]	['tæk taɪl]
65. tests	[tɛsts]	['tɛs təz], ['tɛs tɪz], [tɛs]
66. thorough	['θɝ o]	['θɔɝ o]
67. Tuesday	['tuz de]	['tjuz di], ['tɪuz de]
68. treasurer	['trɛʒ ɚ ɚ]	['trɛʒ ɚ], ['trɛʒ ɚ]
69. understood	[ˌʌn dɚ 'stʊd]	[ˌʌn dɚ 'stʊd]
70. unfamiliar	[ˌʌn fə 'mɪl jɚ]	[ˌʌn fɚ 'mɪl jɚ]
71. ungracious	[ʌn 'gre ʃəs]	[ʌŋ 'gre ʃəs]
72. verbatim	[vɚ 'be tɪm]	[vɚ 'bæt əm]
73. vitriolic	[ˌvɪt ri 'ɑl ɪk]	[ˌvɪt ri 'o lɪk]
74. volatile	['vɑl ə tl̩]	['vɑl ə taɪl]
75. was	[wʌz]	[wʌs], [wɑs]
76. we're	[wiɚ]	[wɝ], [wiʌ]
77. when	[hwɛn]	[hwɪn], [wɪn]
78. youngish	['jʌŋ ɪʃ]	['jʌŋ gɪʃ]
79. you've	[juv]	[jɪv]
80. zealot	['zɛl ət]	['zil ət]

LIST OF FOREIGN WORDS AND PHRASES AND THEIR MEANINGS

1. **ad infinitum** [æd ˌɪn fəˈnɑɪ təm]: LATIN; endlessly, to infinity

2. **a la bonne heure** [ɑ ˌlɑ bo ˈnɝ]: FRENCH; at a good time, well and good

3. **aloha oe** [ɑ ˈlo hɑ ɔɪ]: HAWAIIAN; welcome, love to you, farewell

4. **apres moi le deluge** [ɑ pre ˈmwɑ lə de ˈluʒ]: FRENCH; after me the deluge (a quotation attributed to Louis XV)

5. **a rivederci** [ˌɑ ri ve ˈdɛɝ tʃi]: ITALIAN; farewell, until we meet again

6. **au contraire** [ˌo kon ˈtrɛɝ]: FRENCH; on the contrary

7. **au revoir** [ˌo rəˈvwɑ]: FRENCH; goodbye for now, until we meet again

8. **auf Wiedersehen** [ɑʊf ˈvi dɝˌze ən]: GERMAN; goodbye for now, until we meet again

9. **a votre sante** [ɑ ˈvo trə ˈsɑn te]: FRENCH; to your health (as used in a toast)

10. **bon jour** [bon ˈʒɝ]: FRENCH; good day, good morning

11. **bona fide** [ˈbo nə ˈfɑɪd]: LATIN; in good faith, without fraud

12. **coup d'etat** [ˌku deˈta]: FRENCH; violent or sudden overthrow of a ruler or government, decisive exercise of force in politics to alter rules of government

13. **coup de grace** [ˌku də ˈgrɑs]: FRENCH; stroke of mercy, a death blow to end someone's suffering

14. **Deo gratias** [ˈde o ˈgrat i ɑs]: LATIN; Thanks be to God

290

15. **dramatis personae** ['drɑm ə tɪs pɚ'so nə]: LATIN; characters or persons in a drama

16. **e pluribus unum** [e 'plɝ ə bəs 'u nəm]: LATIN; one among many (motto of the United States)

17. **esprit de corps** [ɛs'pri də 'koɚ]: FRENCH; a common, shared spirit of identity or enthusiasm

18. **et cetera** [ɛt 'sɛt ɚ ə]: LATIN; and others, and so forth

19. **ex libris** [ɛks 'li brəs]: LATIN; from the books (or library) of

20. **faux pas** ['fo 'pɑ]: FRENCH; false step, error in etiquette or manners

21. **gestalt** [gɛ'ʃtɔlt]: GERMAN; a structure or pattern of phenomena which create a functional unit with qualities or properties that are different or not derivable from its parts

22. **hacienda** [ˌhɑ si'ɛn də]: SPANISH; country house or estate

23. **in absentia** [ˌɪn əb 'sɛn ʃi ə]: LATIN; in or during one's absence

24. **laissez faire** [ˌlɛs e 'fɛɚ]: FRENCH; policy of governmental non-intervention in directing economic affairs

25. **n'est-ce pas?** [nɛs 'pɑ]: FRENCH; Isn't it so?

26. **per diem** [pɚ 'dɑɪ əm]: LATIN; by the day, a daily allowance for living

27. **prima facie** ['prɑɪ mə 'fe ʃi]: LATIN; sufficient evidence to win if not disproved, at first view or appearance

28. **raconteur** [ˌræ kɑn'tɝ]: FRENCH; a skillful storyteller

29. **raison d'etre** ['re zon 'dɛt rə]: FRENCH; reason for existing, justification for being

30. **repondez s'il vous plait** [re'pon de sil vu ple]: FRENCH; reply if you please (abbreviated as R.S.V.P. in English invitations)

31. **se habla espanol** [se 'ɑv lɑ ˌes pɑ'njol]: SPANISH; Spanish spoken

32. **s'il vous plait** [sil vu ple]: FRENCH; if you please

33. **sotto voce** ['sɑ to 'vo tʃe]: ITALIAN; under normal voice level, said so as not to be heard easily

34. **tempus fugit** ['tɛm pəs 'fju dʒət]: LATIN; time flies

35. **terra firma** ['tɛɚ ə 'fɚ mə]: LATIN; firm or solid earth, dry land as opposed to water or air

36. **tout le monde** [tu lə mond]: FRENCH; all the world, everyone

37. **verbatim** [vɚ'be tɪm]: LATIN; word for word

38. **wie geht's** [vi 'gets]: GERMAN; How goes it?

APPENDIX 3

TRANSCRIPTIONS THAT CAN FOOL YOU

The following transcriptions look like words written in English. They represent English words that will be written differently from their IPA transcriptions. Pronounce the IPA transcriptions aloud to see why these words can be confusing.

1. [bum]	10. [jets]	19. [sɪns]
2. [jɛt]	11. [bit]	20. [rot]
3. [grin]	12. [wet]	21. [but]
4. [rɑts]	13. [dip]	22. [on]
5. [nut]	14. [glum]	23. [hɑt]
6. [fez]	15. [sit]	24. [win]
7. [siks]	16. [krɪ'tik]	25. [do]
8. [rum]	17. [ɑd]	26. [be]
9. [tɑg]	18. [sun]	27. [tum]

292

28. [ton]

29. [hum]

30. [wɪns]

31. [to]

32. [son]

33. [dim]

34. [we]

35. [ed]

36. [tɑp]

IDENTIFICATION OF COMMON ERRORS IN WORDS

The following words often are mispronounced. The most common error is listed to the left of each word (for example [e-ɪ] means [e] is **substituted** for [ɪ]) and the correct pronunciation is listed **after** the word in IPA symbols. The location of each error is underlined in each IPA transcription. See if you can spot the error in each word.

1. [z-s]: absurd [əb'sɜ˞d]

2. [æ-ə]: abyss [ə'bɪs]

3. [e-i]: academe [ˌækə'dim]

4. omits [k]: accessory [æk'sɛsə˞i]

5. adds [n]: accompanist [ə'kʌmpənɪst]

6. omits [j]: accumulate [ə'kjumjə,let]

7. omits [j]: accuracy ['ækjə˞əsi]

8. adds [j]: acoustic [ə'kustɪk]

9. [ʃ-tʃ]: actually ['æktʃjuəli]

10. adds [ə]: adenoid ['ædn,ɔɪd]

11. [ə-ɚ]: adversary ['ædvɚ,sɛɚi]

12. omits [d]: adverse [æd'vɜ˞s]

13. [t-θ]: aesthetic [æs'θɛtɪk]

14. [ɑɪ-ə]: agile ['ædʒəl], ['ædʒl̩]

15. omits [l]: almighty [ɔl'mɑɪti]

16. omits [l]: almost [ɔl'most]

17. omits [j]: ambulance ['æmbjələns]

18. [æ-ə]: amino [ə'mino]

19. [z-ʒ]: amnesia [æm'niʒɪə]

20. [t-θ]: anesthetist [ə'nɛsθətɪst]

21. [tʃ-k]: archipelago [ˌɑ˞kə'pɛlə,go]

22. adds [r]: asparagus [ə'spæɚ ə gəs]

23. [i-ə]: beautiful ['bjutəfʊl]

24. [ə-ɚ]: berserk [bɚ'sɜ˞k]

25. omits [ʊ]: brochure [bro'ʃʊɚ]

26. [dʒ-ʒ]: camouflage ['kæmə,flɑʒ]

27. [tʃ-ʃ]: chagrin [ʃə'grɪn]

28. [dʒ-ʒ]: corsage [kɔɚ'sɑʒ]

293

29. [ʌ-ju]: culinary ['kjulə,nɛɝi]

30. [s-ʃ]: disheveled ['dɪʃɛvl̩d]

31. adds [j]: dissimilar [dɪ'sɪmələɝ]

32. adds [aɪ]: docile ['dɑsl̩]

33. [ɔɝ-ɝ]: doctoral ['dɑktɝl̩]

34. [ə-ɪ]: elucidate [ɪ'lusə,det]

35. omits [j]: emulate ['ɛmjəlet]

36. [k-t]: etcetera [ɛt 'sɛtɝə]

37. adds [k]: especially [ɛs'pɛʃəli], [ɛs'peʃli]

38. [ɪ-ɛ]: experimental [ɪk,spɛɝə'mɛntl̩]

39. adds [aɪ]: facile ['fæsl̩]

40. [ʌs-æks]: facsimile [fæk'sɪməli]

41. omits [j]: figure ['fɪgjɝ]

42. adds [aɪ]: futile ['fjutl̩]

43. omits [n]: government ['gʌvɝnmɛnt]

44. [o-ʌ]: hover ['hʌvɝ]

45. omits [h]: humane [hju'men]

46. adds [aɪ]: imbecile ['ɪmbəsl̩]

47. [o-ə]: impotent ['ɪmpətənt]

48. [ɛ-ə]: integral ['ɪntəgrəl] (accent changes)

49. adds [o]: isolate ['aɪslet]

50. [kt-s]: lecithin ['lɛsəθɪn]

51. [e-ɛ]: legume [lɛ'gum]

52. [ə-e]: liaison [,li'ezɑn]

53. omits [r]: library ['laɪbrɛɝi]

54. [e-ə]: maintenance ['mentənəns]

55. [e-ɛ]: measure ['mɛʒɝ]

56. [r-ɝ]: perhaps [pɝ 'hæps]

57. adds [r]: prostate ['prɑstet]

58. adds [p]: ptomaine [to'men]

59. [ŋ-m]: pumpkin ['pʌmkɪn]

60. omits [g]: recognize ['rɛkəgnaɪz]

61. [d-dʒ], [ʃ-s]: register, registrar ['rɛdʒɪstɝ], ['rɛdʒɪstrɑɝ]

62. omits [j]: ridiculous [rɪ'dɪkjələs]

63. [ɛ-ɪ]/[tʃ-s]: rinse [rɪns]

64. omits [r], adds [j]: secretary ['sɛkrə,tɛɝi]

65. [lə-l]: sepulcher ['sɛplkɝ]

66. adds [aɪ]: servile ['sɝvl̩]

67. adds [j], [u]: similar ['sɪmələɝ]

68. adds [s]: statistics [stə'tɪstɪks]

69. adds [k]: succinct [sə'sɪŋt]

70. adds [b]: sustain [səs 'ten]

71. adds [w]: sword [sɔɝd]

72. [e-æ]: tapestry ['tæpɪstri]

73. adds [ɪ] or [ə]: tests [tɛsts]

74. [ʃ-stʃ]: textual ['tɛkstʃuəl]

75. [ɔ-ɔɪ]: toilet ['tɔɪlɪt]

76. omits [ɝ]: treasurer ['trɛʒɝɝ]

TRANSLATION OF IPA TRANSCRIPTIONS

The following sentences are transcribed as one might hear them being spoken in daily conversation in the General American dialect. Read them aloud to test your knowledge of the IPA.

1. [ɪf ju no hwɪtʃ 'steʃn̩ plez 'klæsɪkl̩ 'mɪuzɪk æt naɪt, tɛl ʌs.]

2. ['ivn̩ ðo dev med ə hom'rʌn, wi lɔst aʊɝ læst 'besbɔl gem tu ˌɛɝə'zonə stet.]

3. [kʊd wi hæv ə tʃɔɪs əv 'ɛntrez æt aʊɝ 'bʌstɚz 'bænkwɪt?]

4. [hwɛn ʃi sɛd tu tek hɪz æd'vaɪs wɪð ə gren əv sɔlt, ʃi 'dɪdnt min ɪt wʊd bi blænd.]

5. [hwʌtaɪm wɪl ju bi 'pɪkɪŋ əp jɔɝ 'sɪstɚ ɑn 'mʌnde?]

6. ['juʤəli wi hæv aɪs'ti, hɑt dɔgz ænd pə'teto 'sæləd æt aʊɝ klʌb 'pɪknɪk.]

7. ['tɛɝi gɑt ə braɪt rɛd 'snomobil fɔɝ hɝ 'bɝθde.]

8. [wi lind ə'gɛnst ə hjudʒ 'wɪlo tri hwaɪl wi 'wetɪd fɔɝ ðə et e ɛm bʌs.]

9. [aɪ sɔ ə 'lɪtl̩ 'selbot kwaɪt fɑɝ aʊt ɑn 'ɛmɚl̩d lek.]

10. [ən'ʌðɚ 'pɝsn̩ 'ænsɚd ðə fon hwɛn aɪ kɔld maɪ ænts haʊs.]

11. ['sʌmtaɪmz ðə nɔɪz əv 'træfɪk 'goɪŋ pæst hɪz 'ɔfɪs ɪz 'dɛfnɪŋ.]

12. ['ɛni 'mɛmbɚ əv ðə kə'mjunəti kæn gɪv ju dɚ'ɛkʃn̩z tu 'hɪlsaɪd paɝk.]

13. [ɪf 'bɛvɚli 'ɪzn̩t 'rɛdi baɪ ɪ'lɛvn̩, kɔl mi ænd aɪl kʌm 'ovɚ ænd pɪk ju əp.]

14. ['notɪs ɔl ðə 'rozɪz 'blumɪŋ ə'lɔŋ ðɛɝ frʌnt fɛns hwɛn ju draɪv pæst.]

15. [we dɪ'saɪdɪd tu tek aʊɝ tu wik ve'keʃn̩ ɪn ðə ˌkʌlɚ'ado 'maʊntn̩z ðɪs jiɝ.]

16. [hi traɪd tu be 'vɛɝi 'kɔʃəs æz hi kʌt ðə tri lɪm 'hæŋɪŋ 'ovɚ hɪz rʊf.]

17. [ðe 'alwez ɛn'ʤɔɪd 'watʃɪŋ ðə 'ɛɝmen du ðɛɝ 'pɛɝəʃut dʒʌmps.]

18. [aɪm nɑt 'sɝtn̩ bət aɪ θɪŋk ʃi kem hiɝ frəm lə'haɪnə 'maʊi.]

19. [aɪv hæd ə kəm'pjutɚ fɔɝ faɪv jiɝz bət 'haevn̩t 'ɛvɚ kʌm'pjutɪd 'ɛniθɪŋ ən ɪt.]

20. ['kɝəntli ðə 'tɛmpɚətʃɚ ɪz raɪt æt ðə 'frizɪŋ pɔɪnt.]

21. [aɪv hɝd 'mɛni gʊd θɪŋz ə'baʊt ðə sæl'veʃn̩ 'aɝmi.]

22. [nʌn əv ðə 'studn̩ts nu hu hæd 'baɝod ðə bʊk əv 'emi 'loʊl̩z 'poətri.]

23. [ðə hilz əv ðɛɝ ʃuz hæd wɔɝn daʊn.]

24. ['prabəbli ðə 'kaɝtn̩z wɪl ə'raɪv ɑn 'tuzde.]

25. [ɪtʃ taɪm wi 'vɪzɪt vɚ'mɑnt ɪn 'eprɪl, ðə 'mɑʊntn̩z ɑ˞ 'ʃrɑʊdɪd ɪn klɑʊdz.]

26. ['nʌθɪŋ simz tu fɪt 'ɛni mɔ˞ sɪns aɪ bi'gæn 'daɪətɪŋ.]

27. [æz wi wɑtʃt hɚ kæt wɑʃ ɪts fes wi hɚd ə lɑʊd 'pɚɪŋ.]

28. [ə'pɪɚəns me nɑt bi 'ɛvriθɪŋ bət ɪt ɪz 'sʌmθɪŋ tu kən'sɪdɚ.]

29. [ɪf juɚ 'hæpi wɪ ðə rɪ'zʌlts əv jɔ˞ wɚk, juv pæst ðə fɚst tɛst əv æk'sɛptəns.]

30. [hwɛn wi kæn du lɛs wɚk fɔ˞ mɔ˞ 'mʌni, wi bi'gɪn tu bə'liv sʌk'sɛs ɪz dʒʌst ə'rɑʊnd ðə 'kɔ˞nɚ.]

LISTENING AND IDENTIFICATION CHECK

One of the words in each of the following items will be pronounced aloud. Indicate which word is pronounced by circling the letter immediately before the word.

1. a. [livz], b. [lʌvz], c. [lɪvz], d. [laɪvz], e. [lovz]

2. a. ['pritʃɚ], b. ['pɪtʃɚ], c. ['pæstjɚ], d. ['pɪktʃɚ], e. ['pɑstjɚ]

3. a. ['wɑndɚ], b. ['raʊndɚ], c. ['wʌndɚ], d. ['rʌnɚ], e. ['nʌmbɚ,

4. a. ['hɑɚdɪst], b. ['ɑɚtɪst], c. ['ɑɚdɪθ], d. ['hɑɚtiɪst], e. ['hɑɚt ɪz]

5. a. [ri'tʃɛkt], b. [ri'stækt], c. [ri'dʒɛkt], d. [ri'ækt], e. [ri'flɛkt]

6. a. ['hæbɪt], b. ['ræbɪt], c. ['ræbɪd], d. ['ræpɪd], e. [æd 'lɪb]

7. a. ['plʌndʒɚ], b. ['blʌndɚ], c. ['plʌndɚ], d. ['wʌndɚ], e. ['blʌntɚ]

8. a. [ritʃ], b. [rɪdʒ], c. [rɛtʃ], d. [ridz], e. [rɪtʃ]

9. a. [baɪnd], b. ['baɪɪŋ], c. [vaɪn], d. [maɪm], e. ['vaɪɪŋ]

10. a. ['hitɪŋ], b. ['haɪtn̩], c. ['hiðn̩], d. ['hitɪŋ], e. ['hɪdn̩]

11. a. ['plʌʃɪst], b. ['plɛdʒɪz], c. ['plizɪz], d. ['plʌndʒɪz], e. ['plɛdʒɪθ]

12. a. [gɔn], b. [gaʊn], c. [gun], d. [gʌn], e. [gen]

13. a. ['hʌŋgɚ], b. ['ʌmbɚ], c. ['hʌmbl̩], d. ['mʌmbl̩], e. ['nʌmbɚ]

14. a. [θriz], b. [friz], c. [triz], d. [viz], e. [briz]

15. a. ['paʊɚ], b. ['taʊɚ], c. ['saʊɚ], d. ['baʊɚ], e. ['flaʊɚ]

16. a. [tʃuz], b. [dʒuz], c. [juz], d. [suz], e. [ʃuz]

17. a. [kwɪt], b. [kwɪk], c. [hwɪp], d. [kwɪp], e. [wɪt]

18. a. ['krɪtɪk], b. ['krɛdɪt], c. ['krɪkɪt], d. ['krɛtɪd], e. ['krʊkɪd]

19. a. [wɚst], b. [wɚks], c. [wɚdz], d. [wɚθ], e. [hwɚz]

20. a. ['stægnənt], b. ['mægnət], c. ['fregrənt], d. ['flegrənt], e. ['vegrənt]

21. a. [lɔst], b. [kɔst], c. [tɔst], d. [bɔst], e. [kɔzd]

22. a. ['bɑɚtɚ], b. ['hɑɚbɚ], c. ['mɑɚtɚ], d. ['bɑɚbɚ], e. ['hɑɚdɚ]

23. a. [gred], b. [grez], c. [gret], d. [grev], e. [grep]

24. a. ['hɚdl̩], b. ['tɚtl̩], c. ['kɚdl̩], d. ['fɚtl̩], e. ['gɚdl̩]

USING THE CRITIQUE FORM AS A TEACHING/LEARNING TOOL

The critique forms which follow were constructed to eliminate the need for extensive written instructor comments during oral presentations and to give you a simple, consistent format for understanding major areas of difficulty. They will make you aware of cumulative errors which need additional emphasis for your next assignment.

The instructor may ask you to write or type your name and the date on which you are speaking on your critique sheet and hand it in just before you give your presentation. If the instructor tape records the presentation, the letter of the tape (a, b, c, etc.) and the side of the tape (1 or 2) may be circled. Also, a space is included for the instructor to write the beginning and ending numbers on the recorder's digital counter. This information is useful for finding your recorded presentations quickly at a future time.

The critiques contain some of the most common errors in substitution, omission, addition, and transposition of sounds that occur in beginning speech improvement classes. If, for example, you say [mis] for [mɪs] and [kid] for [kɪd], your instructor will place the words "miss" and "kid" after [i-ɪ] in the **SUBSTITUTIONS** section of your critique. You can remember that the symbols indicate you are substituting the first symbol [i] for the second symbol [ɪ]. If you omit the [d] in "didn't" the instructor will write "didn't" after [d] under **OMISSIONS.** If you have errors that aren't listed on the critique, your instructor will write the errors, using IPA symbols, and then will indicate the words in which the errors occur. As you accumulate critiques, you will be able to place them side-by-side and see the areas that continue to give you trouble.

Approximately two-thirds of your critique sheet is devoted to problems in diction. The remaining one-third is devoted to problems in voice. Notice that the instructor will place a check mark or "x" on relative judgment scales to indicate where you fell on each continuum for this assignment. Some space is left at the bottom for brief comments and for the grade the instructor assigns you. The back of the critique may be used for additional comments.

If your instructor requires you to keep a log of cumulative critiques on each of your classmates, you may wish to photocopy this critique form, or use a modified version of it for each speaker. By learning to use the same format in every critique, you will find you can focus your attention on each presentation while quickly writing words in the correct locations on the critique sheets.

Name _____ ( )

Tape: a b c d e f; S: 1 2

Date: Recording #:

SUBSTITUTIONS: Time: 1:   2:   3:   4:

[ɪ-ɛ]
[i-ɪ]
[e-ə]
[u-ʊ]
[ɪ-ʌ]
[ɑ-ɑɪ]
[ɑ-ɔ]
[ɔ-ɑ]
[n-ŋ]
[s-z]
[t/f-θ]
[t-d]   [ə/ɜ-ɚ/ɝ]
[tʃ-dʒ]   [ɑ-ʌ]
[d-ð]
[ʃ-s]
[æʊ-ɑʊ]

OMISSIONS:
[ɔ]   [l]
[u]   [t]
[d]   [   ]
[g]
[i]

ADDITIONS:
[ə/ʌ]
[t]
[ɛ]

TRANSPOSITIONS:
[ks-sk]
[   ]

EXTRA SIBILANCE OR FRICTION: __ lateral
__ frontal
__ hiss

VOCAL QUALITY:
__ nasal   __ denasal   __ tense/harsh
__ guttural/fry
__ breathy   __ hoarse

INFLECTIONAL VARIETY:
little   : : : : :   much

FLUENCY:
broken   : : : : :   smooth

RATE:
slow   : : : : : :   fast

PITCH:
too low   : : : : :   too high

VOLUME/PROJECTION:
too soft   : : : : :   too loud

USE OF INTENSITY/STRESS/EMPHASIS:
too little   : : : : :   too much

GENERAL COMMENTS:

                              GRADE:

Name _____ ( )

Tape: a b c d e f; S: 1 2

Date: Recording #:

SUBSTITUTIONS: Time: 1:   2:   3:   4:

[ɪ-ɛ]
[i-ɪ]
[e-ə]
[u-ʊ]
[ɪ-ʌ]
[ɑ-ɑɪ]
[ɑ-ɔ]
[ɔ-ɑ]
[n-ŋ]
[s-z]
[t/f-θ]
[t-d]   [ə/ɜ-ɚ/ɝ]
[tʃ-dʒ]   [ɑ-ʌ]
[d-ð]
[ʃ-s]
[æʊ-ɑʊ]

OMISSIONS:
[ɔ]   [l]
[u]   [t]
[d]   [   ]
[g]
[j]

ADDITIONS:
[ə/ʌ]
[t]
[ɛ]

TRANSPOSITIONS:
[ks-sk]
[   ]

EXTRA SIBILANCE OR FRICTION: __ lateral
__ frontal
__ hiss

VOCAL QUALITY:
__ nasal   __ denasal   __ tense/harsh
__ guttural/fry
__ breathy   __ hoarse

INFLECTIONAL VARIETY:
little   : : : : :   much

FLUENCY:
broken   : : : : :   smooth

RATE:
slow   : : : : : :   fast

PITCH:
too low   : : : : :   too high

VOLUME/PROJECTION:
too soft   : : : : :   too loud

USE OF INTENSITY/STRESS/EMPHASIS:
too little   : : : : :   too much

GENERAL COMMENTS:

                              GRADE:

Name _____ ( )

Tape:a b c d e f; S: 1 2

Date: Recording #:

SUBSTITUTIONS: Time: 1:   2:   3:   4:

[ɪ-ɛ]
[i-ɪ]
[e-ə]
[u-ʊ]
[ɪ-ʌ]
[ɑ-ɑɪ]
[ɑ-ɔ]
[ɔ-ɑ]
[n-ŋ]
[s-z]
[t/f-θ]
[t-d]   [ə/ɜ-ɚ/ɝ]
[tʃ-dʒ]   [ɑ-ʌ]
[d-ð]
[ʃ-s]
[æʊ-ɑʊ]

OMISSIONS:
[ɔ]   [l]
[u]   [t]
[d]   [ ]
[g]
[i]

ADDITIONS:
[ə/ʌ]
[t]
[ɛ]

TRANSPOSITIONS:
[ks-sk]
[   ]

EXTRA SIBILANCE OR FRICTION: __ lateral
__ frontal
__ hiss

VOCAL QUALITY:
__ nasal   __ denasal   __ tense/harsh
__ guttural/fry
__ breathy   __ hoarse

INFLECTIONAL VARIETY:
little   : : : : :   much

FLUENCY:
broken   : : : : :   smooth

RATE:
slow   : : : : :   fast

PITCH:
too low   : : : : :   too high

VOLUME/PROJECTION:
too soft   : : : : :   too loud

USE OF INTENSITY/STRESS/EMPHASIS:
too little   : : : : :   too much

GENERAL COMMENTS:

                                   GRADE:

Name _____ ( )

Tape:a b c d e f; S: 1 2

Date: Recording #:

SUBSTITUTIONS: Time: 1:   2:   3:   4:

[ɪ-ɛ]
[i-ɪ]
[e-ə]
[u-ʊ]
[ɪ-ʌ]
[ɑ-ɑɪ]
[ɑ-ɔ]
[ɔ-ɑ]
[n-ŋ]
[s-z]
[t/f-θ]
[t-d]   [ə/ɜ-ɚ/ɝ]
[tʃ-dʒ]   [ɑ-ʌ]
[d-ð]
[ʃ-s]
[æʊ-ɑʊ]

OMISSIONS:
[ɔ]   [l]
[u]   [t]
[d]   [ ]
[g]
[j]

ADDITIONS:
[ə/ʌ]
[t]
[ɛ]

TRANSPOSITIONS:
[ks-sk]
[   ]

EXTRA SIBILANCE OR FRICTION: __ lateral
__ frontal
__ hiss

VOCAL QUALITY:
__ nasal   __ denasal   __ tense/harsh
__ guttural/fry
__ breathy   __ hoarse

INFLECTIONAL VARIETY:
little   : : : : :   much

FLUENCY:
broken   : : : : :   smooth

RATE:
slow   : : : : :   fast

PITCH:
too low   : : : : :   too high

VOLUME/PROJECTION:
too soft   : : : : :   too loud

USE OF INTENSITY/STRESS/EMPHASIS:
too little   : : : : :   too much

GENERAL COMMENTS:

                                   GRADE:

Name _____ ( )

Tape: a b c d e f; S: 1 2

Date: Recording #:

SUBSTITUTIONS: Time: 1:   2:   3:   4:

[ɪ-ɛ]

[i-ɪ]

[e-ə]

[u-ʊ]

[ɪ-ʌ]

[ɑ-ɑɪ]

[ɑ-ɔ]

[ɔ-ɑ]

[n-ŋ]

[s-z]

[t/f-θ]

[t-d]   [ə/ɜ-ɚ/ɝ]

[tʃ-dʒ]   [ɑ-ʌ]

[d-ð]

[ʃ-s]

[æʊ-ɑʊ]

OMISSIONS:

[ɔ]   [l]

[u]   [t]

[d]   [   ]

[g]

[j]

ADDITIONS:

[ə/ʌ]

[t]

[ɛ]

TRANSPOSITIONS:

[ks-sk]

[   ]

EXTRA SIBILANCE OR FRICTION: __ lateral

__ frontal

__ hiss

VOCAL QUALITY:

__ nasal   __ denasal   __ tense/harsh

__ guttural/fry

__ breathy   __ hoarse

INFLECTIONAL VARIETY:

little   : : : : : :   much

FLUENCY:

broken   : : : : : :   smooth

RATE:

slow   : : : : : :   fast

PITCH:

too low   : : : : : :   too high

VOLUME/PROJECTION:

too soft   : : : : : :   too loud

USE OF INTENSITY/STRESS/EMPHASIS:

too little   : : : : : :   too much

GENERAL COMMENTS:

                                        GRADE:

Name _____ ( )

Tape: a b c d e f; S: 1 2

Date: Recording #:

SUBSTITUTIONS: Time: 1:   2:   3:   4:

[ɪ-ɛ]

[i-ɪ]

[e-ə]

[u-ʊ]

[ɪ-ʌ]

[ɑ-ɑɪ]

[ɑ-ɔ]

[ɔ-ɑ]

[n-ŋ]

[s-z]

[t/f-θ]

[t-d]   [ə/ɜ-ɚ/ɝ]

[tʃ-dʒ]   [ɑ-ʌ]

[d-ð]

[ʃ-s]

[æʊ-ɑʊ]

OMISSIONS:

[ɔ]   [l]

[u]   [t]

[d]   [   ]

[g]

[j]

ADDITIONS:

[ə/ʌ]

[t]

[ɛ]

TRANSPOSITIONS:

[ks-sk]

[   ]

EXTRA SIBILANCE OR FRICTION: __ lateral

__ frontal

__ hiss

VOCAL QUALITY:

__ nasal   __ denasal   __ tense/harsh

__ guttural/fry

__ breathy   __ hoarse

INFLECTIONAL VARIETY:

little   : : : : : :   much

FLUENCY:

broken   : : : : : :   smooth

RATE:

slow   : : : : : :   fast

PITCH:

too low   : : : : : :   too high

VOLUME/PROJECTION:

too soft   : : : : : :   too loud

USE OF INTENSITY/STRESS/EMPHASIS:

too little   : : : : : :   too much

GENERAL COMMENTS:

                                        GRADE:

Name _____ ( )

Tape: a b c d e f; S: 1 2

Date: Recording #:

SUBSTITUTIONS: Time: 1:   2:   3:   4:

[ɪ-ɛ]

[i-ɪ]

[e-ə]

[u-ʊ]

[ɪ-ʌ]

[ɑ-ɑɪ]

[ɑ-ɔ]

[ɔ-ɑ]

[n-ŋ]

[s-z]

[t/f-θ]

[t-d]   [ə/ɜ-ɚ/ɝ]

[tʃ-dʒ]   [ɑ-ʌ]

[d-ð]

[ʃ-s]

[æʊ-ɑʊ]

OMISSIONS:

[ɔ]   [l]

[u]   [t]

[d]   [   ]

[g]

[i]

ADDITIONS:

[ə/ʌ]

[t]

[ɛ]

TRANSPOSITIONS:

[ks-sk]

[   ]

EXTRA SIBILANCE OR FRICTION: __ lateral

__ frontal

__ hiss

VOCAL QUALITY:

__ nasal   __ denasal   __ tense/harsh

__ guttural/fry

__ breathy   __ hoarse

INFLECTIONAL VARIETY:

little   : : : : :   much

FLUENCY:

broken   : : : : :   smooth

RATE:

slow   : : : : :   fast

PITCH:

too low   : : : : :   too high

VOLUME/PROJECTION:

too soft   : : : : :   too loud

USE OF INTENSITY/STRESS/EMPHASIS:

too little   : : : : :   too much

GENERAL COMMENTS:

                              GRADE:

Name _____ ( )

Tape: a b c d e f; S: 1 2

Date: Recording #:

SUBSTITUTIONS: Time: 1:   2:   3:   4:

[ɪ-ɛ]

[i-ɪ]

[e-ə]

[u-ʊ]

[ɪ-ʌ]

[ɑ-ɑɪ]

[ɑ-ɔ]

[ɔ-ɑ]

[n-ŋ]

[s-z]

[t/f-θ]

[t-d]   [ə/ɜ-ɚ/ɝ]

[tʃ-dʒ]   [ɑ-ʌ]

[d-ð]

[ʃ-s]

[æʊ-ɑʊ]

OMISSIONS:

[ɔ]   [l]

[u]   [t]

[d]   [   ]

[g]

[j]

ADDITIONS:

[ə/ʌ]

[t]

[ɛ]

TRANSPOSITIONS:

[ks-sk]

[   ]

EXTRA SIBILANCE OR FRICTION: __ lateral

__ frontal

__ hiss

VOCAL QUALITY:

__ nasal   __ denasal   __ tense/harsh

__ guttural/fry

__ breathy   __ hoarse

INFLECTIONAL VARIETY:

little   : : : : :   much

FLUENCY:

broken   : : : : :   smooth

RATE:

slow   : : : : :   fast

PITCH:

too low   : : : : :   too high

VOLUME/PROJECTION:

too soft   : : : : :   too loud

USE OF INTENSITY/STRESS/EMPHASIS:

too little   : : : : :   too much

GENERAL COMMENTS:

                              GRADE:

Name _____ ( )

Tape: a b c d e f; S: 1 2
Date: Recording #:
SUBSTITUTIONS: Time: 1:   2:   3:   4:
[ɪ-ɛ]
[i-ɪ]
[e-ə]
[u-ʊ]
[ɪ-ʌ]
[ɑ-ɑɪ]
[ɑ-ɔ]
[ɔ-ɑ]
[n-ŋ]
[s-z]
[t/f-θ]
[t-d]   [ə/ɜ-ɚ/ɝ]
[tʃ-dʒ]   [ɑ-ʌ]
[d-ð]
[ʃ-s]
[æʊ-ɑʊ]
OMISSIONS:
[ɔ]   [l]
[u]   [t]
[d]   [   ]
[g]
[i]

ADDITIONS:
[ə/ʌ]
[t]
[ɛ]
TRANSPOSITIONS:
[ks-sk]
[   ]

EXTRA SIBILANCE OR FRICTION: __ lateral
__ frontal
__ hiss
VOCAL QUALITY:
__ nasal   __ denasal   __ tense/harsh
__ guttural/fry
__ breathy   __ hoarse
INFLECTIONAL VARIETY:
little   : : : : :   much

FLUENCY:
broken   : : : : : :   smooth

RATE:
slow   : : : : : :   fast

PITCH:
too low   : : : : : :   too high

VOLUME/PROJECTION:
too soft   : : : : : :   too loud

USE OF INTENSITY/STRESS/EMPHASIS:
too little   : : : : : :   too much

GENERAL COMMENTS:

                                GRADE:

Name _____ ( )

Tape: a b c d e f; S: 1 2
Date: Recording #:
SUBSTITUTIONS: Time: 1:   2:   3:   4:
[ɪ-ɛ]
[i-ɪ]
[e-ə]
[u-ʊ]
[ɪ-ʌ]
[ɑ-ɑɪ]
[ɑ-ɔ]
[ɔ-ɑ]
[n-ŋ]
[s-z]
[t/f-θ]
[t-d]   [ə/ɜ-ɚ/ɝ]
[tʃ-dʒ]   [ɑ-ʌ]
[d-ð]
[ʃ-s]
[æʊ-ɑʊ]
OMISSIONS:
[ɔ]   [l]
[u]   [t]
[d]   [   ]
[g]
[j]

ADDITIONS:
[ə/ʌ]
[t]
[ɛ]
TRANSPOSITIONS:
[ks-sk]
[   ]

EXTRA SIBILANCE OR FRICTION: __ lateral
__ frontal
__ hiss
VOCAL QUALITY:
__ nasal   __ denasal   __ tense/harsh
__ guttural/fry
__ breathy   __ hoarse
INFLECTIONAL VARIETY:
little   : : : : :   much

FLUENCY:
broken   : : : : : :   smooth

RATE:
slow   : : : : : :   fast

PITCH:
too low   : : : : : :   too high

VOLUME/PROJECTION:
too soft   : : : : : :   too loud

USE OF INTENSITY/STRESS/EMPHASIS:
too little   : : : : : :   too much

GENERAL COMMENTS:

                                GRADE:

GLOSSARY

A

abdomen ['æb də mən]:   body cavity between the diaphragm and pelvic floor (this region often is referred to incorrectly by laypersons as the stomach)

abdominal breathing [æb 'dɑm ən l̩]:   inhalation and exhalation that is controlled largely by expanding and contracting the abdominal muscles and a flattening of the diaphragm

accent ['æk sɛnt]:   stress or emphasis placed on a syllable in a word, or a word in a thought sequence, usually by raising its pitch and/or increasing its volume; also, obvious deviations from a national or regional speech pattern; a dialect

acoustic [ə'ku stɪk]:   pertaining to heard sound, the science of sound, or the act or sense of hearing

Adam's apple ['æd əmz 'æp l̩]:   slight bulge in the front of the throat created by the thyroid cartilage of the larynx

affricate ['æf rə kɪt]:   a new consonant phoneme created by quickly combining adjacent plosive and fricative sounds, as in [dʒ] in "jury" and [t/] in "chest"

alveolar [æl 'vi ə lɚ]:   pertaining to the gum ridge just behind the upper front teeth

articulation [ɑɚ 'tɪk jə 'le ʃn̩], [ʃən]:   diction; modifying and shaping sound to create spoken language

articulators [ɑɚ 'tɪk jə ˌlet ɚz]:   speech organs used to create spoken language including the lips, teeth, tongue, hard and soft palates, and lower jaw

aspiration [ˌæs pɚ 'e ʃn̩], [ʃən]:   release of sound which is accompanied by a puff of air; breathing

assimilation [ə ˌsɪm l̩ 'e ʃn̩], [ʃən]:   mutual influence of adjacent sounds in normal, connected speech, particularly in fast, casual speech as in "betcha" for "bet you"

B

bilabial [bɑɪ 'le bi l̩]:   sounds produced with upper and lower lips including [p], [b], [m], [w] and [hw]; two lips

blending ['blɛnd ɪŋ]:   process of combining two adjacent sounds closely together as in the words "green," and "blue"

breathy ['brɛθ i]:   voice quality characterized by excessive expulsion of breath; somewhat like a whispered voice

C

clavicular [klə'vɪk jə lɚ]:   pertaining to the collarbones or clavicles, as in clavicular breathing during which the collarbones and upper chest are raised and lowered

cognates ['kɑg nets]:   pairs of sounds which are articulated in the same manner and place except for the element of voicing, as in the voiced [d] and voiceless [t]

connotative ['kɑn o ˌte tɪv]:   implied meaning of a word in addition to the literal or denotative meaning; associative or suggested meaning, often resulting from the way a word is said, which can modify or contradict the literal meaning

consonant ['kɑn sən ənt]:   speech sound characterized by partial or complete blockage of the breathstream by the articulators, such as [p], [z], and [v]

continuant [kən 'tɪn ju ənt]:   a consonant which may be prolonged while the articulators remain in the same position; includes all English consonants except [p], [b], [t], [d], [k] and [g]

D

decibel ['dɛs ə ˌbɛl]:   a unit of measurement to express sound wave intensity

denasal [di 'nez l̩]:   quality of voice characterized by inadequate nasalization; lacking nasalization, as when [n] is produced as [d] during nasal congestion

denotative ['di no ˌte tɪv]:   the literal or dictionary meaning of a word

dental ['dɛn tl̩]:   pertaining to the teeth; dental sounds include [f], [v], [θ], and [ð]

diacritical [ˌdaɪ ə 'krɪt ə kl̩]:   pertaining to the symbol system used to indicate how letters are pronounced in words; one of several printed symbol systems used in dictionaries

dialect ['daɪ ə lɛkt]:   distinguishing spoken language traits within the same language, usually defined by geographic, ethnic, or socioeconomic separation

diaphragm ['daɪ ə ˌfræm]:   primary muscle used in breathing which is located between the chest and abdominal cavities

diction ['dɪk ʃn̩], [ʃən]:   articulation, enunciation, or production of speech sounds for a given language

diphthong ['dɪf θɔŋ]:   two vowels which are glided together in the same syllable, without a pause, to produce one phoneme; the IPA symbol for a diphthong includes the original symbols of both sounds, as in [ɑʊ], [ɑɪ], and [ɔɪ]

distinctive feature [dɪs 'tɪŋk tɪv 'fi tʃɚ]:   the one phonetic feature which distinguishes two otherwise identical words in the same language apart, as in the words "s̲ettle" and "n̲ettle" where nasalization becomes a distinctive feature

duration [dɚ 'e ʃn̩], [ʃən]:   length or quantity of time a sound or silence is sustained or prolonged

E

enunciation [i ˌnʌn si 'e ʃn̩], [ʃən]:   diction, enunciation, or production of speech sounds for a given language; usually used in reference to the clarity of articulated sounds

epiglottis [ˌɛp ə 'glɑt ɪs]:   an elongated cartilage at the base of the tongue that lowers to cover the windpipe and vocal folds during the process of swallowing

exhale [ɛks 'hel]:   expel air from the lungs; breathe out; opposite of inhale

312

F

fricative ['frɪk ə tɪv]: voiced or voiceless consonant sound expelled with audible friction as air is forced between two articulators in a narrow channel, as for [s], [z], [f], [v]

fry [fraɪ]: vocal quality produced in the glottis by overly slow movement of the vocal folds which sounds like something frying on a hot griddle; occurs often when pitch and volume drop simultaneously at ends of words

G

General American Speech ['dʒɛn ɚ l ə 'mɛɚ ɪk ən spitʃ]: spoken language used by a majority of speakers of English, and by most major radio and television network newscasters in North America

glide [glaɪd]: a consonant sound produced while the articulators are in continuous motion; semi-vowels including [w] and [j]; process of gradual movement from one sound to another without an intervening break

glottis ['glɑt ɪs]: opening or space between the vocal folds in the larynx; the glottal stop is a sudden stoppage and release of air at the vocal folds

guttural ['gʌt ɚ əl]: quality of voice characterized by a tense or constricted throat, low pitch, and a growling quality; usually associated with anger

H

habituate [hə 'bɪtʃ ju et]: as a result of habit; to make a habit through repetition

hard palate [hɑɚd 'pæl ət]: the bony portion of the roof of the mouth which separates the nasal and oral cavities and to which the soft palate is attached as a fleshy extension

I

inflection [ɪn 'flɛk ʃn̩], [ʃən]: pitch changes which occur within individual sounds, words, or thought sequences to clarify or enhance meaning; pitch changes may be abrupt in steps, or gradual in slides; may be rising, falling, or medial (up and down, or down and up); the term ''vocal variety'' usually is associated with types and numbers of inflections used

intercostal [ˌɪn tɚ 'kɑs tl̩]: muscles between the ribs; during exhalation these muscles pull the ribs downward and inward; considerable chest movement occurs during intercostal breathing

International Phonetic Alphabet (see IPA)

IPA [ɑɪ pi e]: acronym for International Phonetic Alphabet; international symbol system which uses one symbol for each unique spoken sound or phoneme, regardless of the alphabet used or the spelling of the sound

L

labio / labial ['le bi o] ['le bi əl]: pertaining to one or both lips, as in labiodental (lips and teeth) sounds produced by the lower lip coming in contact with the front teeth in the sounds [f] and [v]

larynx ['læɝ ɪŋks]:   the uppermost portion of the trachea containing the vocal folds where sound is first produced; the voice box

lateral ['læt ɚ l]:   emission of breath over the sides, as opposed to the tip, of the tongue, as for [l]; a lateral lisp occurs when air escapes over one or both sides of the tongue for [s] and [z] sounds

lingua ['lɪŋ gwə]:   pertaining to the tongue, as in linguapalatal (tongue and palate) or linguadental (tongue and teeth); also relates to language in general, as in the word "linguist" which relates to one who studies sounds and structures of languages

lungs [lʌngz]:   porous, nonmuscular sacs which fill the chest cavity and are used for storing air while the bloodstream exchanges carbon dioxide for oxygen; serve as the source of breath and power for spoken language

M

melody pattern ['mɛl o di 'pætɚn]:   a repetitive, fairly predictable, and monotonous pattern of inflectional changes within thought sequences which have little relationship to the literal or implied meaning of the thought

monopitch ['mɑn o pɪtʃ]:   monotone; voice which is characterized by the lack of pitch changes; often used as a reference to voices which use few inflectional changes

N

nasal ['nez l]:   pertaining to the nasal cavities or nose; the only nasal sounds in English are [n], [m], and [ŋ]; an excessively nasal voice quality occurs when vowels and diphthongs and nonnasal consonants are allowed to escape through the nose rather than through the mouth

O

omission [o 'mɪ ʃn], [ʃən]:   a diction error which results when one or more phonemes are deleted from a word

optimum pitch ['ɑp tɪ məm pɪtʃ]:   the note on the musical scale which can be said loudest and clearest with the least amount of physical effort; the note on which voice quality is at its best for each individual

orthography [ɔɚ 'θɑg rə fi]:   spelling of words, using the printed or alphabet symbols of a particular language to refer to spoken sounds

overtones ['ov ɚ tonz]:   tones which are higher in pitch than the basic or fundamental tone, produced by the vibration of small portions of the vocal folds (as contrasted with vibration of the entire vocal folds)

P

palate ['pæl ət]:   the hard or soft portions of the roof of the mouth

paralanguage ['pɛɚ ə ˌlæŋ gwɪdʒ]:   vocal modifications in pitch, volume, duration, inflection, pause, intensity, and so on which influence the connotative meaning of the words being spoken; the influence of the vocal message on the verbal message

314

pause [pɔz]: a break in, or absence of sound; silence; temporary cessation of activity for the purpose of filling the lungs, or to influence meaning; break in sound or an interval in meter or music which doesn't necessarily change the overall rhythm

pharynx ['fæɚ ɪŋks]: the throat; connection between the oral and nasal cavities and the esophagus or trachea

phonation [fo 'ne ʃn̩], [ʃən]: production of voiced sounds by vibrating the vocal folds as air passes through them

phoneme ['fo nim]: a basic unique sound (phone) or sound family in a language; a group of phonetically similar sounds (sounds which share distinctive features) in a sound family which may be interchanged without changing meaning

phonemics [fo 'nim ɪks]: study of the phonemes (significantly different sounds) of a language

phonetics [fo 'nɛt ɪks]: study of speech sounds and symbols

pitch [pɪtʃ]: frequency of vibration of a sound wave which is subjectively evaluated by the human ear as a high or low sound on the musical scale

plosive ['plo sɪv]: consonant sound formed by a complete stoppage of the breathstream followed by a quick, explosive release, as in [p], [b], [t], [d], [k], [g]; a vocal stop

projection [pro 'dʒɛk ʃn̩], [ʃən]: focused, forward placement of sound characterized by volume and clarity of sound

Q

quality ['kwɑl ɪ ti]: the combined fundamental and overtone frequencies of an individual's unique sound waves which are modified by the resonating cavities to produce timbre and texture of one's distinctive sounds

R

rate [ret]: speed of speaking which may include considerations of sound duration, number and lengths of pauses, and number of syllables or words spoken per minute

resonation [ˌrɛz n̩ 'e ʃn̩], [ʃən]: enrichment and reinforcement or amplification of sound through secondary vibration or cavity reinforcement; the human resonators are basically the oral, nasal, and throat cavities

respiration [ˌrɛs pɚ 'e ʃn̩], [ʃən]: process of inhaling and exhaling air; breathing

rhythm ['rɪð əm]: repetition of any discernible factor

S

sibilant ['sɪb ə lənt]: characterized by a high frequency sound usually associated with hissing, as in [s], [z]; when too much air is allowed to escape while the tongue pushes hard against the alveolar ridge an excessive amount of sibilance is created

slide [slɑɪd]: a gradual change in pitch from one musical note to another without an intervening pause; a vocal inflection

soft palate [sɔft 'pæl ət]:   the fleshy extension of the hard palate; the velum

step [stɛp]:   an abrupt change in pitch from one musical note to another, without a long, intervening pause; a vocal inflection

stop [stɑp]:   see "plosive"

stressed [strɛst]:   accented; louder and slightly higher pitch than adjacent sounds; may be held slightly longer

strident ['straɪd n̩t], [dɛnt]:   vocal quality characterized by a relatively high pitched, tense, metallic voice

substitution [ˌsʌb stɪ 'tu ʃn̩], [ʃən]:   a diction error which results when one sound replaces another, as in the substitution of [f] for [θ] in the word "mouth"

syntax ['sɪn tæks]:   order or sequence of words in thought sequences such as phrases, clauses, and paragraphs; structure of thought units

T

thorax ['θɔɚ æks]:   the chest; region between the neck and abdomen, enclosed by the ribs

trachea ['trek i ə]:   the windpipe; tubelike structure between the bronchi and pharynx

U

uvula ['juv jə lə]:   fleshy finger which droops from the soft palate in the middle back of the throat

unstressed [ən 'strɛst]:   unaccented; not as loud or as high in pitch as adjacent sounds; may not be held quite as long

V

velum ['vɛl əm]:   soft palate

vocal folds ['vo kl̩ foldz]:   two continuous bands situated in the larynx which vibrate as exhaled air flows through them to create sound; commonly called vocal cords

vocal fry ['vo kl̩ fraɪ]:   see "fry"

voiced [vɔɪst]:   characterized by air which escapes through vibrating vocal folds, as in the sounds [b], [g], and [z]

voiceless ['vɔɪs lɛs]:   characterized by air which escapes through the vocal folds without vibrating; unvoiced

volume ['vɑl jəm]:   degree of loudness of a sound; sound intensity

vowel ['vaʊ əl]:   a group of voiced speech sounds characterized by an open, unobstructed flow of breath; their individual characteristics are formed by changes in the size and shape of the oral cavity and manipulation of the tongue

W

windpipe ['wɪnd paɪp]:   see "trachea"

316

Index